THE LIFE AND LETTERS

OF

LORD MACAULAY.

From a Photograph by Claudet. Engraved by C. Cook.

Macaulay

THE LIFE AND LETTERS

OF

LORD MACAULAY

BY HIS NEPHEW

G. OTTO TREVELYAN

MEMBER OF PARLIAMENT FOR HAWICK DISTRICT OF BURGHS

IN TWO VOLUMES

VOL. I.

NEW YORK
HARPER & BROTHERS, PUBLISHERS
FRANKLIN SQUARE
1876

PREFACE.

THIS work has been undertaken principally from a conviction that it is the performance of a duty which, to the best of my ability, it is incumbent on me to fulfill. Though even on this ground I can not appeal to the forbearance of my readers, I may venture to refer to a peculiar difficulty which I have experienced in dealing with Lord Macaulay's private papers.

To give to the world compositions not intended for publication may be no injury to the fame of writers who, by habit, were careless and hasty workmen; but it is far otherwise in the case of one who made it a rule for himself to publish nothing which was not carefully planned, strenuously labored, and minutely finished. Now, it is impossible to examine Lord Macaulay's journals and correspondence without being persuaded that the idea of their being printed, even in part, never was present to his mind; and I should not feel myself justified in laying them before the public if it were not that their unlabored and spontaneous character adds to their biographical value all, and perhaps more than all, that it detracts from their literary merit.

To the heirs and relations of Mr. Thomas Flower Ellis and Mr. Adam Black; to the Marquis of Lansdowne; to Mr. Macvey Napier; and to the executors of Dr. Whewell, my thanks are due for the courtesy with which they have placed the different portions of my uncle's correspondence at my disposal. Lady Caroline Lascelles has most kindly permitted me to use as much of Lord Carlisle's journal as relates to the subject of this work; and Mr. Charles Cowan, my uncle's old opponent at Edinburgh, has sent me a considerable mass of printed matter bearing upon the elections of 1847 and 1852. The late Sir Edward Ryan, and Mr. Fitzjames Stephen, spared no pains to inform me with regard to Lord Macaulay's work at Calcutta. His early letters, with much that relates to the whole course of his life, have been preserved, studied, and arranged by the affectionate industry of his sister, Miss Macaulay; and material of high interest has been intrusted to my hands by Mr. and the Hon. Mrs. Edward Cropper. I have been assisted throughout the book by the sympathy and the recollections of Lady Holland, the niece to whose custody Lord Macaulay's papers by inheritance descend.

G. O. T.

March, 1876.

CONTENTS.

CHAPTER I.

1800-1818.

CHAPTER II.

1818-1824.

CHAPTER III.

1824-1830.

CHAPTER IV.

1830–1832.

CHAPTER V.

1832–1834.

CHAPTER VI.

1834–1838.

LIFE AND LETTERS

OF

LORD MACAULAY.

CHAPTER I.

1800–1818.

Plan and Scope of the Work.—History of the Macaulay Family.—Aulay.—Kenneth.—Johnson and Boswell.—John Macaulay and his Children.—Zachary Macaulay.—His Career in the West Indies and in Africa.—His Character.—Visit of the French Squadron to Sierra Leone.—Zachary Macaulay's Marriage.—Birth of his Eldest Son.—Lord Macaulay's Early Years.—His Childish Productions.—Mrs. Hannah More.—General Macaulay.—Choice of a School.—Shelford.—Dean Milner.—Macaulay's Early Letters.—Aspenden Hall.—The Boy's Habits and Mental Endowments.—His Home.—The Clapham Set.—The Boy's Relations with his Father.—The Political Ideas among which he was brought up, and their Influence on the Work of his Life.

He who undertakes to publish the memoirs of a distinguished man may find a ready apology in the custom of the age. If we measure the effective demand for biography by the supply, the person commemorated need possess but a very moderate reputation, and have played no exceptional part, in order to carry the reader through many hundred pages of anecdote, dissertation, and correspondence. To judge from the advertisements of our circulating libraries, the public curiosity is keen with regard to some who did nothing worthy of special note, and others who acted so continuously in the face of the world that, when their course was run, there was little left for the world to learn about them. It may, therefore, be taken for granted that a desire exists to hear something authentic about the life of a man who has produced works which are universally known, but which bear little or no indication of the private history and the personal qualities of the author.

This was in a marked degree the case with Lord Macaulay. His two famous contemporaries in English literature have, consciously or unconsciously, told their own story in their books. Those who could see between the lines in "David Copperfield" were aware that they had before them the most delightful of autobiographies: and all who knew how to read Thackeray could trace him in his novels through every stage in his course, on from the day when as a little boy, consigned to the care of English relatives and school-masters, he left his mother on the steps of the landing-place at Calcutta. The dates and names were wanting: but the man was there; while the most ardent admirers of Macaulay will admit that a minute study of his literary productions left them, as far as any but an intellectual knowledge of the writer himself was concerned, very much as it found them. A consummate master of his craft, he turned out works which bore the unmistakable marks of the artificer's hand, but which did not reflect his features. It would be almost as hard to compose a picture of the author from his "History," his "Essays," and his "Lays," as to evolve an idea of Shakspeare from "Henry the Fifth" and "Measure for Measure."

But, besides being a man of letters, Lord Macaulay was a statesman, a jurist, and a brilliant ornament of society, at a time when to shine in society was a distinction which a man of eminence and ability might justly value. In these several capacities, it will be said, he was known well, and known widely. But in the first place, as these pages will show, there was one side of his life (to him, at any rate, the most important) of which even the persons with whom he mixed most freely and confidentially in London drawing-rooms, in the Indian council-chamber, and in the lobbies and on the benches of the House of Commons, were only in part aware. And in the next place, those who have seen his features and heard his voice are few already, and become yearly fewer: while, by a rare fate in literary annals, the number of those who read his books is still rapidly increasing. For every one who sat with him in private company or at the transaction of public business, for every ten who have listened to his oratory in Parliament or from the hustings, there must be tens of thousands whose interest in history and literature he has awakened and informed by his pen, and who would gladly know what manner of man it was that has done them so great a service.

To gratify that most legitimate wish is the duty of those who have the means at their command. His life-like image is indelibly impressed upon their minds (for how could it be otherwise with any who had enjoyed so close relations with such a man?), although the skill which can reproduce that image before the general eye may well be wanting. But his own letters will supply the deficiencies of the biographer. Never did any one leave behind him more copious materials for enabling others to put together a narrative which might be the history, not indeed of his times, but of the man himself. For, in the first place, he so soon showed promise of being one who would give those among whom his early years were passed reason to be proud, and still more certain assurance that he would never afford them cause for shame, that what he wrote was preserved with a care very seldom bestowed on childish compositions; and the value set upon his letters by those with whom he corresponded naturally enough increased as years went on. And, in the next place, he was by nature so incapable of affectation or concealment that he could not write otherwise than as he felt, and, to one person at least, could never refrain from writing all that he felt; so that we may read in his letters, as in a clear mirror, his opinions and inclinations, his hopes and affections, at every succeeding period of his existence. Such letters could never have been submitted to an editor unconnected with both correspondents by the strongest ties: and even one who stands in that position must often be sorely puzzled as to what he has the heart to publish and the right to withhold.

I am conscious that in an undertaking of this nature a near relative has peculiar temptations toward that partiality of the biographer which Lord Macaulay himself so often and so cordially denounced: and the danger is greater in the case of one whose knowledge of him coincided with his later years; for it would not be easy to find a nature which gained more by time than his, and lost less. But, believing, as I do (to use his own words), that "if he were now living he would have sufficient judgment and sufficient greatness of mind" to wish to be shown as himself, I will suppress no trait in his disposition or incident in his career which might provoke blame or question. Such in all points as he was, the world, which has been so indulgent to him, has a right to know him; and those who best love him do not fear the consequences of freely submitting his character and his actions to the public verdict.

The most devout believers in the doctrine of the transmission of family qualities will be content with tracing back descent through four generations: and all favorable hereditary influences, both intellectual and moral, are assured by a genealogy which derives from a Scotch manse. In the first decade of the eighteenth century Aulay Macaulay, the great-grandfather of the historian, was minister of Tiree and Coll; where he was "grievously annoyed by a decreet obtained after instance of the Laird of Ardchattan, taking away his stipend." The Duchess of Argyll of the day appears to have done her best to see him righted: "but his health being much impaired, and there being no church or meeting-house, he was exposed to the violence of the weather at all seasons; and having no manse or glebe, and no fund for communion elements, and no mortification for schools or any pious purpose in either of the islands, and the air being unwholesome, he was dissatisfied:" and so, to the great regret of the parishioners whom he was leaving behind, he migrated to Harris, where he discharged the clerical duties for nearly half a century.

Aulay was the father of fourteen children, of whom one,

Kenneth, the minister of Ardnamurchan, still occupies a very humble niche in the temple of literature. He wrote a "History of St. Kilda," which happened to fall into the hands of Dr. Johnson, who spoke of it more than once with favor. His reason for liking the book is characteristic enough. Mr. Macaulay had recorded the belief prevalent in St. Kilda that, as soon as the factor landed on the island, all the inhabitants had an attack which, from the account, appears to have partaken of the nature both of influenza and bronchitis. This touched the superstitious vein in Johnson, who praised him for his "magnanimity" in venturing to chronicle so questionable a phenomenon: the more so because, said the doctor, "Macaulay set out with a prejudice against prejudice, and wanted to be a smart modern thinker." To a reader of our day the "History of St. Kilda" appears to be innocent of any trace of such pretension; unless it be that the author speaks slightingly of second-sight, a subject for which Johnson always had a strong hankering. In 1773, Johnson paid a visit to Mr. Macaulay, who by that time had removed to Calder, and began the interview by congratulating him on having produced "a very pretty piece of topography"—a compliment which did not seem to the taste of the author. The conversation turned upon rather delicate subjects, and before many hours had passed the guest had said to the host one of the very rudest things recorded by Boswell. Next morning he atoned for his incivility by giving one of the boys of the house a pocket Sallust, and promising to procure him a servitorship at Oxford. Subsequently Johnson pronounced that Mr. Macaulay was not competent to have written the book that went by his name: a decision which, to those who happen to have read the work, will give a very poor notion of my ancestor's abilities.

The eldest son of old Aulay, and the grandfather of Lord Macaulay, was John, born in the year 1720. He was minister successively of Barra, South Uist, and Inverary; the last appointment being a proof of the interest which the family of Argyll continued to take in the fortunes of the Macaulays. He, likewise, during the famous tour in the Hebrides, came across the path of Boswell, who mentions him in an exquisitely absurd paragraph, the first of those in which is described the visit to Inverary Castle on October 25th. Mr. Macaulay afterward passed the evening with the travelers at their inn, and provoked Johnson into what Boswell calls warmth, and any one else would call brutality, by the very proper remark that he had no notion of people being in earnest in good professions if their practice belied them. When we think what well-known ground this was to Lord Macaulay, it is impossible to suppress a wish that the great talker had been at hand to avenge his grandfather and grand-uncle. Next morning "Mr. Macaulay breakfasted with us, nothing hurt or dismayed by his last night's correction. Being a man of good sense, he had a just admiration of Dr. Johnson." He was rewarded by seeing Johnson at his very best, and hearing him declaim some of the finest lines that ever were written, in a manner worthy of his subject.

There is a tradition that, in his younger days, the minister of Inverary proved his Whiggism by giving information to the authorities which almost led to the capture of the young Pretender. It is perhaps a matter of congratulation that this item was not added to the heavy account that the Stuarts have against the Macaulay family. John Macaulay was in high reputation as a preacher, and especially renowned for his fluency. In 1774, he removed to Cardross, in Dumbartonshire, where, on the bank of the noble estuary of the Clyde, he spent the last fifteen years of a useful and honored life. He was twice married. His first wife died at the birth of his first child. Eight years afterward, in 1757, he espoused Margaret, daughter of Colin Campbell, of Inverseger, who survived him by a single year. By her he had the patriarchal number of twelve children, whom he brought up on the old Scotch system—common to the households of minister, man of business, farmer, and peasant alike—on fine air, simple diet, and a solid training in knowledge, human and divine. Two generations after, Mr. Carlyle, during a visit to the late Lord Ashburton at the Grange, caught sight of Macaulay's face in unwonted repose, as he was turning over the pages of a book. "I noticed," said he, "the homely Norse features that you find everywhere in the Western Isles, and I thought to myself: 'Well! any one can see that you are an honest, good sort of fellow, made out of oatmeal.'"

Several of John Macaulay's children obtained position in the world. Aulay, the eldest by his second wife, became a clergyman of the Church of England. His reputation as a scholar and antiquary stood high, and in the capacity of a private tutor he became known even in royal circles. He published pamphlets and treatises, the list of which it is not worth while to record, and meditated several large works that perhaps never got much beyond a title. Of all his undertakings the one best deserving commemoration in these pages was a tour that he made into Scotland in company with Mr. Thomas Babington, the owner of Rothley Temple, in Leicestershire, in the course of which the travelers paid a visit to the manse at Cardross. Mr. Babington fell in love with one of the daughters of the house, Miss Jean Macaulay, and married her in 1787. Nine years afterward, he had an opportunity of presenting his brother-in-law Aulay Macaulay with the very pleasant living of Rothley.

Alexander, another son of John Macaulay, succeeded his father as minister of Cardross. Colin went into the Indian army, and died a general. He followed the example of the more ambitious among his brother officers, and exchanged military for civil duties. In 1799 he acted as secretary to a political and diplomatic commission which accompanied the force that marched under General Harris against Seringapatam. The leading commissioner was Colonel Wellesley, and to the end of General Macaulay's life the great Duke corresponded with him on terms of intimacy, and (so the family flattered themselves) even of friendship. Soon after the commencement of the century, Colin Macaulay became resident at the important native state of Travancore. While on this employment, he happened to light upon a valuable collection of books, and rapidly made himself master of the principal European languages, which he spoke and wrote with a facility surprising in one who had acquired them within a few leagues of Cape Comorin.

There was another son of John Macaulay who in force and elevation of character stood out among his brothers, and who was destined to make for himself no ordinary career. The path which Zachary Macaulay chose to tread did not lead to wealth, or worldly success, or indeed to much worldly happiness. Born in 1768, he was sent out at the age of sixteen by a Scotch house of business as book-keeper to an estate in Jamaica, of which he soon rose to be sole manager. His position brought him into the closest possible contact with negro slavery. His mind was not prepossessed against the system of society which he found in the West Indies. His personal interests spoke strongly in its favor, while his father, whom he justly respected, could see nothing to condemn in an institution recognized by Scripture. Indeed, the religious world still allowed the maintenance of slavery to continue an open question. John Newton, the real founder of that school in the Church of England of which in after-years Zachary Macaulay was a devoted member, contrived to reconcile the business of a slave-trader with the duties of a Christian, and to the end of his days gave scandal to his disciples (who by that time were one and all sworn abolitionists), by refusing to see that there could be no fellowship between light and such darkness.

But Zachary Macaulay had eyes of his own to look about him, a clear head for forming a judgment on what he saw, and a conscience which would not permit him to live otherwise than in obedience to its mandates. The young Scotchman's innate respect for his fellows, and his appreciation of all that instruction and religion can do for men, was shocked at the sight of a population deliberately kept ignorant and heathen. His kind heart was wounded by cruelties practiced at the will and pleasure of a thousand petty despots. He had read his Bible too literally to acquiesce easily in a state of matters under which human beings were bred and raised like a stock of cattle, while outraged morality was revenged on the governing race by the shameless licentiousness which is the inevitable accompaniment of slavery. He was well aware that these evils, so far from being superficial or remediable, were essential to the very existence of a social fabric constituted like that within which he lived. It was not for nothing that he had been behind the scenes in that tragedy of crime and misery. His philanthropy was not learned by the royal road of tracts, and platform speeches, and monthly magazines. What he knew he had spelled out for himself, with no teacher except the aspect of human suffering and degradation and sin.

He was not one of those to whom conviction comes in a day; and, when convinced, he did nothing suddenly. Little more than a boy in age, singularly modest, and constitutionally averse to any course that appeared pretentious or theatrical, he began by a sincere attempt to make the best of his calling. For some years he contented himself with doing what he could (so he writes to a friend) "to alleviate the hardships of a considerable number of my fellow-creatures, and to render the bitter cup of servitude as palatable as possible." But by the time he was four-and-twenty, he became tired of trying to find a compromise between right and wrong, and, refusing really great offers from the people with whom he was connected, he threw up his position and returned to his native country. This step was taken against the wishes of his father, who was not prepared for the construction which his son put upon the paternal precept that a man should make his practice square with his professions.

But Zachary Macaulay soon had more congenial work to do. The young West Indian overseer was not alone in his scruples. Already for some time past a conviction had been abroad that individual citizens could not divest themselves of their share in the responsibility in which the nation was involved by the existence of slavery in our colonies. Already there had been formed the nucleus of the most disinterested, and perhaps the most successful, popular movement which history records. The question of the slave-trade was well before Parliament and the country. Ten years had passed since the freedom of all whose feet touched the soil of our island had been vindicated before the courts at Westminster, and not a few negroes had become their own masters as a consequence of that memorable decision. The patrons of the race were somewhat embarrassed by having these expatriated freedmen on their hands; an opinion prevailed that the traffic in human lives could never be efficiently checked until Africa had obtained the rudiments of civilization; and after long discussion a scheme was matured for the colonization of Sierra Leone by liberated slaves. A company was organized, with a charter from the crown, and a board which included the names of Granville Sharpe and Wilberforce. A large capital was speedily subscribed, and the chair was accepted by Mr. Henry Thornton, a leading City banker and a member of Parliament, whose determined opposition to cruelty and oppression in every form was such as might be expected in one who had inherited from his father the friendship of the poet Cowper. Mr. Thornton heard Macaulay's story from Thomas Babington, with whom he lived on terms of close intimacy and political alliance. The board, by the advice of its chairman, passed a resolution appointing the young man second member in the Sierra Leone Council, and early in the year 1793 he sailed for Africa, where soon after his arrival he succeeded to the position and duties of governor.

The directors had done well to secure a tried man. The colony was at once exposed to the implacable enmity of merchants whose market the agents of the new company spoiled in their capacity of traders, and slave-dealers with whom they interfered in their character of philanthropists. The native tribes in the vicinity, instigated by European hatred and jealousy, began to inflict upon the defenseless authorities of the settlement a series of those monkey-like impertinences which, absurdly as they may read in a narrative, are formidable and ominous when they indicate that savages feel their power. These barbarians, who had hitherto commanded as much rum and gunpowder as they cared to have by selling their neighbors at the nearest barracoon, showed no appreciation for the comforts and advantages of civilization. Indeed, those advantages were displayed in any thing but an attractive shape even within the pale of the company's territory. An aggregation of negroes from Jamaica, London, and Nova Scotia, who possessed no language except an acquired jargon, and shared no associations beyond the recollections of a common servitude, were not very promising apostles for the spread of Western culture and the Christian faith. Things went smoothly enough as long as the business of the colony was mainly confined to eating the provisions that had been brought in the ships; but as soon as the work became real and the commons short, the whole community smoldered down into chronic mutiny.

Zachary Macaulay was the very man for such a crisis. To a rare fund of patience and self-command and perseverance he united a calm courage that was equal to any trial. These qualities were, no doubt, inherent in his disposition; but no one except those who have turned over his voluminous private journals could understand what constant effort and what incessant watchfulness went to maintain, throughout a long life, a course of conduct and a temper of mind which gave every appearance of being the spontaneous fruit of nature. He was not one who dealt in personal experiences: and few among even the friends who loved him like father or brother, and who would have trusted him with all their fortune on his bare word, knew how entirely his outward behavior was the express image of his religious belief. The secret of his character and of his actions lay in perfect humility and an absolute faith. Events did not discompose him, because they were sent by One who best knew his own purposes. He was not fretted by the folly of others, or irritated by their hostility, because he regarded the humblest or the worst of mankind as objects, equally with himself, of the divine love and care. On all other points he examined himself so closely that the meditations of a single evening would fill many pages of diary; but so completely, in his case, had the fear of God cast out all other fear, that, amidst the gravest perils and the most bewildering responsibilities, it never occurred to him to question whether he was brave or not. He worked strenuously and unceasingly, never amusing himself from year's end to year's end, and shrinking from any public praise or recognition as from an unlawful gratification, because he was firmly persuaded that, when all had been accomplished and endured, he was yet but an unprofitable servant, who had done that which was his duty to do. Some, perhaps, will consider such motives as old-fashioned, and such convictions as out of date; but self-abnegation, self-control, and self-knowledge that do not give to self the benefit of any doubt, are virtues which are not old-fashioned, and for which, as time goes on, the world is likely to have as much need as ever.

Sir James Stephen writes thus of his friend Macaulay: "That his understanding was proof against sophistry, and his nerves against fear were, indeed, conclusions to which a stranger arrived at the first interview with him. But what might be suggesting that expression of countenance, at once so earnest and so monotonous—by what manner of feelings those gestures, so uniformly firm and deliberate, were prompted—whence the constant traces of fatigue on those overhanging brows, and on that athletic though ungraceful figure—what might be the charm which excited among his chosen circle a faith approaching to superstition, and a love rising to enthusiasm, toward a man whose demeanor was so inanimate, if not austere: it was a riddle of which neither Gall nor Lavater could have found the key."

That Sir James himself could read the riddle is proved by the concluding words of a passage marked by a force and tenderness of feeling unusual even in him: "His earthward affections, active and all-enduring as they were, could yet thrive without the support of human sympathy, because they were sustained by so abiding a sense of the divine presence, and so absolute a submission to the divine will, as raised him habitually to that higher region where the reproach of man could not reach, and the praise of man might not presume to follow him."

Mr. Macaulay was admirably adapted for the arduous and uninviting task of planting a negro colony. His very deficiencies stood him in good stead; for in presence of the elements with which he had to deal, it was well for him that nature had denied him any sense of the ridiculous. Unconscious of what was absurd around him, and incapable of being flurried, frightened, or fatigued, he stood as a centre of order and authority amidst the seething chaos of inexperience and insubordination. The staff was miserably insufficient, and every officer of the company had to do duty for three in a climate such that a man is fortunate if he can find health for the work of one during a continuous twelvemonth. The governor had to be in the counting-house, the law-court, the school, and even the chapel. He was his own secretary, his own pay-master, his own envoy. He posted ledgers, he decided causes, he conducted correspondence with the directors at home, and visited neighboring potentates on diplomatic missions which made up in danger what they lacked in dignity. In the absence of properly qualified clergymen, with whom he would have been the last to put himself in competition, he preached sermons and performed marriages — a function which must have given honest satisfaction to one who had been so close a witness of the enforced and systematized immorality of a slave-nursery. Before long something fairly resembling order was established, and the settlement began to enjoy a reasonable measure of prosperity. The town was built, the fields were planted, and the schools filled. The governor made a point of allotting the lightest work to the negroes who could read and write: and such was the stimulating effect of this system upon education that he confidently looked forward "to the time when there would be few in the colony unable to read the Bible." A printing-press was in constant operation, and in the use of a copying-machine the little community was three-quarters of a century ahead of the London public offices.

But a severe ordeal was in store for the nascent civilization of Sierra Leone. On a Sunday morning in September, 1794, eight French sail appeared off the coast. The town was about as defensible as Brighton, and it is not difficult to imagine the feelings which the sans-culottes inspired among evangelical colonists whose last advices from Europe dated from the very height of the Reign of Terror. There was a party in favor of escaping into the forest with as much property as could be removed at so short a notice; but the governor insisted that there would be no chance of saving the company's buildings unless the company's servants could make up their minds to remain at their posts and face it out. The squadron moored within musket-shot of the quay, and swept the streets for two hours with grape and bullets; a most gratuitous piece of cruelty that killed a negress and a child, and gave one unlucky English gentleman a fright which ultimately brought him to his grave. The invaders then proceeded to land, and Mr. Macaulay had an opportunity of learning something about the condition of the French marine during the heroic period of the republic.

A personal enemy of his own, the captain of a Yankee slaver, brought a party of sailors straight to the governor's house. What followed had best be told in Mr. Macaulay's own words: "Newell, who was attended by half a dozen sansculottes, almost foaming with rage, presented a pistol to me, and with many oaths demanded instant satisfaction for the slaves who had run away from him to my protection. I made very little reply, but told him he must now *take* such satisfaction as he judged equivalent to his claims, as I was no longer master of my actions. He became so very outrageous that, after bearing with him a little while, I thought it most prudent to repair myself to the French officer, and request his safe-conduct on board the commodore's ship. As I passed along the wharf the scene was curious enough. The Frenchmen, who had come ashore in filth and rags, were now, many of them, dressed out with women's shifts, gowns, and petticoats. Others had quantities of cloth wrapped about their bodies, or perhaps six or seven suits of clothes upon them at a time. The scene which presented itself on my getting on board the flagship was still more singular. The quarter-deck was crowded by a set of ragamuffins whose appearance beggared every previous description, and among whom I sought in vain for some one who looked like a gentleman. The stench and filth exceeded any thing I had ever witnessed in any ship, and the noise and confusion gave me some idea of their famous Mountain. I was ushered into the commodore's cabin, who at least received me civilly. His name was Citizen Allemand. He did not appear to have the right of excluding any of his fellow-citizens even from this place. Whatever might be their rank, they crowded into it, and conversed familiarly with him." Such was the discipline of the fleet that had been beaten by Lord Howe on the 1st of June, and such the raw material of the armies which, under firm hands and on an element more suited to the military genius of their nation, were destined to triumph at Rivoli and Hohenlinden.

Mr. Macaulay, who spoke French with ease and precision, in his anxiety to save the town used every argument which might prevail on the commander, whose Christian name (if one may use such a phrase with reference to a patriot of the year two of the republic), happened, oddly enough, to be the same as his own. He appealed first to the traditional generosity of Frenchmen toward a fallen enemy, but soon discerned that the quality in question had gone out with the old order of things, if indeed it ever existed. He then represented that a people who professed to be waging war with the express object of striking off the fetters of mankind would be guilty of flagrant inconsistency if they destroyed an asylum for liberated slaves: but the commodore gave him to understand that sentiments which sounded very well in the Hall of the Jacobins were out of place on the West Coast of Africa. The governor returned on shore to find the town already completely gutted. It was evident at every turn that, although the republican battalions might carry liberty and fraternity through Europe on the points of their bayonets, the republican sailors had found a very different use for the edge of their cutlasses. "The sight of my own and of the accountant's offices almost sickened me. Every desk and every drawer and every shelf, together with the printing and copying presses, had been completely demolished in the search for money. The floors were strewed with types, and papers, and leaves of books, and I had the mortification to see a great part of my own labor and of the labor of others for several years totally destroyed. At the other end of the house I found telescopes, hygrometers, barometers, thermometers, and electrical machines, lying about in fragments. The view of the town library filled me with lively concern. The volumes were tossed about and defaced with the utmost wantonness, and if they happened to bear any resemblance to Bibles they were torn in pieces and trampled on. The collection of natural curiosities next caught my eye. Plants, seeds, dried birds, insects, and drawings were scattered about in great confusion, and some of the sailors were in the act of killing a beautiful musk-cat, which they afterward eat. Every house was full of Frenchmen, who were hacking and destroying and tearing up every thing which they could not convert to their own use. The destruction of live stock on this and the following day was immense. In my yard alone they killed fourteen dozen of fowls, and there were not less than twelve hundred hogs shot in the town." It was unsafe to walk in the streets of Freetown during the forty-eight hours that followed its capture, because the French crews, with too much of the company's port-wine in their heads to aim straight, were firing at the pigs of the poor freedmen over whom they had achieved such a questionable victory.

To readers of Erckmann-Chatrian it is unpleasant to be taken thus behind the curtain on which those skillful artists have painted the wars of the early Revolution. It is one thing to be told how the crusaders of '93 and '94 were received with blessings and banquets by the populations to whom they brought freedom and enlightenment, and quite another to read the journal in which a quiet, accurate-minded Scotchman tells us how a pack of tipsy ruffians sat abusing Pitt and George to him over a fricassee of his own fowls, and among the wreck of his lamps and mirrors which they had smashed as a protest against aristocratic luxury.

"There is not a boy among them who has not learned to accompany the name of Pitt with an execration. When I went to bed, there was no sleep to be had on account of the sentinels thinking fit to amuse me the whole night through with the revenge they meant to take on him when they got him to Paris. Next morning I went on board the *Experiment.* The commodore and all his officers messed together, and I was admitted among them. They are truly the poorest-looking people I ever saw. Even the commodore has only one suit which can at all distinguish him, not to say from the officers, but from the men. The filth and confusion of their meals were terrible. A chorus of boys usher in the dinner with the Marseilles hymn, and it finishes in the same way. The enthusiasm of all ranks among them is astonishing, but not more so than their blindness. They talk with ecstasy of their revolutionary government, of their bloody executions, of their revolutionary tribunal, of the rapid movement of their revolutionary army with the Corps of Justice and the flying guillotine before it: forgetting that not one of them is not liable to its stroke on the accusation of the greatest vagabond on board. They asked me with triumph if yesterday had not been Sunday. 'Oh,' said they, 'the National Convention have decreed that there is no Sunday, and that the Bible is all a lie.'" After such an experience it is not difficult to account for the keen and almost personal interest with which, to the very day of Waterloo, Mr. Macaulay watched through its varying phases the rise and the downfall of the French power. He followed the progress of the British arms with a minute and intelligent attention which from a very early date communicated itself to his son: and the hearty patriotism of Lord Macaulay is perhaps in no small degree the consequence of what his father suffered from the profane and rapacious sans-culottes of the revolutionary squadron.

Toward the middle of October the republicans took their departure. Even at this distance of time it is provoking to learn that they got back to Brest without meeting an enemy that had teeth to bite. The African climate, however, reduced the squadron to such a plight, that it was well for our frigates that they had not the chance of getting its fever-stricken crews under their hatches. The French never revisited Freetown. Indeed, they had left the place in such a condition that it was not worth their while to return. The houses had been carefully burned to the ground, and the live stock killed. Except the clothes on their backs, and a little brandy and flour, the Europeans had lost every thing they had in the world. Till assistance came from the mother country, they lived upon such provisions as could be recovered from the reluctant hands of the negro settlers, who providentially had not been able to resist the temptation of helping the republicans to plunder the company's stores. Judicious liberality at home, and a year's hard work on the spot, did much to repair the damage; and, when his colony was again upon its feet, Mr. Macaulay sailed to England with the object of recruiting his health, which had broken down under an attack of low fever.

On his arrival he was admitted at once and forever within the innermost circle of friends and fellow-laborers who were united round Wilberforce and Henry Thornton by indissoluble bonds of mutual personal regard and common public ends. As an indispensable part of his initiation into that very pleasant confederacy, he was sent down to be introduced to Hannah More, who was living at Cowslip Green, near Bristol, in the enjoyment of general respect mixed with a good deal of what even those who admire her as she deserved must in conscience call flattery. He there met Selina Mills, a former pupil of the school which the Miss Mores kept in the neighboring city, and a life-long friend of all the sisters. The young lady is said to have been extremely pretty and attractive, as may well be believed by those who saw her in later years. She was the daughter of a member of the Society of Friends, who at one time was a book-seller in Bristol, and who built there a small street, called "Mills Place," in which he himself resided. His grandchildren remembered him as an old man of imposing appearance, with long white hair, talking incessantly of Jacob Boehmen. Mr. Mills had sons, one of whom edited a Bristol journal exceedingly well, and is said to have made some figure in light literature. This uncle of Lord Macaulay was a very lively, clever man, full of good stories, of which only one has survived. Young Mills, while resident in London, had looked in at Rowland Hill's chapel, and had there lost a new hat. When he reported the misfortune to his father, the old Quaker replied, "John, if thee'd gone to the right place of worship, thee'd have kept thy hat upon thy head." Lord Macaulay was accustomed to say that he got his "joviality" from his mother's family. If his power of humor was indeed of Quaker origin, he was rather ungrateful in the use to which he sometimes put it.

Mr. Macaulay fell in love with Miss Mills, and obtained her affection in return. He had to encounter the opposition of her relations, who were set upon her making another and a better match, and of Mrs. Patty More (so well known to all who have studied the somewhat diffuse annals of the More family), who, in the true spirit of romantic friendship, wished her to promise never to marry at all, but to domesticate herself as a youngest sister in the household at Cowslip Green. Miss Hannah, however, took a more unselfish view of the situation, and advocated Mr. Macaulay's cause with firmness and good feeling. Indeed, he must have been, according to her particular notions, the most irreproachable of lovers, until her own Cœlebs was given to the world. By her help he carried his point in so far that the engagement was made and recognized; but the friends of the young lady would not allow her to accompany him to Africa; and, during his absence from England, which began in the early months of 1796, by an arrangement that under the circumstances was very judicious, she spent much of her time with his sister, Mrs. Babington, in Leicestershire.

His first business after arriving at Sierra Leone was to sit in judgment on the ringleaders of a formidable outbreak which had taken place in the colony, and he had an opportunity of proving by example that negro disaffection, from the nature of the race, is peculiarly susceptible to treatment by mild remedies, if only the man in the post of responsibility has got a heart and can contrive to keep his head. He had much more trouble with a batch of missionaries whom he took with him in the ship, and who were no sooner on board than they began to fall out, ostensibly on controversial topics, but more probably from the same motives that so often set the laity quarreling during the incessant and involuntary companionship of a sea-voyage. Mr. Macaulay, finding that the warmth of these debates furnished sport to the captain and other irreligious characters, was forced seriously to exert his authority in order to separate and silence the disputants. His report of these occurrences went in due time to the chairman of the company, who excused himself for an arrangement which had turned out so ill by telling a story of a servant who, having to carry a number of gamecocks from one place to another, tied them up in the same bag, and found, on arriving at his journey's end, that they had spent their time in tearing each other to pieces. When his master called him to account for his stupidity, he replied, "Sir, as they were all your cocks, I thought they would be all on one side."

Things did not go much more smoothly on shore. Mr. Macaulay's official correspondence gives a curious picture of his difficulties in the character of Minister of Public Worship in a black community. "The Baptists under David George are decent and orderly, but there is observable in them a great neglect of family worship, and sometimes an unfairness in their dealings. To Lady Huntingdon's Methodists, as a body, may with great justice be addressed the first verse of the third chapter of the Revelation. The lives of many of them are very disorderly, and rank antinomianism prevails among them." But his sense of religion and decency was most sorely tried by Moses Wilkinson, a so-called Wesleyan Methodist, whose congregation, not a very respectable one to begin with, had recently been swollen by a revival* which had been accompanied by circumstances the reverse of edifying. The governor must have looked back with regret to that period in the history of the colony when he was underhanded in the clerical department.

But his interest in the negro could bear ruder shocks than an occasional outburst of eccentric fanaticism. He liked his work because he liked those for whom he was working.

---

* Lord Macaulay had in his youth heard too much about negro preachers and negro administrators to permit him to entertain any very enthusiastic anticipations with regard to the future of the African race. He writes in his journal for July 8th, 1858: "Motley called. I like him much. We agree wonderfully well about slavery, and it is not often that I meet any person with whom I agree on that subject. For I hate slavery from the bottom of my soul; and yet I am made sick by the cant and the silly mock reasons of the Abolitionists. The nigger driver and the negrophile are two odious things to me. I must make Lady Macbeth's reservation: 'Had he not resembled ——.'"

"Poor people," he writes, "one can not help loving them. With all their trying humors, they have a warmth of affection which is really irresistible." For their sake he endured all the risk and worry inseparable from a long engagement kept by the lady among disapproving friends, and by the gentleman at Sierra Leone. He staid till the settlement had begun to thrive and the company had almost begun to pay, and until the home Government had given marked tokens of favor and protection which some years later developed into a negotiation under which the colony was transferred to the crown. It was not till 1799 that he finally gave up his appointment, and left a region which, alone among men, he quit with unfeigned, and, except in one particular, with unmixed regret. But for the absence of an Eve, he regarded the West Coast of Africa as a veritable paradise, or, to use his own expression, as a more agreeable Montpellier. With a temper which in the intercourse of society was proof against being ruffled by any possible treatment of any conceivable subject, to the end of his life he showed faint signs of irritation if any one ventured in his presence to hint that Sierra Leone was unhealthy.

On his return to England he was appointed secretary to the company, and was married at Bristol on the 26th of August, 1799. A most close union it was, and (though in latter years he became fearfully absorbed in the leading object of his existence, and ceased in a measure to be the companion that he had been), his love for his wife, and deep trust and confidence in her, never failed. They took a small house in Lambeth for the first twelve months. When Mrs. Macaulay was near her confinement, Mrs. Babington, who belonged to the school of matrons who hold that the advantage of country air outweighs that of London doctors, invited her sister-in-law to Rothley Temple; and there, in a room paneled from ceiling to floor, like every corner of the ancient mansion, with oak almost black from age—looking eastward across the park, and southward through an ivy-shaded window into a little garden—Lord Macaulay was born. It was on the 25th of October, 1800, the day of St. Crispin, the anniversary of Agincourt (as he liked to say), that he opened his eyes on a world which he was destined so thoroughly to learn and so intensely to enjoy. His father was as pleased as a father could be; but fate seemed determined that Zachary Macaulay should not be indulged in any great share of personal happiness. The next morning a spinning-jenny set off in a cottage as he was riding past. His horse started and threw him: both arms were broken; and he spent in a sick-room the remainder of the only holiday worth the name which (as far as can be traced in the family records) he ever took during his married life. Owing to this accident, the young couple were detained at Rothley into the winter, and the child was baptized, in the private chapel which formed part of the house, on the 26th of November, 1800, by the names of Thomas Babington, the Rev. Aulay Macaulay and Mr. and Mrs. Babington acting as sponsors.

The two years which followed were passed in a house in Birchin Lane, where the Sierra Leone Company had its office. The only place where the child could be taken for exercise, and what might be called air, was Drapers' Garden, which (already under sentence to be covered with bricks and mortar at an early date) lies behind Throgmorton Street and within a hundred yards of the Stock Exchange. To this dismal yard, containing as much gravel as grass, and frowned upon by a board of rules and regulations almost as large as itself, his mother used to convoy the nurse and the little boy through the crowds that toward noon swarmed along Cornhill and Threadneedle Street, and thither she would return after a due interval to escort them back to Birchin Lane. So strong was the power of association upon Macaulay's mind that in after-years Drapers' Garden was among his favorite haunts. Indeed, his habit of roaming for hours through and through the heart of the City (a habit that never left him as long as he could roam at all), was due in part to the recollection which caused him to regard that region as native ground.

Baby as he was when he quit it, he retained some impression of his earliest home. He remembered standing up at the nursery window by his father's side, looking at a cloud of black smoke pouring out of a tall chimney. He asked if that was hell: an inquiry that was received with a grave displeasure which at the time he could not understand. The kindly father must have been pained almost against his own will at finding what feature of his stern creed it was that had embodied itself in so very material a shape before his little son's imagination. When, in after-days, Mrs. Macaulay was questioned as to how soon she began to detect in the child a promise of the future, she used to say that his sensibilities and affections were remarkably developed at an age which to her hearers appeared next to incredible. He would cry for joy on seeing her after a few hours' absence, and (till her husband put a stop to it) her power of exciting his feelings was often made an exhibition to her friends. She did not regard this precocity as a proof of cleverness, but, like a foolish young mother, only thought that so tender a nature was marked for early death.

The next move which the family made was into as healthy an atmosphere, in every sense, as the most careful parent could wish to select. Mr. Macaulay took a house in the High Street of Clapham, in the part now called the Pavement, on the same side as the Plow Inn, but some doors nearer to the Common. It was a roomy, comfortable dwelling, with a very small garden behind, and in front a very small one indeed, which has entirely disappeared beneath a large shop thrown out toward the roadway by the present occupier, who bears the name of Heywood. Here the boy passed a quiet and most happy childhood. From the time that he was three years old he read incessantly, for the most part lying on the rug before the fire, with his book on the ground, and a piece of bread-and-butter in his hand. A very clever woman who then lived in the house as parlor-maid told how he used to sit in his nankeen frock, perched on the table by her as she was cleaning the plate, and expounding to her out of a volume as big as himself. He did not care for toys, but was very fond of taking his walk, when he would hold forth to his companion, whether nurse or mother, telling interminable stories out of his own head, or repeating what he had been reading in language far above his years. His memory retained without effort the phraseology of the book which he had been last engaged on, and he talked, as the maid said, "quite printed words," which produced an effect that appeared formal, and often, no doubt, exceedingly droll. Mrs. Hannah More was fond of relating how she called at Mr. Macaulay's, and was met by a fair, pretty, slight child, with abundance of light hair, about four years of age, who came to the front door to receive her, and tell her that his parents were out, but that if she would be good enough to come in he would bring her a glass of old spirits: a proposition which greatly startled the good lady, who had never aspired beyond cowslip-wine. When questioned as to what he knew about old spirits he could only say that Robinson Crusoe often had some. About this period his father took him on a visit to Lady Waldegrave at Strawberry Hill, and was much pleased to exhibit to his old friend the fair, bright boy, dressed in a green coat with red collar and cuffs, a frill at the throat, and white trousers. After some time had been spent among the wonders of the Orford Collection, of which he ever after carried a catalogue in his head, a servant who was waiting upon the company in the great gallery spilled some hot coffee over his legs. The hostess was all kindness and compassion, and when, after a while, she asked how he was feeling, the little fellow looked up in her face, and replied, "Thank you, madam, the agony is abated."

But it must not be supposed that his quaint manners proceeded from affectation or conceit; for all testimony declares that a more simple and natural child never lived, or a more lively and merry one. He had at his command the resources of the Common; to this day the most unchanged spot within ten miles of St. Paul's, and which to all appearance will ere long hold that pleasant pre-eminence within ten leagues. That delightful wilderness of gore bushes, and poplar groves, and gravel-pits, and ponds great and small, was to little Tom Macaulay a region of inexhaustible romance and mystery. He explored its recesses; he composed, and almost believed, its legends; he invented for its different features a nomenclature which has been faithfully preserved by two generations of children. A slight ridge intersected by deep ditches toward the west of the Common, the very existence of which no one above eight years old would notice, was dignified with the title of the Alps; while the elevated island, covered with shrubs, that gives a name to the Mount pond, was regarded with infinite awe, as being the nearest approach within the circuit of his observation to a conception of the majesty of Sinai. Indeed, at this period his infant fancy was much exercised with the threats and terrors of the Law. He had a little plot of ground at the back of the house, marked out as his own by a row of oyster-shells, which a maid one day threw away as rubbish. He went straight to the drawing-room, where his mother was entertaining some visitors, walked into the circle, and said, very solemnly, "Cursed be Sally; for it is written, Cursed is he that removeth his neighbor's landmark."

While still the merest child, he was sent as a day-scholar to Mr. Greaves, a shrewd Yorkshireman with a turn for science, who had been originally brought to the neighborhood in order to educate a number of African youths sent over to imbibe Western civilization at the fountain-head. The poor fellows had found as much difficulty in keeping alive at Clapham as Englishmen experience at Sierra Leone; and, in the end, their tutor set up a school for boys of his own color, and at one time had charge of almost the entire rising generation of the Common. Mrs. Macaulay explained to Tom that he must learn to study without the solace of bread-and-butter, to which he replied, "Yes, mama, industry shall be my bread and attention my butter." But, as a matter of fact, no one ever crept more unwillingly to school. Each several afternoon he made piteous entreaties to be excused returning after dinner, and was met by the unvarying formula, "No, Tom, if it rains cats and dogs, you shall go."

His reluctance to leave home had more than one side to it. Not only did his heart stay behind, but the regular lessons of the class took him away from occupations which in his eyes were infinitely more delightful and important; for these were probably the years of his greatest literary activity. As an author he never again had more facility, or any thing like so wide a range. In September, 1808, his mother writes: "My dear Tom continues to show marks of uncommon genius. He gets on wonderfully in all branches of his education, and the extent of his reading, and of the knowledge he has derived from it, are truly astonishing in a boy not yet eight years old. He is at the same time as playful as a kitten. To give you some idea of the activity of his mind, I will mention a few circumstances that may interest you and Colin. You will believe that to him we never appear to regard any thing he does as any thing more than a school-boy's amusement. He took it into his head to write a compendium of universal history about a year ago, and he really contrived to give a tolerably connected view of the leading events from the Creation to the present time, filling about a quire of paper. He told me one day that he had been writing a paper which Henry Daly was to translate into Malabar, to persuade the people of Travancore to embrace the Christian religion. On reading it, I found it to contain a very clear idea of the leading facts and doctrines of that religion, with some strong arguments for its adoption. He was so fired with reading Scott's 'Lay' and 'Marmion,' the former of which he got entirely, and the latter almost entirely, by heart, merely from his delight in reading them, that he determined on writing himself a poem in six cantos which he called 'The Battle of Cheviot.' After he had finished about three of the cantos, of about one hundred and twenty lines each, which he did in a couple of days, he became tired of it. I make no doubt he would have finished his design, but as he was proceeding with it the thought struck him of writing an heroic poem to be called 'Olaus the Great; or, The Conquest of Mona,' in which, after the manner of Virgil, he might introduce in prophetic song the future fortunes of the family—among others, those of the hero who aided in the fall of the tyrant of Mysore, after having long suffered from his tyranny; and of another of his race who had exerted himself for the deliverance of the wretched Africans. He has just begun it. He has composed I know not how many hymns. I send you one as a specimen, in his own handwriting, which he wrote about six months ago on one Monday morning while we were at breakfast."

The affection of the last generation of his relatives has preserved all these pieces, but the piety of this generation will refrain from submitting them to public criticism. A marginal note in which Macaulay has expressed his cordial approval of Uncle Toby's* remark about the great Lipsius, indicates his own wishes in the matter too clearly to leave any choice for those who come after him. But there still may be read in a boyish scrawl the epitome of universal history, from "a new king who knew not Joseph" — down through Rameses, and Dido, and Tydeus, and Tarquin, and Crassus, and Gallienus, and Edward the Martyr—to Louis, who "set off on a crusade against the Albigenses," and Oliver Cromwell, who "was an unjust and wicked man." The hymns remain, which Mrs. Hannah More, surely a consummate judge of the article, pronounced to be "quite extraordinary for such a baby." To a somewhat later period probably belongs a vast pile of blank verse, entitled "Fingal: a Poem in XII Books," two of which are in a complete and connected shape, while the rest of the story is lost amidst a labyrinth of many hundred scattered lines, so transcribed as to suggest a conjecture that the boy's demand for foolscap had outrun the paternal generosity.

Of all his performances that which attracted most attention at the time was undertaken for the purpose of immortalizing Olaus Magnus, King of Norway, from whom the clan to which the bard belonged was supposed to derive its name. Two cantos are extant, of which there are several exemplars, in every stage of caligraphy from the largest round-hand downward, a circumstance which is apparently due to the desire on the part of each of the little Macaulays to possess a copy of the great family epic. The opening stanzas, each of which contains more lines than their author counted years, go swinging along with plenty of animation and no dearth of historical and geographical allusion.

> Day set on Cambria's hills supreme,
> And, Menai, on thy silver stream.

---

* "Tristram Shandy," chap. clxiii.

The star of day had reached the West.
Now in the main it sunk to rest.
Shone great Eleindyn's castle tall:
Shone every battery, every hall:
Shone all fair Mona's verdant plain;
But chiefly shone the foaming main.

And again:

"Long," said the Prince, "shall Olave's name
Live in the high records of fame.
Fair Mona now shall trembling stand
That ne'er before feared mortal hand.
Mona, that isle where Ceres' flower
In plenteous autumn's golden hour
Hides all the fields from man's survey
As locusts hid old Egypt's day."

The passage containing a prophetic mention of his father and uncle, after the manner of the sixth book of the "Æneid," for the sake of which, according to Mrs. Macaulay, the poem was originally designed, can nowhere be discovered. It is possible that in the interval between the conception and the execution the boy happened to light upon a copy of "The Rolliad." If such was the case, he already had too fine a sense of humor to have persevered in his original plan after reading that masterpiece of drollery. It is worthy of note that the voluminous writings of his childhood, dashed off at headlong speed in the odds and ends of leisure from school-study and nursery routine, are not only perfectly correct in spelling and grammar, but display the same lucidity of meaning and scrupulous accuracy in punctuation and the other minor details of the literary art, which characterize his mature works.

Nothing could be more judicious than the treatment that Mr. and Mrs. Macaulay at this time adopted toward their boy. They never handed his productions about, or encouraged him to parade his powers of conversation or memory. They abstained from any word or act which might foster in him a perception of his own genius with as much care as a wise millionaire expends on keeping his son ignorant of the fact that he is destined to be richer than his comrades. "It was scarcely ever," writes one who knew him well from the very first, "that the consciousness was expressed by either of his parents of the superiority of their son over other children. Indeed, with his father I never remember any such expression. What I most observed myself was his extraordinary command of language. When he came to describe to his mother any childish play, I took care to be present, when I could, that I might listen to the way in which he expressed himself, often scarcely exceeded in his later years. Except this trifle, I remember him only as a good-tempered boy, always occupied, playing with his sisters without assumption of any kind." One effect of this early discipline showed itself in his freedom from vanity and susceptibility, those qualities which, coupled together in our modern psychological dialect under the head of "self-consciousness," are supposed to be the besetting defects of the literary character. Another result was his habitual overestimate of the average knowledge possessed by mankind. Judging others by himself, he credited the world at large with an amount of information which certainly few have the ability to acquire or the capacity to retain. If his parents had not been so diligent in concealing from him the difference between his own intellectual stores and those of his neighbors, it is probable that less would have been heard of Lord Macaulay's schoolboy achievements.

The system pursued at home was continued at Barley Wood, the place where the Misses More resided from 1802 onward. Mrs. Macaulay gladly sent her boy to a house where he was encouraged without being spoiled, and where he never failed to be a welcome guest. The kind old ladies made a real companion of him, and greatly relished his conversation; while at the same time, with their ideas on education, they would never have allowed him, even if he had been so inclined, to forget that he was a child. Mrs. Hannah More, who had the rare gift of knowing how to live with both old and young, was the most affectionate and the wisest of friends, and readily undertook the superintendence of his studies, his pleasures, and his health. She would keep him with her for weeks, listening to him as he read prose by the ell, declaimed poetry by the hour, and discussed and compared his favorite heroes, ancient, modern, and fictitious, under all points of view and in every possible combination: coaxing him into the garden under pretense of a lecture on botany; sending him from his books to run round the grounds, or play at cooking in the kitchen; giving him Bible-lessons which invariably ended in a theological argument, and following him with her advice and sympathy through his multifarious literary enterprises. She writes to his father, in 1809: "I heartily hope that the sea-air has been the means of setting you up, and Mrs. Macaulay also, and that the dear little poet has caught his share of bracing. Tell Tom I desire to know how 'Olaus' goes on. The sea, I suppose, furnished him with some new images."

The broader and more genial aspect under which life showed itself to the boy at Barley Wood has left its trace in a series of childish squibs and parodies, which may still be read with an interest that his Cambrian and Scandinavian rhapsodies fail to inspire. The most ambitious of these lighter efforts is a pasquinade occasioned by some local scandal, entitled "Childe Hugh and the Laborer: a Pathetic Ballad." The "Childe" of the story was a neighboring baronet, and the "Abbot" a neighboring rector, and the whole performance, intended, as it was, to mimic the spirit of Percy's "Reliques," irresistibly suggests a reminiscence of "John Gilpin." It is pleasant to know that to Mrs. Hannah More was due the commencement of what eventually became the most readable of libraries, as is shown in a series of letters extending over the entire period of Macaulay's education. When he was six years old, she writes: "Though you are a little boy now, you will one day, if it please God, be a man; but long before you are a man I hope you will be a scholar. I therefore wish you to purchase such books as will be useful and agreeable to you *then*, and that you employ this very small sum in laying a little tiny corner-stone for your future library." And a year or two afterward she thanks him for his "two letters, so neat and free from blots. By this obvious improvement you have entitled yourself to another book. You must go to Hatchard's and choose. I think we have nearly exhausted the epics. What say you to a little good prose? Johnson's "Hebrides," or Walton's "Lives," unless you would like a neat edition of "Cowper's Poems," or "Paradise Lost," for your own eating? In any case, choose something which you do not possess. I want you to become a complete Frenchman, that I may give you Racine, the only dramatic poet I know in any modern language that is perfectly pure and good. I think you have hit off the Ode very well, and I am much obliged to you for the Dedication." The poor little author was already an adept in the traditional modes of requiting a patron.

He had another Mæcenas in the person of General Macaulay, who came back from India in 1810. The boy greeted him with a copy of verses, beginning

> Now safe returned from Asia's parching strand,
> Welcome, thrice welcome to thy native land.

To tell the unvarnished truth, the general's return was not altogether of a triumphant character. After very narrowly escaping with his life from an outbreak at Travancore, incited by a native minister who owed him a grudge, he had given proof of courage and spirit during some military operations which ended in his being brought back to the Residency with flying colors. But, when the fighting was over, he countenanced, and perhaps prompted, measures of retaliation which were ill taken by his superiors at Calcutta. In his congratulatory effusion the nephew presumes to remind the uncle that on European soil there still might be found employment for so redoubtable a sword.

> For many a battle shall be lost and won
> Ere yet thy glorious labors shall be done.

The general did not take the hint, and spent the remainder of his life peacefully enough between London, Bath, and the Continental capitals. He was accustomed to say that his traveling-carriage was his only freehold; and, wherever he fixed his temporary residence, he had the talent of making himself popular. At Geneva he was a universal favorite; he always was welcome at Coppet; and he gave the strongest conceivable proof of a cosmopolitan disposition by finding himself equally at home at Rome and at Clapham. When in England, he lived much with his relations, to whom he was sincerely attached. He was generous in a high degree, and the young people owed to him books which they otherwise could never have obtained, and treats and excursions which formed the only recreations that broke the uniform current of their lives. They regarded their uncle Colin as the man of the world of the Macaulay family.

Zachary Macaulay's circumstances during these years were good, and constantly improving. For some time he held the post of secretary to the Sierra Leone Company, with a salary of £500 per annum. He subsequently entered into partnership with a nephew, and the firm did a large business as African merchants under the names of Macaulay and Babington. The position of the father was favorable to the highest interests of his children. A boy has the best chance of being well brought up in a household where there is solid comfort combined with thrift and simplicity; and the family was increasing too fast to leave any margin for luxurious expenditure. Before the eldest son had completed his thirteenth year he had three brothers and five sisters.

In the course of 1812 it began to be evident that Tom had got beyond the educational capabilities of Clapham; and his father seriously contemplated the notion of removing to London in order to place him as a day-scholar at Westminster. Thorough as was the consideration which the parents gave to the matter, their decision was of more importance than they could at the time foresee. If their son had gone to a public school, it is more than probable that he would have turned out a different man and have done different work. So sensitive and home-loving a boy might for a while have been too depressed to enter fully into the ways of the place; but, as he gained confidence, he could not have withstood the irresistible attractions which the life of a great school exercises over a vivid, eager nature, and he would have sacrificed to passing pleasures and emulations a part, at any rate, of those years which, in order to be what he was, it was necessary that he should spend wholly among his books. Westminster or Harrow might have sharpened his faculties for dealing with affairs and with men, but the world at large would have lost more than he could by any possibility have gained. If Macaulay had received the usual education of a young Englishman, he might in all probability have kept his seat for Edinburgh, but he could hardly have written the essay on Von Ranke, or the description of England in the third chapter of the "History."

Mr. Macaulay ultimately fixed upon a private school, kept by the Rev. Mr. Preston, at Little Shelford, a village in the immediate vicinity of Cambridge. The motives which guided this selection were mainly of a religious nature. Mr. Preston held extreme Low-church opinions, and stood in the good books of Mr. Simeon, whose word had long been law in the Cambridge section of the evangelical circle. But, whatever had been the inducement to make it, the choice proved singularly fortunate. The tutor, it is true, was narrow in his views, and lacked the taste and judgment to set those views before his pupils in an attractive form. Theological topics dragged into the conversation at unexpected moments, inquiries about their spiritual state, and long sermons which had to be listened to under the dire obligation of reproducing them in an epitome, fostered in the minds of some of the boys a reaction against the outward manifestations of religion—a reaction which had already begun under the strict system pursued in their respective homes. But, on the other hand, Mr. Preston knew both how to teach his scholars, and when to leave them to teach themselves. The eminent judge who divided grown men into two sharply defined and most uncomplimentary categories was accustomed to say that private schools made poor creatures, and public schools sad dogs; but Mr. Preston succeeded in giving a practical contradiction to Sir William Maule's proposition. His pupils, who were limited to an average of a dozen at a time, got far beyond their share of honors at the university and of distinction in after-life. George Stainforth, a grandson of Sir Francis Baring, by his success at Cambridge was the first to win the school an honorable name, which was more than sustained by Henry Malden, now

Greek Professor at University College, London, and by Macaulay himself. Shelford was strongly under the influence of the neighboring university: an influence which Mr. Preston, himself an ex-fellow of Trinity, wisely encouraged. The boys were penetrated with Cambridge ambitions and ways of thought, and frequent visitors brought to the table, where master and pupils dined in common, the freshest Cambridge gossip of the graver sort.

Little Macaulay received much kindness from Dean Milner, the president of Queen's College, then at the very summit of a celebrity which is already of the past. Those who care to search among the embers of that once brilliant reputation can form a fair notion of what Samuel Johnson would have been if he had lived a generation later, and had been absolved from the necessity of earning his bread by the enjoyment of ecclesiastical sinecures, and from any uneasiness as to his worldly standing by the possession of academical dignities and functions. The dean, who had boundless good-will for all his fellow-creatures at every period of life, provided that they were not Jacobins or skeptics, recognized the promise of the boy, and entertained him at his college residence on terms of friendliness and almost of equality. After one of these visits, he writes to Mr. Macaulay: "Your lad is a fine fellow. He shall stand before kings. He shall not stand before mean men."

Shelford, February 22d, 1813.

MY DEAR PAPA,—As this is a whole holiday, I can not find a better time for answering your letter. With respect to my health, I am very well, and tolerably cheerful, as Blundell, the best and most clever of all the scholars, is very kind, and talks to me, and takes my part. He is quite a friend of Mr. Preston's. The other boys, especially Lyon, a Scotch boy, and Wilberforce, are very good-natured, and we might have gone on very well had not one ——, a Bristol fellow, come here. He is unanimously allowed to be a queer fellow, and is generally characterized as a foolish boy, and by most of us as an ill-natured one. In my learning I do Xenophon every day, and twice a week the "Odyssey," in which I am classed with Wilberforce, whom all the boys allow to be very clever, very droll, and very impudent. We do Latin verses twice a week, and I have not yet been laughed at, as Wilberforce is the only one who hears them, being in my class. We are exercised also once a week in English composition, and once in Latin composition, and letters of persons renowned in history to each other. We get by heart Greek grammar or Virgil every evening. As for sermon-writing, I have hitherto got off with credit, and I hope I shall keep up my reputation. We have had the first meeting of our debating society the other day, when a vote of censure was moved for upon Wilberforce; but he, getting up, said, "Mr. President, I beg to second the motion." By this means he escaped. The kindness which Mr. Preston shows me is very great. He always assists me in what I can not do, and takes me to walk out with him every now and then. My room is a delightful, snug little chamber, which nobody can enter, as there is a trick about opening the door. I sit like a king, with my writing-desk before me; for (would you believe it?) there is a writing-desk in my chest of drawers; my books on one side, my box of papers on the other, with my arm-chair and my candle; for every boy has a candlestick, snuffers, and extinguisher of his own. Being pressed for room, I will conclude what I have to say to-morrow, and ever remain your affectionate son,

Thomas B. Macaulay.

The youth who on this occasion gave proof of his parentage by his readiness and humor was Wilberforce's eldest son. A fortnight later on, the subject chosen for discussion was "whether Lord Wellington or Marlborough was the greatest general. A very warm debate is expected."

Shelford, April 20th, 1813.

My dear Mama,—Pursuant to my promise, I resume my pen to write to you with the greatest pleasure. Since I wrote to you yesterday, I have enjoyed myself more than I have ever done since I came to Shelford. Mr. Hodson called about twelve o'clock yesterday morning with a pony for me, and took me with him to Cambridge. How surprised and delighted was I to learn that I was to take a bed at Queen's College in Dean Milner's apartments! Wilberforce arrived soon after, and I spent the day very agreeably, the dean amusing me with the greatest kindness. I slept there, and came home on horseback to-day just in time for dinner. The dean has invited me to come again, and Mr. Preston has given his consent. The books which I am at present employed in reading to myself are, in English, "Plutarch's Lives," and Milner's "Ecclesiastical History;" in French, Fénélon's "Dialogues of the Dead." I shall send you back the volumes of Madame de Genlis's *petits romans* as soon as possible, and I should be very much obliged for one or two more of them. Every thing now seems to feel the influence of spring. The trees are all out. The lilacs are in bloom. The days are long, and I feel that I should be happy were it not that I want home. Even yesterday, when I felt more real satisfaction than I have done for almost three months, I could not help feeling a sort of uneasiness, which indeed I have always felt more or less since I have been here, and which is the only thing that hinders me from being perfectly happy. This day two months will put a period to my uneasiness.

Fly fast the hours, and dawn th' expected morn.

Every night when I lie down I reflect that another day is cut off from the tiresome time of absence.

Your affectionate son, THOMAS B. MACAULAY.

Shelford, April 26th, 1813.

MY DEAR PAPA,—Since I have given you a detail of weekly duties, I hope you will be pleased to be informed of my Sunday's occupations. It is quite a day of rest here, and I really look to it with pleasure through the whole of the week. After breakfast we learn a chapter in the Greek Testament, that is, with the aid of our Bibles, and without doing it with a dictionary, like other lessons. We then go to church. We dine almost as soon as we come back, and we are left to ourselves till afternoon church. During this time I employ myself in reading, and Mr. Preston lends me any books for which I ask him, so that I am nearly as well off in this respect as at home, except for one thing, which, though I believe it is useful, is not very pleasant—I can only ask for one book at a time, and can not touch another till I have read it through. We then go to church, and after we come back I read as before till tea-time. After tea we write out the sermon. I can not help thinking that Mr. Preston uses all imaginable means to make us forget it, for he gives us a glass of wine each on Sunday, and on Sunday only, the very day when we want to have all our faculties awake; and some do literally go to sleep during the sermon, and look rather silly when they wake. I, however, have not fallen into this disaster.

Your affectionate son, THOMAS B. MACAULAY.

The constant allusions to home politics and to the progress of the Continental struggle, which occur throughout Zachary Macaulay's correspondence with his son, prove how freely, and on what an equal footing, the parent and child already conversed on questions of public interest. The following letter is curious as a specimen of the eagerness with which the boy habitually flung himself into the subjects which occupied his father's thoughts. The renewal of the East India Company's charter was just then under the consideration of Parliament, and the whole energies of the Evangelical party were exerted in order to signalize the occasion by securing our Eastern dominions as a field for the spread of Christianity. Petitions against the continued exclusion of missionaries were in course of circulation throughout the island, the drafts of which had been prepared by Mr. Macaulay.

Shelford, May 8th, 1813.

MY DEAR PAPA,—As on Monday it will be out of my power to write, since the examination subjects are to be given out then, I write to-day instead to answer your kind and long letter. I am very much pleased that the nation seems to take such interest in the introduction of Christianity into India. My Scotch blood begins to boil at the mention of the seventeen hundred and fifty names that went up from a single country parish. Ask Mama and Selina if they do not now admit my argument with regard to the superior advantages of the Scotch over the English peasantry.

As to my examination preparations, I will, if you please, give you a sketch of my plan. On Monday, the day on which the examination subjects are given out, I shall begin. My first performance will be my verses and my declamation. I shall then translate the Greek and Latin. The first time of going over I shall mark the passages which puzzle me, and then return to them again. But I shall have also to rub up my mathematics (by-the-bye, I begin the second book of Euclid to-day), and to study whatever history may be appointed for the examination. I shall not be able to avoid trembling, whether I know my subjects or not. I am, however, intimidated at nothing but Greek. Mathematics suit my taste, although, before I came, I declaimed against them, and asserted that, when I went to college, it should not be to Cambridge. I am occupied with the hope of lecturing Mama and Selina upon mathematics, as I used to do upon heraldry, and to change Or, and Argent, and Azure, and Gules, for squares, and points, and circles, and angles, and triangles, and rectangles, and rhomboids, and, in a word, "all the pomp and circumstance" of Euclid. When I come home, I shall, if my purse is sufficient, bring a couple of rabbits for Selina and Jane. Your affectionate son,

THOMAS B. MACAULAY.

It will be seen that this passing fondness for mathematics soon changed into bitter disgust.

Clapham, May 28th, 1813.

MY DEAR TOM,—I am very happy to hear that you have so far advanced in your different prize exercises, and with such little fatigue. I know you write with great ease to yourself, and would rather write ten poems than prune one; but remember that excellence is not attained at first. All your pieces are much mended after a little reflection, and therefore take some solitary walks, and think over each separate thing. Spare no time or trouble to render each piece as perfect as you can, and then leave the event without one anxious thought. I have always admired a saying of one of the old heathen philosophers. When a friend was condoling with him that he so well deserved of the gods, and yet that they did not shower their favors on him, as on some others less worthy, he answered, "I will, however, continue to deserve well of them." So do you, my dearest. Do your best, because it is the will of God you should improve every faculty to the utmost now, and strengthen the powers of your mind by exercise, and then in future you will be better enabled to glorify God with all your powers and talents, be they of a more humble or higher order, and you shall not fail to be received into everlasting habitations, with the applauding voice of your Saviour, "Well done, good and faithful servant." You see how ambitious your mother is. She must have the wisdom of her son acknowledged before angels, and an assembled world. My wishes can soar no higher, and they can be content with nothing less for any of my children. The first time I saw your face, I repeated those beautiful lines of Watts's cradle hymn,

> Mayst thou live to know and fear Him,
> Trust and love Him all thy days,
> *Then* go dwell forever near Him,
> See His face, and sing His praise:

and this is the substance of all my prayers for you. In less than a month you and I shall, I trust, be rambling over the Common, which now looks quite beautiful.

I am ever, my dear Tom, your affectionate mother,

SELINA MACAULAY.

The commencement of the second half-year at school, perhaps the darkest season of a boy's existence, was marked by an unusually severe and prolonged attack of home-sickness. It would be cruel to insert the first letter written after the return to Shelford from the summer holidays. That which follows it is melancholy enough.

Shelford, August 14th, 1813.

My dear Mama,—I must confess that I have been a little disappointed at not receiving a letter from home to-day. I hope, however, for one to-morrow. My spirits are far more depressed by leaving home than they were last half-year. Every thing brings home to my recollection. Every thing I read, or see, or hear, brings it to my mind. You told me I should be happy when I once came here, but not an hour passes in which I do not shed tears at thinking of home. Every hope, however unlikely to be realized, affords me some small consolation. The morning on which I went, you told me that possibly I might come home before the holidays. If you can confirm this hope, believe me when I assure you that there is nothing which I would not give for one instant's sight of home. Tell me in your next, expressly, if you can, whether or no there is any likelihood of my coming home before the holidays. If I could gain papa's leave, I should select my birthday on October 25th as the time which I should wish to spend at that home which absence renders still dearer to me. I think I see you sitting by papa just after his dinner, reading my letter, and turning to him, with an inquisitive glance, at the end of the paragraph. I think too that I see his expressive shake of the head at it. Oh, may I be mistaken! You can not conceive what an alteration a favorable answer would produce in me. If your approbation of my request depends upon my advancing in study, I will work like a cart-horse. If you should refuse it, you will deprive me of the most pleasing illusion which I ever experienced in my life. Pray do not fail to write speedily. Your dutiful and affectionate son,

T. B. Macaulay.

His father answered him in a letter of strong religious complexion, full of feeling and even of beauty, but too long for reproduction in a biography that is not his own.

Mr. Macaulay's deep anxiety for his son's welfare sometimes induced him to lend too ready an ear to busybodies who informed him of failings in the boy which would have been treated more lightly, and perhaps more wisely, by a less devoted father. In the early months of 1814 he writes as follows, after hearing the tale of some guest of Mr. Preston whom Tom had no doubt contradicted at table in presence of the assembled household:

London, March 4th, 1814.

My dear Tom,—In taking up my pen this morning a passage in Cowper almost involuntarily occurred to me. You will find it at length in his "Conversation."

> Ye powers who rule the tongue, if such there are,
> And make colloquial happiness your care,
> Preserve me from the thing I dread and hate,
> A duel in the form of a debate.
> Vociferated logic kills me quite.
> A noisy man is always in the right.

You know how much such a quotation as this would fall in with my notions—averse as I am to loud and noisy tones, and self-confident, overwhelming, and yet perhaps very unsound arguments. And you will remember how anxiously I dwelt upon this point while you were at home. I have been in hopes that this half-year would witness a great change in you in this respect. My hopes, however, have been a little damped by something which I heard last week through a friend, who seemed to have received an impression that you had gained a high distinction among the young gentlemen at Shelford by the loudness and vehemence of your tones. Now, my dear Tom, you can not doubt that this gives me pain; and it does so, not so much on account of the thing itself, as because I consider it a pretty infallible test of the mind within. I do long and pray most earnestly that the ornament of a meek and quiet spirit may be substituted for vehemence and self-confidence, and that you may be as much distinguished for the former as ever you have been for the latter. It is a school in which I am not ambitious that any child of mine should take a high degree.

If the people of Shelford be as bad as you represent them in your letters, what are they but an epitome of the world at large? Are they ungrateful to you for your kindnesses? Are they foolish, and wicked, and wayward in the use of their faculties? What is all this but what we ourselves are guilty of every day? Consider how much in our case the guilt of such conduct is aggravated by our superior knowledge. We shall not have ignorance to plead in its extenuation, as many of the people of Shelford may have. Now, instead of railing at the people of Shelford, I think the best thing which you and your school-fellows could do would be to try to reform them. You can buy and distribute useful and striking tracts, as well as Testaments, among such as can read. The cheap Repository and Religious Tract Society will furnish tracts suited to all descriptions of persons; and for those who can not read—why should you not institute a Sunday-school, to be taught by yourselves, and in which, appropriate rewards being given for good behavior, not only at school but through the week, great effects of a moral kind might soon be produced? I have exhausted my paper, and must answer the rest of your letter in a few days. In the mean time,

I am ever your most affectionate father,

ZACHARY MACAULAY.

A father's prayers are seldom fulfilled to the letter. Many years were to elapse before the son ceased to talk loudly and with confidence, and the literature that he was destined to distribute through the world was of another order from that which Mr. Macaulay here suggests. The answer, which is addressed to the mother, affords a proof that the boy could already hold his own. The allusions to the *Christian Observer*, of which his father was editor, and to Dr. Herbert Marsh, with whom the ablest pens of Clapham were at that moment engaged in hot and imbittered controversy, are thrown in with an artist's hand.

Shelford, April 11th, 1814.

MY DEAR MAMA,—The news is glorious indeed. Peace! peace with a Bourbon, with a descendant of Henri Quatre, with a prince who is bound to us by all the ties of gratitude! I have some hopes that it will be a lasting peace, that the troubles of the last twenty years may make kings and nations wiser. I can not conceive a greater punishment to Bonaparte than that which the allies have inflicted on him. How can his ambitious mind support it? All his great projects and schemes which once made every throne in Europe tremble are buried in the solitude of an Italian isle. How miraculously every thing has been conducted! We almost seem to hear the Almighty saying to the fallen tyrant, "For this cause have I raised thee up, that I might show in thee My power."

As I am in very great haste with this letter, I shall have but little time to write. I am sorry to hear that some nameless friend of papa's denounced my voice as remarkably loud. I have accordingly resolved to speak in a moderate key except on the undermentioned special occasions. *Imprimis*, when I am speaking at the same time with three others. Secondly, when I am praising the *Christian Observer*. Thirdly, when I am praising Mr. Preston or his sisters, I may be allowed to speak in my loudest voice, that they may hear me.

I saw to-day that greatest of churchmen, that pillar of Orthodoxy, that true friend to the Liturgy, that mortal enemy to the Bible Society, Herbert Marsh, D.D., Professor of Divinity on Lady Margaret's foundation. I stood looking at him for about ten minutes, and shall always continue to maintain that he is a very ill-favored gentleman as far as outward appearance is concerned. I am going this week to spend a day or two at Dean Milner's, where I hope, nothing unforeseen preventing, to see you in about two months' time.

Ever your affectionate son, T. B. MACAULAY.

In the course of the year 1814 Mr. Preston removed his establishment to Aspenden Hall, near Buntingford, in Hertfordshire—a large old-fashioned mansion, standing amidst extensive shrubberies and a pleasant, undulating domain, sprinkled with fine timber. The house has been rebuilt within the last twenty years, and nothing remains of it except the dark oak paneling of the hall in which the scholars made their recitations on the annual speech-day. The very pretty church, which stands hard by within the grounds, was undergoing restoration in 1873; and by this time the only existing portion of the former internal fittings is the family pew, in which the boys sat on drowsy summer afternoons, doing what they could to keep their impressions of the second sermon distinct from their reminiscences of the morning. Here Macaulay spent four most industrious years, doing less and less in the class-room as time went on, but enjoying the rare advantage of studying Greek and Latin by the side of such a scholar as Malden. The two companions were equally matched in age and classical attainments, and at the university maintained a rivalry so generous as hardly to deserve the name. Each of the pupils had his own chamber, which the others were forbidden to enter under the penalty of a shilling fine. This prohibition was in general not very strictly observed, but the tutor had taken the precaution of placing Macaulay in the room next his own: a proximity which rendered the position of an intruder so exceptionally dangerous that even Malden could not remember having once passed his friend's threshold during the whole of their stay at Aspenden.

In this seclusion, removed from the delight of family intercourse (the only attraction strong enough to draw him from his books), the boy read widely, unceasingly, more than rapidly. The secret of his immense acquirements lay in two invaluable gifts of nature: an unerring memory, and the capacity for taking in at a glance the contents of a printed page. During the first part of his life he remembered whatever caught his fancy, without going through the process of consciously getting it by heart. As a child, during one of the numerous seasons when the social duties devolved upon Mr. Macaulay, he accompanied his father on an afternoon call, and found on a table the "Lay of the Last Minstrel," which he had never before met with. He kept himself quiet with his prize while the elders were talking, and on his return home sat down upon his mother's bed, and repeated to her as many cantos as she had the patience or the strength to listen to. At one period of his life he was known to say that, if by some miracle of vandalism all copies of "Paradise Lost" and "The Pilgrim's Progress" were destroyed off the face of the earth, he would undertake to reproduce them both from recollection whenever a revival of learning came. In 1813, while waiting in a Cambridge coffee-room for a post-chaise which was to take him to his school, he picked up a county newspaper containing two such specimens of provincial poetical talent as in those days might be read in the corner of any weekly journal. One piece was headed "Reflections of an Exile," while the other was a trumpery parody on the Welsh ballad "Ar hyd y nos," referring to some local anecdote of an hostler whose nose had been bitten off by a filly. He looked them once through, and never gave them a thought for forty years, at the end of which time he repeated them both without missing, or, as far as he knew, changing, a single word.

As he grew older, this wonderful power became impaired so far that getting by rote the compositions of others was no longer an involuntary process. He has noted in his Lucan the several occasions on which he committed to memory his favorite passages of an author whom he regarded as unrivaled among rhetoricians, and the dates refer to the year 1836, when he had just turned the middle point of life. During his last years, at his dressing-table in the morning, he would learn by heart one of the little idyls in which Martial expatiates on the enjoyments of a Spanish country-house or a villa-farm in the environs of Rome—those delicious morsels of verse which (considering the sense that modern ideas attach to the name) it is an injustice to class under the head of epigrams.

Macaulay's extraordinary faculty of assimilating printed matter at first sight remained the same through life. To the end he read books faster than other people skimmed them, and skimmed them as fast as any one else could turn the leaves. "He seemed to read through the skin," said one who had often watched the operation. And this speed was not in his case obtained at the expense of accuracy. Any thing which had once appeared in type, from the highest effort of genius down to the most detestable trash that ever consumed ink and paper manufactured for better things, had in his eyes an authority which led him to look upon misquotation as a species of minor sacrilege.

With these endowments, sharpened by an insatiable curiosity, from his fourteenth year onward he was permitted to roam almost at will over the whole expanse of literature. He composed little beyond his school exercises, which themselves bear signs of having been written in a perfunctory manner. At this period he had evidently no heart in any thing but his reading. Before leaving Shelford for Aspenden he had already invoked the epic muse for the last time.

> Arms and the man I sing who strove in vain
> To save green Erin from a foreign reign.

The man was Roderic, King of Connaught, whom he got tired of singing before he had well completed two books of the poem. Thenceforward he appears never to have struck his lyre except in the first enthusiasm aroused by the intelligence of some favorable turn of fortune on the Continent. The flight of Napoleon from Russia was celebrated in a "Pindaric Ode" duly distributed into strophes and antistrophes; and, when the allies entered Paris, the school put his services into requisition to petition for a holiday in honor of the event. He addressed his tutor in a short poem, which begins with a few sonorous and effective couplets, grows more and more like the parody on Fitzgerald in "Rejected Addresses," and ends in a peroration of which the intention is unquestionably mock-heroic:

> Oh, by the glorious posture of affairs,
> By the enormous price that Omnium bears,
> By princely Bourbon's late recovered Crown,
> And by Miss Fanny's safe return from town,
> Oh, do not thou, and thou alone, refuse
> To show thy pleasure at this glorious news!

Touched by the mention of his sister, Mr. Preston yielded; and young Macaulay never turned another verse except at the bidding of his school-master, until, on the eve of his departure for Cambridge, he wrote between three and four hundred lines of a drama, entitled "Don Fernando," marked by force and fertility of diction, but somewhat too artificial to be worthy of publication under a name such as his. Much about the same time he communicated to Malden the commencement of a burlesque poem on the story of Anthony Babington, who by the part that he took in the plots against the life of Queen Elizabeth, had given the family a connection with English history which, however questionable, was in Macaulay's view better than none.

> Each, says the proverb, has his taste. 'Tis true.
> Marsh loves a controversy; Coates a play;
> Bennet a felon; Lewis Way a Jew;
> The Jew the silver spoons of Lewis Way.
> The Gypsy Poetry, to own the truth,
> Has been my love through childhood and in youth.

It is perhaps as well that the project to all appearance stopped with the first stanza, which in its turn was probably written for the sake of a single line. The young man had a better use for his time than to spend it in producing frigid imitations of "Beppo."

He was not unpopular among his fellow-pupils, who regarded him with pride and admiration, tempered by the compassion which his utter inability to play at any sort of game would have excited in every school, private or public alike. He troubled himself very little about the opinion of those by whom he was surrounded at Aspenden. It required the crowd and the stir of a university to call forth the social qualities which he possessed in so large a measure. The tone of his correspondence during these years sufficiently indicates that he lived almost exclusively among books. His letters, which had hitherto been very natural and pretty, began to smack of the library, and please less than those written in early boyhood. His pen was overcharged with the metaphors and phrases of other men, and it was not till maturing powers had enabled him to master and arrange the vast masses of literature which filled his memory that his native force could display itself freely through the medium of a style which was all his own. In 1815 he began a formal literary correspondence, after the taste of the previous century, with Mr. Hudson, a gentleman in the Examiner's Office of the East India House.

Aspenden Hall, August 22d, 1815.

DEAR SIR,—The *Spectator* observes, I believe in his first paper, that we can never read an author with much zest unless we are acquainted with his situation. I feel the same in my epistolary correspondence; and supposing that in this respect we may be alike, I will just tell you my condition. Imagine a house in the middle of pretty large grounds, surrounded by palings. These I never pass. You may therefore suppose that I resemble the Hermit of Parnell:

> As yet by books and swains the world he knew,
> Nor knew if books and swains report it true.

If you substitute newspapers and visitors for books and swains you may form an idea of what I know of the present state of things. Write to me as one who is ignorant of every event except political occurrences. These I learn regularly; but if Lord Byron were to publish melodies or romances, or Scott metrical tales without number, I should never see them, or perhaps hear of them, till Christmas. Retirement of this kind, though it precludes me from studying the works of the hour, is very favorable for the employment of "holding high converse with the mighty dead."

I know not whether "peeping at the world through the loop-holes of retreat" be the best way of forming us for engaging in its busy and active scenes. I am sure it is not a way to my taste. Poets may talk of the beauties of nature, the enjoyments of a country life, and rural innocence; but there is another kind of life which, though unsung by bards, is yet to me infinitely superior to the dull uniformity of country life. London is the place for me. Its smoky atmosphere and its muddy river charm me more than the pure air of Hertfordshire, and the crystal currents of the river Rib. Nothing is equal to the splendid varieties of London life, "the fine flow of London talk," and the dazzling brilliancy of London spectacles. Such are my sentiments; and if ever I publish poetry, it shall not be pastoral. Nature is the last goddess to whom my devoirs shall be paid. Yours most faithfully,

THOMAS B. MACAULAY.

This votary of city life was still two months short of completing his fifteenth year!

Aspenden Hall, August 23d, 1815.

MY DEAR MAMA,—You perceive already in so large a sheet and so small a hand the promise of a long, a very long letter; longer, as I intend it, than all the letters which you send in a half-year together. I have again begun my life of sterile monotony, unvarying labor, the dull return of dull exercises in dull uniformity of tediousness. But do not think that I complain.

> My mind to me a kingdom is.
> Such perfect joy therein I find
> As doth exceed all other bliss
> That God or nature hath assigned.

Assure yourself that I am philosopher enough to be happy, I meant to say not particularly unhappy, in solitude; but man is an animal made for society. I was gifted with reason, not to speculate in Aspenden Park, but to interchange ideas with some person who can understand me. This is what I miss at Aspenden. There are several here who possess both taste and reading, who can criticise Lord Byron and Southey with much tact and "savoir du métier." But here it is not the fashion to think. Hear what I have read since I came here. Hear and wonder! I have in the first place read Boccaccio's "Decameron," a tale of an hundred cantos. He is a wonderful writer. Whether he tells in humorous or familiar strains the follies of the silly Calandrino, or the witty pranks of Buffalmacco and Bruno, or sings in loftier numbers

> Dames, knights, and arms, and love, the feats that spring
> From courteous minds and generous faith,

or lashes with a noble severity and fearless independence the vices of the monks and the priestcraft of the established religion, he is always elegant, amusing, and, what pleases and surprises most in a writer of so unpolished an age, strikingly delicate and chastised. I prefer him infinitely to Chaucer. If you wish for a good specimen of Boccaccio, as soon as you have finished my letter (which will come, I suppose, by dinner-time), send Jane up to the library for Dryden's "Poems," and you will find among them several translations from Boccaccio, particularly one entitled "Theodore and Honoria."

But truly admirable as the bard of Florence is, I must not permit myself to give him more than his due share of my letter. I have likewise read "Gil Blas," with unbounded admiration of the abilities of Le Sage. Malden and I have read "Thalaba" together, and are proceeding to the "Curse of Kehama." Do not think, however, that I am neglecting more important studies than either Southey or Boccaccio. I have read the greater part of the "History of James I.," and Mrs. Montague's essay on Shakspeare, and a great deal of Gibbon. I never devoured so many books in a fortnight. John Smith, Bob Hankinson, and I, went over the "Hebrew Melodies" together. I certainly think far better of them than we used to do at Clapham. Papa may laugh, and indeed he did laugh me out of my taste at Clapham; but I think that there is a great deal of beauty in the first melody, "She walks in beauty," though indeed who it is that walks in beauty is not very exactly defined. My next letter shall contain a production of my muse entitled "An Inscription for the Column of Waterloo," which is to be shown to Mr. Preston to-morrow. What he may think of it I do not know. But I am like my favorite Cicero about my own productions. It is all one to me what others think of them. I never like them a bit less for being disliked by the rest of mankind. Mr. Preston has desired me to bring him up this evening two or three subjects for a declamation. Those which I have selected are as follows: 1st, a speech in the character of Lord Coningsby impeaching the Earl of Oxford; 2d, an essay on the utility of standing armies; 3d, an essay on the policy of Great Britain with regard to Continental possessions. I conclude with sending my love to papa, Selina, Jane, John ("but he is not there," as Fingal pathetically says, when in enumerating his sons who should accompany him to the chase he inadvertently mentions the dead Ryno), Henry, Fanny, Hannah, Margaret, and Charles. Valete. T. B. MACAULAY.

This exhaustive enumeration of his brothers and sisters invites attention to that home where he reigned supreme. Lady Trevelyan thus describes their life at Clapham: "I think that my father's strictness was a good counterpoise to the perfect worship of your uncle by the rest of the family. To us he was an object of passionate love and devotion. To us he could do no wrong. His unruffled sweetness of temper, his unfailing flow of spirits, his amusing talk, all made his presence so delightful that his wishes and his tastes were our law. He hated strangers, and his notion of perfect happiness was to see us all working round him while he read aloud a novel, and then to walk all together on the Common, or, if it rained, to have a frightfully noisy game of hide-and-seek. I have often wondered how our mother could ever have endured our noise in her little house. My earliest recollections speak of the intense happiness of the holidays, beginning with finding him in papa's room in the morning; the awe at the idea of his having reached home in the dark after we were in bed, and the Saturnalia which at once set in; no lessons; nothing but fun and merriment for the whole six weeks. In the year 1816 we were at Brighton for the summer holidays, and he read to us 'Sir Charles Grandison.' It was always a habit in our family to read aloud every evening. Among the books selected, I can recall Clarendon, Burnet, Shakspeare (a great treat when my mother took the volume), Miss Edgeworth, Mackenzie's 'Lounger' and 'Mirror,' and, as a standing dish, the *Quarterly* and the *Edinburgh Review*. Poets, too, especially Scott and Crabbe, were constantly chosen. Poetry and novels, except during Tom's holidays, were forbidden in the daytime, and stigmatized as 'drinking drams in the morning.'"

Morning or evening, Mr. Macaulay disapproved of novel-reading; but, too indulgent to insist on having his own way in any but essential matters, he lived to see himself the head of a family in which novels were more read and better remembered than in any household of the United Kingdom. The first warning of the troubles that were in store for him was an anonymous letter addressed to him as editor of the *Christian Observer*, defending works of fiction, and eulogizing Fielding and Smollett. This he incautiously inserted in his periodical, and brought down upon himself the most violent objurgations from scandalized contributors, one of whom informed the public that he had committed the obnoxious number to the flames, and should thenceforward cease to take in the magazine. The editor replied with becoming spirit, although by that time he was aware that the communication, the insertion of which in an unguarded moment had betrayed him into a controversy for which he had so little heart, had proceeded from the pen of his son. Such was young Macaulay's first appearance in print, if we except the index to the thirteenth volume of the *Christian Observer*, which he drew up during his Christmas holidays of 1814. The place where he performed his earliest literary work can be identified with tolerable certainty. He enjoyed the eldest son's privilege of a separate bed-chamber; and there, at the front window on the top story, farthest from the Common and nearest to London, we can fancy him sitting, apart from the crowded play-room, keeping himself warm as best he might, and traveling steadily through the blameless pages, the contents of which it was his task to classify for the convenience of posterity.

Lord Macaulay used to remark that Thackeray introduced too much of the Dissenting element into his picture of Clapham in the opening chapters of "The Newcomes." The leading people of the place, with the exception of Mr. William Smith, the Unitarian member of Parliament, were one and all stanch Churchmen; though they readily worked in concert with those religious communities which held in the main the same views and pursued the same objects as themselves. Old John Thornton, the earliest of the Evangelical magnates, when he went on his annual tour to the South Coast or the Scotch mountains, would take with him some Independent or Wesleyan minister who was in need of a holiday: and his followers in the next generation had the most powerful motives for maintaining the alliance which he had inaugurated. They could not neglect such doughty auxiliaries in the memorable war which they waged against cruelty, ignorance, and irreligion, and in their less momentous skirmishes with the votaries of the stage, the race-course, and the card-table. Without the aid of non-conformist sympathy, and money, and oratory, and organization, their operations would have been doomed to certain failure. The cordial relations entertained with the members of other denominations by those among whom his youth was passed did much to indoctrinate Macaulay with a lively and genuine interest in sectarian theology. He possessed a minute acquaintance, very rare among men of letters, with the origin and growth of the various forms of faith and practice which have divided the allegiance of his countrymen; not the least important of his qualifications for writing the history of an epoch when the national mind gave itself to religious controversy even more largely than had been its wont.

The method of education in vogue among the Clapham families was simple without being severe. In the spacious gardens, and the commodious houses of an architecture already dating a century back, which surrounded the Common, there was plenty of freedom and good-fellowship, and reasonable enjoyment for young and old alike. Here, again, Thackeray has not done justice to a society that united the mental culture and the intellectual activity which are developed by the neighborhood of a great capital with the wholesome quiet and the homely ways of country life. Hobson and Brian Newcome are not fair specimens of the effect of Clapham influences upon the second generation. There can have been little that was narrow, and nothing vulgar, in a training which produced Samuel Wilberforce, and Sir James Stephen, and Charles and Robert Grant, and Lord Macaulay. The plan on which children were brought up in the chosen home of the Low-church party, during its golden age, will bear comparison with systems about which, in their day, the world was supposed never to tire of hearing, although their ultimate results have been small indeed.

It is easy to trace whence the great bishop and the great writer derived their immense industry. Working came as naturally as walking to sons who could not remember a time when their fathers idled. "Mr. Wilberforce and Mr. Babington have never appeared down-stairs lately, except to take a hasty dinner, and for half an hour after we have supped. The slave-trade now occupies them nine hours daily. Mr. Babington told me last night that he had fourteen hundred folio pages to read, to detect the contradictions, and to collect the answers which corroborate Mr. Wilberforce's assertions in his speeches. These, with more than two thousand pages to be abridged, must be done within a fortnight, and they talk of sitting up one night in every week to accomplish it. The two friends begin to look very ill, but they are in excellent spirits, and at this moment I hear them laughing at some absurd questions in the examination." Passages such as this are scattered broadcast through the correspondence of Wilberforce and his friends. Fortitude and diligence and self-control, and all that makes men good and great, can not be purchased from professional educators. Charity is not the only quality which begins at home. It is throwing away money to spend a thousand a year on the teaching of three boys, if they are to return from school only to find the older members of their family intent on amusing themselves at any cost of time and trouble, or sacrificing self-respect in ignoble efforts to struggle into a social grade above their own. The child will never place his aims high and pursue them steadily unless the parent has taught him what energy and elevation of purpose mean not less by example than by precept.

In that company of indefatigable workers none equaled the labors of Zachary Macaulay. Even now, when he has been in his grave for more than the third of a century, it seems almost an act of disloyalty to record the public services of a man who thought that he had done less than nothing if his exertions met with praise, or even with recognition. The nature and value of those services may be estimated from the terms in which a very competent judge, who knew how to weigh his words, spoke of the part which Mr. Macaulay played in one only of his numerous enterprises—the suppression of slavery and the slave-trade. "That God had called him into being to wage war with this gigantic evil became his immutable conviction. During forty successive years he was ever burdened with this thought. It was the subject of his visions by day and of his dreams by night. To give them reality he labored as men labor for the honors of a profession or for the subsistence of their children. In that service he sacrificed all that a man may lawfully sacrifice—health, fortune, repose, favor, and celebrity. He died a poor man, though wealth was within his reach. He devoted himself to the severest toil, amidst allurements to luxuriate in the delights of domestic and social intercourse, such as few indeed have encountered. He silently permitted some to usurp his hardly earned honors, that no selfish controversy might desecrate their common cause. He made no effort to obtain the praises of the world, though he had talents to command, and a temper peculiarly disposed to enjoy them. He drew upon himself the poisoned shafts of calumny, and, while feeling their sting as generous spirits only can feel it, never turned a single step aside from his path to propitiate or to crush the slanderers."

Zachary Macaulay was no common fanatic. It is difficult to understand when it was that he had time to pick up his knowledge of general literature, or how he made room for it in a mind so crammed with facts and statistics relating to questions of the day, that when Wilberforce was at a loss for a piece of information he used to say, "Let us look it out in Macaulay." His private papers, which are one long register of unbroken toil, do nothing to clear up the problem. Highly cultivated, however, he certainly was, and his society was in request with many who cared little for the objects which to him were every thing. That he should have been esteemed and regarded by Lord Brougham, Francis Horner, and Sir James Mackintosh, seems natural enough; but there is something surprising in finding him in friendly and frequent intercourse with some of his most distinguished French contemporaries. Chateaubriand, Sismondi, the Duc de Broglie, Madame de Staël, and Dumont, the interpreter of Bentham, corresponded with him freely in their own language, which he wrote to admiration. The gratification that his foreign acquaintance felt at the sight of his letters would have been unalloyed but for the pamphlets and blue-books by which they were too often accompanied. It is not difficult to imagine the feelings of a Parisian on receiving two quarto volumes, with the postage only in part prepaid, containing the proceedings of a Committee on Apprenticeship in the West Indies, and including the twelve or fifteen thousand questions and answers on which the Report was founded. It would be hard to meet with a more perfect sample of the national politeness than the passage in which M. Dumont acknowledges one of the less formidable of these unwelcome gifts. "MON CHER AMI,—Je ne laisserai pas partir Mr. Inglis sans le charger de quelques lignes pour vous, afin de vous remercier du *Christian Observer* que vous avez eu la bonté de m'envoyer. Vous savez que j'ai *a great taste for it;* mais il faut vous avouer une triste vérité, c'est que je manque absolument de loisir pour le lire. Ne m'en envoyez plus, car je me sens peiné d'avoir sous les yeux de si bonnes choses dont je n'ai pas le temps de me nourrir."

"In the year 1817," Lady Trevelyan writes, "my parents made a tour in Scotland with your uncle. Brougham gave them a letter to Jeffrey, who hospitably entertained them, but your uncle said that Jeffrey was not at all at his ease, and was apparently so terrified at my father's religious reputation that he seemed afraid to utter a joke. Your uncle complained grievously that they traveled from manse to manse, and always came in for very long prayers and expositions. I think, with all the love and reverence with which your uncle regarded his father's memory, there mingled a shade of bitterness that he had not met quite the encouragement and appreciation from him which he received from others. But such a son as he was! Never a disrespectful word or look, always anxious to please and amuse, and at last he was the entire stay and support of his father's declining years.

"Your uncle was of opinion that the course pursued by his father toward him during his youth was not judicious. But here I am inclined to disagree with him. There was no want of proof of the estimation in which his father held him, corresponding with him from a very early age as with a man, conversing with him freely, and writing of him most fondly. But, in the desire to keep down any conceit, there was certainly in my father a great outward show of repression and depreciation. Then the faults of your uncle were peculiarly those that my father had no patience with. Himself precise in his arrangements, writing a beautiful hand, particular about neatness, very accurate and calm, detesting strong expressions, and remarkably self-controlled—while his eager, impetuous boy, careless of his dress, always forgetting to wash his hands and brush his hair, writing an execrable hand, and folding his letters with a great blotch for a seal, was a constant care and irritation. Many letters to your uncle have I read on these subjects. Sometimes a specimen of the proper way of folding a letter is sent to him (those were the sad days before envelopes were known), and he is desired to repeat the experiment till he succeeds. General Macaulay's fastidious nature led him to take my father's line regarding your uncle, and my youthful soul was often vexed by the constant reprimands for venial transgressions. But the great sin was the idle reading, which was a thorn in my father's side that never was extracted. In truth, he really acknowledged to the full your uncle's abilities, and felt that if he could only add his own *morale*, his unwearied industry, his power of concentrating his energies on the work in hand, his patient, painstaking calmness, to the genius and fervor which his son possessed, then a being might be formed who could regenerate the world. Often in later years I have heard my father, after expressing an earnest desire for some object, exclaim, 'If I had only Tom's power of speech!' But he should have remembered that all gifts are not given to one, and that perhaps such a union as he coveted is even impossible. Parents must be content to see their children walk in their own path, too happy if through any road they attain the same end, the living for the glory of God and the good of man."

From a marvelously early date in Macaulay's life, public affairs divided his thoughts with literature, and, as he grew to manhood, began more and more to divide his aspirations. His father's house was much used as a centre of consultation by members of Parliament who lived in the suburbs on the Surrey side of London, and the boy could hardly have heard more incessant, and assuredly not more edifying political talk if he had been brought up in Downing Street. The future advocate and interpreter of Whig principles was not reared in the Whig faith. Attached friends of Pitt, who in personal conduct and habits of life certainly came nearer to their standard than his great rival, and warmly in favor of a war which to their imagination never entirely lost its early character of an internecine contest with atheism, the Evangelicals in the House of Commons for the most part acted with the Tories. But it may be doubted whether in the long run their party would not have been better without them. By the zeal,* the munificence, the laborious activity with which they pursued their religious and semi-religious enterprises, they did more to teach the world how to get rid of existing institutions than by their votes and speeches at Westminster they contributed to preserve them. With their May meetings, and African institu-

* Macaulay, writing to one of his sisters in 1844, says: "I think Stephen's article on the Clapham sect the best thing he ever did. I do not think with you that the Claphamites were men too obscure for such delineation. The truth is that from that little knot of men emanated all the Bible societies and almost all the missionary societies in the world. The whole organization of the Evangelical party was their work. The share which they had in providing means for the education of the people was great. They were really the destroyers of the slave-trade and of slavery. Many of those whom Stephen describes were public men of the greatest weight. Lord Teignmouth governed India at Calcutta. Grant governed India in Leadenhall Street. Stephen's father was Perceval's right-hand man in the House of Commons. It is needless to speak of Wilberforce. As to Simeon, if you knew what his authority and influence were, and how they extended from Cambridge to the most remote corners of England, you would allow that his real sway in the Church was far greater than that of any primate. Thornton, to my surprise, thinks the passage about my father unfriendly. I defended Stephen. The truth is that he asked my permission to draw a portrait of my father for the *Edinburgh Review*. I told him that I had only to beg that he would not give it the air of a puff: a thing which, for myself and for my friends, I dread far more than any attack. My influence over the *Review* is so well known that a mere eulogy of my father appearing in that work would only call forth derision. I therefore am really glad that Stephen has introduced into his sketch some little characteristic traits which, in themselves, were not beauties."

tions, and antislavery reporters, and their subscriptions of tens of thousands of pounds, and their petitions bristling with hundreds of thousands of signatures, and all the machinery for informing opinion and bringing it to bear on ministers and legislators which they did so much to perfect and even to invent, they can be regarded as nothing short of the pioneers and fuglemen of that system of popular agitation which forms a leading feature in our internal history during the past half-century. At an epoch when the Cabinet which they supported was so averse to manifestations of political sentiment that a Reformer who spoke his mind in England was seldom long out of prison, and in Scotland ran a very serious risk of transportation, Toryism sat oddly enough on men who spent their days in the committee-room and their evenings on the platform, and each of whom belonged to more associations combined for the purpose of influencing Parliament than he could count on the fingers of both his hands.

There was something incongruous in their position, and as time went on they began to perceive the incongruity. They gradually learned that measures dear to philanthropy might be expected to result from the advent to power of their opponents, while their own chief too often failed them at a pinch out of what appeared to them an excessive and humiliating deference to interests powerfully represented on the benches behind him. Their eyes were first opened by Pitt's change of attitude with regard to the object that was next all their hearts. There is something almost pathetic in the contrast between two entries in Wilberforce's diary, of which the first has become classical, but the second is not so generally known. In 1787, referring to the movement against the slave-trade, he says: "Pitt recommended me to undertake its conduct, as a subject suited to my character and talents. At length, I well remember, after a conversation in the open air at the root of an old tree at Holwood, just above the vale of Keston, I resolved to give notice on a fit occasion in the House of Commons of my intention to bring the subject forward." Twelve years later, Mr. Henry Thornton had brought in a bill for confining the trade within certain limits upon the coast of Africa.

"Upon the second reading of this bill," writes Wilberforce, "Pitt coolly put off the debate when I had manifested a design of answering P——'s speech, and so left misrepresentations without a word. William Smith's anger, Henry Thornton's coolness, made a deep impression on me, but conquered, I hope, in a Christian way."

Besides instructing their successors in the art of carrying on a popular movement, Wilberforce and his followers had a lesson to teach, the value of which not so many, perhaps, will be disposed to question. In public life, as in private, they habitually had the fear of God before their eyes. A mere handful as to number, and in average talent very much on a level with the mass of their colleagues; counting in their ranks no orator, or minister, or borough-monger; they commanded the ear of the House, and exerted on its proceedings an influence, the secret of which those who have studied the Parliamentary history of the period find it only too easy to understand. To refrain from gambling and ball-giving, to go much to church and never to the theatre, was not more at variance with the social customs of the day than it was the exception in the political world to meet with men who looked to the facts of the case, and not to the wishes of the minister, and who, before going into the lobby, required to be obliged with a reason instead of with a job. Confidence and respect, and (what in the House of Commons is their unvarying accompaniment), power, were gradually, and to a great extent involuntarily, accorded to this group of members. They were not addicted to crotchets, nor to the obtrusive and unseasonable assertion of conscientious scruples. The occasions on which they made proof of independence and impartiality were such as justified and dignified their temporary renunciation of party ties. They interfered with decisive effect in the debates on the great scandals of Lord Melville and the Duke of York, and in more than one financial or commercial controversy that deeply concerned the national interests, of which the question of the retaining the Orders in Council was a conspicuous instance. A boy who, like young Macaulay, was admitted to the intimacy of politicians such as these, and was accustomed to hear matters of state discussed exclusively from a public point of view without any after-thought of ambition, or jealousy, or self-seeking, could hardly fail to grow up a patriotic and disinterested man. "What is far better and more important than all is this, that I believe Macaulay to be incorruptible. You might lay ribbons, stars, garters, wealth, titles before him in vain. He has an honest, genuine love of his country, and the world would not bribe him to neglect her interests." Thus said Sydney Smith, who of all his real friends was the least inclined to overpraise him.

The memory of Thornton and Babington, and the other worthies of their day and set, is growing dim, and their names already mean little in our ears. Part of their work was so thoroughly done that the world, as its wont is, has long ago taken the credit of that work to itself. Others of their undertakings, in weaker hands than theirs, seem out of date among the ideas and beliefs which now are prevalent. At Clapham, as elsewhere, the old order is changing, and not always in a direction which to them would be acceptable or even tolerable. What was once the home of Zachary Macaulay stands almost within the swing of the bells of a stately and elegant Roman Catholic chapel; and the pleasant mansion of Lord Teignmouth, the cradle of the Bible Society, is now turned into a convent of monks. But, in one shape or another, honest performance always lives, and the gains that accrued from the labors of these men are still on the right side of the national ledger. Among the most permanent of those gains is their undoubted share in the improvement of our political integrity by direct, and still more by indirect, example. It would be ungrateful to forget in how large a measure it is due to them that one whose judgments upon the statesmen of many ages and countries have been delivered to an audience vast beyond all precedent should have framed his decisions in accordance with the dictates of honor and humanity, of ardent public spirit and lofty public virtue.

CHAPTER II.

1818–1824.

Macaulay goes to the University.—His Love for Trinity College.—His Contemporaries at Cambridge.—Charles Austin.—The Union Debating Society.—University Studies, Successes, and Failures.—The Mathematical Tripos.—The Trinity Fellowship.—William the Third.—Letters.—Prize Poems.—Peterloo.—Novel-reading.—The Queen's Trial.—Macaulay's Feeling toward his Mother.—A Reading-party.—Hoaxing an Editor.—Macaulay takes Pupils.

In October, 1818, Macaulay went into residence at Trinity College, Cambridge. Mr. Henry Sykes Thornton, the eldest son of the member for Southwark, was his companion throughout his university career. The young men lived in the same lodgings, and began by reading with the same tutor: a plan which promised well, because, in addition to what was his own by right, each had the benefit of the period of instruction paid for by the other. But two hours were much the same as one to Macaulay, in whose eyes algebra and geometry were so much additional material for lively and interminable argument. Thornton reluctantly broke through the arrangement, and eventually stood highest among the Trinity wranglers of his year: an elevation which he could hardly have attained if he had pursued his studies in company with one who regarded every successive mathematical proposition as an open question. A Parliamentary election took place while the two friends were still quartered in Jesus Lane. A tumult in the neighboring street announced that the citizens were expressing their sentiments by the only channel which was open to them before the days of Reform: and Macaulay, to whom any excitement of a political nature was absolutely irresistible, dragged Thornton to the scene of action, and found the mob breaking the windows of the Hoop Hotel, the head-quarters of the successful candidates. His ardor was cooled by receiving a dead cat full in the face. The man who was responsible for the animal came up and apologized very civilly, assuring him that there was no town-and-gown feeling in the matter, and that the cat had been meant for Mr. Adeane. "I wish," replied Macaulay, "that you had meant it for me, and hit Mr. Adeane."

After no long while he removed within the walls of Trinity, and resided first in the centre rooms of Bishop's Hostel, and subsequently in the Old Court between the Gate and the Chapel. The door which once bore his name is on the ground-floor, to the left hand as you face the staircase. In more recent years under-graduates who are accustomed to be out after lawful hours have claimed a right of way through the window which looks toward the town; to the great annoyance of any occupant who is too good-natured to refuse the accommodation to others, and too steady to need it himself. This power of surreptitious entry had not been discovered in Macaulay's days; and indeed he would have cared very little for the privilege of spending his time outside walls which contained within them as many books as even he could read, and more friends than even he could talk to. Wanting nothing beyond what his college had to give, he reveled in the possession of leisure and liberty, in the almost complete command of his own time, in the power of passing at choice from the most perfect solitude to the most agreeable company. He keenly appreciated a society which cherishes all that is genuine, and is only too outspoken in its abhorrence of pretension and display: a society in which a man lives with those whom he likes and with those only; choosing his comrades for their own sake, and so indifferent to the external distinctions of wealth and position that no one who has entered fully into the spirit of college life can ever unlearn its priceless lesson of manliness and simplicity.

Of all his places of sojourn during his joyous and shining pilgrimage through the world, Trinity, and Trinity alone, had any share with his home in Macaulay's affection and loyalty. To the last he regarded it as an ancient Greek or a mediæval

Italian felt toward his native city. As long as he had place and standing there, he never left it willingly or returned to it without delight. The only step in his course about the wisdom of which he sometimes expressed misgiving was his preference of a London to a Cambridge life. The only dignity that in his later days he was known to covet was an honorary fellowship which would have allowed him again to look through his window upon the college grass-plots, and to sleep within sound of the splashing of the fountain; again to breakfast on commons, and dine beneath the portraits of Newton and Bacon on the daïs of the hall; again to ramble by moonlight round Neville's cloister discoursing the picturesque but somewhat exoteric philosophy which it pleased him to call by the name of metaphysics. From the door of his rooms, along the wall of the chapel, there runs a flagged pathway which affords an acceptable relief from the rugged pebbles that surround it. Here, as a bachelor of arts, he would walk, book in hand, morning after morning, throughout the long vacation, reading with the same eagerness and the same rapidity whether the volume was the most abstruse of treatises, the loftiest of poems, or the flimsiest of novels. That was the spot where in his failing years he specially loved to renew the feelings of the past, and some there are who can never revisit it without the fancy that there, if anywhere, his dear shade must linger.

He was fortunate in his contemporaries. Among his intimate friends were the two Coleridges — Derwent, the son, and Henry Nelson, who was destined to be the son-in-law of the poet; and how exceptional that destiny was, the readers of Sara Coleridge's letters are now aware. Hyde Villiers, whom an untimely death alone prevented from taking an equal place in a trio of distinguished brothers, was of his year, though not of his college.* In the year below were the young men who now bear the titles of Lord Grey, Lord Belper, and Lord Romilly;† and after the same interval came Moultrie,

* Lord Clarendon and his brothers were all Johnians.

† This paragraph was written in the summer of 1874. Three of Macaulay's old college friends, Lord Romilly, Moultrie, and Charles Austin, died in the hard winter that followed, within a few days of each other.

who in his "Dream of Life," with a fidelity which he himself pronounced to have been obtained at some sacrifice of grace, has told us how the heroes of his time looked and lived, and Charles Villiers, who still delights our generation by showing us how they talked. Then there was Praed, fresh from editing the *Etonian*, as a product of collective boyish effort unique in its literary excellence and variety; and Sidney Walker, Praed's gifted school-fellow, whose promise was blighted by premature decay of powers; and Charles Austin, whose fame would now be more in proportion to his extraordinary abilities had not his unparalleled success as an advocate tempted him before his day to retire from the toils of a career of whose rewards he already had enough.

With his vigor and fervor, his depth of knowledge and breadth of humor, his close reasoning illustrated by an expansive imagination, set off, as these gifts were, by the advantage, at that period of life so irresistible, of some experience of the world at home and abroad, Austin was indeed a king among his fellows.

> Grave, sedate,
> And (if the looks may indicate the age),
> Our senior some few years: no keener wit,
> No intellect more subtle, none more bold,
> Was found in all our host.

So writes Moultrie, and the testimony of his verse is borne out by John Stuart Mill's prose. "The impression he gave was that of boundless strength, together with talents which, combined with such apparent force of will and character, seemed capable of dominating the world." He certainly was the only man who ever succeeded in dominating Macaulay. Brimming over with ideas that were soon to be known by the name of Utilitarian, a panegyrist of American institutions, and an unsparing assailant of ecclesiastical endowments and hereditary privileges, he effectually cured the young under-graduate of his Tory opinions, which were never more than skin-deep, and brought him nearer to Radicalism than he ever was before or since. The report of this conversion, of which the most was made by ill-natured tale-bearers who met with more encouragement than they deserved, created some consternation in the family circle: while the reading set at Cambridge was duly scandalized at the influence which one whose classical attainments were rather discursive than exact had gained over a Craven scholar. To this hour men may be found in remote parsonages who mildly resent the fascination which Austin of Jesus exercised over Macaulay of Trinity.

The day and the night together were too short for one who was entering on the journey of life amidst such a band of travelers. So long as a door was open or a light burning in any of the courts, Macaulay was always in the mood for conversation and companionship. Unfailing in his attendance at lecture and chapel, blameless with regard to college laws and college discipline, it was well for his virtue that no curfew was in force within the precincts of Trinity. He never tired of recalling the days when he supped at midnight on milk-punch and roast turkey, drank tea in floods at an hour when older men are intent upon any thing rather than on the means of keeping themselves awake, and made little of sitting over the fire till the bell rang for morning chapel in order to see a friend off by the early coach. In the license of the summer vacation, after some prolonged and festive gathering, the whole party would pour out into the moonlight and ramble for mile after mile through the country till the noise of their wide-flowing talk mingled with the twittering of the birds in the hedges which bordered the Coton pathway or the Madingley road. On such occasions it must have been well worth the loss of sleep to hear Macaulay plying Austin with sarcasms upon the doctrine of the Greatest Happiness, which then had still some gloss of novelty; putting into an ever-fresh shape the time-honored jokes against the Johnians for the benefit of the Villierses; and urging an interminable debate on Wordsworth's merits as a poet, in which the Coleridges, as in duty bound, were ever ready to engage. In this particular field he acquired a skill of fence which rendered him the most redoubtable of antagonists. Many years afterward, at the time when the "Prelude" was fresh from the press, he was maintaining against the opinion of a large and mixed society that the poem was unreadable. At last, overborne by the united indignation of so many of Wordsworth's admirers, he agreed that the question should be referred to the test of personal experience; and on inquiry it was discovered that the only individual present who had got through the "Prelude" was Macaulay himself.

It is not only that the witnesses of these scenes unanimously declare that they have never since heard such conversation in the most renowned of social circles. The partiality of a generous young man for trusted and admired companions may well color his judgment over the space of even half a century. But the estimate of university contemporaries was abundantly confirmed by the outer world. While on a visit to Lord Lansdowne at Bowood, Austin and Macaulay happened to get upon college topics one morning at breakfast. When the meal was finished they drew their chairs to either end of the chimney-piece, and talked at each other across the hearth-rug as if they were in a first-floor room in the Old Court of Trinity. The whole company, ladies, artists, politicians, and diners-out, formed a silent circle round the two Cantabs, and, with a short break for lunch, never stirred till the bell warned them that it was time to dress for dinner.

It has all irrevocably perished. With life before them, and each intent on his own future, none among that troop of friends had the mind to play Boswell to the others. One repartee survives, thrown off in the heat of discussion, but exquisitely perfect in all its parts. Acknowledged without dissent to be the best-applied quotation that ever was made within five miles of the Fitzwilliam Museum, it is unfortunately too strictly classical for reproduction in these pages.

We are more easily consoled for the loss of the eloquence which then flowed so full and free in the debates of the Cambridge Union. In 1820 that society was emerging from a period of tribulation and repression. The authorities of the university, who, as old constituents of Mr. Pitt and warm supporters of Lord Liverpool, had been never very much inclined to countenance the practice of political discussion among the under-graduates, set their faces against it more than ever at an epoch when the temper of the time increased the tendency of young men to run into extremes of partisanship. At length a compromise was extorted from the reluctant hands of the vice-chancellor, and the club was allowed to take into consideration public affairs of a date anterior to the century. It required less ingenuity than the leaders of the Union had at their command to hit upon a method of dealing with the present under the guise of the past. Motions were framed that reflected upon the existing Government under cover of a censure on the cabinets of the previous generation. Resolutions which called upon the meeting to declare that the boon of Catholic Emancipation should have been granted in the year 1795, or that our commercial policy previous to 1800 should have been founded on the basis of free trade, were clearly susceptible of great latitude of treatment. And, again, in its character of a reading-club, the society, when assembled for the conduct of private business, was at liberty to review the political creed of the journals of the day in order to decide which of them it should take in and which it should discontinue. The *Examiner* newspaper was the flag of many a hard-fought battle; the *Morning Chronicle* was voted in and out of the rooms half a dozen times within a single twelvemonth; while a series of impassioned speeches on the burning question of interference in behalf of Greek independence were occasioned by a proposition of Malden's, "that ἡ Ἑλληνίκη σάλπιγξ do lie upon the table."

At the close of the debates, which were held in a large room at the back of The Red Lion in Petty Cury, the most prominent members met for supper in the hotel, or at Moultrie's lodgings, which were situated close at hand. They acted as a self-appointed standing committee, which watched over the general interests of the Union, and selected candidates, whom they put in nomination for its offices. The society did not boast a Hansard: an omission which, as time went on, some among its orators had no reason to regret. Faint recollections still survive of a discussion upon the august topic of the character of George the Third. "To whom do we owe it," asked Macaulay, "that, while Europe was convulsed with anarchy and desolated with war, England alone remained tranquil, prosperous, and secure? To whom but the Good Old King? Why was it that, when neighboring capitals were perishing in the flames, our own was illuminated only for triumphs?* You may find the cause in the same three words: the Good Old King." Praed, on the other hand, would allow his late monarch neither public merits nor private virtues. "A good man! If he had been a plain country gentleman with no wider opportunities for mischief, he would at least have bullied his footman and cheated his steward."

Macaulay's intense enjoyment of all that was stirring and vivid around him undoubtedly hindered him in the race for university honors; though his success was sufficient to inspirit him at the time, and to give him abiding pleasure in the retrospect. He twice gained the chancellor's medal for English verse, with poems admirably planned, and containing passages of real beauty, but which may not be republished in the teeth of the panegyric which, within ten years after they were written, he pronounced upon Sir Roger Newdigate. Sir Roger had laid down the rule that no exercise sent in for the prize which he established at Oxford was to exceed fifty lines. This law, says Macaulay, seems to have more foundation in reason than is generally the case with a literary canon, "for the world, we believe, is pretty well agreed in thinking that the shorter a prize poem is, the better."

Trinity men find it difficult to understand how it was that he missed getting one of the three silver goblets given for the best English declamations of the year. If there is one thing which all Macaulay's friends and all his enemies admit it is that he could declaim English. His own version of the affair was that the senior dean, a relative of the victorious candidate, sent for him, and said, "Mr. Macaulay, as you have not got

* This debate evidently made some noise in the university world. There is an allusion to it in a squib of Praed's, very finished and elegant, and beyond all doubt contemporary. The passage relating to Macaulay begins with the lines—

Then the favorite comes, with his trumpets and drums,
And his arms and his metaphors crossed.

the first cup, I do not suppose that you will care for either of the others." He was consoled, however, by the prize for Latin declamation, and in 1821 he established his classical repute by winning a Craven university scholarship in company with his friend Malden, and Mr. George Long, who was subsequently Professor of Latin at University College, London.

Macaulay detested the labor of manufacturing Greek and Latin verse in cold blood as an exercise, and his hexameters were never up to the best Etonian mark, nor his iambics to the highest standard of Shrewsbury. He defined a scholar as one who reads Plato with his feet on the fender. When already well on in his third year, he writes: "I never practiced composition a single hour since I have been at Cambridge." "Soak your mind with Cicero," was his constant advice to students at that time of life when writing Latin prose is the most lucrative of accomplishments. The advantage of this precept was proved in the fellowship examination of the year 1824, when he obtained the honor which in his eyes was the most desirable that Cambridge had to give. The delight of the young man at finding himself one of the sixty masters of an ancient and splendid establishment; the pride with which he signed his first order for the college plate, and dined for the first time at the high table in his own right; the reflection that these privileges were the fruit, not of favor or inheritance, but of personal industry and ability, were matters on which he loved to dwell long after the world had loaded him with its most envied prizes. Macaulay's feeling on this point is illustrated by the curious reverence which he cherished for those junior members of the college who, some ninety years ago, by a spirited remonstrance addressed to the governing body, brought about a reform in the Trinity fellowship examination that secured to it the character for fair play and efficiency which it has ever since enjoyed. In his copy of the "Cambridge Calendar" for the year 1859 (the last of his life), throughout the list of the old mathematical triposes the words "one of the eight" appear in his handwriting opposite the name of each of these gentlemen. And one, at any rate, among his nephews can never remember the time when it was not diligently impressed upon him that, if he minded his syntax, he might eventually hope to reach a position which would give him three hundred pounds a year, a stable for his horse, six dozen of audit ale every Christmas, a loaf and two pats of butter every morning, and a good dinner for nothing, with as many almonds and raisins as he could eat at dessert.

Macaulay was not chosen a fellow until his third trial, nominally for the amazing reason that his translations from Greek and Latin, while faithfully representing the originals, were rendered into English that was ungracefully bald and inornate. The real cause was, beyond all doubt, his utter neglect of the special study of the place: a liberty which Cambridge seldom allows to be taken with impunity even by her most favored sons. He used to profess deep and lasting regret for his early repugnance to scientific subjects; but the fervor of his penitence in after-years was far surpassed by the heartiness with which he inveighed against mathematics as long as it was his business to learn them. Every one who knows the Senate-house may anticipate the result. When the tripos of 1822 made its appearance, his name did not grace the list. In short, to use the expressive vocabulary of the university, Macaulay was gulfed: a mishap which disabled him from contending for the chancellor's medals, then the crowning trophies of a classical career. "I well remember," says Lady Trevelyan, "that first trial of my life. We were spending the winter at Brighton, when a letter came giving an account of the event. I recollect my mother taking me into her room to tell me; for even then it was known how my whole heart was wrapped up in him, and it was thought necessary to break the news. When your uncle arrived at Brighton I can recall my mother telling him that he had better go at once to his father, and get it over, and I can see him as he left the room on that errand."

During the same year he engaged in a less arduous competition. A certain Mr. Greaves, of Fulbourn, had long since provided a reward of ten pounds for "the junior bachelor of Trinity College who wrote the best essay on the 'Conduct and Character of William the Third.'" As the prize is annual, it is appalling to reflect upon the searching analysis to which the motives of that monarch must by this time have been subjected. The event, however, may be counted as an encouragement to the founders of endowments, for amidst the succession of juvenile critics whose attention was by his munificence turned in the direction of his favorite hero, Mr. Greaves had at last fallen in with the right man. It is more than probable that to this old Cambridgeshire Whig was due the first idea of that "History" in whose pages William of Orange stands as the central figure. The essay is still in existence, in a close neat hand which twenty years of reviewing never rendered illegible. Originally written as a fair copy, but so disfigured, by repeated corrections and additions, as to be unfit for the eyes of the college authorities, it bears evident marks of having been held to the flames, and rescued on second, and in this case, it will be allowed, on better, thoughts. The exercise, which is headed by the very appropriate motto,

> Primus qui legibus urbem
> Fundabit, Curibus parvis et paupere terrâ
> Missus in imperium magnum,

is just such as will very likely be produced in the course of next Easter term by some young man of judgment and spirit who knows his Macaulay by heart, and will paraphrase him without scruple. The characters of James, of Shaftesbury, of William himself; the Popish plot; the struggle over the Exclusion Bill; the reaction from Puritanic rigor into the license of the Restoration, are drawn on the same lines and painted in the same colors as those with which the world is now familiar. The style only wants condensation, and a little of the humor which he had not yet learned to transfer from his conversation to his writings, in order to be worthy of his mature powers. He thus describes William's life-long enemy and rival, whose name he already spells after his own fashion: "Lewis was not a great general. He was not a great legislator. But he was, in one sense of the words, a great king. He was a perfect master of all the mysteries of the science of royalty—of all the arts which at once extend power and conciliate popularity—which most advantageously display the merits, or most dexterously conceal the deficiencies, of a sovereign. He was surrounded by great men, by victorious commanders, by sagacious statesmen. Yet, while he availed himself to the utmost of their services, he never incurred any danger from their rivalry. His was a talisman which extorted the obedience of the proudest and mightiest spirits. The haughty and turbulent warriors whose contests had agitated France during his minority yielded to the irresistible spell, and, like the gigantic slaves of the ring and lamp of Aladdin, labored to decorate and aggrandize a master whom they could have crushed. With incomparable address he appropriated to himself the glory of campaigns which had been planned and counsels which had been suggested by others. The arms of Turenne were the terror of Europe. The policy of Colbert was the strength of France. But in their foreign successes and their internal prosperity the people saw only the greatness and wisdom of Lewis." In the second chapter of the "History" much of this is compressed into the sentence, "He had shown, in an eminent degree, two talents invaluable to a prince—the talent of choosing his servants well, and the talent of appropriating to himself the chief part of the credit of their acts."

In a passage that occurs toward the close of the essay may be traced something more than an outline of the peroration in which, a quarter of a century later on, he summed up the character and results of the Revolution of 1688. "To have been a sovereign, yet the champion of liberty; a revolutionary leader, yet the supporter of social order, is the peculiar glory of William. He knew where to pause. He outraged no national prejudice. He abolished no ancient form. He altered no venerable name. He saw that the existing institutions possessed the greatest capabilities of excellence, and that stronger sanctions and clearer definitions were alone required to make the practice of the British constitution as admirable as the theory. Thus he imparted to innovation the dignity and stability of antiquity. He transferred to a happier order of things the associations which had attached the people to their former Government. As the Roman warrior, before he assaulted Veii, invoked its guardian gods to leave its walls, and to accept the worship and patronize the cause of the besiegers, this great prince, in attacking a system of oppression, summoned to his aid the venerable principles and deeply seated feelings to which that system was indebted for protection."

A letter written during the later years of his life expresses Macaulay's general views on the subject of university honors. "If a man brings away from Cambridge self-knowledge, accuracy of mind, and habits of strong intellectual exertion, he has gained more than if he had made a display of showy superficial Etonian scholarship, got three or four Brown's medals, and gone forth into the world a school-boy, and doomed to be a school-boy to the last. After all, what a man does at Cambridge is, in itself, nothing. If he makes a poor figure in life, his having been senior wrangler or university scholar is never mentioned but with derision. If he makes a distinguished figure, his early honors merge in those of a later date. I hope that I do not overrate my own place in the estimation of society. Such as it is, I would not give a half-penny to add to the consideration which I enjoy all the consideration that I should derive from having been senior wrangler. But I often regret, and even acutely, my want of a senior wrangler's knowledge of physics and mathematics; and I regret still more some habits of mind which a senior wrangler is pretty certain to possess." Like all men who know what the world is, he regarded the triumphs of a college career as of less value than its disappointments. Those are most to be envied who soonest learn to expect nothing for which they have not worked hard, and who never acquire the habit (a habit which an unbroken course of university successes too surely breeds), of pitying themselves overmuch if ever, in after-life, they happen to work in vain.

Cambridge, Wednesday. (Postmark, 1818.)

MY DEAR MOTHER,—King, I am absolutely certain, would take no more pupils on any account. And, even if he would, he has numerous applicants with prior claims. He has already six, who occupy him six hours in the day, and is likewise lecturer to the college. It would, however, be very easy to obtain an excellent tutor. Lefevre and Malkin are men of first-rate mathematical abilities, and both of our college. I can scarcely bear to write on mathematics or mathematicians. Oh for words to express my abomination of that science, if a name sacred to the useful and embellishing arts may be applied to the perception and recollection of certain properties in numbers and figures! Oh that I had to learn astrology, or demonology, or school divinity; oh that I were to pore over Thomas Aquinas, and to adjust the relation of Entity with the two Predicaments, so that I were exempted from this miserable study! "Discipline" of the mind! Say rather starvation, confinement, torture, annihilation! But it must be. I feel myself becoming a personification of algebra, a living trigonometrical canon, a walking table of logarithms. All my perceptions of elegance and beauty gone, or at least going. By the end of the term my brain will be "as dry as the remainder biscuit after a voyage." Oh to change Cam for Isis! But such is my destiny; and since it is so, be the pursuit contemptible, below contempt, or disgusting beyond abhorrence, I shall aim at no second place. But three years! I can not endure the thought. I can not bear to contemplate what I must have to undergo. Farewell, then, Homer and Sophocles and Cicero.

> Farewell, happy fields,
> Where joy forever reigns! Hail, horrors, hail,
> Infernal world!

How does it proceed? Milton's descriptions have been driven out of my head by such elegant expressions as the following:

$$\text{Cos. } x = 1 - \frac{x^2}{1 \cdot 2} + \frac{x^4}{1 \cdot 2 \cdot 3 \cdot 4} - \frac{x^6}{1 \cdot 2 \cdot 3 \cdot 4 \cdot 5 \cdot 6}$$

$$\text{Tan. } \overline{a + b} = \frac{\text{Tan. } a + \text{Tan. } b}{1 - \text{Tan. } a + \text{Tan. } b}.$$

My classics must be Woodhouse, and my amusements summing an infinite series. Farewell; and tell Selina and Jane to be thankful that it is not a necessary part of female education to get a headache daily without acquiring one practical truth or beautiful image in return. Again, and with affectionate love to my father, farewell wishes your most miserable and mathematical son,

T. B. MACAULAY.

Cambridge, November 9th, 1818.

MY DEAR FATHER, — Your letter, which I read with the greatest pleasure, is perfectly safe from all persons who could make a bad use of it. The Emperor Alexander's plans, as detailed in the conversation between him and Clarkson,* are almost superhuman; and tower as much above the common hopes and aspirations of philanthropists as the statue which his Macedonian namesake proposed to hew out of Mount Athos excelled the most colossal works of meaner projectors. As Burke said of Henry the Fourth's wish that every peasant in France might have the chicken in his pot comfortably on a Sunday, we may say of these mighty plans, "The mere wish, the unfulfilled desire, exceeded all that we hear of the splendid professions and exploits of princes." Yet my satisfaction in the success of that noble cause in which the emperor seems to be exerting himself with so much zeal is scarcely so great as my regret for the man who would have traced every step of its progress with anxiety, and hailed its success with the most ardent delight. Poor Sir Samuel Romilly! Quando ullum invenient parem? How long may a penal code, at once too sanguinary and too lenient, half written in blood like Draco's, and half undefined and loose as the common law of a tribe of savages, be the curse and disgrace of the country? How many years may elapse before a man who knows, like him, all that law can teach, and possesses at the same time, like him, a liberality and a discernment of general rights which the technicalities of professional learning rather tend to blunt, shall again rise to ornament and reform our jurisprudence? For such a man, if he had fallen in the maturity of years and honors, and been borne from the bed of sickness to a grave by the side of his prototype Hale amidst the tears of

* Thomas Clarkson, the famous assailant of slavery.

nobles and senators, even then, I think, the public sorrow would have been extreme. But that the last moments of an existence of high thoughts and great virtues should have been passed as his were passed! In my feelings the scene at Claremont* this time last year was mere dust in the balance in comparison. Ever your affectionate son, T. B. M.

Cambridge, Friday, February 5th, 1819.

MY DEAR FATHER,—I have not, of course, had time to examine with attention all your criticisms on "Pompeii."† I certainly am much obliged to you for withdrawing so much time from more important business to correct my effusions. Most of the remarks which I have examined are perfectly just: but as to the more momentous charge, the want of a moral, I think it might be a sufficient defense that, if a subject is given which admits of none, the man who writes without a moral is scarcely censurable. But is it the real fact that no literary employment is estimable or laudable which does not lead to the spread of moral truth or the excitement of virtuous feeling? Books of amusement tend to polish the mind, to improve the style, to give variety to conversation, and to lend a grace to more important accomplishments. He who can effect this has surely done something. Is no useful end served by that writer whose works have soothed weeks of languor and sickness, have relieved the mind exhausted from the pressure of employment by an amusement which delights without enervating, which relaxes the tension of the powers without rendering them unfit for future exercise? I should not be surprised to see these observations refuted; and I shall not be sorry if they are so. I feel personally little interest in the question. If my life be a life of literature, it shall certainly be one of literature directed to moral ends.

At all events, let us be consistent. I was amused in turning over an old volume of the *Christian Observer* to find a gentle-

* The death of Princess Charlotte.

† The subject of the English poem for the chancellor's prize of 1819 was the "Destruction of Pompeii."

man signing himself Excubitor (one of our antagonists in the question of novel-reading), after a very pious argument on the hostility of novels to a religious frame of mind, proceeding to observe that he was shocked to hear a young lady who had displayed extraordinary knowledge of modern ephemeral literature own herself ignorant of Dryden's fables! Consistency with a vengeance! The reading of modern poetry and novels excites a worldly disposition and prevents ladies from reading Dryden's fables! There is a general disposition among the more literary part of the religious world to cry down the elegant literature of our own times, while they are not in the slightest degree shocked at atrocious profaneness or gross indelicacy when a hundred years have stamped them with the title of classical. I say, "If you read Dryden you can have no reasonable objection to reading Scott." The strict antagonist of ephemeral reading exclaims, "Not so. Scott's poems are very pernicious. They call away the mind from spiritual religion and from Tancred and Sigismunda." But I am exceeding all ordinary limits. If these hasty remarks fatigue you, impute it to my desire of justifying myself from a charge which I should be sorry to incur with justice. Love to all at home.

Affectionately yours, T. B. M.

With or without a moral, the poem carried the day. The subject for the next year was "Waterloo." The opening lines of Macaulay's exercise were pretty and simple enough to ruin his chance in an academical competition.

It was the Sabbath morn. How calm and fair
Is the blest dawning of the day of prayer!
Who hath not felt how fancy's mystic power
With holier beauty decks that solemn hour;
A softer lustre in its sunshine sees;
And hears a softer music in its breeze?
Who hath not dreamed that even the sky-lark's throat
Hails that sweet morning with a gentler note?
Fair morn, how gayly shone thy dawning smile
On the green valleys of my native isle!
How gladly many a spire's resounding height
With peals of transport hailed thy new-born light!

> Ah! little thought the peasant then, who blest
> The peaceful hour of consecrated rest,
> And heard the rustic Temple's arch prolong
> The simple cadence of the hallowed song,
> That the same sun illumed a gory field,
> Where wilder song and sterner music pealed;
> Where many a yell unholy rent the air,
> And many a hand was raised—but not in prayer.

The prize fell to a man of another college, and Trinity comforted itself by inventing a story to the effect that the successful candidate had run away from the battle.

In the summer of 1819 there took place a military affair, less attractive than Waterloo as a theme for poets, but which, as far as this country is concerned, has proved even more momentous in its ultimate consequences. On the 16th of August, a Reform demonstration was arranged at Manchester resembling those which were common in the Northern districts during the year 1866, except that in 1819 women formed an important element in the procession. A troop of yeomanry, and afterward two squadrons of hussars, were sent in among the crowd, which was assembled in St. Peter's Fields, the site on which the Free-Trade Hall now stands. The men used their swords freely, and the horses their hoofs. The people, who meant any thing but fighting, trampled each other down in the attempt to escape. Five or six lives were lost, and fifty or sixty persons were badly hurt; but the painful impression wrought upon the national conscience was well worth the price. British blood has never since been shed by British hands in any civic contest that rose above the level of a lawless riot. The immediate result, however, was to concentrate and imbitter party feeling. The grand jury threw out the bills against the yeomen, and found true bills against the popular orators who had called the meeting together. The common councilmen of the city of London, who had presented an address to the prince regent reflecting upon the conduct of the Government, were roundly rebuked for their pains. Earl Fitzwilliam was dismissed from the office of lord lieutenant for taking part in a Yorkshire county gathering which had passed resolutions in the same sense as the address from the City. On the other hand, a Peterloo medal was struck, which is still treasured in such Manchester families as have not learned to be ashamed of the old Manchester politics.

In this heated state of the political atmosphere the expiring Toryism of the antislavery leaders flamed up once again. "I declare," said Wilberforce, "my greatest cause of difference with the democrats is their laying, and causing people to lay, so great a stress on the concerns of this world as to occupy their whole minds and hearts, and to leave a few scanty and lukewarm thoughts for the heavenly treasure." Zachary Macaulay, who never canted, and who knew that on the 16th of August the Manchester magistrates were thinking just as much or as little about religion as the Manchester populace, none the less took the same side as Wilberforce. Having formed for himself, by observations made on the spot, a decided opinion that the authorities ought to be supported, he was much disturbed by reports which came to him from Cambridge.

September, 1819.

My dear Father,—My mother's letter, which has just arrived, has given me much concern. The letter which has, I am sorry to learn, given you and her uneasiness, was written rapidly and thoughtlessly enough, but can scarcely, I think, as far as I remember its tenor, justify some of the extraordinary inferences which it has occasioned. I can only assure you most solemnly that I am not initiated into any democratical societies here, and that I know no people who make politics a common or frequent topic of conversation, except one man who is a determined Tory. It is true that this Manchester business has roused some indignation here, as at other places, and drawn philippics against the powers that be from lips which I never heard opened before but to speak on university contests or university scandal. For myself, I have long made it a rule never to talk on politics except in the most general manner; and I believe that my most intimate associates have no idea of my opinions on the questions of party. I can scarcely be censured, I think, for imparting them to you—which, however, I should scarcely have thought of doing (so much is my mind occupied with other concerns), had not your letter invited me to state my sentiments on the Manchester business.

I hope that this explanation will remove some of your uneasiness. As to my opinions, I have no particular desire to vindicate them. They are merely speculative, and therefore can not partake of the nature of moral culpability. They are early formed, and I am not solicitous that you should think them superior to those of most people at eighteen. I will, however, say this in their defense. Whatever the affectionate alarm of my dear mother may lead her to apprehend, I am not one of the "sons of anarchy and confusion" with whom she classes me. My opinions, good or bad, were learned, not from Hunt and Waithman, but from Cicero, from Tacitus, and from Milton. They are the opinions which have produced men who have ornamented the world and redeemed human nature from the degradation of ages of superstition and slavery. I may be wrong as to the facts of what occurred at Manchester; but, if they be what I have seen them stated, I can never repent speaking of them with indignation. When I cease to feel the injuries of others warmly, to detest wanton cruelty, and to feel my soul rise against oppression, I shall think myself unworthy to be your son.

I could say a great deal more. Above all, I might, I think, ask, with some reason, why a few democratical sentences in a letter, a private letter, of a collegian of eighteen should be thought so alarming an indication of character, when Brougham and other people, who, at an age which ought to have sobered them, talk with much more violence, are not thought particularly ill of? But I have so little room left that I abstain, and will only add thus much. Were my opinions as decisive as they are fluctuating, and were the elevation of a Cromwell or the renown of a Hampden the certain reward of my standing forth in the democratic cause, I would rather have my lips sealed on the subject than give my mother or you one hour of uneasiness. There are not so many people in the world who love me that I can afford to pain them for any object of ambition which it contains. If this assurance be not sufficient, clothe it in what language you please, and believe me to express myself in those words which you think the strongest and most solemn. Affectionate love to my mother and sisters. Farewell. T. B. M.

Cambridge, January 5th, 1820.

MY DEAR FATHER,—Nothing that gives you disquietude can give me amusement. Otherwise I should have been excessively diverted by the dialogue which you have reported with so much vivacity; the accusation; the predictions; and the elegant agnomen of "the novel-reader" for which I am indebted to this incognito. I went in some amazement to Malden, Romilly, and Barlow. Their acquaintance comprehends, I will venture to say, almost every man worth knowing in the university in every field of study. They had never heard the appellation applied to me by any man. Their intimacy with me would of course prevent any person from speaking to them on the subject in an insulting manner; for it is not usual here, whatever your unknown informant may do, for a gentleman who does not wish to be kicked down-stairs to reply to a man who mentions another as his particular friend, "Do you mean the blackguard or the novel-reader?" But I am fully convinced that, had the charge prevailed to any extent, it must have reached the ears of one of those whom I interrogated. At all events, I have the consolation of not being thought a novel-reader by three or four who are entitled to judge upon the subject; and whether their opinion be of equal value with that of this John-a-Nokes against whom I have to plead, I leave you to decide.

But stronger evidence, it seems, is behind. This gentleman was in company with me. Alas that I should never have found out how accurate an observer was measuring my sentiments, numbering the novels which I criticised, and speculating on the probability of my being plucked. "I was familiar with all the novels whose names he had ever heard." If so frightful an accusation did not stun me at once, I might perhaps hint at the possibility that this was to be attributed almost as much to the narrowness of his reading on this subject as to the extent of mine. There are men here who are mere mathematical blocks, who plod on their eight hours a day to the honors of the Senate-house; who leave the groves which witnessed the musings of Milton, of Bacon, and of Gray, without one liberal idea or elegant image, and carry with them into the world minds contracted by unmingled attention to one part of science, and memories stored only with technicalities. How often have I seen such men go forth into society for people to stare at them, and ask each other how it comes that beings so stupid in conversation, so uninformed on every subject of history, of letters, and of taste, could gain such distinction at Cambridge! It is in such circles, which, I am happy to say, I hardly know but by report, that knowledge of modern literature is called novel-reading: a commodious name, invented by ignorance and applied by envy, in the same manner as men without learning call a scholar a pedant, and men without principle call a Christian a Methodist. To me the attacks of such men are valuable as compliments. The man whose friend tells him that he is known to be extensively acquainted with elegant literature may suspect that he is flattering him; but he may feel real and secure satisfaction when some Johnian sneers at him for a novel-reader.

As to the question whether or not I am wasting time, I shall leave that for time to answer. I can not afford to sacrifice a day every week in defense and explanation as to my habits of reading. I value, most deeply value, that solicitude which arises from your affection for me; but let it not debar me from justice and candor. Believe me ever, my dear father,

Your most affectionate son, T. B. M.

The father and son were in sympathy upon what, at this distance of time, appears as the least inviting article of the Whig creed. They were both partisans of the queen. Zachary Macaulay was inclined in her favor by sentiments alike of friendship and of the most pardonable resentment. Brougham, her illustrious advocate, had for ten years been the main hope and stay of the movement against slavery and the slave-trade; while the *John Bull*, whose special mission it was to write her down, honored the Abolitionist party with its declared animosity. However full its columns might be of libels upon the honor of the wives and daughters of Whig statesmen, it could always find room for calumnies against Mr. Macaulay which in ingenuity of fabrication and in cruelty of intention were conspicuous even among the contents of the most discreditable publication that ever issued from the London press. When Queen Caroline landed from the Continent in June, 1820, the young Trinity under-graduate greeted her majesty with a complimentary ode, which certainly little resembled those effusions that in the old courtly days a university was accustomed to lay at the feet of its sovereign. The piece has no literary value, and is curious only as reflecting the passion of the hour. The first and last stanzas run as follows:

Let mirth on every visage shine,
  And glow in every soul.
Bring forth, bring forth, the oldest wine,
  And crown the largest bowl.
Bear to her home, while banners fly
  From each resounding steeple,
And rockets sparkle in the sky,
  The Daughter of the People.
E'en here, for one triumphant day,
  Let want and woe be dumb,
And bonfires blaze, and school-boys play.
  Thank Heaven our queen is come!

* * * * *

Though tyrant hatred still denies
  Each right that fits thy station,
To thee a people's love supplies
  A nobler coronation:
A coronation all unknown
  To Europe's royal vermin:
For England's heart shall be thy throne,
  And purity thine ermine;
Thy Proclamation our applause,
  Applause denied to some;
Thy crown our love; thy shield our laws.
  Thank Heaven our queen is come!

Early in November, warned by growing excitement outside the House of Lords, and by dwindling majorities within, Lord Liverpool announced that the king's ministers had come to the determination not to proceed further with the Bill of Pains and Penalties. The joy which this declaration spread through the country has been described as "beyond the scope of record."

Cambridge, November 13th, 1820.

My dear Father, — All here is ecstasy. "Thank God, the country is saved," were my first words when I caught a glimpse of the papers of Friday night. "Thank God, the country is saved," is written on every face, and echoed by every voice. Even the symptoms of popular violence, three days ago so terrific, are now displayed with good humor, and received with cheerfulness. Instead of curses on the Lords, on every post and every wall is written, "All is as it should be;" "Justice done at last," and similar mottoes expressive of the sudden turn of public feeling. How the case may stand in London, I do not know; but here the public danger, like all dangers which depend merely on human opinions and feelings, has disappeared from our sight almost in the twinkling of an eye. I hope that the result of these changes may be the secure re-establishment of our commerce, which I suppose political apprehensions must have contributed to depress. I hope, at least, that there is no danger to our own fortunes of the kind at which you seem to hint. Be assured, however, my dear father, that, be our circumstances what they may, I feel firmly prepared to encounter the worst with fortitude, and to do my utmost to retrieve it by exertion. The best inheritance you have already secured to me, an unblemished name and a good education. And for the rest, whatever calamities befall us, I would not, to speak without affectation, exchange adversity consoled, as with us it must ever be, by mutual affection and domestic happiness, for any thing which can be possessed by those who are destitute of the kindness of parents and sisters like mine. But I think, on referring to your letter, that I insist too much upon the signification of a few words. I hope so, and trust that every thing will go well. But it is chapel time, and I must conclude. Ever most affectionately yours,

T. B. MACAULAY.

Trin. Coll., March 25th, 1821.

MY DEAR MOTHER,—I entreat you to entertain no apprehensions about my health. My fever, cough, and sore-throat have all disappeared for the last four days. Many thanks for your intelligence about poor dear John's recovery, which has much exhilarated me. Yet I do not know whether illness to him is not rather a prerogative than an evil. I am sure that it is well worth while being sick to be nursed by a mother. There is nothing which I remember with such pleasure as the time when you nursed me at Aspenden. The other night, when I lay on my sofa very ill and hypochondriac, I was thinking over that time. How sick, and sleepless, and weak I was, lying in bed, when I was told that you were come! How well I remember with what an ecstasy of joy I saw that face approaching me, in the middle of people that did not care if I died that night, except for the trouble of burying me! The sound of your voice, the touch of your hand, are present to me now, and will be, I trust in God, to my last hour. The very thought of these things invigorated me the other day; and I almost blessed the sickness and low spirits which brought before me associated images of a tenderness and an affection, which, however imperfectly repaid, are deeply remembered. Such scenes and such recollections are the bright half of human nature and human destiny. All objects of ambition, all rewards of talent, sink into nothing compared with that affection which is independent of good or adverse circumstances, excepting that it is never so ardent, so delicate, or so tender as in the hour of languor or distress. But I must stop. I had no intention of pouring out on paper what I am much more used to think than to express. Farewell, my dear mother. Ever yours, affectionately,

T. B. MACAULAY.

Macaulay liked Cambridge too well to spend the long vacation elsewhere except under strong compulsion: but in 1821, with the terrors of the mathematical tripos already close at hand, he was persuaded into joining a reading-party in Wales, with a Mr. Bird as tutor. Eardley Childers, the father of the statesman of that name, has preserved a pleasant little memorial of the expedition.

To Charles Smith Bird, Eardley Childers, Thos. B. Macaulay, William Clayton Walters, Geo. B. Paley, Robert Jarratt, Thos. Jarratt, Edwin Kempson, Ebenezer Ware, Wm. Cornwall, John Greenwood, J. Lloyd, and Jno. Wm. Gleadall, Esquires:

Gentlemen,—We, the undersigned, for ourselves and the inhabitants in general of the town of Llanrwst, in the county of Denbigh, consider it our duty to express to you the high sense we entertain of your general good conduct and demeanor during your residence here, and we assure you that we view with much regret the period of your separation and departure from among us. We are very sensible of the obligation we are under for your uniformly benevolent and charitable exertions upon several public occasions, and we feel peculiar pleasure in thus tendering to you individually our gratitude and thanks.

Wishing you all possible prosperity and happiness in your future avocations, we subscribe ourselves with unfeigned respect, gentlemen, your most obedient servants,

Rev. John Tiltey, etc., etc.
(25 signatures.)

In one respect Macaulay hardly deserved his share of this eulogium. A scheme was on foot in the town to found an auxiliary branch of the Bible Society. A public meeting was called, and Mr. Bird urged his eloquent pupil to aid the project with a specimen of Union rhetoric. Macaulay, however, had had enough of the Bible Society at Clapham, and sturdily refused to come forward as its champion at Llanrwst.

Llanrwst, July —, 1821.

My dear Mother,—You see I know not how to date my letter. My calendar in this sequestered spot is as irregular as

Robinson Crusoe's after he had missed one day in his calculation. I have no intelligence to send you, unless a battle between a drunken attorney and an impudent publican which took place here yesterday may deserve the appellation. You may, perhaps, be more interested to hear that I sprained my foot, and am just recovering from the effects of the accident by means of opodeldoc which I bought at the tinker's; for all trades and professions here lie in a most delightful confusion. The druggist sells hats; the shoe-maker is the sole book-seller, if that dignity may be allowed him on the strength of the three Welsh Bibles and the Guide to Caernarvon which adorn his window; ink is sold by the apothecary; the grocer sells ropes (a commodity which, I fear, I shall require before my residence here is over) and tooth-brushes. A clothes-brush is a luxury yet unknown to Llanrwst. As to books, for want of any other English literature, I intend to learn "Paradise Lost" by heart at odd moments. But I must conclude. Write to me often, my dear mother, and all of you at home, or you may have to answer for my drowning myself, like Gray's bard, in "Old Conway's foaming flood," which is most conveniently near for so poetical an exit.

Ever most affectionately yours, T. B. M.

Llanrwst, August 31st, 1821.

My dear Father,—I have just received your letter, and can not but feel concerned at the tone of it. I do not think it quite fair to attack me for filling my letters with remarks on the king's Irish expedition. It has been the great event of this part of the world. I was at Bangor when he sailed. His bows, and the Marquis of Anglesea's fête, were the universal subjects of conversation; and some remarks on the business were as natural from me as accounts of the coronation from you in London. In truth, I have little else to say. I see nothing that connects me with the world except the newspapers. I get up, breakfast, read, play at quoits, and go to bed. This is the history of my life. It will do for every day of the last fortnight.

As to the king, I spoke of the business, not at all as a political, but as a moral, question, as a point of correct feeling and of private decency. If Lord —— were to issue tickets for a gala ball immediately after receiving intelligence of the sudden death of his divorced wife, I should say the same. I pretend to no great insight into party politics; but the question whether it is proper for any man to mingle in festivities while his wife's body lies unburied is one, I confess, which I thought myself competent to decide. But I am not anxious about the fate of my remarks, which I have quite forgotten, and which, I dare say, were very foolish. To me it is of little importance whether the king's conduct were right or wrong; but it is of great importance that those whom I love should not think me a precipitate, silly, shallow sciolist in politics, and suppose that every frivolous word that falls from my pen is a dogma which I mean to advance as indisputable; and all this only because I write to them without reserve; only because I love them well enough to trust them with every idea which suggests itself to me. In fact, I believe that I am not more precipitate or presumptuous than other people, but only more open. You can not be more fully convinced than I am how contracted my means are of forming a judgment. If I chose to weigh every word that I uttered or wrote to you, and, whenever I alluded to politics, were to labor and qualify my expressions as if I were drawing up a state paper, my letters might be a great deal wiser, but would not be such letters as I should wish to receive from those whom I loved. Perfect love, we are told, casteth out fear. If I say, as I know I do, a thousand wild and inaccurate things, and employ exaggerated expressions about persons or events in writing to you or to my mother, it is not, I believe, that I want power to systematize my ideas or to measure my expressions, but because I have no objection to letting you see my mind in deshabille. I have a court dress for days of ceremony and people of ceremony, nevertheless. But I would not willingly be frightened into wearing it with you; and I hope you do not wish me to do so.

Ever yours, T. B. M.

To hoax a newspaper has, time out of mind, been the special

ambition of under-graduate wit. In the course of 1821 Macaulay sent to the *Morning Post* a burlesque copy of verses, entitled "Tears of Sensibility." The editor fell an easy victim, but unfortunately did not fall alone.

No pearl of ocean is so sweet
  As that in my Zuleika's eye.
No earthly jewel can compete
  With tears of sensibility.

Like light phosphoric on the billow,
  Or hermit ray of evening sky,
Like ripplings round a weeping willow
  Are tears of sensibility.

Like drops of iris-colored fountains
  By which Endymion loved to lie,
Like dew-gems on untrodden mountains
  Are tears of sensibility.

While Zephyr broods o'er moonlight rill
  The flowerets droop as if to die,
And from their chaliced cups distill
  The tears of sensibility.

The heart obdurate never felt
  One link of Nature's magic tie,
If ne'er it knew the bliss to melt
  In tears of sensibility.

The generous and the gentle heart
  Is like that balmy Indian tree
Which scatters from the wounded part
  The tears of sensibility.

Then, oh! ye fair, if Pity's ray
  E'er taught your snowy breasts to sigh,
Shed o'er my contemplative lay
  The tears of sensibility.

November 2d, 1821.

My dear Mother,—I possess some of the irritability of a poet, and it has been a good deal awakened by your criticisms. I could not have imagined that it would have been necessary for me to have said that the execrable trash entitled "Tears of Sensibility" was merely a burlesque on the style of the magazine verses of the day. I could not suppose that you could have suspected me of *seriously* composing such a farrago of false metaphor and unmeaning epithet. It was meant solely for a caricature on the style of the poetasters of newspapers and journals; and (though I say it who should not say it) has excited more attention and received more praise at Cambridge than it deserved. If you have it, read it over again, and do me the justice to believe that such a compound of jargon, nonsense, false images, and exaggerated sentiment is not the product of my serious labors. I sent it to the *Morning Post*, because that paper is the ordinary receptacle of trash of the description which I intended to ridicule, and its admission therefore pointed the jest. I see, however, that for the future I must mark more distinctly when I intend to be ironical. Your affectionate son, T. B. M.

Cambridge, July 26th, 1822.

My dear Father,—I have been engaged to take two pupils for nine months of the next year. They are brothers whose father, a Mr. Stoddart, resides at Cambridge. I am to give them an hour a day each, and am to receive a hundred guineas. It gives me great pleasure to be able even in this degree to relieve you from the burden of my expenses here. I begin my tutorial labors to-morrow. My pupils are young, one being fifteen and the other thirteen years old; but I hear excellent accounts of their proficiency, and I intend to do my utmost for them. Farewell. T. B. M.

A few days later on he writes: "I do not dislike teaching; whether it is that I am more patient than I had imagined, or that I have not yet had time to grow tired of my new vocation. I find, also, what at first sight may appear paradoxical, that I read much more in consequence, and that the regularity of habits necessarily produced by a periodical employment which can not be procrastinated fully compensates for the loss of the time which is consumed in tuition."

Trinity College, Cambridge, October 1st, 1824.

My dear Father,—I was elected Fellow this morning, shall be sworn in to-morrow, and hope to leave Cambridge on Tuesday for Rothley Temple. The examiners speak highly of the manner in which I acquitted myself, and I have reason to believe that I stood first of the candidates.

I need not say how much I am delighted by my success, and how much I enjoy the thought of the pleasure which it will afford to you, my mother, and our other friends. Till I become a master of arts next July, the pecuniary emolument which I shall derive will not be great. For seven years from that time it will make me almost an independent man.

Malden is elected. You will take little interest in the rest of our Cambridge successes and disappointments.

Yours most affectionately, T. B. M.

CHAPTER III.

1824-1830.

Macaulay is Called to the Bar.—Does not Make it a Serious Profession.—Speech before the Antislavery Society.—Knight's *Quarterly Magazine.*—The *Edinburgh Review* and the "Essay on Milton."—Macaulay's Personal Appearance and Mode of Existence.—His Defects and Virtues, Likings and Antipathies.—Croker.—Sadler.—Zachary Macaulay's Circumstances.—Description of the Family Habits of Life in Great Ormond Street.—Macaulay's Sisters.—Lady Trevelyan.—"The Judicious Poet." Macaulay's Humor in Conversation.—His Articles in the *Review.*—His Attacks on the Utilitarians and on Southey.—*Blackwood's Magazine.*—Macaulay is made Commissioner of Bankruptcy.—Enters Parliament.—Letters from Circuit and Edinburgh.

MACAULAY was called to the bar in 1826, and joined the Northern Circuit at Leeds. On the evening that he first appeared at mess, when the company were retiring for the night, he was observed to be carefully picking out the longest candle. An old king's counsel, who noticed that he had a volume under his arm, remonstrated with him on the danger of reading in bed, upon which he rejoined with immense rapidity of utterance: "I always read in bed at home; and if I am not afraid of committing parricide and matricide and fratricide, I can hardly be expected to pay any special regard to the lives of the bagmen of Leeds." And, so saying, he left his hearers staring at one another, and marched off to his room, little knowing that before many years were out he would have occasion to speak much more respectfully of the Leeds bagmen.

Under its social aspect, Macaulay heartily enjoyed his legal career. He made an admirable literary use of the Saturnalia which the Northern Circuit calls by the name of "Grand Night," when personalities of the most pronounced description are welcomed by all except the object of them, and forgiven even by him. His hand may be recognized in a macaronic poem, written in Greek and English, describing the feast at which Alexander murdered Clitus. The death of the victim is treated with an exuberance of fantastic drollery; and a song, put into the mouth of Nearchus, the admiral of the Macedonian fleet, and beginning with the lines,

> When as first I did come back from plowing the salt water,
> They paid me off at Salamis, three minæ and a quarter,

is highly Aristophanic in every sense of the word.

He did not seriously look to the bar as a profession. No persuasion would induce him to return to his chambers in the evening, according to the practice then in vogue. After the first year or two of the period during which he called himself a barrister he gave up even the pretense of reading law, and spent many more hours under the gallery of the House of Commons than in all the courts together. The person who knew him best said of him: "Throughout life he never really applied himself to any pursuit that was against the grain." Nothing is more characteristic of the man than the contrast between his unconquerable aversion to the science of jurisprudence at the time when he was ostensibly preparing himself to be an advocate, and the zest with which, on his voyage to India, he mastered that science, in principle and detail, as soon as his imagination was fired by the prospect of the responsibilities of a lawgiver.

He got no business worth mention, either in London or on circuit. Zachary Macaulay, who was not a man of the world, did what he could to make interest with the attorneys, and, as a last resource, proposed to his son to take a brief in a suit which he himself had instituted against the journal that had so grossly libeled him. "I am rather glad," writes Macaulay from York in March, 1827, "that I was not in London, if your advisers thought it right that I should have appeared as your counsel. Whether it be contrary to professional etiquette I do not know; but I am sure that it would be shocking to public feeling, and particularly imprudent against adversaries whose main strength lies in detecting and exposing indecorum or eccentricity. It would have been difficult to avoid a quarrel with Sugden, with Wetherell, and with old Lord Eldon himself. Then the *John Bull* would have been upon us with every advantage. The personal part of the consideration it would have been my duty, and my pleasure and pride also, to overlook, but your interests must have suffered."

Meanwhile he was busy enough in fields better adapted than the law to his talents and his temperament. He took a part in the meeting of the Antislavery Society held at Freemasons' Tavern, on the 25th of June, 1824, with the Duke of Gloucester in the chair. The *Edinburgh Review* described his speech as "a display of eloquence so signal for rare and matured excellence, that the most practiced orator may well admire how it should have come from one who then for the first time addressed a public assembly."

Those who know what the annual meeting of a well-organized and disciplined association is may imagine the whirlwind of cheers which greeted the declaration that the hour was at hand when "the peasant of the Antilles will no longer crawl in listless and trembling dejection round a plantation from whose fruits he must derive no advantage, and a hut whose door yields him no protection; but, when his cheerful and voluntary labor is performed, he will return with the firm step and erect brow of a British citizen from the field which is his freehold to the cottage which is his castle.

Surer promise of aptitude for political debate was afforded by the skill with which the young speaker turned to account the recent trial for sedition, and death in prison, of Smith, the Demerara missionary: an event which was fatal to slavery in the West Indies in the same degree as the execution of John Brown was its death-blow in the United States. "When this country has been endangered, either by arbitrary power or popular delusion, truth has still possessed one irresistible organ, and justice one inviolable tribunal. That organ has been an English press, and that tribunal an English jury. But in those wretched islands we see a press more hostile to truth than any censor, and juries more insensible to justice than any Star Chamber. In those islands alone is exemplified the full meaning of the most tremendous of the curses denounced against the apostate Hebrews, 'I will curse your blessings.' We can prove this assertion out of the mouth of our adversaries. We remember, and God Almighty forbid that we ever should forget, how, at the trial of Mr. Smith, hatred regulated every proceeding, was substituted for every law, and allowed its victim no sanctuary in the house of mourning, no refuge in the very grave. Against the members of that court-martial the country has pronounced its verdict. But what is the line of defense taken by its advocates? It has been solemnly and repeatedly declared in the House of Commons that a jury composed of planters would have acted with far more injustice than did this court: this court, which has never found a single lawyer to stake his professional character on the legality of its proceedings. The argument is this. Things have doubtless been done which should not have been done. The court-martial sat without a jurisdiction; it convicted without evidence; it condemned to a punishment not warranted by law. But we must make allowances. We must judge by comparison. 'Mr. Smith ought to have been very thankful that it was no worse. Only think what would have been his fate if he had been tried by a jury of planters!' Sir, I have always lived under the protection of the British laws, and therefore I am unable to imagine what could be worse: but, though I have small knowledge, I have a large faith: I by no means presume to set any limits to the possible injustice of a West Indian judicature. And since the colonists maintain that a jury composed of their own body not only possibly might, but necessarily must, have acted with more iniquity than this court-martial, I certainly shall not dispute the assertion, though I am utterly unable to conceive the mode."

That was probably the happiest half-hour of Zachary Macaulay's life. "My friend," said Wilberforce, when his turn came to speak, "would doubtless willingly bear with all the base falsehoods, all the vile calumnies, all the detestable artifices which have been aimed against him, to render him the martyr and victim of our cause, for the gratification he has this day enjoyed in hearing one so dear to him plead such a cause in such a manner." Keen as his pleasure was, he took it in his own sad way. From the first moment to the last, he never moved a muscle of his countenance, but sat with his eyes fixed on a piece of paper, on which he seemed to be writing with a pencil. While talking with his son that evening, he referred to what had passed only to remark that it was ungraceful in so young a man to speak with folded arms in the presence of royalty.

In 1823 the leading members of the cleverest set of boys who ever were together at a public school found themselves collected once more at Cambridge. Of the former staff of the *Etonian*, Praed, Moultrie, Derwent Coleridge, and, among others, Mr. Edmond Beales, so well known to our generation as an ardent politician, were now in residence at King's or Trinity. Mr. Charles Knight, too enterprising a publisher to let such a quantity of youthful talent run to waste, started a periodical, which was largely supported by under-graduates and bachelors of arts, among whom the veterans of the Eton press formed a brilliant, and, as he vainly hoped, a reliable nucleus of contributors.

Knight's *Quarterly Magazine* is full of Macaulay, and of Macaulay in the attractive shape which a great author wears while he is still writing to please no one but himself. He unfortunately did not at all please his father. In the first number, besides a great deal of his that is still worth reading, there were printed, under his adopted signature of Tristram Merton, two little poems, the nature of which may be guessed from Praed's editorial comments. "Tristram Merton, I have a strong curiosity to know who Rosamond is. But you will not tell me; and, after all, as far as your verses are concerned, the surname is nowise germane to the matter. As poor Sheridan said, it is too formal to be registered in love's calendar." And again: "Tristram, I hope Rosamond and your Fair Girl of France will not pull caps; but I can not forbear the temptation of introducing your Roxana and Statira to an admiring public." The verses were such as any man would willingly look back to having written at two-and-twenty; but their appearance occasioned real misery to Zachary Macaulay, who indeed disapproved of the whole publication from beginning to end, with the exception of an article on West Indian slavery which his son had inserted with the most filial intention, but which, it must be allowed, was not quite in keeping with the general character of the magazine.

July 9th, 1823.

My dear Father,—I have seen the two last letters which you have sent to my mother. They have given me deep pain; but pain without remorse. I am conscious of no misconduct, and whatever uneasiness I may feel arises solely from sympathy for your distress.

You seem to imagine that the book is edited, or principally written, by friends of mine. I thought that you had been aware that the work is conducted in London, and that my friends and myself are merely contributors, and form a very small proportion of the contributors. The manners of almost all of my acquaintances are so utterly alien from coarseness, and their morals from libertinism, that I feel assured that no objection of that nature can exist to their writings. As to my own contributions, I can only say that the Roman story was read to my mother before it was published, and would have been read to you if you had happened to be at home. Not one syllable of censure was uttered.

The essay on the "Royal Society of Literature" was read to you. I made the alterations which I conceived that you desired, and submitted them afterward to my mother. As to the poetry which you parallel with Little's, if any thing vulgar or licentious has been written by myself, I am willing to bear the consequences. If any thing of that cast has been written by my friends, I allow that a certain degree of blame attaches to me for having chosen them at least indiscreetly. If, however, a book-seller of whom we knew nothing has coupled improper productions with ours in a work over which we had no control, I can not plead guilty to any thing more than misfortune: a misfortune in which some of the most rigidly moral and religious men of my acquaintance have participated in the present instance.

I am pleading at random for a book which I never saw. I

am defending the works of people most of whose names I never heard. I am therefore writing under great disadvantages. I write also in great haste. I am unable even to read over what I have written. Affectionately yours,

T. B. M.

Moved by the father's evident unhappiness, the son promised never to write again for the obnoxious periodical. The second number was so dull and decorous that Zachary Macaulay, who felt that, if the magazine went on through successive quarters reforming its tone in the same proportion, it would soon be on a level of virtue with the *Christian Observer*, withdrew his objection; and the young man wrote regularly till the short life of the undertaking ended in something very like a quarrel between the publisher and his contributors. It is not the province of biography to dilate upon works which are already before the world, and the results of Macaulay's literary labor during the years 1823 and 1824 have been, perhaps, only too freely reproduced in the volumes which contain his miscellaneous writings. It is, however, worthy of notice that among his earlier efforts in literature his own decided favorite was "the conversation between Mr. Abraham Cowley and Mr. John Milton touching the great civil war." But an author, who is exempt from vanity, is inclined to rate his own works rather according as they are free from faults than as they abound in beauties: and Macaulay's readers will very generally give the preference to two fragmentary sketches of Roman and Athenian society which sparkle with life, and humor, and a masculine, vigorous fancy that had not yet learned to obey the rein. Their crude but genuine merit suggests a regret that he did not in after-days enrich the *Edinburgh Review* with a couple of articles on classical subjects, as a sample of that ripened scholarship which produced the "Prophecy of Capys," and the episode relating to the Phalaris controversy in the essay on "Sir William Temple."

Rothley Temple, October 7th, 1824.

MY DEAR FATHER,—As to Knight's magazine, I really do

not think that, considering the circumstances under which it is conducted, it can be much censured. Every magazine must contain a certain quantity of mere ballast, of no value but as it occupies space. The general tone and spirit of the work will stand a comparison, in a moral point of view, with any periodical publication not professedly religious. I will venture to say that nothing has appeared in it, at least since the first number, from the pen of any of my friends, which can offend the most fastidious. Knight is absolutely in our hands, and most desirous to gratify us all, and me in particular. When I see you in London I will mention to you a piece of secret history which will show you how important our connection with this work may possibly become.

Yours affectionately, T. B. M.

The "piece of secret history" above referred to was beyond a doubt the commencement of Macaulay's connection with the *Edinburgh Review*. That famous periodical, which for three-and-twenty-years had shared in and promoted the rising fortunes of the Liberal cause, had now attained its height—a height unequaled before or since—of political, social, and literary power. To have the entry of its columns was to command the most direct channel for the spread of opinions, and the shortest road to influence and celebrity. But already the anxious eye of the master seemed to discern symptoms of decline. Jeffrey, in Lord Cockburn's phrase, was "growing feverish about new writers." In January, 1825, he says, in a letter to a friend in London: "Can you not lay your hands on some clever young man who would write for us? The original supporters of the work are getting old, and either too busy or too stupid, and here the young men are mostly Tories." Overtures had already been made to Macaulay, and that same year his article on Milton appeared in the August number.

The effect on the author's reputation was instantaneous. Like Lord Byron, he awoke one morning and found himself famous. The beauties of the work were such as all men could recognize, and its very faults pleased. The redundance of youthful enthusiasm, which he himself unsparingly condemns in the preface to his collected essays, seemed graceful enough in the eyes of others, if it were only as a relief from the perverted ability of that elaborate libel on our great epic poet which goes by the name of Dr. Johnson's "Life of Milton." Murray declared that it would be worth the copyright of "Childe Harold" to have Macaulay on the staff of the *Quarterly*. The family breakfast-table in Bloomsbury was covered with cards of invitation to dinner from every quarter of London, and his father groaned in spirit over the conviction that thenceforward the law would be less to him than ever. A warm admirer of Robert Hall, Macaulay heard with pride how the great preacher, then well-nigh worn out with that long disease, his life, was discovered lying on the floor, employed in learning, by aid of grammar and dictionary, enough Italian to enable him to verify the parallel between Milton and Dante. But the compliment that of all others came most nearly home—the only commendation of his literary talent which even in the innermost domestic circle he was ever known to repeat—was the sentence with which Jeffrey acknowledged the receipt of his manuscript, "The more I think, the less I can conceive where you picked up that style."

Macaulay's outward man was never better described than in two sentences of Praed's Introduction to Knight's *Quarterly Magazine*. "There came up a short manly figure, marvelously upright, with a bad neckcloth, and one hand in his waistcoat-pocket. Of regular beauty he had little to boast; but in faces where there is an expression of great power, or of great good-humor, or both, you do not regret its absence." This picture, in which every touch is correct, tells all that there is to be told. He had a massive head, and features of a powerful and rugged cast; but so constantly lighted up by every joyful and ennobling emotion that it mattered little if, when absolutely quiescent, his face was rather homely than handsome. While conversing at table, no one thought him otherwise than good-looking; but when he rose, he was seen to be short and stout in figure. "At Holland House, the other day," writes his sister Margaret, in September, 1831, "Tom met Lady Lyndhurst for the first time. She said to him, 'Mr. Macaulay, you are so different to what I expected. I thought you were dark and thin, but you are fair, and, really, Mr. Macaulay, you are fat.'" He at all times sat and stood straight, full, and square; and in this respect Woolner, in the fine statue at Cambridge, has missed what was undoubtedly the most marked fact in his personal appearance. He dressed badly, but not cheaply. His clothes, though ill put on, were good, and his wardrobe was always enormously overstocked. Later in life he indulged himself in an apparently inexhaustible succession of handsome embroidered waistcoats, which he used to regard with much complacency. He was unhandy to a degree quite unexampled in the experience of all who knew him. When in the open air, he wore perfectly new dark kid gloves, into the fingers of which he never succeeded in inserting his own more than half-way. After he had sailed for India, there were found in his chambers between fifty and sixty strops, hacked into strips and splinters, and razors without beginning or end. About the same period he hurt his hand, and was reduced to send for a barber. After the operation, he asked what was to pay. "Oh, sir," said the man, "whatever you usually give the person who shaves you." "In that case," said Macaulay, "I should give you a great gash on each cheek."

During an epoch when, at our principal seats of education, athletic pursuits are regarded as a leading object of existence, rather than as a means of health and recreation, it requires some boldness to confess that Macaulay was utterly destitute of bodily accomplishments, and that he viewed his deficiencies with supreme indifference. He could neither swim, nor row, nor drive, nor skate, nor shoot. He seldom crossed a saddle, and never willingly. When in attendance at Windsor, as a cabinet minister, he was informed that a horse was at his disposal. "If her majesty wishes to see me ride," he said, "she must order out an elephant." The only exercise in which he can be said to have excelled was that of threading crowded streets with his eyes fixed upon a book. He might be seen in such thoroughfares as Oxford Street and Cheapside walking as fast as other people walked, and reading a great deal faster than any body else could read. As a pedestrian he was, indeed, above the average. Till he had passed fifty, he thought nothing of going on foot from the Albany to Clapham, and from Clapham on to Greenwich, and, while still in the prime of life, he was forever on his feet indoors as well as out. "In those days," says his cousin, Mrs. Conybeare, "he walked rapidly up and down a room as he talked. I remember on one occasion, when he was making a call, he stopped short in his walk in the midst of a declamation on some subject, and said, 'You have a brick floor here.' The hostess confessed that it was true, though she hoped that it had been disguised by double matting and a thick carpet. He said that his habit of always walking enabled him to tell accurately the material he was treading on.'"

His faults were such as give annoyance to those who dislike a man rather than anxiety to those who love him. Vehemence, overconfidence, the inability to recognize that there are two sides to a question or two people in a dialogue, are defects which during youth are perhaps inseparable from gifts like those with which he was endowed. Moultrie, speaking of his under-graduate days, tells us that

> To him
> There was no pain like silence—no constraint
> So dull as unanimity. He breathed
> An atmosphere of argument, nor shrunk
> From making, where he could not find, excuse
> For controversial fight.

At Cambridge he would say of himself that whenever any body enunciated a proposition all possible answers to it rushed into his mind at once, and it was said of him by others that he had no politics except the opposite of those held by the persons with whom he was talking. To that charge, at any rate, he did not long continue liable. He left college a stanch and vehement Whig, eager to maintain against all comers and at any moment that none but Whig opinions had a leg to stand upon. His cousin, George Babington, a rising surgeon, with whom at one time he lived in the closest intimacy, was always ready to take up the Tory cudgels. The two friends "would walk up and down the room, crossing each other for hours, shouting one another down with a continuous simultaneous storm of words, until George at length yielded to arguments and lungs combined. Never, so far as I remember, was there any loss of temper. It was a fair, good-humored battle, in not very mannerly lists."

Even as a very young man nine people out of ten liked nothing better than to listen to him: which was fortunate; because in his early days he had scanty respect of persons, either as regarded the choice of his topics or the quantity of his words. But with his excellent temper, and entire absence of conceit, he soon began to learn consideration for others in small things as well as in great. By the time he was fairly launched in London, he was agreeable in company as well as forcible and amusing. Wilberforce speaks of his "unruffled good humor." Sir Robert Inglis, a good observer, with ample opportunity of forming a judgment, pronounced that he conversed, and did not dictate, and that he was loud, but never overbearing. As far back as the year 1826, Crabb Robinson gave a very favorable account of his demeanor in society, which deserves credence as the testimony of one who liked his share of talk, and was not willing to be put in the background for any body. "I went to James Stephen, and drove with him to his house at Hendon. A dinner-party. I had a most interesting companion in young Macaulay, one of the most promising of the rising generation I have seen for a long time. He has a good face—not the delicate features of a man of genius and sensibility, but the strong lines and well-knit limbs of a man sturdy in body and mind. Very eloquent and cheerful. Overflowing with words, and not poor in thought. Liberal in opinion, but no radical. He seems a correct as well as a full man. He showed a minute knowledge of subjects not introduced by himself."

So loyal and sincere was Macaulay's nature that he was unwilling to live upon terms of even apparent intimacy with people whom he did not like, or could not esteem; and, as far as civility allowed, he avoided their advances, and especially their hospitality. He did not choose, he said, to eat salt with a man for whom he could not say a good word in all companies.

He was true throughout life to those who had once acquired his regard and respect. Moultrie says of him:

> His heart was pure and simple as a child's
> Unbreathed on by the world: in friendship warm,
> Confiding, generous, constant; and, though now
> He ranks among the great ones of the earth,
> And hath achieved such glory as will last
> To future generations, he, I think,
> Would sup on oysters with as right good-will
> In this poor home of mine as e'er he did
> On Petty Cury's classical first-floor
> Some twenty years ago.

He loved to place his purse, his influence, and his talents at the disposal of a friend; and any one whom he called by that name he judged with indulgence, and trusted with a faith that would endure almost any strain. If his confidence proved to have been egregiously misplaced, which he was always the last to see, he did not resort to remonstrance or recrimination. His course under such circumstances he described in a couplet from an old French comedy:*

> Le bruit est pour le fat, la plainte pour le sot;
> L'honnête homme trompé s'éloigne et ne dit mot.

He was never known to take part in any family quarrel, or personal broil of any description whatsoever. His conduct in this respect was the result of self-discipline, and did not proceed from any want of sensibility. "He is very sensitive," said his sister Margaret, "and remembers long, as well as feels deeply, any thing in the form of slight." Indeed, at college his friends used to tell him that his leading qualities were "generosity and vindictiveness." Courage he certainly did not lack. During the years when his spirit was high, and his pen cut deep, and when the habits of society were different

* La Coquette Corrigée. Comédie par Mr. Delanoue, 1756. In his Journal of February 15th, 1851, after quoting the couplet, Macaulay adds: "Odd that two lines of a damned play, and, it should seem, a justly damned play, should have lived near a century, and have become proverbial."

from what they are at present, more than one adversary displayed symptoms of a desire to meet him elsewhere than on paper. On these occasions, while showing consideration for his opponent, he evinced a quiet but very decided sense of what was due to himself which commanded the respect of all who were implicated, and brought difficulties that might have been grave to an honorable and satisfactory issue.

He reserved his pugnacity for quarrels undertaken on public grounds and fought out, with the world looking on as umpire. In the lists of criticism and of debate it can not be denied that, as a young man, he sometimes deserved the praise which Dr. Johnson pronounced upon a good hater. He had no mercy for bad writers, and notably for bad poets, unless they were in want of money; in which case he became, within his means, the most open-handed of patrons. He was too apt to undervalue both the heart and the head of those who desired to maintain the old system of civil and religious exclusion, and who grudged political power to their fellow-countrymen, or at any rate to those of their fellow-countrymen whom he was himself prepared to enfranchise. Independent, frank, and proud almost to a fault, he detested the whole race of jobbers and time-servers, parasites and scandal-mongers, led-captains, led-authors, and led-orators. Some of his antipathies have stamped themselves indelibly upon literary history. He attributed to the Right Honorable John Wilson Croker, Secretary to the Admiralty during the twenty years preceding 1830, qualities which excited his disapprobation beyond control, and possibly beyond measure. In a singularly powerful letter, written as late as 1843, he recites in detail certain unsavory portions of that gentleman's private life which were not only part of the stock-gossip of every bow-window in St. James's Street, but which had been brought into the light of day in the course either of Parliamentary or judicial investigations. After illustrating these transactions with evidence which proved that he did not take up an antipathy on hearsay, Macaulay comments on them in such terms as clearly indicate that his animosity to Croker arose from incompatibility of moral sentiments, and not of political opinions. He then proceeds to remark on "the scandals of Croker's literary life;" "his ferocious insults to women, to Lady Morgan, Mrs. Austin, and others;" his twitting Harriet Martineau with deafness; his twitting Madame D'Arblay with concealing her age. "I might add," he says, "a hundred other charges. These, observe, are things done by a privy councilor, by a man who has a pension from the country of two thousand pounds a year, by a man who affects to be a champion of order and religion." Macaulay's judgment has been confirmed by the public voice, which, rightly or wrongly, identifies Croker with the character of Rigby in Mr. Disraeli's "Coningsby."

Macaulay was the more formidable as an opponent, because he could be angry without losing his command of the situation. His first onset was terrific; but in the fiercest excitement of the mêlée he knew when to call a halt. A certain member of Parliament named Michael Thomas Sadler had fallen foul of Malthus, and very foul, indeed, of Macaulay, who in two short and telling articles* took revenge enough for both. He writes on this subject to Mr. Macvey Napier, who, toward the close of 1829, had succeeded Jeffrey in the editorship of the *Edinburgh Review:* "The position which we have now taken up is absolutely impregnable; and if we were to quit it, though we might win a more splendid victory we should expose ourselves to some risk. My rule in controversy has always been that to which the Lacedæmonians adhered in war: never to break the ranks for the purpose of pursuing a beaten enemy." He had, indeed, seldom occasion to strike twice. Where he set his mark, there was no need of a second impression. The unduly severe fate of those who crossed his path during the years when his blood was hot teaches a serious lesson on the responsibilities of genius. Croker, and Sadler, and poor Robert Montgomery, and the

---

* Macaulay writes to Mr. Napier in February, 1831: "People here think that I have answered Sadler completely. Empson tells me that Malthus is well pleased, which is a good sign. As to Blackwood's trash, I could not get through it. It bore the same relation to Sadler's pamphlet that a bad hash bears to a bad joint."

other less eminent objects of his wrath, appear likely to enjoy just so much notoriety, and of such a nature, as he has thought fit to deal out to them in his pages; and it is possible that even Lord Ellenborough may be better known to our grandchildren by Macaulay's oration on the gates of Somnauth than by the noise of his own deeds, or the echo of his own eloquence.

When Macaulay went to college, he was justified in regarding himself as one who would not have to work for his bread. His father, who believed himself to be already worth a hundred thousand pounds, had statedly declared to the young man his intention of making him, in a modest way, an eldest son; and had informed him that, by doing his duty at the university, he would earn the privilege of shaping his career at choice. In 1818 the family removed to London, and set up an establishment on a scale suited to their improved circumstances in Cadogan Place, which, in every thing except proximity to Bond Street, was then hardly less rural than Clapham. But the prosperity of the house of Macaulay Babington was short-lived. The senior member of the firm gave his whole heart, and five-sixths of his time, to objects unconnected with his business; and he had selected a partner who did not possess the qualities necessary to compensate for his own deficiencies. In 1819, the first indications of possible disaster begin to show themselves in the letters to and from Cambridge; while waiting for a fellowship, Macaulay was glad to make a hundred guineas by taking pupils; and, as time went on, it became evident that he was to be an eldest son only in the sense that throughout the coming years of difficulty and distress his brothers and sisters would depend mainly upon him for comfort, guidance, and support. He acknowledged the claim cheerfully, lovingly, and indeed almost unconsciously. It was not in his disposition to murmur over what was inevitable, or to plume himself upon doing what was right. He quietly took up the burden which his father was unable to bear; and, before many years had elapsed, the fortunes of all for whose welfare he considered himself responsible were abundantly assured. In the course of the efforts which he expended on the accomplishment of this result, he unlearned the very notion of framing his method of life with a view to his own pleasure; and such was his high and simple nature that it may well be doubted whether it ever crossed his mind that to live wholly for others was a sacrifice at all.

He resided with his father in Cadogan Place, and accompanied him when, under the pressure of pecuniary circumstances, he removed to a less fashionable quarter of the town. In 1823 the family settled in 50 Great Ormond Street, which runs east and west for some three hundred yards through the region bounded by the British Museum, the Foundling Hospital, and Gray's Inn Road. It was a large, rambling house, at the corner of Powis Place, and was said to have been the residence of Lord Chancellor Thurlow at the time when the Great Seal was stolen from his custody. It now forms the east wing of a homeopathic hospital. Here the Macaulays remained till 1831. "Those were to me," says Lady Trevelyan, "years of intense happiness. There might be money troubles, but they did not touch us. Our lives were passed after a fashion which would seem, indeed, strange to the present generation. My father, ever more and more engrossed in one object, gradually gave up all society, and my mother never could endure it. We had friends, of course, with whom we staid out for months together, and we dined with the Wilberforces, the Buxtons, Sir Robert Inglis, and others; but what is now meant by 'society' was utterly unknown to us.

"In the morning there was some pretense of work and study. In the afternoon your uncle always took my sister Margaret and myself a long walk. We traversed every part of the City, Islington, Clerkenwell, and the parks, returning just in time for a six-o'clock dinner. What anecdotes he used to pour out about every street, and square, and court, and alley! There are many places I never pass without the tender grace of a day that is dead coming back to me. Then, after dinner, he always walked up and down the drawing-room between us chatting till tea-time. Our noisy mirth, his wretched puns, so many a minute, so many an hour! Then we sung, none of us having any voices, and he, if possible, least of all; but still the old nursery songs were set to music and chanted. My father, sitting at his own table, used to look up occasionally, and push back his spectacles, and, I dare say, wonder, in his heart, how we could so waste our time. After tea the book then in reading was produced. Your uncle very seldom read aloud himself of an evening, but walked about listening, and commenting, and drinking water.

"The Sundays were in some respects trying days to him. My father's habit was to read a long sermon to us all in the afternoon, and again after evening service another long sermon was read at prayer-time to the servants. Our doors were open to sons of relations or friends; and cousins who were medical students, or clerks in merchants' houses, came in regularly to partake of our Sunday dinner and sermons. Sunday walking, for walking's sake, was never allowed, and even going to a distant church was discouraged. When in Cadogan Place, we always crossed the Five Fields, where Belgrave Square now stands, to hear Dr. Thorpe at the Lock Chapel, and bring him home to dine with us. From Great Ormond Street, we attended St. John's Chapel in Bedford Row, then served by Daniel Wilson, afterward Bishop of Calcutta. He was succeeded in 1826 by the Rev. Baptist Noel. Your uncle generally went to church with us in the morning, and latterly formed the habit of walking out of town, alone or with a friend, in the after-part of the day. I never heard that my father took any notice of this, and, indeed, in the interior of his own family, he never attempted in the smallest degree to check his son in his mode of life or in the expression of his opinions.

"I believe that breakfast was the pleasantest part of the day to my father. His spirits were then at their best, and he was most disposed to general conversation. He delighted in discussing the newspaper with his son, and lingered over the table long after the meal was finished. On this account he felt it extremely when, in the year 1829, your uncle went to live in chambers, and often said to my mother that the change had taken the brightness out of his day. Truly he was, to old and young alike, the sunshine of our home; and I believe that no one who did not know him there ever knew him in his most brilliant, witty, and fertile vein."

That home was never more cheerful than during the eight years which followed the close of Macaulay's college life. There had been much quiet happiness at Clapham, and much in Cadogan Place; but it was round the house in Great Ormond Street that the dearest associations gathered. More than forty years afterward, when Lady Trevelyan was dying, she had herself driven to the spot, as the last drive she ever took, and sat silent in her carriage for many minutes with her eyes fixed upon those well-known walls.

While warmly attached to all his nearest relations, Macaulay lived in the closest and most frequent companionship with his sisters Hannah and Margaret, younger than himself by ten and twelve years respectively. His affection for these two, deep and enduring as it was, had in it no element of blindness or infatuation. He never said, wrote, or printed any thing resembling those flights of extravagant, and sometimes grotesque, panegyric which render the last half of John Stuart Mill's "Autobiography" one long domestic apotheosis. Even in the privacy of a diary, or the confidence of the most familiar correspondence, Macaulay knew better than to render those whom he loved ridiculous by fond exaggeration of their merits. Margaret, as will be seen in the course of this narrative, died young, leaving a memory of outward graces, and sweet and noble mental qualities, which is treasured by all among whom her short existence was passed. As regards the other sister, there are many alive who knew her for what she was; and, for those who did not know her, if this book proves how much of her brother's heart she had, and how well it was worth having, her children will feel that they have repaid their debt even to her.

Education in the Macaulay family was not on system. Of what are ordinarily called accomplishments, the daughters had but few, and Hannah fewest of any; but ever since she could remember any thing, she had enjoyed the run of a good standard library, and had been allowed to read at her own time and according to her own fancy. There were two traits in her nature which are seldom united in the same person: a vivid, practical interest in the realities which surrounded her, joined with the power of passing at will into a world of literature and romance, in which she found herself entirely at home. The feeling with which Macaulay and his sister regarded books differed from that of other people in kind rather than in degree. When they were discoursing together about a work of history or biography, a by-stander would have supposed that they had lived in the times of which the author treated, and had a personal acquaintance with every human being who was mentioned in his pages. Pepys, Addison, Horace Walpole, Dr. Johnson, Madame de Genlis, the Duc de St. Simon, and the several societies in which those worthies moved, excited in their minds precisely the same sort of concern, and gave matter for discussions of exactly the same type as most people bestow upon the proceedings of their own contemporaries. The past was to them as the present, and the fictitious as the actual. The older novels, which had been the food of their early years, had become part of themselves to such an extent that in speaking to each other they frequently employed sentences from dialogues in those novels to express the idea, or even the business, of the moment. On matters of the street or of the household they would use the very language of Mrs. Elton and Mrs. Bennet, Mr. Woodhouse, Mr. Collins, and John Thorpe, and the other inimitable actors on Jane Austen's unpretending stage, while they would debate the love affairs and the social relations of their own circle in a series of quotations from "Sir Charles Grandison" or "Evelina."

The effect was at times nothing less than bewildering. When Lady Trevelyan married, her husband, whose reading had lain anywhere rather than among the circulating libraries, used at first to wonder who the extraordinary people could be with whom his wife and his brother-in-law appeared to have lived. This style of thought and conversation had for young minds a singular and a not unhealthy fascination. Lady Trevelyan's children were brought up among books (to use the homely simile of an American author), as a stable-boy among horses. The shelves of the library, instead of frowning on us as we played and talked, seemed alive with kindly and familiar faces. But death came, and came again, and then all was changed, and changed as in an instant. There were many favorite volumes out of which the spirit seemed to vanish at once and forever. We endeavored unsuccessfully to revive by our own efforts the amusement which we had been taught to find in the faded flatteries and absurdities that passed between Miss Seward and her admirers, or to retrace for ourselves the complications of female jealousy which played round Cowper's tea-table at Olney. We awoke to the discovery that the charm was not in us, nor altogether in the books themselves. The talisman which endowed with life and meaning all that it touched had passed away from among us, leaving recollections which are our most cherished, as they must ever be our proudest, possession.

Macaulay thought it probable that he could rewrite "Sir Charles Grandison" from memory, and certainly he might have done so with his sister's help. But his intimate acquaintance with a work was no proof of its merit. "There was a certain prolific author," says Lady Trevelyan, "named Mrs. Meeke, whose romances he all but knew by heart; though he quite agreed in my criticism that they were one just like another, turning on the fortunes of some young man in a very low rank of life who eventually proves to be the son of a duke. Then there was a set of books by a Mrs. Kitty Cuthbertson, most silly, though readable, productions, the nature of which may be guessed from their titles: 'Santo Sebastiano; or, The Young Protector;' 'The Forest of Montalbano;' 'The Romance of the Pyrenees;' and 'Adelaide; or, The Countercharm.' I remember how, when 'Santo Sebastiano' was sold by auction in India, he and Miss Eden bid against each other till he secured it at a fabulous price; and I possess it still."

As an indication of the thoroughness with which this literary treasure had been studied, there appears on the last page an elaborate computation of the number of fainting-fits that occur in the course of the five volumes.

Julia de Clifford	11
Lady Delamore	4
Lady Theodosia	4
Lord Glenbrook	2
Lord Delamore	2
Lady Enderfield	1
Lord Ashgrove	1
Lord St. Orville	1
Henry Mildmay	1

A single passage, selected for no other reason than because it is the shortest, will serve as a specimen of these catastrophes: "One of the sweetest smiles that ever animated the face of mortal now diffused itself over the countenance of Lord St. Orville, as he fell at the feet of Julia in a death-like swoon."

The fun that went on in Great Ormond Street was of a jovial, and sometimes uproarious, description. Even when the family was by itself, the school-room and the drawing-room were full of young people; and friends and cousins flocked in numbers to a resort where so much merriment was perpetually on foot. There were seasons during the school holidays when the house overflowed with noise and frolic from morning to night; and Macaulay, who at any period of his life could literally spend whole days in playing with children, was master of the innocent revels. Games of hide-and-seek, that lasted for hours, with shouting, and the blowing of horns up and down the stairs and through every room, were varied by ballads, which, like the scalds of old, he composed during the act of recitation, while the others struck in with the chorus. He had no notion whatever of music, but an infallible ear for rhythm. His knack of improvisation he at all times exercised freely. The verses which he thus produced, and which he invariably attributed to an anonymous author whom he styled "the Judicious Poet," were exclusively for home consumption. Some of these effusions illustrate a sentiment in his disposition which was among the most decided, and the most frequently and loudly expressed. Macaulay was only too easily bored, and those whom he considered fools he by no means suffered gladly. He once amused his sisters by pouring out whole Iliads of extempore doggerel upon the head of an unfortunate country squire of their acquaintance who had a habit of detaining people by the button, and who was especially addicted to the society of the higher order of clergy.

His Grace Archbishop Manners Sutton
Could not keep on a single button.
As for Right Reverend John of Chester,
His waistcoats open at the breast are.
Our friend* has filled a mighty trunk
With trophies torn from Doctor Monk,
And he has really tattered foully
The vestments of Archbishop Howley.
No button could I late discern on
The garments of Archbishop Vernon,
And never had his fingers mercy
Upon the garb of Bishop Percy.
The buttons fly from Bishop Ryder
Like corks that spring from bottled cider,

and so on throughout the entire bench, until, after a good half-hour of hearty and spontaneous nonsense, the girls would go laughing back to their Italian and their drawing-boards.

He did not play upon words as a habit, nor did he interlard his talk with far-fetched or overstrained witticisms. His humor, like his rhetoric, was full of force and substance, and arose naturally from the complexion of the conversation or the circumstance of the moment. But when alone with his sisters, and, in after-years, with his nieces, he was fond of setting himself deliberately to manufacture conceits resembling those on the heroes of the Trojan war which have been thought worthy of publication in the collected works of Swift. When walking in London he would undertake to give some droll turn to the name of every shop-keeper in the street, and, when traveling, to the name of every station along the line. At home he would run through the countries of Europe, the States of the Union, the chief cities of our Indian Empire, the

* The name of this gentleman has been concealed, as not being sufficiently known by all to give point, but well enough remembered by some to give pain.

provinces of France, the prime ministers of England, or the chief writers and artists of any given century; striking off puns, admirable, endurable, and execrable, but all irresistibly laughable, which followed each other in showers like sparks from flint. Capping verses was a game of which he never tired. "In the spring of 1829," says his cousin, Mrs. Conybeare, "we were staying in Ormond Street. My chief recollection of your uncle during that visit is on the evenings when we capped verses. All the family were quick at it, but his astounding memory made him supereminent. When the time came for him to be off to bed at his chambers, he would rush out of the room after uttering some long-sought line, and would be pursued to the top of the stairs by one of the others who had contrived to recall a verse which served the purpose, in order that he might not leave the house victorious; but he, with the hall-door open in his hand, would shriek back a crowning effort, and go off triumphant."

Nothing of all this can be traced in his letters before the year 1830. Up to that period he corresponded regularly with no one but his father, between whom and himself there existed a strong regard, but scanty sympathy or similarity of pursuits. It was not until he poured out his mind almost daily to those who approached him more nearly in age and in tastes, that the lighter side of his nature began to display itself on paper. Most of what he addressed to his parents between the time when he left Cambridge and the time when he entered the House of Commons may be characterized as belonging to the type of duty-letters, treating of politics, legal gossip, personal adventures, and domestic incidents, with some reticence, and little warmth or ease of expression. The periodical insertion on the son's part of anecdotes and observations bearing upon the question of slavery reminds the reader of those presents of tall recruits with which at judiciously chosen intervals Frederic the Great used to conciliate his terrible father. As between the Macaulays, these little filial attentions acquire a certain gracefulness from the fact that, in the circumstances of the family, they could be prompted by no other motive than a dutiful and disinterested affection.

It must not be supposed—no one who examines the dates of his successive essays will for a moment suppose—that his attention was distracted or his energy dissipated by trifles. Besides the finished study of Machiavelli, and the masterly sketch of our great civil troubles known as the article on "Hallam's Constitutional History," he produced much that his mature judgment would willingly have allowed to die, but which had plenty of life in it when it first appeared between the blue and yellow covers. His most formidable enterprise during the five earliest years of his connection with the great *Review* was that passage of arms against the champions of the Utilitarian philosophy in which he touched the mighty shields of James Mill and Jeremy Bentham, and rode slashing to right and left through the ranks of their less distinguished followers. Indeed, while he sincerely admired the chiefs of the school, he had a young man's prejudice against their disciples, many of whom he regarded as "persons who, having read little or nothing, are delighted to be rescued from the sense of their own inferiority by some teacher who assures them that the studies which they have neglected are of no value, puts five or six phrases into their mouths, lends them an odd number of the *Westminster Review*, and in a month transforms them into philosophers." It must be allowed that there was some color for his opinion. The Benthamite training may have stimulated the finer intellects (and they were not few) which came within its influence; but it is impossible to conceive any thing more dreary than must have been the condition of a shallow mind, with a native predisposition to sciolism, after its owner had joined a society "composed of young men agreeing in fundamental principles, acknowledging Utility as their standard in ethics and politics," "meeting once a fortnight to read essays and discuss questions conformably to the premises thus agreed on," and "expecting the regeneration of mankind, not from any direct action on the sentiments of unselfish benevolence and love of justice, but from the effect of educated intellect enlightening the selfish feelings." John Stuart Mill, with that candor which is the rarest of his great qualities, gave a generous and authoritative testimony to the merit of these attacks upon his father and his father's creed which Macaulay himself lived to wish that he had left unwritten.

He was already famous enough to have incurred the inevitable penalty of success in the shape of the pronounced hostility of *Blackwood's Magazine.* The feelings which the leading contributors to that periodical habitually entertained toward a young and promising writer were in his case sharpened by political partisanship; and the just and measured severity which he infused into his criticism on Southey's "Colloquies of Society" brought down upon him the bludgeon to whose strokes poetic tradition has attributed the death of Keats. Macaulay was made of harder stuff, and gave little heed to a string of unsavory invectives compounded out of such epithets as "ugly," "splay-footed," and "shapeless;" such phrases as "stuff and nonsense," "malignant trash," "impertinent puppy," and "audacity of impudence;" and other samples from the polemical vocabulary of the personage who, by the irony of fate, filled the chair of moral philosophy at Edinburgh. The substance of Professor Wilson's attacks consisted in little more than the reiteration of that charge of intellectual juvenility which never fails to be employed as the last resource against a man whose abilities are undoubted and whose character is above detraction: a charge which came with an ill grace from one who, at the age of forty-five, considered the production of twenty columns a month of Bacchanalian gossip a worthy and becoming occupation for his own powers.

"*North.* He's a clever lad, James.

"*Shepherd.* Evidently; and a clever lad he'll remain, depend ye upon that, a' the days of his life. A clever lad thirty years auld and some odds is to ma mind the maist melancholy sight in nature. Only think of a clever lad o' threescore and ten, on his death-bed, wha can look back on nae greater achievement than haeing aince, or aiblins ten times, abused Mr. Southey in the *Embro' Review.*"

The prophecies of jealousy seldom come true. Southey's book died before its author: with the exception of the passages extracted by Macaulay, which have been reproduced in his essay a hundred times and more for once that they were printed in the volumes from which he selected them for his animadversion.

The chambers in which he ought to have been spending his days, and did actually spend his nights, between the years 1829 and 1834, were within five minutes' walk of the house in Great Ormond Street. The building of which those chambers formed a part, 8 South Square, Gray's Inn, has since been pulled down to make room for an extension of the library; a purpose which, in Macaulay's eyes, would amply compensate for the loss of such associations as might otherwise have attached themselves to the locality. His Trinity fellowship brought him in nearly three hundred pounds annually, and the *Edinburgh Review* almost as much again. In January, 1828, during the interregnum that separated the resignation of Lord Goderich and the acceptance of the premiership by the Duke of Wellington, Lord Lyndhurst made him a commissioner of bankruptcy: a rare piece of luck at a time when, as Lord Cockburn tells us, "a youth of a Tory family, who was discovered to have a leaning toward the doctrines of the opposition, was considered as a lost son." "The commission is welcome," Macaulay writes to his father, "and I am particularly glad that it has been given at a time when there is no ministry, and when the acceptance of it implies no political obligation. To Lord Lyndhurst I, of course, feel personal gratitude, and I shall always take care how I speak of him."

The emoluments of the office made up his income, for the three or four years during which he held it, to about a thousand pounds per annum. His means were more than sufficient for his wants, but too small and far too precarious for the furtherance of the political aspirations which now were uppermost in his mind. "Public affairs," writes Lady Trevelyan, "were become intensely interesting to him. Canning's accession to power, then his death, the repeal of the Test Act, the emancipation of the Catholics, all in their turn filled his heart and soul. He himself longed to be taking his part in Parliament, but with a very hopeless longing.

"In February, 1830, I was staying at Mr. Wilberforce's, at

Highwood Hill, when I got a letter from your uncle, inclosing one from Lord Lansdowne, who told him that he had been much struck by the articles on Mill, and that he wished to be the means of first introducing their author to public life by proposing to him to stand for the vacant seat at Calne. Lord Lansdowne expressly added that it was your uncle's high moral and private character which had determined him to make the offer, and that he wished in no respect to influence his votes, but to leave him quite at liberty to act according to his conscience. I remember flying into Mr. Wilberforce's study, and, absolutely speechless, putting the letter into his hands. He read it with much emotion, and returned it to me, saying, 'Your father has had great trials, obloquy, bad health, many anxieties. One must feel as if Tom were given him for a recompense.' He was silent for a moment, and then his mobile face lighted up, and he clapped his hand to his ear, and cried, 'Ah! I hear that shout again. Hear! hear! What a life it was!'"

And so, on the eve of the most momentous conflict that ever was fought out by speech and vote within the walls of a senate-house, the young recruit went gayly to his post in the ranks of that party whose coming fortunes he was prepared loyally to follow, and the history of whose past he was destined eloquently, and perhaps imperishably, to record.

York, April 2d, 1826.

My dear Father,—I am sorry that I have been unable to avail myself of the letters of introduction which you forwarded to me. Since I received them I have been confined to the house with a cold; and, now that I am pretty well recovered, I must take my departure for Pontefract. But if it had been otherwise, I could not have presented these recommendations. Letters of this sort may be of great service to a barrister, but the barrister himself must not be the bearer of them. On this subject the rule is most strict, at least on our circuit. The hugging of the Bar, like the simony of the Church, must be altogether carried on by the intervention of third persons. We are sensible of our dependence on the attorneys, and proportioned to that sense of dependence is our affectation of superiority. Even to take a meal with an attorney is a high misdemeanor. One of the most eminent men among us brought himself into a serious scrape by doing so. But to carry a letter of introduction, to wait in the outer room while it is being read, to be then ushered into the presence, to receive courtesies which can only be considered as the condescensions of a patron, to return courtesies which are little else than the blessings of a beggar, would be an infinitely more terrible violation of our professional code. Every barrister to whom I have applied for advice has most earnestly exhorted me on no account whatever to present the letters myself. I should perhaps add that my advisers have been persons who can not by any possibility feel jealous of me.

In default of any thing better, I will eke out my paper with some lines which I made in bed last night—an inscription for a picture of Voltaire.

> If thou would'st view one more than man and less,
>   Made up of mean and great, of foul and fair,
> Stop here; and weep and laugh, and curse and bless,
>   And spurn and worship; for thou seest Voltaire.
>
> That flashing eye blasted the conqueror's spear,
>   The monarch's sceptre, and the Jesuit's beads;
> And every wrinkle in that haggard sneer
>   Hath been the grave of Dynasties and Creeds.
>
> In very wantonness of childish mirth
>   He puffed Bastilles, and thrones, and shrines away,
> Insulted Heaven, and liberated earth.
>   Was it for good or evil? Who shall say?

Ever affectionately yours, T. B. M.

York, July 21st, 1826.

MY DEAR FATHER,—The other day as I was changing my neckcloth which my wig had disfigured, my good landlady knocked at the door of my bedroom, and told me that Mr. Smith wished to see me, and was in my room below. Of all names by which men are called, there is none which conveys a less determinate idea to the mind than that of Smith. Was he on the circuit? For I do not know half the names of my companions. Was he a special messenger from London? Was he a York attorney coming to be preyed upon, or a beggar coming to prey upon me; a barber to solicit the dressing of my wig, or a collector for the Jews' Society? Down I went, and, to my utter amazement, beheld the Smith of Smiths, Sydney Smith, alias Peter Plymley. I had forgotten his very existence till I discerned the queer contrast between his black coat and his snow-white head, and the equally curious contrast between the clerical amplitude of his person and the most unclerical wit, whim, and petulance of his eye. I shook hands with him very heartily; and on the Catholic question we immediately fell, regretted Evans,* triumphed over Lord George Beresford, and abused the bishops. He then very kindly urged me to spend the time between the close of the Assizes and the commencement of the Sessions at his house; and was so hospitably pressing that I at last agreed to go thither on Saturday afternoon. He is to drive me over again into York on Monday morning. I am very well pleased at having this opportunity of becoming better acquainted with a man who, in spite of innumerable affectations and oddities, is certainly one of the wittiest and most original writers of our times. Ever yours affectionately, T. B. M.

Bradford, July 26th, 1826.

MY DEAR FATHER,—On Saturday I went to Sydney Smith's. His parish lies three or four miles out of any frequented road. He is, however, most pleasantly situated. "Fifteen years ago," said he to me, as I alighted at the gate of his shrubbery, "I was taken up in Piccadilly and set down here. There was no house, and no garden; nothing but a bare field." One service this eccentric divine has certainly rendered to the Church—he has built the very neatest, most commodious, and most appropriate rectory that I ever saw. All its decorations

* These allusions refer to the general election which had recently taken place.

are in a peculiarly clerical style, grave, simple, and Gothic. The bed-chambers are excellent, and excellently fitted up; the sitting-rooms handsome; and the grounds sufficiently pretty. Tindal and Parke (not the judge, of course), two of the best lawyers, best scholars, and best men in England, were there. We passed an extremely pleasant evening, had a very good dinner, and many amusing anecdotes.

After breakfast the next morning, I walked to church with Sydney Smith. The edifice is not at all in keeping with the rectory. It is a miserable little hovel, with a wooden belfry. It was, however, well filled, and with decent people, who seemed to take very much to their pastor. I understand that he is a very respectable apothecary; and most liberal of his skill, his medicine, his soup, and his wine among the sick. He preached a very queer sermon—the former half too familiar, and the latter half too florid, but not without some ingenuity of thought and expression.

Sydney Smith brought me to York on Monday morning, in time for the stage-coach which runs to Skipton. We parted with many assurances of good-will. I have really taken a great liking to him. He is full of wit, humor, and shrewdness. He is not one of those show-talkers who reserve all their good things for special occasions. It seems to be his greatest luxury to keep his wife and daughters laughing for two or three hours every day. His notions of law, government, and trade are surprisingly clear and just. His misfortune is to have chosen a profession at once above him and below him. Zeal would have made him a prodigy; formality and bigotry would have made him a bishop; but he could neither rise to the duties of his order, nor stoop to its degradations.

He praised my articles in the *Edinburgh Review* with a warmth which I am willing to believe sincere, because he qualified his compliments with several very sensible cautions. My great danger, he said, was that of taking a tone of too much asperity and contempt in controversy. I believe that he is right, and I shall try to mend.

Ever affectionately yours, T. B. M.

Lancaster, September 1st, 1827.

MY DEAR FATHER,—Thank Hannah from me for her pleasant letter. I would answer it if I had any thing equally amusing to say in return; but here we have no news, except what comes from London, and is as stale as inland fish before it reaches us. We have circuit anecdotes, to be sure; and perhaps you will be pleased to hear that Brougham has been rising through the whole of this struggle. At York, Pollock decidedly took the lead. At Durham, Brougham overtook him, passed him at Newcastle, and got immensely ahead of him at Carlisle and Appleby, which, to be sure, are the places where his own connections lie. We have not been here quite long enough to determine how he will succeed with the Lancastrians. This has always hitherto been his least favorable place. He appears to improve in industry and prudence. He learns his story more thoroughly, and tells it more clearly than formerly. If he continues to manage causes as well as he has done of late, he must rise to the summit of the profession. I can not say quite so much for his temper, which this close and constant rivalry does not improve. He squabbles with Pollock more than, in generosity or policy, he ought to do. I have heard several of our younger men wondering that he does not show more magnanimity. He yawns while Pollock is speaking—a sign of weariness which, in their present relation to each other, he would do well to suppress. He has said some very good, but very bitter, things. There was a case of a lead-mine. Pollock was for the proprietors, and complained bitterly of the encroachments which Brougham's clients had made upon this property, which he represented as of immense value. Brougham said that the estimate which his learned friend formed of the property was vastly exaggerated, but that it was no wonder that a person who found it so easy to get gold for his lead should appreciate that heavy metal so highly. The other day Pollock laid down a point of law rather dogmatically. "Mr. Pollock," said Brougham, "perhaps, before you rule the point, you will suffer his lordship to submit a few observations on it to your consideration."

I received the Edinburgh paper which you sent me. Silly and spiteful as it is, there is a little truth in it. In such cases I always remember those excellent lines of Boileau:

> Moi, qu'une humeur trop libre, un esprit peu soumis,
> De bonne heure a pourvu d'utiles ennemis,
> Je dois plus à leur haine (il faut que je l'avoue)
> Qu'au faible et vain talent dont la France me loue.
> Sitôt que sur un vice ils pensent me confondre,
> C'est en me guérissant que je sais leur répondre.

This place disagrees so much with me that I shall leave it as soon as the dispersion of the circuit commences—that is, after the delivery of the last batch of briefs; always supposing, which may be supposed without much risk of mistake, that there are none for me.

Ever yours affectionately, T. B. M.

It was about this period that the Cambridge Senate came to a resolution to petition against the Catholic Claims. The minority demanded a poll, and conveyed a hint to their friends in London. Macaulay, with one or two more to help him, beat up the Inns of Court for recruits, chartered a stage-coach, packed it inside and out with young Whig masters of arts, and drove up King's Parade just in time to turn the scale in favor of Emancipation. The whole party dined in triumph at Trinity, and got back to town the same evening; and the Tory journalists were emphatic in their indignation at the deliberate opinion of the university having been overridden by a coachful of "godless and briefless barristers."

Court-house, Pomfret, April 15th, 1828.

MY DEAR MOTHER,—I address this epistle to you as the least undeserving of a very undeserving family. You, I think, have sent me one letter since I left London. I have nothing here to do but to write letters; and, what is not very often the case, I have members of Parliament in abundance to frank them, and abundance of matter to fill them with. My Edinburgh expedition has given me so much to say that, unless I write off some of it before I come home, I shall talk you all to death, and be voted a bore in every house which I visit. I will commence with Jeffrey himself. I had almost forgotten his person; and, indeed, I should not wonder if even now I were to forget it again. He has twenty faces, almost as unlike each other as my father's to Mr. Wilberforce's, and infinitely more unlike to each other than those of near relatives often are; infinitely more unlike, for example, than those of the two Grants. When absolutely quiescent, reading a paper, or hearing a conversation in which he takes no interest, his countenance shows no indication whatever of intellectual superiority of any kind. But as soon as he is interested, and opens his eyes upon you, the change is like magic. There is a flash in his glance, a violent contortion in his frown, an exquisite humor in his sneer, and a sweetness and brilliancy in his smile, beyond any thing that ever I witnessed. A person who had seen him in only one state would not know him if he saw him in another. For he has not, like Brougham, marked features which in all moods of mind remain unaltered. The mere outline of his face is insignificant. The expression is every thing; and such power and variety of expression I never saw in any human countenance, not even in that of the most celebrated actors. I can conceive that Garrick may have been like him. I have seen several pictures of Garrick, none resembling another, and I have heard Hannah More speak of the extraordinary variety of countenance by which he was distinguished, and of the unequaled radiance and penetration of his eye. The voice and delivery of Jeffrey resemble his face. He possesses considerable power of mimicry, and rarely tells a story without imitating several different accents. His familiar tone, his declamatory tone, and his pathetic tone are quite different things. Sometimes Scotch predominates in his pronunciation; sometimes it is imperceptible. Sometimes his utterance is snappish and quick to the last degree; sometimes it is remarkable for rotundity and mellowness. I can easily conceive that two people who had seen him on different days might dispute about him as the travelers in the fable disputed about the chameleon.

In one thing, as far as I observed, he is always the same;

and that is the warmth of his domestic affections. Neither Mr. Wilberforce nor my uncle Babington comes up to him in this respect. The flow of his kindness is quite inexhaustible. Not five minutes pass without some fond expression or caressing gesture to his wife or his daughter. He has fitted up a study for himself; but he never goes into it. Law papers, reviews, whatever he has to write, he writes in the drawing-room or in his wife's boudoir. When he goes to other parts of the country on a retainer he takes them in the carriage with him. I do not wonder that he should be a good husband; for his wife is a very amiable woman. But I was surprised to see a man so keen and sarcastic, so much of a scoffer, pouring himself out with such simplicity and tenderness in all sorts of affectionate nonsense. Through our whole journey to Perth he kept up a sort of mock quarrel with his daughter; attacked her about novel-reading, laughed her into a pet, kissed her out of it, and laughed her into it again. She and her mother absolutely idolize him, and I do not wonder at it.

His conversation is very much like his countenance and his voice, of immense variety; sometimes plain and unpretending even to flatness; sometimes whimsically brilliant and rhetorical almost beyond the license of private discourse. He has many interesting anecdotes, and tells them very well. He is a shrewd observer; and so fastidious that I am not surprised at the awe in which many people seem to stand when in his company. Though not altogether free from affectation himself, he has a peculiar loathing for it in other people, and a great talent for discovering and exposing it. He has a particular contempt, in which I most heartily concur with him, for the *fadaises* of blue-stocking literature, for the mutual flatteries of coteries, the handing about of *vers de société*, the albums, the conversaziones, and all the other nauseous trickeries of the Sewards, Hayleys, and Sothebys. I am not quite sure that he has escaped the opposite extreme, and that he is not a little too desirous to appear rather a man of the world, an active lawyer, or an easy, careless gentleman, than a distinguished writer. I must own that when Jeffrey and I were by ourselves, he talked much and very well on literary topics. His kindness and hospitality to me were, indeed, beyond description; and his wife was as pleasant and friendly as possible. I liked every thing but the hours. We were never up till ten, and never retired till two hours at least after midnight. Jeffrey, indeed, never goes to bed till sleep comes on him overpoweringly, and never rises till forced up by business or hunger. He is extremely well in health; so that I could not help suspecting him of being very hypochondriac; for all his late letters to me have been filled with lamentations about his various maladies. His wife told me, when I congratulated her on his recovery, that I must not absolutely rely on all his accounts of his own diseases. I really think that he is, on the whole, the youngest-looking man of fifty that I know, at least when he is animated.

His house is magnificent. It is in Moray Place, the newest pile of buildings in the town, looking out to the Forth on one side, and to a green garden on the other. It is really equal to the houses in Grosvenor Square. Fine, however, as is the new quarter of Edinburgh, I decidedly prefer the Old Town. There is nothing like it in the island. You have been there; but you have not seen the town: and no lady ever sees a town. It is only by walking on foot through all corners at all hours that cities can be really studied to good purpose. There is a new pillar to the memory of Lord Melville; very elegant, and very much better than the man deserved. His statue is at the top, with a wreath on the head very like a night-cap drawn over the eyes. It is impossible to look at it without being reminded of the fate which the original most richly merited. But my letter will overflow even the ample limits of a frank, if I do not conclude. I hope that you will be properly penitent for neglecting such a correspondent when you receive so long a dispatch written amidst the bellowing of justices, lawyers, criers, witnesses, prisoners, and prisoners' wives and mothers. Ever yours affectionately, T. B. M.

Lancaster, March 14th, 1829.

MY DEAR FATHER,—A single line to say that I am at Lancaster. Where you all are I have not the very slightest notion. Pray let me hear. That dispersion of the Gentiles which our friends the prophets foretell seems to have commenced with our family.

Every thing here is going on in the common routine. The only things of peculiar interest are those which we get from the London papers. All minds seem to be perfectly made up as to the certainty of Catholic Emancipation having come at last. The feeling of approbation among the barristers is all but unanimous. The quiet towns-people here, as far as I can see, are very well contented. As soon as I arrived I was asked by my landlady how things had gone. I told her the division, which I had learned from Brougham at Garstang. She seemed surprised at the majority. I asked her if she was against the measure. "No; she only wished that all Christians would live in peace and charity together." A very sensible speech, and better than one at least of the members for the county ever made in his life.

I implore you above every thing, my dear father, to keep up your health and spirits. Come what may, the conveniences of life, independence, our personal respectability, and the exercise of the intellect and the affections, we are almost certain of retaining; and every thing else is a mere superfluity, to be enjoyed, but not to be missed. But I ought to be ashamed of reading you a lecture on qualities which you are so much more competent to teach than myself.

Ever yours very affectionately, T. B. M.

To Macvey Napier, Esq.

50 Great Ormond Street, London, January 25th, 1830.

My dear Sir,—I send off by the mail of to-day an article on Southey—too long, I fear, to meet your wishes, but as short as I could make it.

There were, by-the-bye, in my last article a few omissions made, of no great consequence in themselves; the longest, I think, a paragraph of twelve or fourteen lines. I should scarcely have thought this worth mentioning, as it certainly by no means exceeds the limits of that editorial prerogative which I most willingly recognize, but that the omissions seemed to me, and to one or two persons who had seen the article in its original state, to be made on a principle which, however sound in itself, does not, I think, apply to compositions of this description. The passages omitted were the most pointed and ornamented sentences in the review. Now, for high and grave works, a history, for example, or a system of political or moral philosophy, Dr. Johnson's rule—that every sentence which the writer thinks fine ought to be cut out—is excellent. But periodical works like ours, which, unless they strike at the first reading are not likely to strike at all, whose whole life is a month or two, may, I think, be allowed to be sometimes even viciously florid. Probably, in estimating the real value of any tinsel which I may put upon my articles, you and I should not materially differ. But it is not by his own taste, but by the taste of the fish, that the angler is determined in his choice of bait.

Perhaps, after all, I am ascribing to system what is mere accident. Be assured, at all events, that what I have said is said in perfect good-humor, and indicates no mutinous disposition.

The Jews are about to petition Parliament for relief from the absurd restrictions which lie on them—the last relic of the old system of intolerance. I have been applied to by some of them, in the name of the managers of the scheme, to write for them in the *Edinburgh Review*. I would gladly further a cause so good, and you, I think, could have no objection.

Ever yours truly, T. B. MACAULAY.

Bowood, February 10th, 1830.

MY DEAR FATHER,—I am here in a very nice room, with perfect liberty, and a splendid library at my command. It seems to be thought desirable that I should stay in the neighborhood, and pay my compliments to my future constituents every other day.

The house is splendid and elegant, yet more remarkable for comfort than for either elegance or splendor. I never saw any great place so thoroughly desirable for a residence. Lord Kerry tells me that his uncle left every thing in ruin—trees cut down, and rooms unfurnished—and sold the library, which was extremely fine. Every book and picture in Bowood has been bought by the present lord, and certainly the collection does him great honor.

I am glad that I staid here. A burgess of some influence, who, at the last election, attempted to get up an opposition to the Lansdowne interest, has just arrived. I called on him this morning, and, though he was a little ungracious at first, succeeded in obtaining his promise. Without him, indeed, my return would have been secure; but both from motives of interest and from a sense of gratitude I think it best to leave nothing undone which may tend to keep Lord Lansdowne's influence here unimpaired against future elections.

Lord Kerry seems to me to be going on well. He has been in very good condition, he says, this week; and hopes to be at the election, and at the subsequent dinner. I do not know when I have taken so much to so young a man. In general my intimacies have been with my seniors; but Lord Kerry is really quite a favorite of mine—kind, lively, intelligent, modest, with the gentle manners which indicate a long intimacy with the best society, and yet without the least affectation. We have oceans of beer and mountains of potatoes for dinner. Indeed, Lady Lansdowne drank beer most heartily on the only day which she passed with us; and when I told her, laughing, that she set me at ease on a point which had given me much trouble, she said that she would never suffer any dandy novelist to rob her of her beer or her cheese.

The question between law and politics is a momentous one. As far as I am myself concerned, I should not hesitate; but the interest of my family is also to be considered. We shall see, however, before long, what my chance of success as a public man may prove to be. At present it would clearly be wrong in me to show any disposition to quit my profession.

I hope that you will be on your guard as to what you may say to Brougham about this business. He is so angry at it that he can not keep his anger to himself. I know that he has blamed Lord Lansdowne in the robing-room of the Court of King's Bench. The seat ought, he says, to have been given to another man. If he means Denman, I can forgive, and even respect him, for the feeling which he entertains.

Believe me ever yours most affectionately, T. B. M.

CHAPTER IV.

1830–1832.

State of Public Affairs when Macaulay entered Parliament.—His Maiden Speech.—The French Revolution of July, 1830.—Macaulay's Letters from Paris.—The Palais Royal.—Lafayette.—Lardner's Cabinet "Cyclopedia."—The New Parliament Meets.—Fall of the Duke of Wellington.—Scene with Croker.—The Reform Bill.—Political Success.—House of Commons Life.—Macaulay's Party Spirit.—London Society.—Mr. Thomas Flower Ellis.—Visit to Cambridge.—Rothley Temple.—Margaret Macaulay's Journal.—Lord Brougham.—Hopes of Office.—Macaulay as a Politician.—Letters to Lady Trevelyan, Mr. Napier, and Mr. Ellis.

THROUGHOUT the last two centuries of our history there never was a period when a man conscious of power, impatient of public wrongs, and still young enough to love a fight for its own sake, could have entered Parliament with a fairer prospect of leading a life worth living, and doing work that would requite the pains, than at the commencement of the year 1830.

In these volumes, which only touch politics in order to show to what extent Macaulay was a politician, and for how long, controversies can not appropriately be started or revived. This is not the place to enter into a discussion on the vexed question as to whether Mr. Pitt and his successors, in pursuing their system of repression, were justified by the necessities of the long French war. It is enough to assert, what few or none will deny, that, for the space of more than a generation from 1790 onward, our country had, with a short interval, been governed on declared reactionary principles. We in whose days Whigs and Tories have often exchanged office, and still more often interchanged policies, find it difficult to imagine what must have been the condition of the kingdom when one and the same party almost continuously held not only place, but power, over a period when to an unexampled degree "public life was exasperated by hatred, and the charities of private life soured by political aversion." Fear, religion, ambition, and self-interest — every thing that could tempt and every thing that could deter—were enlisted on the side of the dominant opinions. To profess Liberal views was to be hopelessly excluded from all posts of emolument, from all functions of dignity, from the opportunities of business, from the amenities of society. Quiet tradesmen, who ventured to maintain that there was something in Jacobinism besides the guillotine, soon found their town or village too hot to hold them, and were glad to place the Atlantic between themselves and their neighbors. Clergymen suspected of thinking that in the "Vindiciæ Gallicæ" Mackintosh had got the better of Burke, were ousted from their college fellowships as atheists, or left to starve without a curacy as radicals. Political animosity and political favoritism made themselves felt in departments of life which had hitherto been free from their encroachments. Whig merchants had a difficulty in getting money for their paper, and Whig barristers in obtaining acceptance for their arguments. Whig statesmen, while enjoying that security for life and liberty which even in the worst days of our recent history has been the reward of eminence, were powerless in the Commons and isolated in the Lords. No motive but disinterested conviction kept a handful of veterans steadfast round a banner which was never raised except to be swept contemptuously down by the disciplined and overwhelming strength of the ministerial phalanx. Argument and oratory were alike unavailing under a constitution which was, indeed, a despotism of privilege. The county representation of England was an anomaly, and the borough representation little better than a scandal. The constituencies of Scotland, with so much else that of right belonged to the public, had got into Dundas's pocket. In the year 1820 all the towns north of Tweed together contained fewer voters than are now on the rolls of the single burgh of Hawick, and all the counties together contained fewer voters than are now on the register of Roxburghshire. So small a band of electors was easily manipulated by a party leader who had the patronage of India at his command. The three presidencies were flooded with the sons and nephews of men who were lucky enough to have a seat in a town-council or a superiority in a rural district; and fortunate it was for our empire that the responsibilities of that noblest of all careers soon educated young civil servants into something higher than mere adherents of a political party.

While the will of the nation was paralyzed within the senate, effectual care was taken that its voice should not be heard without. The press was gagged in England, and throttled in Scotland. Every speech, or sermon, or pamphlet, the substance of which a crown lawyer could torture into a semblance of sedition, sent its author to the jail, the hulks, or the pillory. In any place of resort where an informer could penetrate, men spoke their minds at imminent hazard of ruinous fines and protracted imprisonment. It was vain to appeal to Parliament for redress against the tyranny of packed juries and panic-driven magistrates. Sheridan endeavored to retain for his countrymen the protection of Habeas Corpus, but he could only muster forty-one supporters. Exactly as many members followed Fox into the lobby when he opposed a bill which, interpreted in the spirit that then actuated our tribunals, made attendance at an open meeting summoned for the consideration of Parliamentary Reform a service as dangerous as night-poaching and far more dangerous than smuggling. Only ten more than that number ventured to protest against the introduction of a measure, still more inquisitorial in its provisions and ruthless in its penalties, which rendered every citizen who gave his attention to the removal of public grievances liable at any moment to find himself in the position of a criminal—that very measure in behalf of which Bishop Horsley had stated in the House of Peers that he did not know what the mass of the people of any country had to do with the laws except to obey them.

Amidst a population which had once known freedom, and was still fit to be intrusted with it, such a state of matters could not last forever. Justly proud of the immense success that they had bought by their resolution, their energy, and their perseverance, the ministers regarded the fall of Napoleon as a party triumph which could only serve to confirm their power. But the last cannon-shot that was fired on the 18th of June, 1815, was in truth the death-knell of the Golden Age of Toryism. When the passion and ardor of the war gave place to the discontent engendered by a protracted period of commercial distress, the opponents of progress began to perceive that they had to reckon, not with a small and disheartened faction, but with a clear majority of the nation led by the most enlightened and the most eminent of its sons. Agitators and incendiaries retired into the background, as will always be the case when the country is in earnest; and statesmen who had much to lose, but were not afraid to risk it, stepped quietly and firmly to the front. The men, and the sons of the men, who had so long endured exclusion from office imbittered by unpopularity, at length reaped their reward. Earl Grey, who forty years before had been hooted through the streets of North Shields with cries of "No Popery," lived to bear the most respected name in England; and Brougham, whose opinions differed little from those for expressing which Dr. Priestley, in 1791, had his house burned about his ears by the Birmingham mob, was now the popular idol beyond all comparison or competition.

In the face of such unanimity of purpose, guided by so much worth and talent, the ministers lost their nerve, and, like all rulers who do not possess the confidence of the governed, began first to make mistakes and then to quarrel among themselves. Throughout the years of Macaulay's early manhood the ice was breaking fast. He was still quite young when the concession of Catholic emancipation* gave a moral shock to

---

* Macaulay was fond of repeating an answer made to him by Lord Clarendon in the year 1829. The young men were talking over the situation, and Macaulay expressed curiosity as to the terms in which the Duke of Wellington would recommend the Catholic Relief Bill to the Peers. "Oh," said the other, "it will be easy enough. He'll say, 'My lords, attention! Right about face! March!'"

the Tory party from which it never recovered until the old order of things had finally passed away. It was his fortune to enter into other men's labors after the burden and heat of the day had already been borne, and to be summoned into the field just as the season was at hand for gathering in a ripe and long-expected harvest of beneficent legislation.

On the 5th of April, 1830, he addressed the House of Commons on the second reading of Mr. Robert Grant's bill for the removal of Jewish disabilities. Sir James Mackintosh rose with him, but Macaulay got the advantage of the preference that has always been conceded to one who speaks for the first time after gaining his seat during the continuance of a Parliament—a privilege which, by a stretch of generosity, is now extended to new members who have been returned at a general election. Sir James subsequently took part in the debate; not, as he carefully assured his audience, "to supply any defects in the speech of his honorable friend, for there were none that he could find, but principally to absolve his own conscience." Indeed, Macaulay, addressing himself to his task with an absence of pretension such as never fails to conciliate the good-will of the House toward a maiden speech, put clearly and concisely enough the arguments in favor of the bill—arguments which, obvious and almost commonplace as they appear under this straightforward treatment, had yet to be repeated during a space of six-and-thirty years before they commended themselves to the judgment of our Upper Chamber.

"The power of which you deprive the Jew consists in maces, and gold chains, and skins of parchment with pieces of wax dangling from their edges. The power which you leave the Jew is the power of principal over clerk, of master over servant, of landlord over tenant. As things now stand, a Jew may be the richest man in England. He may possess the means of raising this party and depressing that; of making East Indian directors; of making members of Parliament. The influence of a Jew may be of the first consequence in a war which shakes Europe to the centre. His power may come into play in assisting or thwarting the greatest plans of the greatest princes; and yet, with all this confessed, acknowledged, undenied, you would have him deprived of power! Does not wealth confer power? How are we to permit all the consequences of that wealth but one? I can not conceive the nature of an argument that is to bear out such a position. If we were to be called on to revert to the day when the warehouses of Jews were torn down and pillaged, the theory would be comprehensible. But we have to do with a persecution so delicate that there is no abstract rule for its guidance. You tell us that the Jews have no legal right to power, and I am bound to admit it; but in the same way, three hundred years ago they had no legal right to be in England, and six hundred years ago they had no legal right to the teeth in their heads. But, if it is the moral right we are to look at, I hold that on every principle of moral obligation the Jew has a right to political power."

He was on his legs once again, and once only, during his first session; doing more for future success in Parliament by his silence than he could have effected by half a dozen brilliant perorations. A crisis was rapidly approaching when a man gifted with eloquence, who by previous self-restraint had convinced the House that he did not speak for speaking's sake, might rise almost in a day to the very summit of influence and reputation. The country was under the personal rule of the Duke of Wellington, who had gradually squeezed out of his Cabinet every vestige of Liberalism and even of independence, and who at last stood so completely alone that he was generally supposed to be in more intimate communication with Prince Polignac than with any of his own colleagues. The duke had his own way in the Lords; and on the benches of the Commons the Opposition members were unable to carry, or even visibly to improve their prospect of carrying, the measures on which their hearts were set. The Reformers were not doing better in the division lobby than in 1821, and their question showed no signs of having advanced since the day when it had been thrown over by Pitt on the eve of the French Revolution.

But the outward aspect of the situation was very far from answering to the reality. While the leaders of the popular party had been spending themselves in efforts that seemed each more abortive than the last—dividing only to be enormously outvoted, and vindicating with calmness and moderation the first principles of constitutional government only to be stigmatized as the apostles of anarchy—a mighty change was surely but imperceptibly effecting itself in the collective mind of their fellow-countrymen.

> For, while the tired waves, vainly breaking,
> Seem here no painful inch to gain,
> Far back, through creeks and inlets making,
> Comes silent, flooding in, the main.

Events were at hand which unmistakably showed how different was the England of 1830 from the England of 1790. The king died; Parliament was dissolved on the 24th of July; and in the first excitement and bustle of the elections, while the candidates were still on the road and the writs in the mail-bag, came the news that Paris was in arms. The troops fought as well as Frenchmen ever can be got to fight against the tricolor; but by the evening of the 29th it was all over with the Bourbons. The minister whose friendship had reflected such unpopularity on our own premier succumbed to the detestation of the victorious people, and his sacrifice did not save the dynasty. What was passing among our neighbors for once created sympathy, and not repulsion, on this side the Channel. One French revolution had condemned English Liberalism to forty years of subjection, and another was to be the signal which launched it on as long a career of supremacy. Most men said, and all felt, that Wellington must follow Polignac; and the public temper was such as made it well for the stability of our throne that it was filled by a monarch who had attracted to himself the hopes and affection of the nation, and who shared its preferences and antipathies with regard to the leading statesmen of the day.

One result of political disturbance in any quarter of the globe is to fill the scene of action with young members of Parliament, who follow revolutions about Europe as assiduously as Jew brokers attend upon the movements of an invading army. Macaulay, whose re-election for Calne had been a thing of course, posted off to Paris at the end of August, journeying by Dieppe and Rouen, and eagerly enjoying a first taste of continental travel. His letters during the tour were such as, previously to the age of railroads, brothers who had not been abroad before used to write for the edification of sisters who expected never to go abroad at all. He describes in minute detail manners and institutions that to us are no longer novelties, and monuments which an educated Englishman of our time knows as well as Westminster Abbey, and a great deal better than the Tower. Every thing that he saw, heard, eat, drank, paid, and suffered, was noted down in his exuberant diction to be read aloud and commented on over the breakfast-table in Great Ormond Street.

"At Rouen I was struck by the union of venerable antiquity with extreme liveliness and gayety. We have nothing of the sort in England. Till the time of James the First, I imagine, our houses were almost all of wood, and have, in consequence, disappeared. In York there are some very old streets; but they are abandoned to the lowest people, and the gay shops are in the newly built quarter of the town. In London, what with the fire of 1666, and what with the natural progress of demolition and rebuilding, I doubt whether there are fifty houses that date from the Reformation. But in Rouen you have street after street of lofty, stern-looking masses of stone, with Gothic carvings. The buildings are so high, and the ways so narrow, that the sun can scarcely reach the pavements. Yet in these streets, monastic in their aspect, you have all the glitter of Regent Street or the Burlington Arcade. Rugged and dark above, below they are a blaze of ribbons, gowns, watches, trinkets, artificial flowers; grapes, melons, and peaches such as Covent Garden does not furnish, filling the windows of the fruiterers; showy women swimming smoothly over the uneasy stones, and stared at by national guards swaggering by in full uniform. It is the Soho Bazaar transplanted into the gloomy cloisters of Oxford."

He writes to a friend just before he started on his tour: "There is much that I am impatient to see, but two things specially—the Palais Royal, and the man who called me the Aristarchus of Edinburgh." Who this person might be, and whether Macaulay succeeded in meeting him, are questions which his letters leave unsolved; but he must have been a constant visitor at the Palais Royal if the hours that he spent in it bore any relation to the number of pages which it occupies in his correspondence. The place was indeed well worth a careful study; for in 1830 it was not the orderly and decent bazaar of the Second Empire, but was still that compound of Parnassus and Bohemia which is painted in vivid colors in the "Grand Homme de Provence" of Balzac—still the paradise of such ineffable rascals as Diderot has drawn, with terrible fidelity, in his "Neveu de Rameau."

"If I were to select the spot in all the earth in which the good and evil of civilization are most strikingly exhibited, in which the arts of life are carried to the highest perfection, and in which all pleasures, high and low, intellectual and sensual, are collected in the smallest space, I should certainly choose the Palais Royal. It is the Covent Garden Piazza, the Paternoster Row, the Vauxhall, the Albion Tavern, the Burlington Arcade, the Crockford's, the Finish, the Athenæum of Paris, all in one. Even now, when the first dazzling effect has passed off, I never traverse it without feeling bewildered by its magnificent variety. As a great capital is a country in miniature, so the Palais Royal is a capital in miniature—an abstract and epitome of a vast community, exhibiting at a glance the politeness which adorns its higher ranks, the coarseness of its populace, and the vices and the misery which lie underneath its brilliant exterior. Every thing is there, and every body. Statesmen, wits, philosophers, beauties, dandies, blacklegs, adventurers, artists, idlers, the king and his court, beggars with matches crying for charity, wretched creatures dying of disease and want in garrets. There is no condition of life which is not to be found in this gorgeous and fantastic fairy-land."

He had excellent opportunities for seeing behind the scenes during the closing acts of the great drama that was being played out through those summer months. The Duc de Broglie, then prime minister, treated him with marked attention both as an Englishman of distinction and as his father's son. He was much in the Chamber of Deputies, and witnessed that strange and pathetic historical revival when, after an interval of forty such years as mankind had never known before, the aged La Fayette again stood forth in the character of a disinterested dictator between the hostile classes of his fellow-countrymen.

"De La Fayette is so overwhelmed with work that I scarcely knew how to deliver even Brougham's letter, which was a letter of business, and should have thought it absurd to send him Mackintosh's, which was a mere letter of introduction. I fell in with an English acquaintance who told me that he had an appointment with La Fayette, and who undertook to deliver them both. I accepted his offer, for if I had left them with the porter, ten to one they would never have been opened. I hear that hundreds of letters are lying in the lodge of the hotel. Every Wednesday morning, from nine to eleven, La Fayette gives audience to any body who wishes to speak with him; but about ten thousand people attend on these occasions, and fill not only the house, but all the court-yard and half the street. La Fayette is commander-in-chief of the National Guard of France. The number of these troops in Paris alone is upward of forty thousand. The Government finds a musket and bayonet; but the uniform, which costs about ten napoleons, the soldiers provide themselves. All the shopkeepers are enrolled, and I can not sufficiently admire their patriotism. My landlord, Meurice, a man who, I suppose, has realized a million francs or more, is up one night in four with his firelock, doing the duty of a common watchman.

"There is, however, something to be said as an explanation of the zeal with which the bourgeoisie give their time and money to the public. The army received so painful a humiliation in the battles of July that it is by no means inclined to serve the new system faithfully. The rabble behaved nobly during the conflict, and have since shown rare humanity and moderation. Yet those who remember the former Revolution feel an extreme dread of the ascendency of mere multitude; and there have been signs, trifling in themselves, but such as may naturally alarm people of property. Workmen have struck. Machinery has been attacked. Inflammatory handbills have appeared upon the walls. At present all is quiet; but the thing may happen, particularly if Polignac and Peyronnet should not be put to death. The Peers wish to save them. The lower orders, who have had five or six thousand of their friends and kinsmen butchered by the frantic wickedness of these men, will hardly submit. 'Eh! eh!' said a fierce old soldier of Napoleon to me the other day. 'L'on dit qu'ils seront déportés; mais ne m'en parle pas. Non! non! Coupez leur le cou. Sacré! Ça ne passera pas comme ça.'

"This long political digression will explain to you why Monsieur de La Fayette is so busy. He has more to do than all the ministers together. However, my letters were presented, and he said to my friend that he had a soirée every Tuesday, and should be most happy to see me there. I drove to his house yesterday night. Of the interest which the common Parisians take in politics you may judge by this: I told my driver to wait for me, and asked his number. 'Ah! monsieur, c'est un beau numéro. C'est un brave numéro. C'est 221.' You may remember that the number of Deputies who voted the intrepid address to Charles the Tenth which irritated him into his absurd *coup d'état* was 221. I walked into the hotel through a crowd of uniforms, and found the reception-rooms as full as they could hold. I was not able to make my way to La Fayette, but I was glad to see him. He looks like the brave, honest, simple, good-natured man that he is."

Besides what is quoted above, there is very little of general interest in these journal letters; and their publication would serve no purpose except that of informing the present leader of the monarchists what his father had for breakfast and dinner during a week of 1830, and of enabling him to trace changes in the disposition of the furniture of the De Broglie Hotel. "I believe," writes Macaulay, "that I have given the inventory of every article in the duke's *salon*. You will think that I have some intention of turning upholsterer."

His thoughts and observations on weightier matters he kept

for an article on "The State of Parties in France," which he intended to provide for the October number of the *Edinburgh Review*. While he was still at Paris, this arrangement was rescinded by Mr. Napier, in compliance with the wish, or the whim, of Brougham; and Macaulay's surprise and annoyance vented themselves in a burst of indignant rhetoric* strong enough to have upset a government. His wrath, or that part of it, at least, which was directed against the editor, did not survive an interchange of letters; and he at once set to work upon turning his material into the shape of a volume for the series of Lardner's "Cabinet Cyclopædia," under the title of "The History of France, from the Restoration of the Bourbons to the Accession of Louis Philippe." Ten years ago, proofs of the first eighty-eight pages were found in Messrs. Spottiswoode's printing-office, with a note on the margin to the effect that most of the type was broken up before the sheets had been pulled. The task, as far as it went, was faithfully performed; but the author soon arrived at the conclusion that he might find a more profitable investment for his labor. With his head full of Reform, Macaulay was loath to spend in epitomizing history the time and energy that would be better employed in helping to make it.

When the new Parliament met on the 26th of October, it was already evident that the Government was doomed. Where the elections were open, Reform had carried the day. Brougham was returned for Yorkshire, a constituency of tried independence, which before 1832 seldom failed to secure the triumph of a cause into whose scale it had thrown its enormous weight. The counties had declared for the Whigs by a majority of eight to five, and the great cities by a majority of eight to one. Of the close boroughs in Tory hands many were held by men who had not forgotten Catholic Emancipation, and who did not mean to pardon their leaders until they had ceased to be ministers.

In the debate on the Address, the Duke of Wellington uttered his famous declaration that the Legislature possessed,

---

* See, on page 183 the letter to Mr. Napier, of September 16th, 1831.

and deserved to possess, the full and entire confidence of the country; that its existing constitution was not only practically efficient, but theoretically admirable; and that if he himself had to frame a system of representation, he should do his best to imitate so excellent a model, though he admitted that the nature of man was incapable at a single effort of attaining to such mature perfection. His bewildered colleagues could only assert in excuse that their chief was deaf, and wish that every body else had been deaf too. The second ministerial feat was of a piece with the first. Their majesties had accepted an invitation to dine at Guildhall on the 9th of November. The lord mayor elect informed the Home Office that there was danger of riot, and the premier (who could not be got to see that London was not Paris because his own political creed happened to be much the same as Polignac's) advised the king to postpone his visit to the City, and actually talked of putting Lombard Street and Cheapside in military occupation. Such a step taken at such a time by such a man had its inevitable result. Consols, which the duke's speech on the Address had brought from 84 to 80, fell to 77 in an hour and a half: jewelers and silversmiths sent their goods to the banks: merchants armed their clerks and barricaded their warehouses: and when the panic subsided, fear only gave place to the shame and annoyance which a loyal people, whose loyalty was at that moment more active than ever, experienced from the reflection that all Europe was discussing the reasons why our king could not venture to dine in public with the chief magistrate of his own capital. A strong minister, who sends the funds down seven per cent. in as many days, is an anomaly that no nation will consent to tolerate; the members of the Cabinet looked forward with consternation to a scheme of Reform which, with the approbation of his party, Brougham had undertaken to introduce on the 15th of November; and when, within twenty-four hours of the dreaded debate, they were defeated on a motion for a committee on the civil list, their relief at having obtained an excuse for retiring at least equaled that which the country felt at getting rid of them.

Earl Grey came in, saying (and meaning what he said) that

the principles on which he stood were "amelioration of abuses, promotion of economy, and the endeavor to preserve peace consistently with the honor of the country." Brougham, who was very sore at having been forced to postpone his notice on Reform on account of the ministerial crisis, had gratuitously informed the House of Commons on two successive days that he had no intention of taking office. A week later on, he accepted the chancellorship with an inconsistency which his friends readily forgave, for they knew that, when he resolved to join the Cabinet, he was thinking more of his party than of himself; a consideration that naturally enough only sharpened the relish with which his adversaries pounced upon this first of his innumerable scrapes. When the new writ for Yorkshire was moved, Croker commented sharply on the position in which the chancellor was placed, and remarked that he had often heard Brougham declare that "the characters of public men formed part of the wealth of England"—a reminiscence which was delivered with as much gravity and unction as if it had been Mackintosh discoursing on Romilly. Unfortunately for himself, Croker ruined his case by referring to a private conversation, an error which the House of Commons always takes at least an evening to forgive; and Macaulay had his audience with him as he vindicated the absent orator with a generous warmth which at length carried him so far that he was interrupted by a call to order from the chair: "The noble lord had but a few days for deliberation, and that at a time when great agitation prevailed, and when the country required a strong and efficient ministry to conduct the government of the state. At such a period a few days are as momentous as months would be at another period. It is not by the clock that we should measure the importance of the changes that might take place during such an interval. I owe no allegiance to the noble lord who has been transferred to another place; but, as a member of this House, I can not banish from my memory the extraordinary eloquence of that noble person within these walls—an eloquence which has left nothing equal to it behind: and when I behold the departure of the great man from among us, and when I see the place in which he sat, and from which he has so often astonished us by the mighty powers of his mind, occupied this evening by the honorable member who has commenced this debate, I can not express the feelings and emotions to which such circumstances give rise."

Parliament adjourned over Christmas, and on the 1st of March, 1831, Lord John Russell introduced the Reform Bill amidst breathless silence, which was at length broken by peals of contemptuous laughter from the Opposition benches as he read the list of the hundred and ten boroughs which were condemned to partial or entire disfranchisement. Sir Robert Inglis led the attack upon a measure that he characterized as revolution in the guise of a statute. Next morning, as Sir Robert was walking into town over Westminster Bridge, he told his companion that up to the previous night he had been very anxious, but that his fears were now at an end, inasmuch as the shock caused by the extravagance of the ministerial proposals would infallibly bring the country to its senses. On the evening of that day Macaulay made the first of his Reform speeches. When he sat down, the Speaker sent for him, and told him that, in all his prolonged experience, he had never seen the House in such a state of excitement. Even at this distance of time, it is impossible to read aloud the last thirty sentences without an emotion which suggests to the mind what must have been their effect when declaimed by one who felt every word that he spoke, in the midst of an assembly agitated by hopes and apprehensions such as living men have never known or have long forgotten. Sir Thomas Denman, who rose later on in the discussion, said, with universal acceptance, that the orator's words remained tingling in the ears of all who heard them, and would last in their memories as long as they had memories to employ. That sense of proprietorship in an effort of genius which the House of Commons is ever ready to entertain effaced for a while all distinctions of party. Portions of the speech, said Sir Robert Peel, "were as beautiful as any thing I have ever heard or read. It reminded one of the old times." The names of Fox, Burke, and Canning were during that evening in every body's mouth;

and Macaulay overheard with delight a knot of old members illustrating their criticisms by recollections of Lord Plunket. He had reason to be pleased; for he had been thought worthy of the compliment which the judgment of Parliament reserves for a supreme occasion. In 1866, on the second reading of the Franchise Bill, when the crowning oration of that memorable debate had come to its close amidst a tempest of applause, one or two veterans of the lobby, forgetting Macaulay on Reform—forgetting, it may be, Mr. Gladstone himself on the Conservative Budget of 1852—pronounced, amidst the willing assent of a younger generation, that there had been nothing like it since Plunket.

The unequivocal success of the first speech into which he had thrown his full power decided for some time to come the tenor of Macaulay's career. During the next three years he devoted himself to Parliament, rivaling Stanley in debate, and Hume in the regularity of his attendance. He entered with zest into the animated and many-sided life of the House of Commons, of which so few traces can ordinarily be detected in what goes by the name of political literature. The biographers of a distinguished statesman too often seem to have forgotten that the subject of their labors passed the best part of his waking hours during the half of every year in a society of a special and deeply marked character, the leading traits of which are, at least, as well worth recording as the fashionable or diplomatic gossip that fills so many volumes of memoirs and correspondence. Macaulay's letters sufficiently indicate how thoroughly he enjoyed the ease, the freedom, the hearty good-fellowship, that reign within the precincts of our national senate; and how entirely he recognized that spirit of noble equality, so prevalent among its members, which takes little or no account of wealth, or title, or, indeed, of reputation won in other fields, but which ranks a man according as the value of his words, and the weight of his influence, bear the test of a standard which is essentially its own.

In February, 1831, he writes to Whewell: "I am impatient for Praed's début. The House of Commons is a place in which I would not promise success to any man. I have great doubts even about Jeffrey. It is the most peculiar audience in the world. I should say that a man's being a good writer, a good orator at the bar, a good mob-orator, or a good orator in debating clubs, was rather a reason for expecting him to fail than for expecting him to succeed in the House of Commons. A place where Walpole succeeded and Addison failed; where Dundas succeeded and Burke failed; where Peel now succeeds and where Mackintosh fails; where Erskine and Scarlett were dinner-bells; where Lawrence and Jekyll, the two wittiest men, or nearly so, of their time, were thought bores, is surely a very strange place. And yet I feel the whole character of the place growing upon me. I begin to like what others about me like, and to disapprove what they disapprove. Canning used to say that the House, as a body, had better taste than the man of best taste in it, and I am very much inclined to think that Canning was right."

The readers of Macaulay's letters will, from time to time, find reason to wish that the young Whig of 1830 had more frequently practiced that studied respect for political opponents which now does so much to correct the intolerance of party among men who can be adversaries without ceasing to regard each other as colleagues. But that honorable sentiment was the growth of later days; and, at an epoch when the system of the past and the system of the future were night after night in deadly wrestle on the floor of St. Stephen's, the combatants were apt to keep their kindliness, and even their courtesies, for those with whom they stood shoulder to shoulder in the fray. Politicians, Conservative and Liberal alike, who were themselves young during the sessions of 1866 and 1867, and who can recall the sensations evoked by a contest of which the issues were far less grave and the passions less strong than of yore, will make allowances for one who, with the imagination of a poet and the temperament of an orator, at thirty years old was sent straight into the thickest of the tumult which then raged round the standard of Reform, and will excuse him for having borne himself in that battle of giants as a determined and a fiery partisan.

If to live intensely be to live happily, Macaulay had an enviable lot during those stirring years; and if the old song-writers had reason on their side when they celebrated the charms of a light purse, he certainly possessed that element of felicity. Among the earliest economical reforms undertaken by the new Government was a searching revision of our bankruptcy jurisdiction, in the course of which his commissionership was swept away without leaving him a penny of compensation. "I voted for the Bankruptcy Court Bill," he said, in answer to an inquisitive constituent. "There were points in that bill of which I did not approve, and I only refrained from stating those points because an office of my own was at stake." When this source fell dry he was for a while a poor man; for a member of Parliament who has others to think of besides himself is any thing but rich on sixty or seventy pounds a quarter as the produce of his pen, and a college income which has only a few more months to run. At a time when his Parliamentary fame stood at its highest he was reduced to sell the gold medals which he had gained at Cambridge; but he was never for a moment in debt; nor did he publish a line prompted by any lower motive than the inspiration of his political faith or the instinct of his literary genius. He had none but pleasant recollections connected with the period when his fortunes were at their lowest. From the secure prosperity of after-life he delighted in recalling the time when, after cheering on the fierce debate for twelve or fifteen hours together, he would walk home by daylight to his chambers, and make his supper on a cheese which was a present from one of his Wiltshire constituents, and a glass of the audit ale which reminded him that he was still a fellow of Trinity.

With political distinction came social success more rapid and more substantial, perhaps, than has ever been achieved by one who took so little trouble to win or to retain it. The circumstances of the time were all in his favor. Never did our higher circles present so much that would attract a new-comer, and never was there more readiness to admit within them all who brought the honorable credentials of talent and celebrity. In 1831 the exclusiveness of birth was passing away, and the exclusiveness of fashion had not set in. The Whig party, during its long period of depression, had been drawn together by the bonds of common hopes, and endeavors, and disappointments; and personal reputation, whether literary, political, or forensic, held its own as against the advantages of rank and money to an extent that was never known before and never since. Macaulay had been well received in the character of an *Edinburgh Reviewer*, and his first great speech in the House of Commons at once opened to him all the doors in London that were best worth entering. Brought up, as he had been, in a household which was perhaps the strictest and the homeliest among a set of families whose creed it was to live outside the world, it put his strength of mind to the test when he found himself courted and observed by the most distinguished and the most formidable personages of the day. Lady Holland listened to him with unwonted deference, and scolded him with a circumspection that was in itself a compliment. Rogers spoke *of* him with friendliness and *to* him with positive affection, and gave him the last proof of his esteem and admiration by asking him to name the morning for a breakfast-party. He was treated with almost fatherly kindness by the able and worthy man who is still remembered by the name of Conversation Sharp. Indeed, his deference for the feelings of all whom he liked and respected, which an experienced observer could detect beneath the eagerness of his manner and the volubility of his talk, made him a favorite among those of a generation above his own. He bore his honors quietly, and enjoyed them with the natural and hearty pleasure of a man who has a taste for society, but whose ambitions lie elsewhere. For the space of three seasons he dined out almost nightly, and spent many of his Sundays in those suburban residences which, as regards the company and the way of living, are little else than sections of London removed into a purer air.

Before very long his habits and tastes began to incline in the direction of domesticity, and even of seclusion: and, indeed, at every period of his life he would gladly desert the haunts of those whom Pope and his contemporaries used to term "the great," to seek the cheerful and cultured simplicity of his home, or the conversation of that one friend who had a share in the familiar confidence which Macaulay otherwise reserved for his nearest relatives. This was Mr. Thomas Flower Ellis, whose reports of the proceedings in King's Bench, extending over a whole generation, have established and perpetuated his name as that of an acute and industrious lawyer. He was older than Macaulay by four years. Though both fellows of the same college, they missed each other at the university, and it was not until 1827, on the northern circuit, that their acquaintance began. "Macaulay has joined," writes Mr. Ellis: "an amusing person; somewhat boyish in his manner, but very original." The young barristers had in common an insatiable love of the classics; and similarity of character, not very perceptible on the surface, soon brought about an intimacy which ripened into an attachment as important to the happiness of both concerned as ever united two men through every stage of life and vicissitude of fortune. Mr. Ellis had married early, but in 1839 he lost his wife; and Macaulay's helpful and heart-felt participation in his great sorrow riveted the links of a chain that was already indissoluble. The letters contained in these volumes will tell, better than the words of any third person, what were the points of sympathy between the two companions, and in what manner they lived together till the end came. Mr. Ellis survived his friend little more than a year; not complaining or lamenting, but going about his work like a man from whose day the light had departed.

Brief and rare were the vacations of the most hard-worked Parliament that had sat since the times of Pym and Hampden. In the late autumn of 1831, the defeat of the Reform Bill in the House of Lords delivered over the country to agitation, resentment, and alarm, and gave a short holiday to public men who were not ministers, magistrates, or officers in the yeomanry. Hannah and Margaret Macaulay accompanied their brother on a visit to Cambridge, where they met with the welcome which young masters of arts delight in providing for the sisters of a comrade of whom they are fond and proud.

"On the evening that we arrived," says Lady Trevelyan, "we met at dinner Whewell, Sedgwick, Airy, and Thirlwall; and how pleasant they were, and how much they made of us, two happy girls, who were never tired of seeing and hearing and admiring!* We breakfasted, lunched, and dined with one or the other of the set during our stay, and walked about the colleges all day with the whole train. Whewell was then tutor: rougher, but less pompous and much more agreeable than in after-years, though I do not think that he ever cordially liked your uncle. We then went on to Oxford, which, from knowing no one there, seemed terribly dull to us by comparison with Cambridge, and we rejoiced our brother's heart by sighing after Trinity."

During the first half of his life, Macaulay spent months of every year at the seat of his uncle, Mr. Babington, who kept open house for his nephews and nieces throughout the summer and autumn. Rothley Temple, which lies in a valley beyond the first ridge that separates the flat, unattractive country immediately round Leicester from the wild and beautiful scenery of Charnwood Forest, is well worth visiting as a singularly unaltered specimen of an old English home. The stately trees; the grounds, half park and half meadow; the cattle grazing up to the very windows; the hall, with its stone pavement rather below than above the level of the soil, hung with armor rude and rusty enough to dispel the suspicion of its having passed through a collector's hands; the low ceilings; the dark oak wainscot, carved after primitive designs, that covered every inch of wall in bedroom and corridor; the general air which the whole interior presented of having been put to rights at the date of the Armada and left alone ever since—all this antiquity contrasted quaintly, but prettily enough, with the youth and gayety that lighted up every corner of the ever-crowded though comfortable mansion. In wet

* A reminiscence from that week of refined and genial hospitality survives in the "Essay on Madame D'Arblay." The reception which Miss Burney would have enjoyed at Oxford, if she had visited it otherwise than as an attendant on royalty, is sketched off with all the writer's wonted spirit, and more than his wonted grace.

weather there was always a merry group sitting on the staircase or marching up and down the gallery; and wherever the noise and fun were most abundant, wherever there were to be heard the loudest laughter and the most vehement expostulation, Macaulay was the centre of a circle which was exclaiming at the levity of his remarks about the Blessed Martyr; disputing with him on the comparative merits of Pascal, Racine, Corneille, Molière, and Boileau; or checking him as he attempted to justify his godparents by running off a list of all the famous Thomases in history. The place is full of his memories. His favorite walk was a mile of field-road and lane which leads from the house to a lodge on the highway; and his favorite point of view in that walk was a slight acclivity whence the traveler from Leicester catches his first sight of Rothley Temple, with its background of hill and greenwood. He is remembered as sitting at the window in the hall, reading Dante to himself, or translating it aloud as long as any listener cared to remain within ear-shot. He occupied, by choice, a very small chamber on the ground-floor, through the window of which he could escape unobserved while afternoon callers were on their way between the front door and the drawing-room. On such occasions he would take refuge in a boat moored under the shade of some fine oaks which still exist, though the ornamental water on whose bank they stood has since been converted into dry land.

A journal kept at intervals by Margaret Macaulay, some extracts from which have here been arranged in the form of a continuous narrative, affords a pleasant and faithful picture of her brother's home-life during the years 1831 and 1832. With an artless candor from which his reputation will not suffer, she relates the alternations of hope and disappointment through which the young people passed when it began to be a question whether or not he would be asked to join the Administration.

"I think I was about twelve when I first became very fond of my brother, and from that time my affection for him has gone on increasing during a period of seven years. I shall never forget my delight and enchantment when I first found that he seemed to like talking to me. His manner was very flattering to such a child, for he always took as much pains to amuse me, and to inform me on any thing I wished to know, as he could have done to the greatest person in the land. I have heard him express great disgust toward those people who, lively and agreeable abroad, are a dead-weight in the family circle. I think the remarkable clearness of his style proceeds in some measure from the habit of conversing with very young people, to whom he has a great deal to explain and impart.

"He reads his works to us in the manuscript, and when we find fault, as I very often do, with his being too severe upon people, he takes it with the greatest kindness, and often alters what we do not like. I hardly ever, indeed, met with a sweeter temper than his. He is rather hasty, and when he has not time for an instant's thought he will sometimes return a quick answer, for which he will be sorry the moment he has said it. But in a conversation of any length, though it may be on subjects that touch him very nearly, and though the person with whom he converses may be very provoking and extremely out of temper, I never saw him lose his. He never uses this superiority, as some do, for the purpose of irritating another still more by coolness, but speaks in a kind, good-natured manner, as if he wished to bring the other back to temper without appearing to notice that he had lost it.

"He at one time took a very punning turn, and we laid a wager in books, my 'Mysteries of Udolpho' against his 'German Theatre,' that he could not make two hundred puns in an evening. He did it, however, in two hours, and, although they were of course most of them miserably bad, yet it was a proof of great quickness.

"*Saturday, February 26th,* 1831.—At dinner we talked of the Grants. Tom said he had found Mr. Robert Grant walking about in the lobbies of the House of Commons, and saying that he wanted somebody to defend his place in the Government, which he heard was going to be attacked. 'What did you say to him?' we asked. 'Oh, I said nothing; but, if they'll give me the place, I'll defend it. When I am judge advocate, I promise you that I will not go about asking any one to defend me.'

"After dinner we played at capping verses, and after that at a game in which one of the party thinks of something for the others to guess at. Tom gave the slug that killed Perceval, the lemon that Wilkes squeezed for Dr. Johnson, the pork-chop which Thurtell eat after he had murdered Weare, and Sir Charles Macarthy's jaw, which was sent by the Ashantees as a present to George the Fourth.

"Some one mentioned an acquaintance who had gone to the West Indies, hoping to make money, but had only ruined the complexions of his daughters. Tom said:

Mr. Walker was sent to Berbice
By the greatest of statesmen and earls.
He went to bring back yellow boys,
But he only brought back yellow girls.

"I never saw any thing like the fun and humor that kindle in his eye when a repartee or verse is working in his brain.

"*March* 3*d*, 1831.—Yesterday morning Hannah and I walked part of the way to his chambers with Tom, and, as we separated, I remember wishing him good luck and success that night. He went through it most triumphantly, and called down upon himself admiration enough to satisfy even his sister. I like so much the manner in which he receives compliments. He does not pretend to be indifferent, but smiles in his kind and animated way, with 'I am sure it is very kind of you to say so,' or something of that nature. His voice, from cold and overexcitement, got quite into a scream toward the last part. A person told him that he had not heard such speaking since Fox. 'You have not heard such screaming since Fox,' he said.

"*March* 24*th*, 1831.—By Tom's account, there never was such a scene of agitation as the House of Commons presented at the passing of the second reading of the Reform Bill the day before yesterday, or rather yesterday, for they did not divide till three or four in the morning. When dear Tom came the next day he was still very much excited, which I found to my cost, for when I went out to walk with him, he walked so very fast that I could scarcely keep up with him at all. With sparkling eyes he described the whole scene of the preceding evening in the most graphic manner.

"'I suppose the ministers are all in high spirits,' said mamma. 'In spirits, ma'am? I'm sure I don't know. In bed, I'll answer for it.' Mamma asked him for franks, that she might send his speech to a lady* who, though of high Tory principles, is very fond of Tom, and has left him in her will her valuable library. 'Oh no,' he said, 'don't send it. If you do, she'll cut me off with a prayer-book.'

"Tom is very much improved in his appearance during the last two or three years. His figure is not so bad for a man of thirty as for a man of twenty-two. He dresses better, and his manners, from seeing a great deal of society, are very much improved. When silent and occupied in thought, walking up and down the room, as he always does, his hands clenched, and muscles working with the intense exertion of his mind, strangers would think his countenance stern; but I remember a writing-master of ours, when Tom had come into the room and left it again, saying, 'Ladies, your brother looks like a lump of good humor!'

"*March* 30*th*, 1831.—Tom has just left me, after a very interesting conversation. He spoke of his extreme idleness. He said: 'I never knew such an idle man as I am. When I go in to Empson or Ellis his tables are always covered with books and papers. I can not stick at any thing for above a day or two. I mustered industry enough to teach myself Italian. I wish to speak Spanish. I know I could master the difficulties in a week, and read any book in the language at the end of a month, but I

---

* This lady was Mrs. Hannah More.

have not the courage to attempt it. If there had not been really something in me, idleness would have ruined me.'

"I said that I was surprised at the great accuracy of his information, considering how desultory his reading had been. 'My accuracy as to facts,' he said, 'I owe to a cause which many men would not confess. It is due to my love of castle-building. The past is, in my mind, soon constructed into a romance.' He then went on to describe the way in which from his childhood his imagination had been filled by the study of history. 'With a person of my turn,' he said, 'the minute touches are of as great interest, and perhaps greater, than the most important events. Spending so much time as I do in solitude, my mind would have rusted by gazing vacantly at the shop-windows. As it is, I am no sooner in the streets than I am in Greece, in Rome, in the midst of the French Revolution. Precision in dates, the day or hour in which a man was born or died, becomes absolutely necessary. A slight fact, a sentence, a word, are of importance in my romance. "Pepys's Diary" formed almost inexhaustible food for my fancy. I seem to know every inch of Whitehall. I go in at Hans Holbein's gate, and come out through the matted gallery. The conversations which I compose between great people of the time are long, and sufficiently animated: in the style, if not with the merits, of Sir Walter Scott's. The old parts of London, which you are sometimes surprised at my knowing so well, those old gates and houses down by the river, have all played their part in my stories.' He spoke, too, of the manner in which he used to wander about Paris, weaving tales of the Revolution, and he thought that he owed his command of language greatly to this habit.

"I am very sorry that the want both of ability and memory should prevent my preserving with greater truth a conversation which interested me very much.

"*May* 21*st*, 1831.—Tom was from London at the time my mother's death occurred, and things fell out in such a manner that the first information he received of it was from the newspapers. He came home directly. He was in an agony of distress, and gave way at first to violent bursts of feeling. During the whole of the week he was with us all day, and was the greatest comfort to us imaginable. He talked a great deal of our sorrow, and led the conversation by degrees to other subjects, bearing the whole burden of it himself, and interesting us without jarring with the predominant feeling of the time. I never saw him appear to greater advantage—never loved him more dearly.

"*September*, 1831.—Of late we have walked a good deal. I remember pacing up and down Brunswick Square and Lansdowne Place for two hours one day, deep in the mazes of the most subtle metaphysics; up and down Cork Street, engaged over Dryden's poetry and the great men of that time; making jokes all the way along Bond Street, and talking politics everywhere.

"Walking in the streets with Tom and Hannah, and talking about the hard work the heads of his party had got now, I said: 'How idle they must think you, when they meet you here in the busy part of the day!' 'Yes, here I am,' said he, 'walking with two* unidea'd girls. However, if one of the ministry says to me, "Why walk you here all the day idle?" I shall say, "Because no man has hired me."'

"We talked of eloquence, which he has often compared to fresco-painting: the result of long study and meditation, but at the moment of execution thrown off with the greatest rapidity: what has apparently been the work of a few hours being destined to last for ages.

"Mr. Tierney said he was sure Sir Philip Francis had written 'Junius,' for he was the proudest man he ever knew, and no one ever heard of any thing he had done to be proud of.

"*November* 14*th*, 1831, *Half-past Ten.*—On Friday last Lord Grey sent for Tom. His note was received too late to be acted on that day. On Saturday came another, asking him to East Sheen on that day, or Sunday. Yesterday, accordingly, he went, and staid the night, promising to be here as early as possible to-day. So much depends upon the result of this visit! That he will be offered a place I have not the least doubt. He will refuse a lordship of the treasury, a lordship of the admiralty, or the mastership of the ordnance. He will accept the secretaryship of the Board of Control, but will not thank them for it; and would not accept that, but that he thinks it will be a place of importance during the approaching discussions on the East Indian monopoly.

"If he gets a sufficient salary, Hannah and I shall most likely live with him. Can I possibly look forward to any thing happier? I can not imagine a course of life that would suit him better than thus to enjoy the pleasures of domestic life without its restraints; with sufficient business, but not, I hope, too much.

"At one o'clock he came. I went out to meet him. 'I have nothing to tell you. Nothing. Lord Grey sent for me to speak about a matter of importance, which must be strictly private.'

"*November* 27*th*.—I am just returned from a long walk, during which the conversation turned entirely on one subject. After a little previous talk about a certain great personage,† I asked Tom when the present coolness between them began. He said: 'Nothing could exceed my respect and admiration for him in early days. I saw at that time private letters in

---

* Boswell relates in his tenth chapter how Johnson scolded Langton for leaving "his social friends, to go and sit with a set of wretched unidea'd girls."

† The personage was Lord Brougham, who at this time was too formidable for the poor girl to venture to write his name at length even in a private journal.

which he spoke highly of my articles, and of me as the most rising man of the time. After a while, however, I began to remark that he became extremely cold to me, hardly ever spoke to me on circuit, and treated me with marked slight. If I were talking to a man, if he wished to speak to him on politics or any thing else that was not in any sense a private matter, he always drew him away from me instead of addressing us both. When my article on Hallam came out, he complained to Jeffrey that I took up too much of the *Review;* and when my first article on Mill appeared, he foamed with rage, and was very angry with Jeffrey for having printed it.'

"'But,' said I, 'the Mills are friends of his, and he naturally did not like them to be attacked.'

"'On the contrary,' said Tom, 'he had attacked them fiercely himself; but he thought I had made a hit, and was angry accordingly. When a friend of mine defended my articles to him, he said: "I know nothing of the articles. I have not read Macaulay's articles." What can be imagined more absurd than his keeping up an angry correspondence with Jeffrey about articles he has never read? Well, the next thing was that Jeffrey, who was about to give up the editorship, asked me if I would take it. I said that I would gladly do so, if they would remove the head-quarters of the *Review* to London. Jeffrey wrote to him about it. He disapproved of it so strongly that the plan was given up. The truth was that he felt that his power over the *Review* diminished as mine increased, and he saw that he would have little, indeed, if I were editor.

"'I then came into Parliament. I do not complain that he should have preferred Denman's claims to mine, and that he should have blamed Lord Lansdowne for not considering him. I went to take my seat. As I turned from the table at which I had been taking the oaths, he stood as near to me as you do now, and he cut me dead. We never spoke in the House, excepting once, that I can remember, when a few words passed between us in the lobby. I have sat close to him when many men of whom I knew nothing have introduced themselves to me to shake hands, and congratulate me after making a speech, and he has never said a single word. I know that it is jealousy, because I am not the first man whom he has used in this way. During the debate on the Catholic claims he was so enraged because Lord Plunket had made a very splendid display, and because the Catholics had chosen Sir Francis Burdett instead of him to bring the bill forward, that he threw every difficulty in its way. Sir Francis once said to him, "Really, Mr. ——, you are so jealous that it is impossible to act with you." I never will serve in an administration of which he is the head. On that I have most firmly made up my mind. I do not believe that it is in his nature to be a month in office without caballing against his colleagues.*

---

* "There never was a direct personal rival, or one who was in a position

"'He is, next to the king, the most popular man in England. There is no other man whose entrance into any town in the kingdom would be so certain to be with huzzaing and taking off of horses. At the same time, he is in a very ticklish situation, for he has no real friends. Jeffrey, Sydney Smith, Mackintosh, all speak of him as I now speak to you. I was talking to Sydney Smith of him the other day, and said that, great as I felt his faults to be, I must allow him a real desire to raise the lower orders, and do good by education, and those methods upon which his heart has been always set. Sydney would not allow this, or any other, merit. Now, if those who are called his friends feel toward him, as they all do, angry and sore at his overbearing, arrogant, and neglectful conduct, when those reactions in public feeling, which must come, arrive, he will have nothing to return upon, no place of refuge, no band of such tried friends as Fox and Canning had to support him. You will see that he will soon place himself in a false position before the public. His popularity will go down, and he will find himself alone. Mr. Pitt, it is true, did not study to strengthen himself by friendships; but this was not from jealousy. I do not love the man, but I believe he was quite superior to that. It was from a solitary pride he had. I heard at Holland House the other day that Sir Philip Francis said that, though he hated Pitt, he must confess there was something fine in seeing how he maintained his post by himself. "The lion walks alone," he said. "The jackals herd together."'"

This conversation, to those who have heard Macaulay talk, bears unmistakable signs of having been committed to paper while the words, or, at any rate, the outlines, of some of the most important sentences were fresh in his sister's mind. Nature had predestined the two men to mutual antipathy. Macaulay, who knew his own range and kept within it, and who gave the world nothing except his best and most finished work, was fretted by the slovenly omniscience of Brougham, who affected to be a walking encyclopedia, "a kind of semi-Solomon, half knowing every thing from the cedar to the hyssop." The student, who, in his later years, never left his library for the House of Commons without regret, had little in common with one who, like Napoleon, held that a great reputation was a great noise; who could not change horses without making

---

which, however reluctantly, implied rivalry, to whom he has been just; and on the fact of this ungenerous jealousy I do not understand that there is any difference of opinion."—*Lord Cockburn's Journal.*

a speech, see the Tories come in without offering to take a judgeship, or allow the French to make a revolution without proposing to naturalize himself as a citizen of the new republic. The statesman who never deserted an ally or distrusted a friend could have no fellowship with a free-lance, ignorant of the very meaning of loyalty; who, if the surfeited pen of the reporter had not declined its task, would have enriched our collections of British oratory by at least one philippic against every colleague with whom he had ever acted. The many who read this conversation by the light of the public history of Lord Melbourne's administration, and, still more, the few who have access to the secret history of Lord Grey's cabinet, will acknowledge that seldom was a prediction so entirely fulfilled, or a character so accurately read. And that it was not a prophecy composed after the event, is proved by the circumstance that it stands recorded in the handwriting of one who died before it was accomplished.

"*January 3d*, 1832.—Yesterday Tom dined at Holland House, and heard Lord Holland tell this story: Some paper was to be published by Mr. Fox, in which mention was made of Mr. Pitt having been employed at a club in a manner that would have created scandal. Mr. Wilberforce went to Mr. Fox, and asked him to omit the passage. 'Oh, to be sure,' said Mr. Fox; 'if there are any good people who would be scandalized, I will certainly put it out.' Mr. Wilberforce then preparing to take his leave, he said: 'Now, Mr. Wilberforce, if, instead of being about Mr. Pitt, this had been an account of my being seen gaming at White's on a Sunday, would you have taken so much pains to prevent it being known?' 'I asked this,' said Mr. Fox, 'because I wanted to see what he would say; for I knew he would not tell a lie about it. He threw himself back, as his way was, and only answered, "Oh, Mr. Fox, you are always so pleasant!"'

"*January 8th*, 1832.—Yesterday Tom dined with us, and staid late. He talked almost uninterruptedly for six hours. In the evening he made a great many impromptu charades in verse. I remember he mentioned a piece of impertinence of Sir Philip Francis. Sir Philip was writing a history of his own time, with characters of its eminent men, and one day asked Mr. Tierney if he should like to hear his own character. Of course, he said, 'Yes,' and it was read to him. It was very flattering, and he expressed his gratification for so favorable a description of himself. 'Subject to revision, you must remember, Mr. Tierney,' said Sir Philip, as he laid the manuscript by; 'subject to revision according to what may happen in the future.'

"I am glad Tom has reviewed old John Bunyan. Many are reading it who never read it before. Yesterday, as he was sitting in the Athenæum, a gentleman called out, 'Waiter, is there a copy of "The Pilgrim's Progress" in the library?' As might be expected, there was not.

"*February* 12*th*, 1832.—This evening Tom came in, Hannah and I being alone. He was in high boyish spirits. He had seen Lord Lansdowne in the morning, who had requested to speak with him. His lordship said that he wished to have a talk about his taking office, not with any particular thing in view, as there was no vacancy at present and none expected, but that he should be glad to know his wishes in order that he might be more able to serve him in them.

"Tom, in answer, took rather a high tone. He said he was a poor man, but that he had as much as he wanted, and, as far as he was personally concerned, had no desire for office. At the same time he thought that, after the Reform Bill had passed, it would be absolutely necessary that the Government should be strengthened; that he was of opinion that he could do it good service; that he approved of its general principles, and should not be unwilling to join it. Lord Lansdowne said that they all—and he particularly mentioned Lord Grey—felt of what importance to them his help was, and that he now perfectly understood his views.

"*February* 13*th*, 1832.—It has been much reported, and has even appeared in the newspapers, that the ministers were doing what they could to get Mr. Robert Grant out of the way to make room for Tom. Last Sunday week it was stated in the *John Bull* that Madras had been offered to the judge advocate for this purpose, but that he had refused it. Two or three nights since, Tom, in endeavoring to get to a high bench in the House, stumbled over Mr. Robert Grant's legs, as he was stretched out half asleep. Being roused, he apologized in the usual manner, and then added, oddly enough, 'I am very sorry, indeed, to stand in the way of your mounting.'

"*March* 15*th*, 1832.—Yesterday Hannah and I spent a very agreeable afternoon with Tom.

"He began to talk of his idleness. 'He really came and dawdled with us all day long: he had not written a line of his review of Burleigh's Life, and he shrunk from beginning on such a great work.' I asked him to put it by for the present, and write a light article on novels. This he seemed to think he should like, and said he could get up an article on Richardson in a very short time; but he knew of no book that he could hang it on. Hannah advised that he should place at the head of his article a fictitious title in Italian of a critique on 'Clarissa Harlowe,' published at Venice. He seemed taken with this idea, but said that if he did such a thing he must never let his dearest friend know.

"I was amused with a parody of Tom's on the nursery song 'Twenty Pounds shall marry me,' as applied to the creation of peers.

What though now opposed I be?
Twenty peers shall carry me.
If twenty won't, thirty will,
For I'm his majesty's bouncing Bill.

Sir Robert Peel has been extremely complimentary to him. One sentence he repeated to us: 'My only feeling toward that gentleman is a not ungenerous envy, as I listened to that wonderful flow of natural and beautiful language, and to that utterance which, rapid as it is, seems scarcely able to convey its rich freight of thought and fancy!' People say that these words were evidently carefully prepared.

"I have just been looking round our little drawing-room, as if trying to impress every inch of it on my memory, and thinking how in future years it will rise before my mind as the scene of many hours of light-hearted mirth: how I shall again see him, lolling indolently on the old blue sofa, or strolling round the narrow confines of our room. With such a scene will come the remembrance of his beaming countenance, happy, affectionate smile, and joyous laugh; while, with every one at ease around him, he poured out the stores of his full mind in his own peculiarly beautiful and expressive language, more delightful here than anywhere else, because more perfectly unconstrained. The name which passes through this little room in the quiet, gentle tones of sisterly affection is a name which will be repeated through distant generations, and go down to posterity linked with eventful times and great deeds."

The last words here quoted will be very generally regarded as the tribute of a sister's fondness. Many, who readily admit that Macaulay's name will go down to posterity linked with eventful times and great deeds, make that admission with reference to times not his own, and deeds in which he had no part except to commemorate them with his pen. To him, as to others, a great reputation of a special order brought with it the consequence that the credit which he deserved for what he had done well was overshadowed by the renown of what he did best. The world, which has forgotten that Newton excelled as an administrator and Voltaire as a man of business, remembers somewhat faintly that Macaulay was an eminent orator, and, for a time at least, a strenuous politician. The universal voice of his contemporaries during the first three years of his parliamentary career testifies to the leading part which he played in the House of Commons so long as with all his heart he cared, and with all his might he tried, to play it. Jeffrey (for it is well to adduce none but first-rate evidence) says, in his account of an evening's discussion on the second reading of the Reform Bill: "Not a very striking debate. There was but one exception, and it was a brilliant one. I mean Macaulay, who surpassed his former appearance in closeness, fire, and vigor, and very much improved the effect of it by a more steady and graceful delivery. It was prodigiously cheered, as it deserved, and, I think, puts him clearly at the head of the great speakers, if not the debaters, of the House." And again, on the 17th of December: "Macaulay made, I think, the best speech he has yet delivered; the most condensed, at least, and with the greatest weight of matter. It contained, indeed, the only argument to which any of the speakers who followed him applied themselves." Lord Cockburn, who sat under the gallery for twenty-seven hours during the last three nights of the bill, pronounced Macaulay's speech to have been "by far the best;" though, like a good Scotchman, he asserts that he heard nothing at Westminster which could compare with Dr. Chalmers in the General Assembly. Sir James Mackintosh writes from the library of the House of Commons, "Macaulay and Stanley have made two of the finest speeches ever spoken in Parliament;" and a little further on he classes together the two young orators as "the chiefs of the next, or rather of this, generation."

To gain and keep the position that Mackintosh assigned him, Macaulay possessed the power, and in early days did not lack the will. He was prominent on the parliamentary stage, and active behind the scenes; the soul of every honorable project which might promote the triumph of his principles and the ascendency of his party. One among many passages in his correspondence may be quoted without a very serious breach of ancient and time-worn confidences. On the 17th of September, 1831, he writes to his sister Hannah: "I have been very busy since I wrote last, moving heaven and earth to render it certain that, if our ministers are so foolish as to resign in the event of a defeat in the Lords, the Commons may be firm and united; and I think that I have arranged a plan which will secure a bold and instant declaration on our part if necessary. Lord Ebrington is the man whom I have in my eye as our leader. I have had much conversation with him, and with several of our leading county members. They are all stanch; and I will answer for this—that, if the ministers should throw us over, we will be ready to defend ourselves."

The combination of public spirit, political instinct, and legitimate self-assertion which was conspicuous in Macaulay's character, pointed him out to some whose judgment had been trained by long experience of affairs as a more than possible leader in no remote future; and it is not for his biographer to deny that they had grounds for their conclusion. The prudence, the energy, the selfreliance, which he displayed in another field might have been successfully directed to the conduct of an executive policy and the management of a popular assembly. Macaulay never showed himself deficient in the qualities which enable a man to trust his own sense; to feel responsibility, but not to fear it; to venture where others shrink; to decide while others waver; with all else that belongs to the vocation of a ruler in a free country. But it was not his fate: it was not his work: and the rank which he might have claimed among the statesmen of Britain was not ill exchanged for the place which he occupies in the literature of the world.

To Macvey Napier, Esq.

York, March 22d, 1830.

My dear Sir,—I was in some doubt as to what I should be able to do for Number 101, and I deferred writing till I could make up my mind. If my friend Ellis's article on "Greek History," of which I have formed high expectations, could have been ready, I should have taken a holiday. But as there is no chance of that for the next number, I ought, I think, to consider myself as his bail, and to surrender myself to your disposal in his stead.

I have been thinking of a subject, light and trifling enough, but perhaps not the worse for our purpose on that account. We seldom want a sufficient quantity of heavy matter. There is a wretched poetaster of the name of Robert Montgomery who has written some volumes of detestable verses on religious subjects, which by mere puffing in magazines and newspapers have had an immense sale, and some of which are now in their tenth or twelfth edition. I have for some time past thought that the trick of puffing, as it is now practiced both by authors and publishers, is likely to degrade the literary character and to deprave the public taste in a frightful degree. I really think that we ought to try what effect satire will have upon this nuisance, and I doubt whether we can ever find a better opportunity. Yours, very faithfully,

T. B. Macaulay.

To Macvey Napier, Esq.

London, August 19th, 1830.

My dear Sir,—The new number appeared this morning in the shop windows. The article on Niebuhr contains much that is very sensible; but it is not such an article as so noble a subject required. I am not, like Ellis, Niebuhr-mad; and I agree with many of the remarks which the reviewer has made both on this work and on the school of German critics and historians. But surely the reviewer ought to have given an account of the system of exposition which Niebuhr has adopted, and of the theory which he advances respecting the institutions of Rome. The appearance of the book is really an era in the intellectual history of Europe, and I think that the *Edinburgh Review* ought at least to have given a luminous abstract of it. The very circumstance that Niebuhr's own arrangement and style are obscure, and that his translators have need of translators to make them intelligible to the multitude, rendered it more desirable that a clear and neat statement of the points in controversy should be laid before the public. But it is useless to talk of what can not be mended. The best editors can not always have good writers, and the best writers can not always write their best.

I have no notion on what ground Brougham imagines that I am going to review his speech. He never said a word to me on the subject. Nor did I ever say either to him or to any one else a single syllable to that effect. At all events, I shall not make Brougham's speech my text. We have had quite enough of puffing and flattering each other in the *Review*. It is a vile taste for men united in one literary undertaking to exchange their favors.

I have a plan of which I wish to know your opinion. In ten days or thereabouts I set off for France, where I hope to pass six weeks. I shall be in the best society, that of the Duc de Broglie, Guizot, and so on. I think of writing an article on the politics of France since the Restoration, with characters of the principal public men, and a parallel between the present state of France and that of England. I think that this might be made an article of extraordinary interest. I do not say that I could make it so. It must, you will perceive, be a long paper, however concise I may try to be; but as the subject is important, and I am not generally diffuse, you must not stint me. If you like this scheme, let me know as soon as possible. Ever yours truly, T. B. MACAULAY.

It can not be denied that there was some ground for the imputation of systematic puffing which Macaulay urges with a freedom that a modern editor would hardly permit to the most valued contributor. Brougham had made a speech on slavery in the House of Commons; but time was wanting to get the Corrected Report published soon enough for him to obtain his tribute of praise in the body of the *Review*. The unhappy Mr. Napier was actually reduced to append a notice to the July number regretting that "this powerful speech, which, as we are well informed, produced an impression on those who heard it not likely to be forgotten, or to remain barren of effects, should have reached us at a moment when it was no longer possible for us to notice its contents at any length..... On the eve of a general election to the first Parliament of a new reign, we could have wished to be able to contribute our aid toward the facts and arguments here so strikingly and commandingly stated and enforced, among those who are about to exercise the elective franchise..... We trust that means will be taken to give the widest possible circulation to the Corrected Report. Unfortunately, we can, at present, do nothing more than lay before our readers its glowing peroration — so worthy of this great orator, this unwearied friend of liberty and humanity."

To Macvey Napier, Esq.

Paris, September 16th, 1830.

My dear Sir,—I have just received your letter, and I can not deny that I am much vexed at what has happened. It is not very agreeable to find that I have thrown away the labor, the not unsuccessful labor, as I thought, of a month, particularly as I have not many months of perfect leisure. This would not have happened if Brougham had notified his intentions to you earlier, as he ought, in courtesy to you, and to every body connected with the *Review*, to have done. He must have known that this French question was one on which many people would be desirous to write.

I ought to tell you that I had scarcely reached Paris when I received a letter containing a very urgent application from a very respectable quarter. I was desired to write a sketch, in one volume, of the late Revolution here. Now, I really hesitated whether I should not make my excuses to you, and accept this proposal; not on account of the pecuniary terms, for about these I have never much troubled myself, but because I should have had ampler space for this noble subject than the *Review* would have afforded. I thought, however, that this would not be a fair or friendly course toward you. I accordingly told the applicants that I had promised you an article, and that I could not well write twice in one month on the same subject without repeating myself. I therefore declined, and recommended a person whom I thought quite capable of producing an attractive book on these events. To that person my correspondent has probably applied. At all events, I can not revive the negotiation. I can not hawk my rejected articles up and down Paternoster Row.

I am, therefore, a good deal vexed at this affair; but I am not at all surprised at it. I see all the difficulties of your situation. Indeed, I have long foreseen them. I always knew that in every association, literary or political, Brougham would wish to domineer. I knew, also, that no editor of the *Edin-*

burgh Review could, without risking the ruin of the publication, resolutely oppose the demands of a man so able and powerful. It was because I was certain that he would exact submissions which I am not disposed to make that I wished last year to give up writing for the *Review*. I had long been meditating a retreat. I thought Jeffrey's abdication a favorable time for effecting it; not, as I hope you are well assured, from any unkind feeling toward you, but because I knew that, under any editor, mishaps such as that which has now occurred would be constantly taking place. I remember that I predicted to Jeffrey what has now come to pass almost to the letter.

My expectations have been exactly realized. The present constitution of the *Edinburgh Review* is this: that at whatever time Brougham may be pleased to notify his intention of writing on any subject, all previous engagements are to be considered as annulled by that notification. His language translated into plain English is this: "I must write about this French Revolution, and I will write about it. If you have told Macaulay to do it, you may tell him to let it alone. If he has written an article, he may throw it behind the grate. He would not himself have the assurance to compare his own claims with mine. I am a man who acts a prominent part in the world: he is nobody. If he must be reviewing, there is my speech about the West Indies. Set him to write a puff on that. What have people like him to do, except to eulogize people like me?" No man likes to be reminded of his inferiority in such a way, and there are some particular circumstances in this case which render the admonition more unpleasant than it would otherwise be. I know that Brougham dislikes me; and I have not the slightest doubt that he feels great pleasure in taking this subject out of my hands, and at having made me understand, as I do most clearly understand, how far my services are rated below his. I do not blame you in the least. I do not see how you could have acted otherwise. But, on the other hand, I do not see why I should make any efforts or sacrifices for a *Review* which lies under an intolerable dictation. Whatever my writings may be worth, it is not for want of strong solicitations and tempting offers from other quarters that I have continued to send them to the *Edinburgh Review*. I adhered to the connection solely because I took pride and pleasure in it. It has now become a source of humiliation and mortification.

I again repeat, my dear sir, that I do not blame you in the least. This, however, only makes matters worse. If you had used me ill, I might complain, and might hope to be better treated another time. Unhappily, you are in a situation in which it is proper for you to do what it would be improper in me to endure. What has happened now may happen next quarter, and must happen before long, unless I altogether refrain from writing for the *Review*. I hope you will forgive me if I say that I feel what has passed too strongly to be inclined to expose myself to a recurrence of the same vexations. Yours most truly, T. B. MACAULAY.

A few soft words induced Macaulay to reconsider his threat of withdrawing from the *Review*; but even before Mr. Napier's answer reached him the feeling of personal annoyance had already been effaced by a greater sorrow: a letter arrived announcing that his sister Jane had died suddenly and most unexpectedly. She was found in the morning lying as though still asleep, having passed away so peacefully as not to disturb a sister who had spent the night in the next room, with a door open between them. Mrs. Macaulay never recovered from this shock. Her health gave way, and she lived into the coming year only so long as to enable her to rejoice in the first of her son's Parliamentary successes.

Paris, September 26th.

MY DEAR FATHER,—This news has broken my heart. I am fit neither to go nor to stay. I can do nothing but sit in my room, and think of poor dear Jane's kindness and affection. When I am calmer, I will let you know my intentions. There will be neither use nor pleasure in remaining here. My present purpose, as far as I can form one, is to set off in two or three days for England, and in the mean time to see nobody, if I can help it, but Dumont, who has been very kind to me. Love to all—to all who are left me to love. We must love each other better. T. B. M.

London, March 30th, 1831.

Dear Ellis,—I have little news for you, except what you will learn from the papers as well as from me. It is clear that the Reform Bill must pass, either in this or in another Parliament. The majority of one does not appear to me, as it does to you, by any means inauspicious. We should perhaps have had a better plea for a dissolution if the majority had been the other way. But surely a dissolution under such circumstances would have been a most alarming thing. If there should be a dissolution now, there will not be that ferocity in the public mind which there would have been if the House of Commons had refused to entertain the bill at all. I confess that, till we had a majority, I was half inclined to tremble at the storm which we had raised. At present I think that we are absolutely certain of victory, and of victory without commotion.

Such a scene as the division of last Tuesday I never saw, and never expect to see again. If I should live fifty years, the impression of it will be as fresh and sharp in my mind as if it had just taken place. It was like seeing Cæsar stabbed in the Senate-house, or seeing Oliver taking the mace from the table; a sight to be seen only once, and never to be forgotten. The crowd overflowed the House in every part. When the strangers were cleared out, and the doors locked, we had six hundred and eight members present—more by fifty-five than ever were in a division before. The ayes and noes were like two volleys of cannon from opposite sides of a field of battle. When the opposition went out into the lobby,* an operation which took up twenty minutes or more, we spread ourselves over the benches on both sides of the House; for there were many of us who had not been able to find a seat during the

* "The practice in the Commons, until 1836, was to send one party forth into the lobby, the other remaining in the House."—Sir T. Erskine May's *Parliamentary Practice*.

evening. When the doors were shut we began to speculate on our numbers. Every body was desponding. "We have lost it. We are only two hundred and eighty at most. I do not think we are two hundred and fifty. They are three hundred. Alderman Thompson has counted them. He says they are two hundred and ninty-nine." This was the talk on our benches. I wonder that men who have been long in Parliament do not acquire a better *coup d'œil* for numbers. The House, when only the ayes were in it, looked to me a very fair House—much fuller than it generally is even on debates of considerable interest. I had no hope, however, of three hundred. As the tellers passed along our lowest row on the left-hand side the interest was insupportable—two hundred and ninety-one—two hundred and ninety-two—we were all standing up and stretching forward, telling with the tellers. At three hundred there was a short cry of joy—at three hundred and two another—suppressed, however, in a moment; for we did not yet know what the hostile force might be. We knew, however, that we could not be severely beaten. The doors were thrown open, and in they came. Each of them, as he entered, brought some different report of their numbers. It must have been impossible, as you may conceive, in the lobby, crowded as they were, to form any exact estimate. First we heard that they were three hundred and three; then that number rose to three hundred and ten; then went down to three hundred and seven. Alexander Barry told me that he had counted, and that they were three hundred and four. We were all breathless with anxiety, when Charles Wood, who stood near the door, jumped up on a bench and cried out, "They are only three hundred and one." We set up a shout that you might have heard to Charing Cross, waving our hats, stamping against the floor, and clapping our hands. The tellers scarcely got through the crowd; for the House was thronged up to the table, and all the floor was fluctuating with heads like the pit of a theatre. But you might have heard a pin drop as Duncannon read the numbers. Then again the shouts broke out, and many of us shed tears. I could scarcely refrain. And the jaw of Peel fell; and the face of Twiss was as the face of a damned soul; and Herries looked like Judas taking his neck-tie off for the last operation. We shook hands, and clapped each other on the back, and went out laughing, crying, and huzzaing into the lobby. And no sooner were the outer doors opened than another shout answered that within the House. All the passages and the stairs into the waiting-rooms were thronged by people who had waited till four in the morning to know the issue. We passed through a narrow lane between two thick masses of them; and all the way down they were shouting and waving their hats, till we got into the open air. I called a cabriolet, and the first thing the driver asked was, "Is the bill carried?" "Yes, by one." "Thank God for it, sir!" And away I rode to Gray's Inn—and so ended a scene which will probably never be equaled till the reformed Parliament wants reforming; and that I hope will not be till the days of our grandchildren—till that truly orthodox and apostolical person, Dr. Francis Ellis, is an archbishop of eighty.

As for me, I am for the present a sort of lion. My speech has set me in the front rank, if I can keep there; and it has not been my luck hitherto to lose ground when I have once got it. Sheil and I are on very civil terms. He talks largely concerning Demosthenes and Burke. He made, I must say, an excellent speech; too florid and queer, but decidedly successful.

Why did not Price speak? If he was afraid, it was not without reason; for a more terrible audience there is not in the world. I wish that Praed had known to whom he was speaking. But, with all his talent, he has no tact, and he has fared accordingly. Tierney used to say that he never rose in the House without feeling his knees tremble under him; and I am sure that no man who has not some of that feeling will ever succeed there. Ever yours, T. B. MACAULAY.

London, May 27th, 1831.

MY DEAR HANNAH,—Let me see if I can write a letter *à la* Richardson: a little less prolix it must be, or it will exceed my ounce. By-the-bye, I wonder that Uncle Selby never grudged the postage of Miss Byron's letters. According to the nearest calculation that I can make, her correspondence must have enriched the post-office of Ashby Canons by something more than the whole annual interest of her fifteen thousand pounds.

I reached Lansdowne House by a quarter to eleven, and passed through the large suite of rooms to the great Sculpture Gallery. There were seated and standing perhaps three hundred people listening to the performers, or talking to each other. The room is the handsomest and largest, I am told, in any private house in London. I inclose our musical bill of fare. Fanny, I suppose, will be able to expound it better than I. The singers were more showily dressed than the auditors, and seemed quite at home. As to the company, there was just every body in London (except that little million and a half that you wot of)—the Chancellor, and the First Lord of the Admiralty, and Sydney Smith, and Lord Mansfield, and all the Barings and the Fitzclarences, and a hideous Russian spy, whose face I see everywhere, with a star on his coat. During the interval between the delights of "I tuoi frequenti," and the ecstasies of "Se tu m' ami," I contrived to squeeze up to Lord Lansdowne. I was shaking hands with Sir James Macdonald, when I heard a command behind us, "Sir James, introduce me to Mr. Macaulay;" and we turned, and there sat a large bold-looking woman, with the remains of a fine person, and the air of Queen Elizabeth. "Macaulay," said Sir James, "let me present you to Lady Holland." Then was her ladyship gracious beyond description, and asked me to dine and take a bed at Holland House next Tuesday. I accepted the dinner, but declined the bed, and I have since repented that I so declined it. But I probably shall have an opportunity of retracting on Tuesday.

To-night I go to another musical party at Marshall's, the late M.P. for Yorkshire. Every body is talking of Paganini and his violin. The man seems to be a miracle. The newspapers say that long streamy flakes of music fall from his string, interspersed with luminous points of sound which ascend the air and appear like stars. This eloquence is quite beyond me. Ever yours, T. B. M.

London, May 28th, 1831.

My dear Hannah,—More gayeties and music-parties; not so fertile of adventures as that memorable masquerade whence Harriet Byron was carried away; but still I hope that the narrative of what passed there will gratify "the venerable circle." Yesterday I dressed, called a cab, and was whisked away to Hill Street. I found old Marshall's house a very fine one. He ought, indeed, to have a fine one; for he has, I believe, at least thirty thousand a year. The carpet was taken up, and chairs were set out in rows, as if we had been at a religious meeting. Then we had flute-playing by the first flute-player in England, and pianoforte-strumming by the first pianoforte-strummer in England, and singing by all the first singers in England, and Signor Rubini's incomparable tenor, and Signor Curioni's incomparable counter-tenor, and Pasta's incomparable expression. You who know how airs much inferior to this take my soul and lap it in Elysium, will form some faint conception of my transport. Sharp beckoned me to sit by him in the back row. These old fellows are so selfish. "Always," said he, "establish yourself in the middle of the row against the wall; for, if you sit in the front or next the edges, you will be forced to give up your seat to the ladies who are standing." I had the gallantry to surrender mine to a damsel who had stood for a quarter of an hour; and I lounged into the anterooms, where I found Samuel Rogers. Rogers and I sat together on a bench in one of the passages, and had a good deal of very pleasant conversation. He was—as indeed he has always been to me—extremely kind, and told me that if it were in his power he would contrive to be at Holland House with me, to give me an insight into its ways. He is the great oracle of that circle.

He has seen the king's letter to Lord Grey respecting the Garter, or at least has authentic information about it. It is a happy stroke of policy, and will, they say, decide many wavering votes in the House of Lords. The king, it seems, requests Lord Grey to take the order, as a mark of royal confidence in him "at so critical a time"—significant words, I think.

Ever yours, T. B. Macaulay.

To Hannah More Macaulay.

London, May 30th, 1831.

Well, my dear, I have been to Holland House. I took a glass coach, and arrived, through a fine avenue of elms, at the great entrance toward seven o'clock. The house is delightful—the very perfection of the old Elizabethan style—a considerable number of very large and very comfortable rooms, rich with antique carving and gilding, but carpeted and furnished with all the skill of the best modern upholsterers. The library is a very long room—as long, I should think, as the gallery at Rothley Temple—with little cabinets for study branching out of it, warmly and snugly fitted up, and looking out on very beautiful grounds. The collection of books is not, like Lord Spencer's, curious; but it contains almost every thing that one ever wished to read. I found nobody there when I arrived but Lord Russell, the son of the Marquess of Tavistock. We are old House of Commons friends; so we had some very pleasant talk, and in a little while in came Allen, who is warden of Dulwich College, and who lives almost entirely at Holland House. He is certainly a man of vast information and great conversational powers. Some other gentlemen dropped in, and we chatted till Lady Holland made her appearance. Lord Holland dined by himself on account of his gout. We sat down to dinner in a fine long room, the wainscot of which is rich with gilded coronets, roses, and portcullises. There were Lord Albemarle, Lord Alvanley, Lord Russell, Lord Mahon—a violent Tory, but a very agreeable companion and a very good scholar. There was Cradock, a fine fellow, who was the Duke of Wellington's aid-de-camp in 1815, and some other people whose names I did not catch. What, however, is more to the purpose, there was a most excellent dinner. I have always heard that Holland House is famous for its good cheer, and certainly the reputation is not unmerited. After dinner Lord Holland was wheeled in and placed very near me. He was extremely amusing and good-natured.

In the drawing-room I had a long talk with Lady Holland about the antiquities of the house, and about the purity of the

English language wherein she thinks herself a critic. I happened, in speaking about the Reform Bill, to say that I wished that it had been possible to form a few commercial constituencies, if the word constituency were admissible. "I am glad you put that in," said her ladyship. "I was just going to give it you. It is an odious word. Then there is *talented*, and *influential*, and *gentlemanly*. I never could break Sheridan of *gentlemanly*, though he allowed it to be wrong." We talked about the word *talents* and its history. I said that it had first appeared in theological writing, that it was a metaphor taken from the parable in the New Testament, and that it had gradually passed from the vocabulary of divinity into common use. I challenged her to find it in any classical writer on general subjects before the Restoration, or even before the year 1700. I believe that I might safely have gone down later. She seemed surprised by this theory, never having, so far as I could judge, heard of the parable of the talents. I did not tell her, though I might have done so, that a person who professes to be a critic in the delicacies of the English language ought to have the Bible at his fingers' ends.

She is certainly a woman of considerable talents and great literary acquirements. To me she was excessively gracious; yet there is a haughtiness in her courtesy which, even after all that I had heard of her, surprised me. The centurion did not keep his soldiers in better order than she keeps her guests. It is to one "Go," and he goeth; and to another "Do this," and it is done. "Ring the bell, Mr. Macaulay." "Lay down that screen, Lord Russell; you will spoil it." "Mr. Allen, take a candle and show Mr. Cradock the picture of Bonaparte." Lord Holland is, on the other hand, all kindness, simplicity, and vivacity. He talked very well both on politics and on literature. He asked me in a very friendly manner about my father's health, and begged to be remembered to him.

When my coach came, Lady Holland made me promise that I would on the first fine morning walk out to breakfast with them and see the grounds; and, after drinking a glass of very good iced lemonade, I took my leave, much amused and pleased. The house certainly deserves its reputation for pleasantness, and her ladyship used me, I believe, as well as it is her way to use any body. Ever yours, T. B. M.

To Hannah M. Macaulay.

Court of Commissioners, Basinghall Street, May 31st, 1831.

My dear Sister,—How delighted I am that you like my letters, and how obliged by yours! But I have little more than my thanks to give for your last. I have nothing to tell about great people to-day. I heard no fine music yesterday, saw nobody above the rank of a baronet, and was shut up in my own room reading and writing all the morning. This day seems likely to pass in much the same way, except that I have some bankruptcy business to do, and a couple of sovereigns to receive. So here I am, with three of the ugliest attorneys that ever deserved to be transported sitting opposite to me: a disconsolate-looking bankrupt, his hands in his empty pockets, standing behind; a lady scolding for her money, and refusing to be comforted because it is not; and a surly butcher-like-looking creditor, growling like a house-dog, and saying, as plainly as looks can say, "If I sign your certificate, blow me, that's all." Among these fair and interesting forms, on a piece of official paper, with a pen and with ink found at the expense of the public, am I writing to Nancy.

These dirty courts, filled with Jew money-lenders, sheriffs' officers, attorneys' runners, and a crowd of people who live by giving sham bail and taking false oaths, are not by any means such good subjects for a lady's correspondent as the sculpture gallery at Lansdowne House, or the conservatory at Holland House, or the notes of Pasta, or the talk of Rogers. But we can not be always fine. When my Richardsonian epistles are published there must be dull as well as amusing letters among them; and this letter is, I think, as good as those sermons of Sir Charles to Geronymo which Miss Byron hypocritically asked for, or as the greater part of that stupid last volume.

We shall soon have more attractive matter. I shall walk out to breakfast at Holland House; and I am to dine with

Sir George Philips, and with his son, the member for Steyning, who have the best of company; and I am going to the fancy ball of —— the Jew. He met me in the street, and implored me to come. "You need not dress more than for an evening party. You had better come. You will be delighted. It will be so very pretty." I thought of Dr. Johnson* and the herdsman with his "See, such pretty goats." However, I told my honest Hebrew that I would come. I may perhaps, like the Benjamites, steal away some Israelite damsel in the middle of her dancing.

But the noise all round me is becoming louder, and a baker in a white coat is bellowing for the book to prove a debt of nine pounds fourteen shillings and fourpence. So I must finish my letter, and fall to business. Ever yours,

T. B. M.

To Hannah M. Macaulay.

London, June 1st, 1831.

My dear Sister,—My last letter was a dull one. I mean this to be very amusing. My last was about Basinghall Street, attorneys, and bankrupts. But for this—take it dramatically in the German style.

Fine morning. Scene, the great entrance of Holland House.

Enter Macaulay, *and* Two Footmen *in livery.*

First Footman. Sir, may I venture to demand your name?
Macaulay. Macaulay, and thereto I add M.P.
And that addition, even in these proud halls,
May well insure the bearer some respect.
Second Footman. And art thou come to breakfast with our lord?
Macaulay. I am; for so his hospitable will,
And hers—the peerless dame ye serve—hath bade.
First Footman. Ascend the stair, and thou above shalt find,
On snow-white linen spread, the luscious meal.

(*Exit* Macaulay *upstairs.*)

In plain English prose, I went this morning to breakfast at Holland House. The day was fine, and I arrived at twenty min-

* See Boswell's "Tour to the Hebrides," September 1st, 1773.

utes after ten. After I had lounged a short time in the dining-room, I heard a gruff, good-natured voice asking, "Where is Mr. Macaulay? Where have you put him?" and in his arm-chair Lord Holland was wheeled in. He took me round the apartments, he riding, and I walking. He gave me the history of the most remarkable portraits in the library, where there is, by-the-bye, one of the few bad pieces of Lawrence that I have seen—a head of Charles James Fox, an ignominious failure. Lord Holland said that it was the worst ever painted of so eminent a man by so eminent an artist. There is a very fine head of Machiavelli, and another of Earl Grey, a very different sort of man. I observed a portrait of Lady Holland, painted some thirty years ago. I could have cried to see the change. She must have been a most beautiful woman. She still looks, however, as if she had been handsome, and shows in one respect great taste and sense: she does not rouge at all, and her costume is not youthful, so that she looks as well in the morning as in the evening. We came back to the dining-room. Our breakfast party consisted of my lord and lady, myself, Lord Russell, and Luttrell. You must have heard of Luttrell. I met him once at Rogers's; and I have seen him, I think, in other places. He is a famous wit—the most popular, I think, of all the professed wits—a man who has lived in the highest circles, a scholar, and no contemptible poet. He wrote a little volume of verse entitled "Advice to Julia"—not first-rate, but neat, lively, piquant, and showing the most consummate knowledge of fashionable life.

We breakfasted on very good coffee, and very good tea, and very good eggs, butter kept in the midst of ice, and hot rolls. Lady Holland told us her dreams; how she had dreamed that a mad dog bit her foot, and how she set off to Brodie, and lost her way in St. Martin's Lane, and could not find him. She hoped, she said, the dream would not come true. I said that I had had a dream which admitted of no such hope, for I had dreamed that I heard Pollock speak in the House of Commons, that the speech was very long, and that he was coughed down. This dream of mine diverted them much.

After breakfast Lady Holland offered to conduct me to her

own drawing-room, or, rather, commanded my attendance. A very beautiful room it is, opening on a terrace, and wainscoted with miniature paintings interesting from their merit, and interesting from their history. Among them I remarked a great many—thirty I should think—which even I, who am no great connoisseur, saw at once could come from no hand but Stothard's. They were all on subjects from Lord Byron's poems. "Yes," said she; "poor Lord Byron sent them to me a short time before the separation. I sent them back, and told him that, if he gave them away, he ought to give them to Lady Byron. But he said that he would not, and that if I did not take them the bailiffs would, and that they would be lost in the wreck." Her ladyship then honored me so far as to conduct me through her dressing-room into the great family bed-chamber to show me a very fine picture, by Reynolds, of Fox, when a boy, bird'snesting. She then consigned me to Luttrell, asking him to show me the grounds.

Through the grounds we went, and very pretty I thought them. In the Dutch garden is a fine bronze bust of Napoleon, which Lord Holland put up in 1817, while Napoleon was a prisoner at St. Helena. The inscription was selected by his lordship, and is remarkably happy. It is from Homer's "Odyssey." I will translate it, as well as I can extempore, into a measure which gives a better idea of Homer's manner than Pope's sing-song couplet.

For not, be sure, within the grave
Is hid that prince, the wise, the brave;
But in an islet's narrow bound,
With the great ocean roaring round,
The captive of a foeman base,
He pines to view his native place.

There is a seat near the spot which is called Rogers's seat. The poet loves, it seems, to sit there. A very elegant inscription by Lord Holland is placed over it:

Here Rogers sat; and here forever dwell
With me those pleasures which he sung so well.

Very neat and condensed, I think. Another inscription by

Luttrell hangs there. Luttrell adjured me with mock pathos to spare his blushes; but I am author enough to know what the blushes of authors mean. So I read the lines, and very pretty and polished they were, but too many to be remembered from one reading.

Having gone round the grounds, I took my leave, very much pleased with the place. Lord Holland is extremely kind. But that is of course; for he is kindness itself. Her ladyship too, which is by no means of course, is all graciousness and civility. But, for all this, I would much rather be quietly walking with you: and the great use of going to these fine places is to learn how happy it is possible to be without them. Indeed, I care so little for them that I certainly should not have gone to-day, but that I thought that I should be able to find materials for a letter which you might like.

Farewell. T. B. MACAULAY.

To Hannah M. Macaulay.

London, June 3d, 1831.

MY DEAR SISTER,—I can not tell you how delighted I am to find that my letters amuse you. But sometimes I must be dull like my neighbors. I paid no visits yesterday, and have no news to relate to-day. I am sitting again in Basinghall Street; and Basil Montagu* is haranguing about Lord Verulam and the way of inoculating one's mind with truth; and all this apropos of a lying bankrupt's balance-sheet.

Send me some gossip, my love. Tell me how you go on with German. What novel have you commenced? or, rather, how many dozen have you finished? Recommend me one. What say you to "Destiny?" Is "The Young Duke" worth reading? And what do you think of "Laurie Todd?"

I am writing about Lord Byron so pathetically that I make Margaret cry, but so slowly that I am afraid I shall make Na-

* "Those who are acquainted with the courts in which Mr. Montagu practices with so much ability and success will know how often he enlivens the discussion of a point of law by citing some weighty aphorism, or some brilliant illustration, from the 'De Augmentis' or the 'Novum Organum.'"—MACAULAY'S *Review of Basil Montagu's Edition of Bacon.*

pier wait. Rogers, like a civil gentleman, told me last week to write no more reviews, and to publish separate works, adding, what for him is a very rare thing, a compliment, "You may do any thing, Mr. Macaulay." See how vain and insincere human nature is! I have been put into so good a temper with Rogers, that I have paid him, what is as rare with me as with him, a very handsome compliment in my review. It is not undeserved, but I confess that I can not understand the popularity of his poetry. It is pleasant and flowing enough, less monotonous than most of the imitations of Pope and Goldsmith, and calls up many agreeable images and recollections. But that such men as Lord Granville, Lord Holland, Hobhouse, Lord Byron, and others of high rank in intellect, should place Rogers, as they do, above Southey, Moore, and even Scott himself, is what I can not conceive. But this comes of being in the highest society of London. What Lady Jane Granville called the Patronage of Fashion can do as much for a middling poet as for a plain girl like Miss Arabella Falconer.*

But I must stop. This rambling talk has been scrawled in the middle of haranguing, squabbling, swearing, and crying. Since I began it, I have taxed four bills, taken forty depositions, and rated several perjured witnesses.

Ever yours, T. B. M.

To Hannah and Margaret Macaulay.

London, June 7th, 1831.

Yesterday I dined at Marshall's, and was almost consoled for not meeting Ramohun Roy by a very pleasant party. The great sight was the two wits, Rogers and Sydney Smith. Singly I have often seen them; but to see them both together was a novelty, and a novelty not the less curious because their mutual hostility is well known, and the hard hits which they have given to each other are in every body's mouth. They were very civil, however. But I was struck by the truth of what

* Lady Jane and Miss Arabella appear in Miss Edgeworth's "Patronage."

Matthew Bramble, a person of whom you probably never heard, says in Smollett's "Humphry Clinker"—that one wit in a company, like a knuckle of ham in soup, gives a flavor, but two are too many. Rogers and Sydney Smith would not come into conflict. If one had possession of the company, the other was silent; and, as you may conceive, the one who had possession of the company was always Sydney Smith, and the one who was silent was always Rogers. Sometimes, however, the company divided, and each of them had a small congregation. I had a good deal of talk with both of them; for, in whatever they may disagree, they agree in always treating me with very marked kindness.

I had a good deal of pleasant conversation with Rogers. He was telling me of the curiosity and interest which attached to the persons of Sir Walter Scott and Lord Byron. When Sir Walter Scott dined at a gentleman's in London some time ago, all the servant-maids in the house asked leave to stand in the passage and see him pass. He was, as you may conceive, greatly flattered. About Lord Byron, whom he knew well, he told me some curious anecdotes. When Lord Byron passed through Florence, Rogers was there. They had a good deal of conversation, and Rogers accompanied him to his carriage. The inn had fifty windows in front. All the windows were crowded with women, mostly English women, to catch a glance at their favorite poet. Among them were some at whose houses he had often been in England, and with whom he had lived on friendly terms. He would not notice them, or return their salutations. Rogers was the only person that he spoke to.

The worst thing that I know about Lord Byron is the very unfavorable impression which he made on men who certainly were not inclined to judge him harshly, and who, as far as I know, were never personally ill-used by him. Sharp and Rogers both speak of him as an unpleasant, affected, splenetic person. I have heard hundreds and thousands of people who never saw him rant about him; but I never heard a single expression of fondness for him fall from the lips of any of those who knew him well. Yet, even now, after the lapse of five-

and-twenty years, there are those who can not talk for a quarter of an hour about Charles Fox without tears.

Sydney Smith leaves London on the 20th, the day before Parliament meets for business. I advised him to stay, and see something of his friends who would be crowding to London. "My flock!" said this good shepherd. "My dear sir, remember my flock!

"The hungry sheep look up, and are not fed."

I could say nothing to such an argument, but I could not help thinking that, if Mr. Daniel Wilson had said such a thing, it would infallibly have appeared in his funeral sermon, and in his "Life" by Baptist Noel. But in poor Sydney's mouth it sounded like a joke. He begged me to come and see him at Combe Florey. "There I am, sir, the priest of the Flowery Valley, in a delightful parsonage, about which I care a good deal, and a delightful country, about which I do not care a straw." I told him that my meeting him was some compensation for missing Ramohun Roy. Sydney broke forth: "Compensation! Do you mean to insult me? A beneficed clergyman, an orthodox clergyman, a nobleman's chaplain, to be no more than compensation for a Brahmin; and a heretic Brahmin too, a fellow who has lost his own religion and can't find another; a vile heterodox dog, who, as I am credibly informed, eats beefsteaks in private! A man who has lost his caste; who ought to have melted lead poured down his nostrils, if the good old Vedas were in force as they ought to be."

These are some Boswelliana of Sydney, not very clerical, you will say, but indescribably amusing to the hearers, whatever the readers may think of them. Nothing can present a more striking contrast to his rapid, loud, laughing utterance, and his rector-like amplitude and rubicundity, than the low, slow, emphatic tone, and the corpse-like face of Rogers. There is as great a difference in what they say as in the voice and look with which they say it. The conversation of Rogers is remarkably polished and artificial. What he says seems to have been long meditated, and might be published with little correction. Sydney talks from the impulse of the moment, and his fun is quite inexhaustible. Ever yours,

T. B. M.

To Hannah M. Macaulay.

London, June 8th, 1831.

My dear Sister,—Yesterday night I went to the Jew's. I had indeed no excuse for forgetting the invitation; for, about a week after I had received the green varnished billet and answered it, came another in the self-same words and addressed to Mr. Macaulay, Jun. I thought that my answer had miscarried; so down I sat, and composed a second epistle to the Hebrews. I afterward found that the second invitation was meant for Charles.

I set off a little after ten, having attired myself simply as for a dinner-party. The house is a very fine one. The door was guarded by peace-officers and besieged by starers. My host met me in a superb court-dress, with his sword at his side. There was a most sumptuous-looking Persian, covered with gold lace. Then there was an Italian bravo with a long beard. Two old gentlemen, who ought to have been wiser, were fools enough to come in splendid Turkish costumes at which every body laughed. The fancy dresses were worn almost exclusively by the young people. The ladies for the most part contented themselves with a few flowers and ribbons oddly disposed. There was, however, a beautiful Mary Queen of Scots, who looked as well as dressed the character perfectly; an angel of a Jewess in a Highland plaid; and an old woman, or rather a woman—for through her disguise it was impossible to ascertain her age—in the absurdest costume of the last century. These good people soon began their quadrilles and galopades, and were enlivened by all the noise that twelve fiddlers could make for their lives.

You must not suppose that the company was made up of these mummers. There was Dr. Lardner, and Long, the Greek professor in the London University, and Sheil, and Strutt, and Romilly, and Owen, the philanthropist. Owen laid hold on Sheil, and gave him a lecture on Co-operation which lasted for half an hour. At last Sheil made his escape. Then Owen seized Mrs. Sheil, a good Catholic, and a very agreeable woman, and began to prove to her that there could be no such thing as moral responsibility. I had fled at the first sound of his discourse, and was talking with Strutt and Romilly, when, behold! I saw Owen leave Mrs. Sheil and come toward us. So I cried out, "Sauve qui peut!" and we ran off. But before we had got five feet from where we were standing, who should meet us face to face but old Basil Montagu? "Nay, then," said I, "the game is up. The Prussians are on our rear. If we are to be bored to death, there is no help for it." Basil seized Romilly; Owen took possession of Strutt; and I was blessing myself on my escape, when the only human being worthy to make a third with such a pair, J——, caught me by the arm, and begged to have a quarter of an hour's conversation with me. While I was suffering under J——, a smart, impudent-looking young dog, dressed like a sailor in a blue jacket and check shirt, marched up, and asked a Jewish-looking damsel near me to dance with him. I thought that I had seen the fellow before; and, after a little looking, I perceived that it was Charles; and most knowingly, I assure you, did he perform a quadrille with Miss Hilpah Manasses.

If I were to tell you all that I saw, I should exceed my ounce. There was Martin, the painter, and Procter, alias Barry Cornwall, the poet or poetaster. I did not see one peer, or one star, except a foreign order or two, which I generally consider as an intimation to look to my pockets. A German knight* is a dangerous neighbor in a crowd. After seeing a galopade very prettily danced by the Israelitish women, I went down-stairs, reclaimed my hat, and walked into the dining-room. There, with some difficulty, I squeezed myself between a Turk and a Bernese peasant, and obtained an ice, a macaroon, and glass of wine. Charles was there, very active in his attendance on his fair Hilpah. I bid him good-night. "What!" said young hopeful, "are you going yet?" It was near one o'clock; but this joyous tar seemed to think it im-

* Macaulay ended by being a German knight himself.

possible that any body could dream of leaving such delightful enjoyments till day-break. I left him staying Hilpah with flagons, and walked quietly home. But it was some time before I could get to sleep. The sound of fiddles was in mine ears, and gaudy dresses, and black hair, and Jewish noses, were fluctuating up and down before mine eyes.

There is a fancy ball for you. If Charles writes a history of it, tell me which of us does it best. Ever yours,

T. B. M.

To Hannah M. Macaulay.

London, June 10th, 1831.

My dear Sister,—I am at Basinghall Street, and I snatch this quarter of an hour, the only quarter of an hour which I am likely to secure during the day, to write to you. I will not omit writing two days running, because, if my letters give you half the pleasure which your letters give me, you will, I am sure, miss them. I have not, however, much to tell. I have been very busy with my article on Moore's "Life of Byron." I never wrote any thing with less heart. I do not like the book; I do not like the hero: I have said the most I could for him, and yet I shall be abused for speaking as coldly of him as I have done.

I dined the day before yesterday at Sir George Philips's with Sotheby, Morier, the author of "Hadji Baba," and Sir James Mackintosh. Morier began to quote Latin before the ladies had left the room, and quoted it by no means to the purpose. After their departure he fell to repeating Virgil, choosing passages which every body else knows and does not repeat. He, though he tried to repeat them, did not know them, and could not get on without my prompting. Sotheby was full of his translation of Homer's "Iliad," some specimens of which he has already published. It is a complete failure; more literal than that of Pope, but still tainted with the deep radical vice of Pope's version—a thoroughly modern and artificial manner. It bears the same kind of relation to the "Iliad" that Robertson's narrative bears to the story of Joseph in the Book of Genesis.

There is a pretty allegory in Homer—I think in the last

book, but I forget precisely where—about two vessels, the one filled with blessings and the other with sorrow, which stand, says the poet, on the right and left hand of Jupiter's throne, and from which he dispenses good and evil at his pleasure among men. What word to use for these vessels has long posed the translators of Homer. Pope, who loves to be fine, calls them *urns*. Cowper, who loves to be coarse, calls them *casks*—a translation more improper than Pope's; for a cask is, in our general understanding, a wooden vessel, and the Greek word means an earthen vessel. There is a curious letter of Cowper's to one of his female correspondents about this unfortunate word. She begged that Jupiter might be allowed a more elegant piece of furniture for his throne than a cask. But Cowper was peremptory. I mentioned this incidentally when we were talking about translations. This set Sotheby off. "I," said he, "have translated it *vase*. I hope that meets your ideas. Don't you think vase will do? Does it satisfy you?" I told him, sincerely enough, that it satisfied me; for I must be most unreasonable to be dissatisfied at any thing that he chooses to put in a book which I never shall read. Mackintosh was very agreeable; and, as usually happens when I meet him, I learned something from him.

The great topic now in London is not, as you perhaps fancy, Reform, but Cholera. There is a great panic; as great a panic as I remember, particularly in the City. Rice shakes his head, and says that this is the most serious thing that has happened in his time; and assuredly, if the disease were to rage in London as it has lately raged in Riga, it would be difficult to imagine any thing more horrible. I, however, feel no uneasiness. In the first place, I have a strong leaning toward the doctrines of the anti-contagionists. In the next place, I repose a great confidence in the excellent food and the cleanliness of the English.

I have this instant received your letter of yesterday with the inclosed proof-sheets. Your criticism is to a certain extent just; but you have not considered the whole sentence together. *Depressed* is in itself better than *weighed down*; but "the oppressive privileges which had depressed industry" would be a horrible cacophony. I hope that word convinces you. I have often observed that a fine Greek compound is an excellent substitute for a reason.

I met Rogers at the Athenæum. He begged me to breakfast with him, and name my day, and promised that he would procure me as agreeable a party as he could find in London. Very kind of the old man, is it not? and, if you knew how Rogers is thought of, you would think it as great a compliment as could be paid to a duke. Have you seen what the author of "The Young Duke" says about me; how rabid I am, and how certain I am to rat? Ever yours, T. B. M.

Macaulay's account of the allusion to himself in "The Young Duke" is perfectly accurate; and yet, when read as a whole, the passage* in question does not appear to have been ill-naturedly meant. It is much what any young literary man outside the House of Commons might write of another who had only been inside that House for a few weeks; and it was probably forgotten by the author within twenty-four hours after the ink was dry. It is to be hoped that the commentators of the future will not treat it as an authoritative record of Mr. Disraeli's estimate of Lord Macaulay's political character.

To Hannah M. Macaulay.

London, June 25th, 1831.

My dear Sister,—There was, as you will see, no debate on Lord John Russell's motion. The Reform Bill is to be brought in, read once, and printed, without discussion. The contest will be on the second reading, and will be protracted, I should think, through the whole of the week after next—next week it will be, when you read this letter.

---

* "I hear that Mr. Babington Macaulay is to be returned. If he speaks half as well as he writes, the House will be in fashion again. I fear that he is one of those who, like the individual whom he has most studied, will give up to a party what was meant for mankind. At any rate, he must get rid of his rabidity. He writes now on all subjects as if he certainly intended to be a renegade, and was determined to make the contrast complete."—*The Young Duke,* book v., chap. vi.

I breakfasted with Rogers yesterday. There was nobody there but Moore. We were all on the most friendly and familiar terms possible; and Moore, who is, Rogers tells me, excessively pleased with my review of his book, showed me very marked attention. I was forced to go away early on account of bankrupt business; but Rogers said that we must have the talk out; so we are to meet at his house again to breakfast. What a delightful house it is! It looks out on the Green Park just at the most pleasant point. The furniture has been selected with a delicacy of taste quite unique. Its value does not depend on fashion, but must be the same while the fine arts are held in any esteem. In the drawing-room, for example, the chimney-pieces are carved by Flaxman into the most beautiful Grecian forms. The book-case is painted by Stothard, in his very best manner, with groups from Chaucer, Shakspeare, and Boccaccio. The pictures are not numerous; but every one is excellent. In the dining-room there are also some beautiful paintings. But the three most remarkable objects in that room are, I think, a cast of Pope taken after death by Roubiliac; a noble model in terra-cotta by Michael Angelo, from which he afterward made one of his finest statues, that of Lorenzo de' Medici; and, lastly, a mahogany table on which stands an antique vase.

When Chantrey dined with Rogers some time ago, he took particular notice of the vase, and the table on which it stands, and asked Rogers who made the table. "A common carpenter," said Rogers. "Do you remember the making of it?" said Chantrey. "Certainly," said Rogers, in some surprise: "I was in the room while it was finished with the chisel, and gave the workman directions about placing it." "Yes," said Chantrey, "I was the carpenter. I remember the room well and all the circumstances." A curious story, I think, honorable both to the talent which raised Chantrey, and to the magnanimity which kept him from being ashamed of what he had been. Ever yours affectionately, T. B. M.

To Hannah M. Macaulay.

London, June 29th, 1831.

MY DEAR SISTER,—We are not yet in the full tide of Parliamentary business. Next week the debates will be warm and long. I should not wonder if we had a discussion of five nights. I shall probably take a part in it.

I have breakfasted again with Rogers. The party was a remarkable one—Lord John Russell, Tom Moore, Tom Campbell, and Luttrell. We were all very lively. An odd incident took place after breakfast, while we were standing at the window and looking into the Green Park. Somebody was talking about diners-out. "Ay," said Campbell—

"'Ye diners-out from whom we guard our spoons.'"

Tom Moore asked where the line was. "Don't you know?" said Campbell. "Not I," said Moore. "Surely," said Campbell, "it is your own." "I never saw it in my life," said Moore. "It is in one of your best things in the *Times*," said Campbell. Moore denied it. Hereupon I put in my claim, and told them that it was mine. Do you remember it? It is in some lines called the "Political Georgics," which I sent to the *Times* about three years ago. They made me repeat the lines, and were vociferous in praise of them. Tom Moore then said, oddly enough, "There is another poem in the *Times* that I should like to know the author of, 'A Parson's Account of his Journey to the Cambridge Election.'" I laid claim to that also. "That is curious," said Moore. "I begged Barnes to tell me who wrote it. He said that he had received it from Cambridge, and touched it up himself, and pretended that all the best strokes were his. I believed that he was lying, because I never knew him to make a good joke in his life. And now the murder is out." They asked me whether I had put any thing else in the *Times*. Nothing, I said, except the "Sortes Virgilianæ," which Lord John remembered well. I never mentioned the "Cambridge Journey" or the "Georgics" to any but my own family; and I was therefore, as you may conceive, not a little flattered to hear in one day Moore praising one of them, and Campbell praising the other.

I find that my article on Byron is very popular, one among a thousand proofs of the bad taste of the public. I am to review Croker's edition of Bozzy. It is wretchedly ill done. The notes are poorly written and shamefully inaccurate. There is, however, much curious information in it. The whole of "The Tour to the Hebrides" is incorporated with "The Life." So are most of Mrs. Thrale's anecdotes, and much of Sir John Hawkins's lumbering book. The whole makes five large volumes. There is a most laughable sketch of Bozzy, taken by Sir T. Lawrence, when young. I never saw a character so thoroughly hit off. I intend the book for you when I have finished my criticism on it. You are, next to myself, the best-read Boswellite that I know. The lady whom Johnson abused for flattering him* was certainly, according to Croker, Hannah More. Another ill-natured sentence about a Bath lady† whom Johnson called "empty-headed" is also applied to your godmother. Ever yours,

T. B. M.

To Hannah M. Macaulay.

London, July 6th, 1831.

MY DEAR SISTER,—I have been so busy during the last two or three days that I have found no time to write to you. I have now good news for you. I spoke yesterday night with a success beyond my utmost expectations. I am half ashamed to tell you the compliments which I have received; but you well know that it is not from vanity, but to give you pleasure, that I tell you what is said about me. Lord Althorp told me twice that it was the best speech he had ever heard; Graham, and Stanley, and Lord John Russell spoke of it in the same way; and O'Connell followed me out of the House to pay me the most enthusiastic compliments. I delivered my speech much

---

* See Boswell's "Life of Johnson," April 15th, 1778.

† "He would not allow me to praise a lady then at Bath, observing, 'She does not gain upon me, sir; I think her empty-headed.'"

more slowly than any that I have before made, and it is, in consequence, better reported than its predecessors, though not well. I send you several papers. You will see some civil things in the leading articles of some of them. My greatest pleasure in the midst of all this praise is to think of the pleasure which my success will give to my father and my sisters. It is happy for me that ambition has in my mind been softened into a kind of domestic feeling, and that affection has at least as much to do as vanity with my wish to distinguish myself. This I owe to my dear mother, and to the interest which she always took in my childish successes. From my earliest years the gratification of those whom I love has been associated with the gratification of my own thirst for fame, until the two have become inseparably joined in my mind.

Ever yours, T. B. M.

To Hannah M. Macaulay.

London, July 8th, 1831.

My dear Sister,—Do you want to hear all the compliments that are paid to me? I shall never end, if I stuff my letters with them; for I meet nobody who does not give me joy. Baring tells me that I ought never to speak again. Howick sent a note to me yesterday to say that his father wished very much to be introduced to me, and asked me to dine with them yesterday, as by great good luck there was nothing to do in the House of Commons. At seven I went to Downing Street, where Earl Grey's official residence stands. It is a noble house. There are two splendid drawing-rooms which overlook St. James's Park. Into these I was shown. The servant told me that Lord Grey was still at the House of Lords, and that her ladyship had just gone to dress. Howick had not mentioned the hour in his note. I sat down, and turned over two large port-folios of political caricatures. Earl Grey's own face was in every print. I was very much diverted. I had seen some of them before; but many were new to me, and their merit is extraordinary. They were the caricatures of that remarkably able artist who calls himself H. B. In about half an hour Lady Georgiana Grey, and the countess, made their appearance. We had some pleasant talk, and they made many apologies. The earl, they said, was unexpectedly delayed by a question which had arisen in the Lords. Lady Holland arrived soon after, and gave me a most gracious reception, shook my hand very warmly, and told me in her imperial, decisive manner that she had talked with all the principal men on our side about my speech, that they all agreed that it was the best that had been made since the death of Fox, and that it was more like Fox's speaking than any body's else. Then she told me that I was too much worked, that I must go out of town, and absolutely insisted on my going to Holland House to dine and take a bed on the next day on which there is no Parliamentary business. At eight we went to dinner. Lord Howick took his father's place, and we feasted very luxuriously. At nine Lord Grey came from the House, with Lord Durham, Lord Holland, and the Duke of Richmond. They dined on the remains of our dinner with great expedition, as they had to go to a cabinet council at ten. Of course I had scarcely any talk with Lord Grey. He was, however, extremely polite to me, and so were his colleagues. I liked the ways of the family.

I picked up some news from these cabinet ministers. There is to be a coronation on quite a new plan: no banquet in Westminster Hall, no feudal services, no champion, no procession from the Abbey to the Hall and back again. But there is to be a service in the Abbey. All the peers are to come in state and in their robes, and the king is to take the oaths, and be crowned and anointed, in their presence. The spectacle will be finer than usual to the multitude out-of-doors. The few hundreds who could obtain admittance to the Hall will be the only losers. Ever yours, T. B. M.

To Hannah M. Macaulay.

London, July 11th, 1831.

MY DEAR SISTER,—Since I wrote to you I have been out to dine and sleep at Holland House. We had a very agreeable and splendid party; among others, the Duke and Duchess of Richmond, and the Marchioness of Clanricarde, who, you know, is the daughter of Canning. She is very beautiful, and very like her father, with eyes full of fire, and great expression in all her features. She and I had a great deal of talk. She showed much cleverness and information, but, I thought, a little more of political animosity than is quite becoming in a pretty woman. However, she has been placed in peculiar circumstances. The daughter of a statesman who was a martyr to the rage of faction may be pardoned for speaking sharply of the enemies of her parent: and she did speak sharply. With knitted brows, and flashing eyes, and a look of feminine vengeance about her beautiful mouth, she gave me such a character of Peel as he would certainly have had no pleasure in hearing.

In the evening Lord John Russell came; and, soon after, old Talleyrand. I had seen Talleyrand in very large parties, but had never been near enough to hear a word that he said. I now had the pleasure of listening for an hour and a half to his conversation. He is certainly the greatest curiosity that I ever fell in with. His head is sunk down between two high shoulders. One of his feet is hideously distorted. His face is as pale as that of a corpse, and wrinkled to a frightful degree. His eyes have an odd glassy stare quite peculiar to them. His hair, thickly powdered and pomatumed, hangs down his shoulders on each side as straight as a pound of tallow-candles. His conversation, however, soon makes you forget his ugliness and infirmities. There is a poignancy without effort in all that he says, which reminded me a little of the character which the wits of Johnson's circle give of Beauclerk. For example, we talked about Metternich and Cardinal Mazarin. "J'y trouve beaucoup à redire. Le cardinal trompait; mais il ne mentait pas. Or M. de Metternich ment toujours, et ne trompe jamais." He mentioned M. de Saint-Aulaire—now one of the most distinguished public men of France. I said: "M. de Saint-Aulaire est beau-père de M. le duc de Cazes, n'est-ce pas?" "Non, monsieur," said Talleyrand; "l'on disait, il y a douze ans, que M. de Saint-Aulaire était beau-père* de M. de Cazes; l'on dit maintenant que M.

* This saying remained in Macaulay's mind. He quotes it on the mar-

de Cazes est gendre de M. de Saint-Aulaire." It was not easy to describe the change in the relative positions of two men more tersely and more sharply; and these remarks were made in the lowest tone, and without the slightest change of muscle, just as if he had been remarking that the day was fine. He added: "M. de Saint-Aulaire a beaucoup d'esprit. Mais il est dévot, et, ce qui pis est, dévot honteux. Il va se cacher dans quelque hameau pour faire ses Pâques." This was a curious remark from a bishop. He told several stories about the political men of France: not of any great value in themselves: but his way of telling them was beyond all praise; concise, pointed, and delicately satirical. When he had departed, I could not help breaking out into admiration of his talent for relating anecdotes. Lady Holland said that he had been considered for nearly forty years as the best teller of a story in Europe, and that there was certainly nobody like him in that respect.

When the prince was gone we went to bed. In the morning Lord John Russell drove me back to London in his cabriolet, much amused with what I had seen and heard. But I must stop. Ever yours, T. B. M.

To Hannah M. Macaulay.

Basinghall Street, July 15th, 1831.

My dear Sister,—The rage of faction at the present moment exceeds any thing that has been known in our day. Indeed, I doubt whether, at the time of Mr. Pitt's first becoming premier, at the time of Sir Robert Walpole's fall, or even during the desperate struggles between the Whigs and Tories at the close of Anne's reign, the fury of party was so fearfully violent. Lord Mahon said to me yesterday that friendships of long standing were everywhere giving way, and that the schism between the reformers and the anti-reformers was spreading from the House of Commons into every private

---

gin of his Aulus Gellius as an illustration of the passage in the nineteenth book in which Julius Cæsar is described, absurdly enough, as "perpetuus ille dictator, Cneii Pompeii socer."

circle. Lord Mahon himself is an exception. He and I are on excellent terms. But Praed and I become colder every day.

The scene of Tuesday night beggars description. I left the House at about three, in consequence of some expressions of Lord Althorp's which indicated that the ministry was inclined to yield on the question of going into committee on the bill. I afterward much regretted that I had gone away; not that my presence was necessary, but because I should have liked to have sat through so tremendous a storm. Toward eight in the morning the Speaker was almost fainting. The ministerial members, however, were as true as steel. They furnished the ministry with the resolution which it wanted. "If the noble lord yields," said one of our men, "all is lost." Old Sir Thomas Baring sent for his razor, and Benett, the member for Wiltshire, for his night-cap; and they were both resolved to spend the whole day in the House rather than give way. If the opposition had not yielded, in two hours half London would have been in Old Palace Yard.

Since Tuesday the Tories have been rather cowed. But their demeanor, though less outrageous than at the beginning of the week, indicates what would in any other time be called extreme violence. I have not been once in bed till three in the morning since last Sunday. To-morrow we have a holiday. I dine at Lansdowne House. Next week I dine with Littleton, the member for Staffordshire, and his handsome wife. He told me that I should meet two men whom I am curious to see—Lord Plunket and the Marquess Wellesley: let alone the Chancellor, who is not a novelty to me.

Ever yours, T. B. M.

To Hannah M. Macaulay.

London, July 25th, 1831.

My dear Sister,—On Saturday evening I went to Holland House. There I found the Dutch Embassador, M. de Weissembourg, Mr. and Mrs. Vernon Smith, and Admiral Adam, a son of the old Adam who fought the duel with Fox. We dined like emperors, and jabbered in several languages. Her ladyship, for an *esprit fort*, is the greatest coward that I ever saw. The last time that I was there she was frightened out of her wits by the thunder. She closed all the shutters, drew all the curtains, and ordered candles in broad day to keep out the lightning, or rather the appearance of the lightning. On Saturday she was in a terrible taking about the cholera; talked of nothing else; refused to eat any ice, because somebody said that ice was bad for the cholera; was sure that the cholera was at Glasgow; and asked me why a cordon of troops was not instantly placed around that town to prevent all intercourse between the infected and the healthy spots. Lord Holland made light of her fears. He is a thoroughly good-natured, open, sensible man; very lively; very intellectual; well read in politics, and in the lighter literature both of ancient and modern times. He sets me more at ease than almost any person that I know by a certain good-humored way of contradicting that he has. He always begins by drawing down his shaggy eyebrows, making a face extremely like his uncle, wagging his head, and saying: "Now do you know, Mr. Macaulay, I do not quite see that. How do you make it out?" He tells a story delightfully, and bears the pain of his gout, and the confinement and privations to which it subjects him, with admirable fortitude and cheerfulness. Her ladyship is all courtesy and kindness to me; but her demeanor to some others, particularly to poor Allen, is such as it quite pains me to witness. He is really treated like a negro slave. "Mr. Allen, go into my drawing-room and bring my reticule." "Mr. Allen, go and see what can be the matter that they do not bring up dinner." "Mr. Allen, there is not enough turtle-soup for you. You must take gravy-soup or none." Yet I can scarcely pity the man. He has an independent income, and if he can stoop to be ordered about like a footman, I can not so much blame her for the contempt with which she treats him. Perhaps I may write again to-morrow. Ever yours,

T. B. M.

To Hannah M. Macaulay.

Library of the House of Commons, July 26th, 1831.

MY DEAR SISTER,—Here I am seated, waiting for the debate on the borough of St. Germains with a very quiet party—Lord

Milton, Lord Tavistock, and George Lamb. But, instead of telling you in dramatic form* my conversations with cabinet ministers, I shall, I think, go back two or three days, and complete the narrative which I left imperfect in my epistle of yesterday.

At half-after seven on Sunday I was set down at Littleton's palace, for such it is, in Grosvenor Place. It really is a noble house; four superb drawing-rooms on the first floor hung round with some excellent pictures—a Hobbema (the finest by that artist in the world, it is said), and Lawrence's charming portrait of Mrs. Littleton. The beautiful original, by-the-bye, did not make her appearance. We were a party of gentlemen. But such gentlemen! Listen, and be proud of your connection with one who is admitted to eat and drink in the same room with beings so exalted. There were two chancellors, Lord Brougham and Lord Plunket. There was Earl Gower; Lord St. Vincent; Lord Seaford; Lord Duncannon; Lord Ebrington; Sir James Graham; Sir John Newport; the two secretaries of the treasury, Rice and Ellice; George Lamb; Denison; and half a dozen more lords and distinguished commoners, not to mention Littleton himself. Till

---

* This refers to a passage in a former letter, likewise written from the Library of the House.

"'Macaulay!' Who calls Macaulay? Sir James Graham. What can he have to say to me? Take it dramatically:

"*Sir J. G.* Macaulay!

"*Macaulay.* What?

"*Sir J. G.* Whom are you writing to, that you laugh so much over your letter?

"*Macaulay.* To my constituents at Calne, to be sure. They expect news of the Reform Bill every day.

"*Sir J. G.* Well, writing to constituents is less of a plague to you than to most people, to judge by your face.

"*Macaulay.* How do you know that I am not writing a billetdoux to a lady?

"*Sir J. G.* You look more like it, by Jove!

"*Cutler Fergusson, M.P. for Kirkcudbright.* Let ladies and constituents alone, and come into the House. We are going on to the case of the borough of Great Bedwin immediately."

last year he lived in Portman Square. When he changed his residence his servants gave him warning. They could not, they said, consent to go into such an unheard-of part of the world as Grosvenor Place. I can only say that I have never been in a finer house than Littleton's, Lansdowne House excepted, and perhaps Lord Milton's, which is also in Grosvenor Place. He gave me a dinner of dinners. I talked with Denison, and with nobody else. I have found out that the real use of conversational powers is to put them forth in tête-à-tête. A man is flattered by your talking your best to him alone. Ten to one he is piqued by your overpowering him before a company. Denison was agreeable enough. I heard only one word from Lord Plunket, who was remarkably silent. He spoke of Doctor Thorpe, and said that, having heard the doctor in Dublin, he should like to hear him again in London. "Nothing easier," quoth Littleton; "his chapel is only two doors off; and he will be just mounting the pulpit." "No," said Lord Plunket; "I can't lose my dinner." An excellent saying, though one which a less able man than Lord Plunket might have uttered.

At midnight I walked away with George Lamb, and went —where, for a ducat? "To bed," says Miss Hannah. Nay, my sister, not so; but to Brooks's. There I found Sir James Macdonald; Lord Duncannon, who had left Littleton's just before us; and many other Whigs and ornaments of human nature. As Macdonald and I were rising to depart we saw Rogers, and I went to shake hands with him. You can not think how kind the old man was to me. He shook my hand over and over, and told me that Lord Plunket longed to see me in a quiet way, and that he would arrange a breakfast-party in a day or two for that purpose.

Away I went from Brooks's—but whither? "To bed now, I am sure," says little Anne. No, but on a walk with Sir James Macdonald to the end of Sloane Street, talking about the Ministry, the Reform Bill, and the East India question.

Ever yours, T. B. M.

To Hannah M. Macaulay.

House of Commons Smoking-room, Saturday.

My dear Sister,—The newspapers will have explained the reason of our sitting to-day. At three this morning I left the House. At two this afternoon I have returned to it, with the thermometer at boiling-heat, and four hundred and fifty people stowed together like negroes in the pious John Newton's slave-ship. I have accordingly left Sir Francis Burdett on his legs, and repaired to the smoking-room; a large, wainscoted, uncarpeted place, with tables covered with green baize and writing materials. On a full night it is generally thronged toward twelve o'clock with smokers. It is then a perfect cloud of fume. There have I seen (tell it not to the West Indians) Buxton blowing fire out of his mouth. My father will not believe it. At present, however, all the doors and windows are open, and the room is pure enough from tobacco to suit my father himself.

Get Blackwood's new number. There is a description of me in it. What do you think he says that I am? "A little, splay-footed, ugly, dumpling of a fellow, with a mouth from ear to ear." Conceive how such a charge must affect a man so enamored of his own beauty as I am.

I said a few words the other night. They were merely in reply, and quite unpremeditated, and were not ill received. I feel that much practice will be necessary to make me a good debater on points of detail, but my friends tell me that I have raised my reputation by showing that I was quite equal to the work of extemporaneous reply. My manner, they say, is cold and wants care. I feel this myself. Nothing but strong excitement and a great occasion overcomes a certain reserve and *mauvaise honte* which I have in public speaking; not a *mauvaise honte* which in the least confuses me or makes me hesitate for a word, but which keeps me from putting any fervor into my tone or my action. This is perhaps in some respects an advantage; for, when I *do* warm, I am the most vehement speaker in the House, and nothing strikes an audience so much as the animation of an orator who is generally cold.

I ought to tell you that Peel was very civil, and cheered me loudly; and that impudent, leering Croker congratulated the House on the proof which I had given of my readiness. He was afraid, he said, that I had been silent so long on account of the many allusions which had been made to Calne. Now that I had risen again he hoped that they should hear me often. See whether I do not dust that varlet's jacket for him in the next number of the *Blue and Yellow*.* I detest him more than cold boiled veal.

After the debate I walked about the streets with Bulwer till nearly three o'clock. I spoke to him about his novels with perfect sincerity, praising warmly, and criticising freely. He took the praise as a greedy boy takes apple-pie, and the criticism as a good, dutiful boy takes senna-tea. He has one eminent merit, that of being a most enthusiastic admirer of mine; so that I may be the hero of a novel yet, under the name of Delamere or Mortimer. Only think what an honor!

Bulwer is to be editor of the *New Monthly Magazine.* He begged me very earnestly to give him something for it. I would make no promises; for I am already over head and ears in literary engagements. But I may possibly now and then send him some trifle or other. At all events, I shall expect him to puff me well. I do not see why I should not have my puffers as well as my neighbors.

I am glad that you have read Madame de Staël's "Allemagne." The book is a foolish one in some respects; but it abounds with information, and shows great mental power. She was certainly the first woman of her age; Miss Edgeworth, I think, the second; and Miss Austen the third.

Ever yours, T. B. M.

---

* "By-the-bye," Macaulay writes elsewhere, "you never saw such a scene as Croker's oration on Friday night. He abused Lord John Russell, he abused Lord Althorp, he abused the lord advocate, and we took no notice—never once groaned or cried 'No!' But he began to praise Lord Fitzwilliam—'a venerable nobleman, an excellent and amiable nobleman,' and so forth; and we all broke out together with 'Question!' 'No, no!' 'This is too bad!' 'Don't, don't!' He then called Canning his right honorable friend. 'Your friend! d—n your impudent face!' said the member who sat next me."

To Hannah M. Macaulay.

London, August 29th, 1831.

My dear Sister,—Here I am again settled, sitting up in the House of Commons till three o'clock five days in the week, and getting an indigestion at great dinners the remaining two. I dined on Saturday with Lord Althorp, and yesterday with Sir James Graham. Both of them gave me exactly the same dinner; and though I am not generally copious on the repasts which my hosts provide for me, I must tell you, for the honor of official hospitality, how our ministers regale their supporters. Turtle, turbot, venison, and grouse formed part of both entertainments.

Lord Althorp was extremely pleasant at the head of his own table. We were a small party—Lord Ebrington, Hawkins, Captain Spencer, Stanley, and two or three more. We all of us congratulated Lord Althorp on his good health and spirits. He told us that he never took exercise now; that from his getting up, till four o'clock, he was engaged in the business of his office; that at four he dined, went down to the House at five, and never stirred till the House rose, which is always after midnight; that he then went home, took a basin of arrowroot with a glass of sherry in it, and went to bed, where he always dropped asleep in three minutes. "During the week," said he, "which followed my taking office I did not close my eyes for anxiety. Since that time I have never been awake a quarter of an hour after taking off my clothes." Stanley laughed at Lord Althorp's arrowroot, and recommended his own supper—cold meat and warm negus; a supper which I will certainly begin to take when I feel a desire to pass the night with a sensation as if I were swallowing a nutmeg-grater every third minute.

We talked about timidity in speaking. Lord Althorp said that he had only just got over his apprehensions. "I was as much afraid," he said, "last year as when first I came into Parliament. But now I am forced to speak so often that I am quite hardened. Last Thursday I was up forty times." I was not much surprised at this in Lord Althorp, as he is certainly one of the most modest men in existence. But I was surprised to hear Stanley say that he never rose without great uneasiness. "My throat and lips," he said, "when I am going to speak, are as dry as those of a man who is going to be hanged." Nothing can be more composed and cool than Stanley's manner. His fault is on that side. A little hesitation at the beginning of a speech is graceful, and many eminent speakers have practiced it merely in order to give the appearance of unpremeditated reply to prepared speeches. Stanley speaks like a man who never knew what fear, or even modesty, was. Tierney, it is remarkable, who was the most ready and fluent debater almost ever known, made a confession similar to Stanley's. He never spoke, he said, without feeling his knees knock together when he rose.

My opinion of Lord Althorp is extremely high. In fact, his character is the only stay of the ministry. I doubt whether any person has ever lived in England who, with no eloquence, no brilliant talents, no profound information, with nothing, in short, but plain good sense and an excellent heart, possessed so much influence both in and out of Parliament. His temper is an absolute miracle. He has been worse used than any minister ever was in debate, and he has never said one thing inconsistent, I do not say with gentleman-like courtesy, but with real benevolence. Lord North, perhaps, was his equal in suavity and good nature; but Lord North was not a man of strict principles. His administration was not only an administration hostile to liberty, but it was supported by vile and corrupt means—by direct bribery, I fear, in many cases. Lord Althorp has the temper of Lord North with the principles of Romilly. If he had the oratorical powers of either of those men, he might do any thing. But his understanding, though just, is slow, and his elocution painfully defective. It is, however, only justice to him to say that he has done more service to the Reform Bill even as a debater than all the other ministers together, Stanley excepted.

We are going—by *we* I mean the members of Parliament who are for reform—as soon as the bill is through the Commons, to give a grand dinner to Lord Althorp and Lord John

Russell, as a mark of our respect. Some people wished to have the other cabinet ministers included; but Grant and Palmerston are not in sufficiently high esteem among the Whigs to be honored with such a compliment.

Ever yours, T. B. M.

To Hannah M. Macaulay.

London, September 9th, 1831.

My dear Sister,—I scarcely know where to begin, or where to end, my story of the magnificence of yesterday. No pageant can be conceived more splendid. The newspapers will happily save me the trouble of relating minute particulars. I will therefore give you an account of my own proceedings, and mention what struck me most. I rose at six. The cannon awaked me; and, as soon as I got up, I heard the bells pealing on every side from all the steeples in London. I put on my court-dress, and looked a perfect Lovelace in it. At seven the glass coach which I had ordered for myself and some of my friends came to the door. I called in Hill Street for William Marshall, M. P. for Beverley, and in Cork Street for Strutt, the member for Derby, and Hawkins, the member for Tavistock. Our party being complete, we drove through crowds of people and ranks of horse-guards in cuirasses and helmets to Westminster Hall, which we reached as the clock struck eight.

The House of Commons was crowded, and the whole assembly was in uniform. After prayers we went out in order by lot, the Speaker going last. My county, Wiltshire, was among the first drawn; so I got an excellent place in the Abbey, next to Lord Mahon, who is a very great favorite of mine, and a very amusing companion, though a bitter Tory.

Our gallery was immediately over the great altar. The whole vast avenue of lofty pillars was directly in front of us. At eleven the guns fired, the organ struck up, and the procession entered. I never saw so magnificent a scene. All down that immense vista of gloomy arches there was one blaze of scarlet and gold. First came heralds in coats stiff with embroidered lions, unicorns, and harps; then nobles bearing the regalia, with pages in rich dresses carrying their coronets on cushions; then the dean and prebendaries of Westminster in copes of cloth of gold; then a crowd of beautiful girls and women, or at least of girls and women who at a distance looked altogether beautiful, attending on the queen. Her train of purple velvet and ermine was borne by six of these fair creatures. All the great officers of state in full robes, the Duke of Wellington with his marshal's staff, the Duke of Devonshire with his white rod, Lord Grey with the sword of state, and the chancellor with his seals, came in procession. Then all the royal dukes with their trains borne behind them, and last the king leaning on two bishops. I do not, I dare say, give you the precise order. In fact, it was impossible to discern any order. The whole abbey was one blaze of gorgeous dresses, mingled with lovely faces.

The queen behaved admirably, with wonderful grace and dignity. The king very awkwardly. The Duke of Devonshire looked as if he came to be crowned instead of his master. I never saw so princely a manner and air. The chancellor looked like Mephistopheles behind Margaret in the church. The ceremony was much too long, and some parts of it were carelessly performed. The archbishop mumbled. The Bishop of London preached, well enough indeed, but not so effectively as the occasion required; and, above all, the bearing of the king made the foolish parts of the ritual appear monstrously ridiculous, and deprived many of the better parts of their proper effect. Persons who were at a distance, perhaps, did not feel this; but I was near enough to see every turn of his finger and every glance of his eye. The moment of the crowning was extremely fine. When the archbishop placed the crown on the head of the king, the trumpets sounded, and the whole audience cried out, "God save the King." All the peers and peeresses put on their coronets, and the blaze of splendor through the Abbey seemed to be doubled. The king was then conducted to the raised throne, where the peers successively did him homage, each of them kissing his cheek and touching the crown. Some of them were cheered, which I thought indecorous in such a place and on such an occasion.

The Tories cheered the Duke of Wellington; and our people, in revenge, cheered Lord Grey and Brougham.

You will think this a very dull letter for so great a subject; but I have only had time to scrawl these lines in order to catch the post. I have not a minute to read them over. I lost yesterday, and have been forced to work to-day. Half my article on Boswell went to Edinburgh the day before yesterday. I have, though I say it who should not say it, beaten Croker black and blue. Impudent as he is, I think he must be ashamed of the pickle in which I leave him.

Ever yours, T. B. M.

To Hannah M. Macaulay.

London, September 13th, 1831.

My dear Sister,—I am in high spirits at the thought of soon seeing you all in London, and being again one of a family, and of a family which I love so much. It is well that one has something to love in private life; for the aspect of public affairs is very menacing—fearful, I think, beyond what people in general imagine. Three weeks, however, will probably settle the whole, and bring to an issue the question, Reform or Revolution. One or the other I am certain that we must and shall have. I assure you that the violence of the people, the bigotry of the lords, and the stupidity and weakness of the ministers, alarm me so much that even my rest is disturbed by vexation and uneasy forebodings; not for myself, for I may gain and can not lose; but for this noble country, which seems likely to be ruined without the miserable consolation of being ruined by great men. All seems fair as yet, and will seem fair for a fortnight longer. But I know the danger from information more accurate and certain than, I believe, any body not in power possesses; and I perceive, what our men in power do not perceive, how terrible the danger is.

I called on Lord Lansdowne on Sunday. He told me distinctly that he expected the bill to be lost in the Lords, and that, if it were lost, the ministers must go out. I told him, with as much strength of expression as was suited to the nature of our connection and to his age and rank, that if the ministers receded before the Lords, and hesitated to make peers, they and the Whig party were lost; that nothing remained but an insolent oligarchy on the one side, and an infuriated people on the other; and that Lord Grey and his colleagues would become as odious and more contemptible than Peel and the Duke of Wellington. Why did they not think of all this earlier? Why put their hand to the plow and look back? Why begin to build without counting the cost of finishing? Why raise the public appetite, and then balk it? I told him that the House of Commons would address the king against a Tory ministry. I feel assured that it would do so. I feel assured that, if those who are bidden will not come, the highways and hedges will be ransacked to get together a reforming cabinet. To one thing my mind is made up. If nobody else will move an address to the crown against a Tory ministry, I will. Ever yours, T. B. M.

London, October 17th, 1831.

My dear Ellis,—I should have written to you before, but that I mislaid your letter and forgot your direction. When shall you be in London? Of course you do not mean to sacrifice your professional business to the work of numbering the gates and telling the towers of boroughs* in Wales. You will come back, I suppose, with your head full of ten-pound householders instead of ἥρωες, and of Caermarthen and Denbigh instead of Carians and Pelasgians. Is it true, by-the-bye, that the commissioners are whipped on the boundaries of the boroughs by the beadles, in order that they may not forget the precise line which they have drawn? I deny it wherever I go, and assure people that some of my friends who are in the commission would not submit to such degradation.

You must have been hard-worked indeed, and soundly whipped too, if you have suffered as much for the Reform Bill as we who debated it. I believe that there are fifty members of the House of Commons who have done irreparable in-

* Mr. Ellis was one of the commissioners appointed to arrange the boundaries of parliamentary boroughs in connection with the Reform Bill.

jury to their health by attendance on the discussions of this session. I have got through pretty well, but I look forward, I confess, with great dismay to the thought of recommencing; particularly as Wetherell's cursed lungs seem to be in as good condition as ever.

I have every reason to be gratified by the manner in which my speeches have been received. To say the truth, the station which I now hold in the House is such that I should not be inclined to quit it for any place which was not of considerable importance. What you saw about my having a place was a blunder of a stupid reporter's. Croker was taunting the Government with leaving me to fight their battle and to rally their followers; and said that the honorable and learned member for Calne, though only a practicing barrister in title, seemed to be in reality the most efficient member of the Government. By-the-bye, my article on Croker has not only smashed his book, but has hit the *Westminster Review* incidentally. The Utilitarians took on themselves to praise the accuracy of the most inaccurate writer that ever lived, and gave as an instance of it a note in which, as I have shown, he makes a mistake of twenty years and more. John Mill is in a rage, and says that they are in a worse scrape than Croker; John Murray says that it is a d d nuisance; and Croker looks across the House of Commons at me with a leer of hatred which I repay with a gracious smile of pity.

I am ashamed to have said so much about myself. But you asked for news about me. No request is so certain to be granted, or so certain to be a curse to him who makes it, as that which you have made to me. Ever yours,

T. B. Macaulay.

London, January 9th, 1832.

Dear Napier,—I have been so much engaged by bankrupt business, as we are winding up the affairs of many estates, that I shall not be able to send off my article about Hampden till Thursday, the 12th. It will be, I fear, more than forty pages long. As Pascal said of his eighteenth letter, I would have made it shorter if I could have kept it longer.

You must indulge me, however, for I seldom offend in that way.

It is in part a narrative. This is a sort of composition which I have never yet attempted. You will tell me, I am sure with sincerity, how you think that I succeed in it. I have said as little about Lord Nugent's book as I decently could.

Ever yours, T. B. M.

London, January 19th, 1832.

DEAR NAPIER,—I will try the "Life of Lord Burleigh," if you will tell Longman to send me the book. However bad the work may be, it will serve as a heading for an article on the times of Elizabeth. On the whole, I thought it best not to answer Croker. Almost all the little pamphlet which he published (or rather printed, for I believe it is not for sale), is made up of extracts from *Blackwood:* and I thought that a contest with your grog-drinking, cock-fighting, cudgel-playing professor of moral philosophy would be too degrading. I could have demolished every paragraph of the defense. Croker defended his θνητοὶ φίλοι* by quoting a passage of Euripides which, as every scholar knows, is corrupt; which is nonsense and false metre if read as he reads it; and which Markland and Matthiæ have set right by a most obvious correction. But, as nobody seems to have read his vindication, we can gain nothing by refuting it. Ever yours, T. B. MACAULAY.

---

* "Mr. Croker has favored us with some Greek of his own. 'At the altar,' says Dr. Johnson, 'I recommended my θ φ.' 'These letters,' says the editor (which Dr. Strahan seems not to have understood), 'probably mean θνητοὶ φίλοι, *departed friends*.' Johnson was not a first-rate Greek scholar; but he knew more Greek than most boys when they leave school; and no school-boy could venture to use the word θνητοὶ in the sense which Mr. Croker ascribes to it without imminent danger of a flogging."—*Macaulay's Review of Croker's Boswell.*

CHAPTER V.

1832–1834.

Macaulay is Invited to stand for Leeds.—The Reform Bill passes.—Macaulay appointed Commissioner of the Board of Control.—His Life in Office.—Letters to his Sister.—Contested Election at Leeds.—Macaulay's Bearing as a Candidate.—Canvassing.—Pledges.—Intrusion of Religion into Politics. —Placemen in Parliament. —Liverpool.— Margaret Macaulay's Marriage.—How it Affected her Brother.—He is Returned for Leeds.—Becomes Secretary of the Board of Control.—Letters to Lady Trevelyan.—Session of 1832.—Macaulay's Speech on the India Bill.—His Regard for Lord Glenelg.—Letters to Lady Trevelyan.—The West Indian Question.—Macaulay resigns Office.—He gains his Point, and resumes his Place.—Emancipation of the Slaves.—Death of Wilberforce.—Letters to Lady Trevelyan.—Macaulay is appointed Member of the Supreme Council of India.—Letters to Lady Trevelyan, Lord Lansdowne, and Mr. Napier.—Altercation between Lord Althorp and Mr. Sheil.—Macaulay's Appearance before the Committee of Investigation.—He sails for India.

During the earlier half of the year 1832 the vessel of Reform was still laboring heavily; but long before she was through the breakers, men had begun to discount the treasures which she was bringing into port. The time was fast approaching when the country would be called upon to choose its first Reformed Parliament. As if the spectacle of what was doing at Westminster did not satisfy their appetite for political excitement, the constituencies of the future could not refrain from anticipating the fancied pleasures of an electoral struggle. Impatient to exercise their privileges, and to show that they had as good an eye for a man as those patrons of nomination seats whose discernment was being vaunted nightly in a dozen speeches from the opposition benches of the House of Commons, the great cities were vying with each other to seek representatives worthy of the occasion and of themselves. The Whigs of Leeds, already provided with one candidate in a member of the great local firm of the Marshalls, resolved to seek for another among the distinguished politicians of their party. As early as October, 1831, Macaulay had received a requisition from that town, and had pledged himself to stand as soon as it had been elevated into a parliamentary borough. The Tories, on their side, brought forward Mr. Michael Sadler, the very man on whose behalf the Duke of Newcastle had done "what he liked with his own" in Newark, and, at the last general election, had done it in vain. Sadler, smarting from the lash of the *Edinburgh Review*, infused into the contest an amount of personal bitterness that, for his own sake, might better have been spared; and, during more than a twelvemonth to come, Macaulay lived the life of a candidate whose own hands are full of public work at a time when his opponent has nothing to do except to make himself disagreeable. But, having once undertaken to fight the battle of the Leeds Liberals, he fought it stoutly and cheerily, and would have been the last to claim it as a merit, that, with numerous opportunities of a safe and easy election at his disposal, he remained faithful to the supporters who had been so forward to honor him with their choice.

The old system died hard; but in May, 1832, came its final agony. The Reform Bill had passed the Commons, and had been read a second time in the Upper House; but the facilities which committee affords for maiming and delaying a measure of great magnitude and intricacy proved too much for the self-control of the Lords. The king could not bring himself to adopt that wonderful expedient by which the unanimity of the three branches of our legislature may, in the last resort, be secured. Deceived by an utterly fallacious analogy, his majesty began to be persuaded that the path of concession would lead him whither it had led Louis the Sixteenth, and he resolved to halt on that path at the point where his ministers advised him to force the hands of their lordships by creating peers. The supposed warnings of the French Revolution, which had been dinned into the ears of the country by every Tory orator from Peel to Sibthorpe, at last had produced their effect on the royal imagination. Earl

Grey resigned, and the Duke of Wellington, with a loyalty which certainly did not stand in need of such an unlucky proof, came forward to meet the storm. But its violence was too much even for his courage and constancy. He could not get colleagues to assist him in the Cabinet, or supporters to vote with him in Parliament, or soldiers to fight for him in the streets; and it was evident that in a few days his position would be such as could only be kept by fighting.

The revolution had, in truth, commenced. At a meeting of the political unions on the slope of Newhall Hill at Birmingham, a hundred thousand voices had sung the words:

> God is our guide. No swords we draw.
> We kindle not war's battle fires.
> By union, justice, reason, law,
> We claim the birthright of our sires.

But those very men were now binding themselves by a declaration that, unless the bill passed, they would pay no taxes, nor purchase property distrained by the tax-gatherer. In thus renouncing the first obligation of a citizen, they did in effect draw the sword, and they would have been cravens if they had left it in the scabbard. Lord Milton did something to enhance the claim of his historic house upon the national gratitude by giving practical effect to this audacious resolve; and, after the lapse of two centuries, another Great Rebellion, more effectual than its predecessor, but so brief and bloodless that history does not recognize it as a rebellion at all, was inaugurated by the essentially English proceeding of a quiet country gentleman telling the collector to call again. The crisis lasted just a week. The duke had no mind for a succession of Peterloos, on a vaster scale, and with a different issue. He advised the king to recall his ministers; and his majesty, in his turn, honored the refractory lords with a most significant circular letter, respectful in form, but unmistakable in tenor. A hundred peers of the opposition took the hint, and contrived to be absent whenever Reform was before the House. The bill was read for a third time by a majority of five to one on the 4th of June; a strange, and not very complimentary, method of celebrating old George the Third's birthday. On the 5th it received the last touches in the Commons; and on the 7th it became an act, in very much the same shape, after such and so many vicissitudes, as it wore when Lord John Russell first presented it to Parliament.

Macaulay, whose eloquence had signalized every stage of the conflict, and whose printed speeches are, of all its authentic records, the most familiar to readers of our own day, was not left without his reward. He was appointed one of the commissioners of the Board of Control, which, for three quarters of a century, from 1784 onward, represented the crown in its relations to the East Indian directors. His duties, like those of every individual member of a commission, were light or heavy as he chose to make them; but his own feeling with regard to those duties must not be deduced from the playful allusions contained in letters dashed off during the momentary leisure of an overbusy day for the amusement of two girls who barely numbered forty years between them. His speeches and essays teem with expressions of a far deeper than official interest in India and her people; and his minutes remain on record to prove that he did not affect the sentiment for a literary or oratorical purpose. The attitude of his own mind with regard to our Eastern empire is depicted in the passage on Burke, in the essay on Warren Hastings, which commences with the words "His knowledge of India," and concludes with the sentence "Oppression in Bengal was to him the same thing as oppression in the streets of London." That passage, unsurpassed as it is in force of language and splendid fidelity of detail by any thing that Macaulay ever wrote or uttered, was inspired, as all who knew him could testify, by sincere and entire sympathy with that great statesman of whose humanity and breadth of view it is the merited, and not inadequate, panegyric.

In Margaret Macaulay's journal there occurs more than one mention of her brother's occasional fits of contrition on the subject of his own idleness; but these regrets and confessions must be taken for what they are worth, and for no more. He worked much harder than he gave himself credit for. His nature was such that whatever he did was done with all his heart and all his power, and he was constitutionally incapable of doing it otherwise. He always underestimated the tension and concentration of mind which he brought to bear upon his labors, as compared with that which men in general bestow on whatever business they may have in hand; and toward the close of life this honorable self-deception no doubt led him to draw far too largely upon his failing strength, under the impression that there was nothing unduly severe in the efforts to which he continued to brace himself with ever-increasing difficulty.

During the eighteen months that he passed at the Board of Control he had no time for relaxation, and very little for the industry which he loved the best. Giving his days to India, and his nights to the inexorable demands of the Treasury whip, he could devote a few hours to the *Edinburgh Review* only by rising at five when the rules of the House of Commons had allowed him to get to bed betimes on the previous evening. Yet, under these conditions, he contrived to provide Mr. Napier with the highly finished articles on Horace Walpole and Lord Chatham, and to gratify a political opponent who was destined to be a life-long friend by his kindly criticism and spirited summary of Lord Mahon's "History of the War of the Succession in Spain." And, in the "Friendship's Offering" of 1833, one of those mawkish annual publications of the album species which were then in fashion, appeared his poem of "The Armada;" whose swinging couplets read as if somewhat out of place in the company of such productions as "The Mysterious Stranger; or, The Bravo of Banff;" "Away to the Greenwood, a Song;" and, "Lines on a Window that had been Frozen," beginning with,

> Pellucid pane, this morn on thee
> My fancy shaped both tower and tree.

To Hannah and Margaret Macaulay.

Bath, June 10th, 1832.

My dear Sisters,—Every thing has gone wrong with me. The people at Calne fixed Wednesday for my re-election on taking office; the very day on which I was to have been at a public dinner at Leeds. I shall therefore remain here till Wednesday morning, and read Indian politics in quiet. I am already deep in Zemindars, Ryots, Polygars, Courts of Phoujdary, and Courts of Nizamut Adawlut. I can tell you which of the native powers are subsidiary and which independent, and read you lectures of an hour on our diplomatic transactions at the courts of Lucknow, Nagpore, Hydrabad, and Poonah. At Poonah, indeed, I need not tell you that there is no court; for the Paishwa, as you are doubtless aware, was deposed by Lord Hastings in the Pindarree war. Am I not in fair training to be as great a bore as if I had myself been in India—that is to say, as great a bore as the greatest?

I am leading my watering-place life here; reading, writing, and walking all day; speaking to nobody but the waiter and the chamber-maid; solitary in a great crowd, and content with solitude. I shall be in London again on Thursday, and shall also be an M.P. From that day you may send your letters as freely as ever; and pray do not be sparing of them. Do you read any novels at Liverpool? I should fear that the good Quakers would twitch them out of your hands, and appoint their portion in the fire. Yet probably you have some safe place, some box, some drawer with a key, wherein a marble-covered book may lie for Nancy's Sunday reading. And, if you do not read novels, what do you read! How does Schiller go on? I have sadly neglected Calderon; but whenever I have a month to spare, I shall carry my conquests far and deep into Spanish literature. Ever yours, T. B. M.

To Hannah and Margaret Macaulay.

London, July 2d, 1832.

MY DEAR SISTERS,—I am, I think, a better correspondent than you two put together. I will venture to say that I have written more letters by a good many than I have received, and this with India and the *Edinburgh Review* on my hands; the "Life of Mirabeau" to be criticised; the Rajah of Travancore to be kept in order; and the bad money, which the Emperor of the Burmese has had the impudence to send us by way of tribute, to be exchanged for better. You have nothing to do but to be good, and write. Make no excuses, for your excuses are contradictory. If you see sights, describe them; for then you have subjects. If you stay at home, write; for then you have time. Remember that I never saw the cemetery or the railroad. Be particular, above all, in your accounts of the Quakers. I enjoin this especially on Nancy; for from Meg I have no hope of extracting a word of truth.

I dined yesterday at Holland House: all lords except myself. Lord Radnor, Lord Poltimore, Lord King, Lord Russell, and his uncle Lord John. Lady Holland was very gracious, praised my article on Burleigh to the skies, and told me, among other things, that she had talked on the preceding day for two hours with Charles Grant upon religion, and had found him very liberal and tolerant. It was, I suppose, the cholera which sent her ladyship to the only saint in the ministry for ghostly counsel. Poor Macdonald's case was most undoubtedly cholera. It is said that Lord Amesbury also died of cholera, though no very strange explanation seems necessary to account for the death of a man of eighty-four. Yesterday it was rumored that the three Miss Molyneuxes, of whom, by-the-way, there are only two, were all dead in the same way; that the Bishop of Worcester and Lord Barham were no more; and many other foolish stories. I do not believe there is the slightest ground for uneasiness, though Lady Holland apparently considers the case so serious that she has taken her conscience out of Allen's keeping and put it into the hands of Charles Grant.

Here I end my letter; a great deal too long already for so busy a man to write, and for such careless correspondents to receive.

T. B. M.

To Hannah and Margaret Macaulay.

London, July 6th, 1832.

Be you Foxes, be you Pitts,
You must write to silly chits.
Be you Tories, be you Whigs,
You must write to sad young gigs.

> On whatever board you are—
> Treasury, Admiralty, War,
> Customs, Stamps, Excise, Control—
> Write you must, upon my soul.

So sings the Judicious Poet: and here I sit in my parlor, looking out on the Thames, and divided, like Garrick in Sir Joshua's picture, between Tragedy and Comedy—a letter to you, and a bundle of papers about Hydrabad, and the firm of Palmer & Co., late bankers to the Nizan.

Poor Sir Walter Scott is going back to Scotland by sea to-morrow. All hope is over; and he has a restless wish to die at home. He is many thousand pounds worse than nothing. Last week he was thought to be so near his end that some people went, I understand, to sound Lord Althorp about a public funeral. Lord Althorp said, very like himself, that if public money was to be laid out, it would be better to give it to the family than to spend it in one day's show. The family, however, are said to be not ill off.

I am delighted to hear of your proposed tour, but not so well pleased to be told that you expect to be bad correspondents during your stay at Welsh inns. Take pens and ink with you, if you think that you shall find none at The Bard's Head, or The Glendower Arms. But it will be too bad if you send me no letters during a tour which will furnish so many subjects. Why not keep a journal, and minute down in it all that you see and hear? and remember that I charge you, as the venerable circle charged Miss Byron, to tell me of every person who "regards you with an eye of partiality."

What can I say more? as the Indians end their letters. Did not Lady Holland tell me of some good novels? I remember "Henry Masterton," three volumes, an amusing story and a happy termination. Smuggle it in, next time that you go to Liverpool, from some circulating library; and deposit it in a lock-up place out of the reach of them that are clothed in drab; and read it together at the curling hour.

My article on Mirabeau will be out in the forthcoming number. I am not a good judge of my own compositions, I fear; but I think that it will be popular. A Yankee has written to me to say that an edition of my works is about to be published in America with my life prefixed, and that he shall be obliged to me to tell him when I was born, whom I married, and so forth. I guess I must answer him slick right away. For, as the Judicious Poet observes,

> Though a New England man lolls back in his chair,
> With a pipe in his mouth, and his legs in the air,
> Yet surely an Old England man such as I
> To a kinsman by blood should be civil and spry.

How I run on in quotation! But when I begin to cite the verses of our great writers I never can stop. Stop I must, however. Yours, T. B. M.

To Hannah and Margaret Macaulay.

London, July 18th, 1832.

My dear Sisters,—I have heard from Napier. He speaks rapturously of my article on Dumont,* but sends me no money. Allah blacken his face! as the Persians say. He has not yet paid me for Burleigh.

We are worked to death in the House of Commons, and we are henceforth to sit on Saturdays. This, indeed, is the only way to get through our business. On Saturday next we shall, I hope, rise before seven, as I am engaged to dine on that day with pretty, witty Mrs. ——. I fell in with her at Lady Grey's great crush, and found her very agreeable. Her husband is nothing in society. Rogers has some very good stories about their domestic happiness—stories confirming a theory of mine which, as I remember, made you very angry. When they first married, Mrs. —— treated her husband with great respect. But, when his novel came out and failed completely, she changed her conduct, and has, ever since that unfortunate publication, hen-pecked the poor author unmercifully. And the case, says Rogers, is the harder, because it is suspected that she wrote part of the book herself. It is like the

* Dumont's "Life of Mirabeau." See the "Miscellaneous Writings of Lord Macaulay."

scene in Milton where Eve, after tempting Adam, abuses him for yielding to temptation. But do you not remember how I told you that much of the love of women depended on the eminence of men? And do you not remember how, on behalf of your sex, you resented the imputation?

As to the present state of affairs abroad and at home, I can not sum it up better than in these beautiful lines of the poet:

Peel is preaching, and Croker is lying.
The cholera's raging, the people are dying.
When the House is the coolest, as I am alive,
The thermometer stands at a hundred and five.
We debate in a heat that seems likely to burn us,
Much like the three children who sung in the furnace.
The disorders at Paris have not ceased to plague us:
Don Pedro, I hope, is ere this on the Tagus:
In Ireland no tithe can be raised by a parson:
Mr. Smithers is just hanged for murder and arson:
Dr. Thorpe has retired from the Lock, and 'tis said
That poor little Wilks will succeed in his stead.

Ever yours, T. B. M.

To Hannah and Margaret Macaulay.

London, July 21st, 1832.

MY DEAR SISTERS,—I am glad to find that there is no chance of Nancy's turning Quaker. She would, indeed, make a queer kind of female Friend.

What the Yankees will say about me I neither know nor care. I told them the dates of my birth, and of my coming into Parliament. I told them also that I was educated at Cambridge. As to my early bon-mots, my crying for holidays, my walks to school through showers of cats and dogs, I have left all those for the "Life of the late Right Honorable Thomas Babington Macaulay, with large extracts from his correspondence, in two volumes, by the Very Rev. J. Macaulay, Dean of Durham, and Rector of Bishopsgate, with a superb portrait from the picture by Pickersgill in the possession of the Marquis of Lansdowne."

As you like my verses, I will some day or other write you a whole rhyming letter. I wonder whether any man ever wrote doggerel so easily. I run it off just as fast as my pen can move, and that is faster by about three words in a minute than any other pen that I know. This comes of a school-boy habit of writing verses all day long. Shall I tell you the news in rhyme? I think I will send you a regular sing-song gazette.

We gained a victory last night as great as e'er was known.
We beat the opposition upon the Russian loan.
They hoped for a majority, and also for our places.
We won the day by seventy-nine. You should have seen their faces.
Old Croker, when the shout went down our rank, looked blue with rage.
You'd have said he had the cholera in the spasmodic stage.
Dawson was red with ire as if his face were smeared with berries;
But of all human visages the worst was that of Herries.
Though not his friend, my tender heart I own could not but feel
A little for the misery of poor Sir Robert Peel!
But hang the dirty Tories! and let them starve and pine!
Huzza for the majority of glorious seventy-nine!

Ever yours, T. B. M.

To Hannah and Margaret Macaulay.

House of Commons Smoking-room, July 23d, 1832.

MY DEAR SISTERS,—I am writing here, at eleven at night, in this filthiest of all filthy atmospheres, and in the vilest of all vile company; with the smell of tobacco in my nostrils, and the ugly, hypocritical face of Lieutenant —— before my eyes. There he sits writing opposite to me. To whom, for a ducat? To some secretary of an Hibernian Bible Society; or to some old woman who gives cheap tracts, instead of blankets, to the starving peasantry of Connemara; or to some good Protestant lord who bullies his Popish tenants. Reject not my letter, though it is redolent of cigars and genuine pigtail; for this is the room—

The room—but I think I'll describe it in rhyme,
That smells of tobacco and chloride of lime.
The smell of tobacco was always the same:
But the chloride was brought since the cholera came.

But I must return to prose, and tell you all that has fallen out since I wrote last. I have been dining with the Listers, at Knightsbridge. They are in a very nice house next, or almost next, to that which the Wilberforces had. We had quite a family party. There were George Villiers, and Hyde Villiers, and Edward Villiers. Charles was not there. George and Hyde rank very high in my opinion. I liked their behavior to their sister much. She seems to be the pet of the whole family; and it is natural that she should be so. Their manners are softened by her presence; and any roughness and sharpness which they have in intercourse with men vanish at once. They seem to love the very ground that she treads on; and she is undoubtedly a charming woman—pretty, clever, lively, and polite.

I was asked yesterday evening to go to Sir John Burke's to meet another heroine who was very curious to see me. Whom do you think? Lady Morgan. I thought, however, that, if I went, I might not improbably figure in her next novel; and, as I am not ambitious of such an honor, I kept away. If I could fall in with her at a great party, where I could see unseen and hear unheard, I should very much like to make observations on her; but I certainly will not, if I can help it, meet her face to face, lion to lioness.

That confounded, chattering —— has just got into an argument about the Church with an Irish papist who has seated himself at my elbow; and they keep such a din that I can not tell what I am writing. There they go. The lord lieutenant—the Bishop of Derry—Magee—O'Connell—your Bible meetings—your Agitation meetings—the propagation of the Gospel—Maynooth College—the Seed of the Woman shall bruise the Serpent's head. My dear lieutenant, you will not only bruise but break my head with your clatter. Mercy! mercy! However, here I am at the end of my letter, and I shall leave the two demoniacs to tear each other to pieces.

Ever yours, T. B. M.

To Hannah and Margaret Macaulay.

Library of the H. of C., July 30th, 1832, 11 o'clock at night.

My dear Sisters,—Here I am. Daniel Whittle Harvey is

speaking: the House is thin; the subject is dull; and I have stolen away to write to you. Lushington is scribbling at my side. No sound is heard but the scratching of our pens, and the ticking of the clock. We are in a far better atmosphere than in the smoking-room, whence I wrote to you last week; and the company is more decent, inasmuch as that naval officer, whom Nancy blames me for describing in just terms, is not present.

By-the-bye, you know doubtless the lines which are in the mouth of every member of Parliament, depicting the comparative merits of the two rooms. They are, I think, very happy.

If thou goest into the smoking-room
Three plagues will thee befall—
The chloride of lime, the tobacco-smoke,
And the captain, who's worst of all—
The canting sea-captain,
The prating sea-captain,
The captain, who's worst of all.

If thou goest into the library
Three good things will thee befall—
Very good books, and very good air,
And M*c**l*y, who's best of all—
The virtuous M*c**l*y,
The prudent M*c**l*y,
M*c**l*y, who's best of all.

Oh, how I am worked! I never see Fanny from Sunday to Sunday. All my civilities wait for that blessed day; and I have so many scores of visits to pay that I can scarcely find time for any of that Sunday reading in which, like Nancy, I am in the habit of indulging. Yesterday, as soon as I was fixed in my best and had breakfasted, I paid a round of calls to all my friends who had the cholera. Then I walked to all the clubs of which I am a member to see the newspapers. The first of these two works you will admit to be a work of mercy; the second, in a political man, one of necessity. Then, like a good brother, I walked under a burning sun to Kensington to ask Fanny how she did, and staid there two hours. Then I went to Knightsbridge to call on Mrs. Lister, and chatted with her till it was time to go and dine at the Athenæum. Then I dined, and after dinner, like a good young man, I sat and read Bishop Heber's journal till bed-time. There is a Sunday for you! I think that I excel in the diary line. I will keep a journal, like the bishop, that my memory may

Smell sweet and blossom in the dust.

Next Sunday I am to go to Lord Lansdowne's at Richmond, so that I hope to have something to tell you. But on second thoughts I will tell you nothing, nor ever will write to you again, nor ever speak to you again. I have no pleasure in writing to undutiful sisters. Why do you not send me longer letters? But I am at the end of my paper, so that I have no more room to scold. Ever yours, T. B. M.

To Hannah and Margaret Macaulay.

London, August 14th, 1832.

My dear Sisters,—Our work is over at last; not, however, till it has half killed us all.* On Saturday we met for the last time, I hope, on business. When the House rose, I set off for Holland House. We had a small party, but a very distinguished one. Lord Grey, the Chancellor, Lord Palmerston, Luttrell, and myself were the only guests. Allen was of course at the end of the table, carving the dinner and sparring with my lady. The dinner was not so good as usual; for the French cook was ill; and her ladyship kept up a continued lamentation during the whole repast. I should never have

* On the 8th of August, 1832, Macaulay writes to Lord Mahon: "We are now strictly on duty. No furloughs even for a dinner engagement, or a sight of Taglioni's legs, can be obtained. It is very hard to keep forty members in the House. Sibthorpe and Leader are on the watch to count us out; and from six till two we never venture farther than the smoking-room without apprehension. In spite of all our exertions, the end of the session seems farther and farther off every day. If you would do me the favor of inviting Sibthorpe to Chevening Park you might be the means of saving my life, and that of thirty or forty more of us, who are forced to swallow the last dregs of the oratory of this Parliament; and nauseous dregs they are."

found out that every thing was not as it should be but for her criticisms. The soup was too salt; the cutlets were not exactly *comme il faut;* and the pudding was hardly enough boiled. I was amused to hear from the splendid mistress of such a house the same sort of apologies which —— made when her cook forgot the joint and sent up too small a dinner to table. I told Luttrell that it was a comfort to me to find that no rank was exempted from these afflictions.

They talked about ——'s marriage. Lady Holland vehemently defended the match; and, when Allen said that —— had caught a Tartar, she quite went off into one of her tantrums: "She a Tartar! Such a charming girl a Tartar! He is a very happy man, and your language is insufferable; insufferable, Mr. Allen." Lord Grey had all the trouble in the world to appease her. His influence, however, is very great. He prevailed on her to receive Allen again into favor, and to let Lord Holland have a slice of melon, for which he had been petitioning most piteously, but which she had steadily refused on account of his gout. Lord Holland thanked Lord Grey for his intercession. "Ah, Lord Grey, I wish you were always here. It is a fine thing to be prime minister." This tattle is worth nothing, except to show how much the people whose names will fill the history of our times resemble in all essential matters the quiet folks who live in Mecklenburg Square and Brunswick Square.

I slept in the room which was poor Mackintosh's. The next day, Sunday, —— came to dinner. He scarcely ever speaks in the society of Holland House. Rogers, who is the bitterest and most cynical observer of little traits of character that ever I knew, once said to me of him: "Observe that man. He never talks to men; he never talks to girls; but, when he can get into a circle of old tabbies, he is just in his element. He will sit clacking with an old woman for hours together. That always settles my opinion of a young fellow."

I am delighted to find that you like my review on Mirabeau, though I am angry with Margaret for grumbling at my Scriptural allusions, and still more angry with Nancy for denying my insight into character. It is one of my strong points. If she knew how far I see into hers, she would be ready to hang herself. Ever yours, T. B. M.

To Hannah and Margaret Macaulay.

London, August 16th, 1832.

MY DEAR SISTERS,—We begin to see a hope of liberation. To-morrow, or on Saturday at furthest, we hope to finish our business. I did not reach home till four this morning, after a most fatiguing and yet rather amusing night. What passed will not find its way into the papers, as the gallery was locked during most of the time. So I will tell you the story.

There is a bill before the House prohibiting those processions of Orangemen which have excited a good deal of irritation in Ireland. This bill was committed yesterday night. Shaw, the Recorder of Dublin, an honest man enough, but a bitter Protestant fanatic, complained that it should be brought forward so late in the session. Several of his friends, he said, had left London believing that the measure had been abandoned. It appeared, however, that Stanley and Lord Althorp had given fair notice of their intention; so that if the absent members had been mistaken, the fault was their own; and the House was for going on. Shaw said warmly that he would resort to all the means of delay in his power, and moved that the chairman should leave the chair. The motion was negatived by forty votes to two. Then the first clause was read. Shaw divided the House again on that clause. He was beaten by the same majority. He moved again that the chairman should leave the chair. He was beaten again. He divided on the second clause. He was beaten again. He then said that he was sensible that he was doing very wrong; that his conduct was unhandsome and vexatious; that he heartily begged our pardons; but that he had said that he would delay the bill as far as the forms of the House would permit; and that he must keep his word. Now came a discussion by which Nancy, if she had been in the ventilator,* might have

* A circular ventilator, in the roof of the House of Commons, was the only Ladies' Gallery that existed in the year 1832.

been greatly edified, touching the nature of vows; whether a man's promise given to himself—a promise from which nobody could reap any advantage, and which every body wished him to violate—constituted an obligation. Jephtha's daughter was a case in point, and was cited by somebody sitting near me. Peregrine Courtenay on one side of the House, and Lord Palmerston on the other, attempted to enlighten the poor Orangeman on the question of casuistry. They might as well have preached to any madman out of St. Luke's. "I feel," said the silly creature, "that I am doing wrong, and acting very unjustifiably. If gentlemen will forgive me, I will never do so again. But I must keep my word." We roared with laughter every time he repeated his apologies. The orders of the House do not enable any person absolutely to stop the progress of a bill in committee, but they enable him to delay it grievously. We divided seventeen times, and between every division this vexatious Irishman made us a speech of apologies and self-condemnation. Of the two who had supported him at the beginning of his freak one soon sneaked away. The other, Sibthorpe, staid to the last, not expressing remorse like Shaw, but glorying in the unaccommodating temper he showed and in the delay which he produced. At last the bill went through. Then Shaw rose; congratulated himself that his vow was accomplished; said that the only atonement he could make for conduct so unjustifiable was to vow that he would never make such a vow again; promised to let the bill go through its future stages without any more divisions; and contented himself with suggesting one or two alterations in the details. "I hint at these amendments," he said. "If the Secretary for Ireland approves of them, I hope he will not refrain from introducing them because they are brought forward by me. I am sensible that I have forfeited all claim to the favor of the House. I will not divide on any future stage of the bill." We were all heartily pleased with these events; for the truth was that the seventeen divisions occupied less time than a real hard debate would have done, and were infinitely more amusing. The oddest part of the business is that Shaw's frank, good-natured way of proceeding, absurd as it was, has made him popular. He was never so great a favorite with the House as after harassing it for two or three hours with the most frivolous opposition. This is a curious trait of the House of Commons. Perhaps you will find this long story, which I have not time to read over again, very stupid and unintelligible. But I have thought it my duty to set before you the evil consequences of making vows rashly and adhering to them superstitiously; for in truth, my Christian brethren, or rather my Christian sisters, let us consider, etc., etc., etc.

But I reserve the sermon on promises, which I had intended to preach, for another occasion. Ever yours, T. B. M.

To Hannah and Margaret Macaulay.

London, August 17th, 1832.

My dear Sisters,—I brought down my story of Holland House to dinner-time on Saturday evening. To resume my narrative, I slept there on Sunday night. On Monday morning, after breakfast, I walked to town with Luttrell, whom I found a delightful companion. Before we went, we sat and chatted with Lord Holland in the library for a quarter of an hour. He was very entertaining. He gave us an account of a visit which he paid long ago to the court of Denmark, and of King Christian, the madman, who was at last deprived of all real share in the government on account of his infirmity. "Such a Tom of Bedlam I never saw," said Lord Holland. "One day the Neapolitan Embassador came to the levee, and made a profound bow to his majesty. His majesty bowed still lower. The Neapolitan bowed down his head almost to the ground; when, behold! the king clapped his hands on his excellency's shoulders, and jumped over him like a boy playing at leap-frog. Another day the English Embassador was sitting opposite the king at dinner. His majesty asked him to take wine. The glasses were filled. The embassador bowed, and put the wine to his lips. The king grinned hideously, and threw his wine into the face of one of the footmen. The other guests kept the most profound gravity; but the Englishman, who had but lately come to Copenhagen, though a practiced diplomatist, could not help giving some signs of astonishment. The king immediately addressed him in French: 'Eh, mais, Monsieur l'Envoyé d'Angleterre, qu'avez-vous donc? Pourquoi riez-vous? Est-ce qu'il y ait quelque chose qui vous ait diverti? Faites-moi le plaisir de me l'indiquer. J'aime beaucoup les ridicules.'"

Parliament is up at last. We official men are now left alone at the West End of London, and are making up for our long confinement in the mornings by feasting together at night. On Wednesday I dined with Labouchere at his official residence in Somerset House. It is well that he is a bachelor; for he tells me that the ladies, his neighbors, make bitter complaints of the unfashionable situation in which they are cruelly obliged to reside gratis. Yesterday I dined with Will Brougham, and an official party, in Mount Street. We are going to establish a Club to be confined to members of the House of Commons in place under the present Government, who are to dine together weekly at Grillon's Hotel, and to settle the affairs of the state better, I hope, than our masters at their cabinet dinners. Ever yours, T. B. M.

To Hannah M. Macaulay.

London, September 20th, 1832.

My dear Sister,—I am at home again from Leeds, where every thing is going on as well as possible. I, and most of my friends, feel sanguine as to the result. About half my day was spent in speaking, and hearing other people speak; in squeezing and being squeezed; in shaking hands with people whom I never saw before, and whose faces and names I forget within a minute after being introduced to them. The rest was passed in conversation with my leading friends, who are very honest, substantial manufacturers. They feed me on roast-beef and Yorkshire pudding; at night they put me into capital bedrooms; and the only plague which they give me is that they are always begging me to mention some food or wine for which I have a fancy, or some article of comfort and convenience which I may wish them to procure.

I traveled to town with a family of children who eat without intermission from Market Harborough, where they got into the coach, to the Peacock at Islington, where they got out of it. They breakfasted as if they had fasted all the preceding day. They dined as if they had never breakfasted. They eat on the road one large basket of sandwiches, another of fruit, and a boiled fowl: besides which there was not an orange-girl, or an old man with cakes, or a boy with filberts, who came to the coach-side when we stopped to change horses, of whom they did not buy something.

I am living here by myself, with no society, or scarcely any, except my books. I read a play of Calderon before I breakfast; then look over the newspaper; frank letters; scrawl a line or two to a foolish girl in Leicestershire; and walk to my office. There I stay till near five, examining claims of money-lenders on the native sovereigns of India, and reading Parliamentary papers. I am beginning to understand something about the Bank, and hope, when next I go to Rothley Temple, to be a match for the whole firm of Mansfield and Babington on questions relating to their own business. When I leave the board, I walk for two hours; then I dine; and I end the day quietly over a basin of tea and a novel.

On Saturday I go to Holland House, and stay there till Monday. Her ladyship wants me to take up my quarters almost entirely there; but I love my own chambers and independence, and am neither qualified nor inclined to succeed Allen in his post. On Friday week, that is to-morrow week, I shall go for three days to Sir George Philips's, at Weston, in Warwickshire. He has written again in terms half complaining; and, though I can ill spare time for the visit, yet, as he was very kind to me when his kindness was of some consequence to me, I can not, and will not, refuse. Ever yours,

T. B. M.

To Hannah M. Macaulay.

London, September 25th, 1832.

My dear Sister,—I went on Saturday to Holland House, and staid there Sunday. It was legitimate Sabbath employment—visiting the sick—which, as you well know, always stands first among the works of mercy enumerated in good books. My lord was ill, and my lady thought herself so. He was, during the greater part of the day, in bed. For a few hours he lay on his sofa, wrapped in flannels. I sat by him about twenty minutes, and was then ordered away. He was very weak and languid; and, though the torture of the gout was over, was still in pain; but he retained all his courage, and all his sweetness of temper. I told his sister that I did not think that he was suffering much. "I hope not," said she; "but it is impossible to judge by what he says; for through the sharpest pain of the attack he never complained." I admire him more, I think, than any man whom I know. He is only fifty-seven or fifty-eight. He is precisely the man to whom health would be particularly valuable, for he has the keenest zest for those pleasures which health would enable him to enjoy. He is, however, an invalid and a cripple. He passes some weeks of every year in extreme torment. When he is in his best health he can only limp a hundred yards in a day. Yet he never says a cross word. The sight of him spreads good humor over the face of every one who comes near him. His sister, an excellent old maid as ever lived, and the favorite of all the young people of her acquaintance, says that it is quite a pleasure to nurse him. She was reading "The Inheritance" to him as he lay in bed, and he enjoyed it amazingly. She is a famous reader; more quiet and less theatrical than most famous readers, and therefore the fitter for the bedside of a sick man. Her ladyship had fretted herself into being ill, could eat nothing but the breast of a partridge, and was frightened out of her wits by hearing a dog howl. She was sure that this noise portended her death, or my lord's. Toward the evening, however, she brightened up, and was in very good spirits. My visit was not very lively. They dined at four, and the company was, as you may suppose at this season, but scanty. Charles Greville, commonly called, Heaven knows why, Punch Greville, came on the Saturday. Byng, named from his hair Poodle Byng, came on the Sunday. Allen, like the poor, we had with us always. I was grateful, however, for many pleasant evenings passed there when London was full and Lord Holland out of bed. I therefore did my best to keep the house alive. I had the library and the delightful gardens to myself during most of the day, and I got through my visit very well.

News you have in the papers. Poor Scott is gone; and I can not be sorry for it. A powerful mind in ruins is the most heart-breaking thing which it is possible to conceive. Ferdinand of Spain is gone too; and, I fear, old Mr. Stephen is going fast. I am safe at Leeds. Poor Hyde Villiers is very ill. I am seriously alarmed about him. Kindest love to all. Ever yours,

T. B. M.

To Hannah M. Macaulay.

Weston House, September 29th, 1832.

My dear Sister,—I came hither yesterday, and found a handsome house, pretty grounds, and a very kind host and hostess. The house is really very well planned. I do not know that I have ever seen so happy an imitation of the domestic architecture of Elizabeth's reign. The oriels, towers, terraces, and battlements are in the most perfect keeping; and the building is as convenient within as it is picturesque without. A few weather-stains, or a few American creepers, and a little ivy, would make it perfect: and all that will come, I suppose, with time. The terrace is my favorite spot. I always liked "the trim gardens" of which Milton speaks, and thought that Brown and his imitators went too far in bringing forests and sheep-walks up to the very windows of drawing-rooms.

I came through Oxford. It was as beautiful a day as the second day of our visit, and the High Street was in all its glory. But it made me quite sad to find myself there without you and Margaret. All my old Oxford associations are gone. Oxford, instead of being, as it used to be, the magnificent old city of the seventeenth century—still preserving its antique character among the improvements of modern times, and exhibiting in the midst of upstart Birminghams and Manchesters the same aspect which it wore when Charles held his court at Christchurch, and Rupert led his cavalry over Magdalene Bridge—is now to me only the place where I was so happy with my little sisters. But I was restored to mirth, and even to indecorous mirth, by what happened after we had left the fine old place behind us. There was a young fellow of about five-and-twenty, mustached and smartly dressed, in the coach with me. He was not absolutely uneducated, for he was reading a novel, "The Hungarian Brothers," the whole way. We rode, as I told you, through the High Street. The coach stopped to dine; and this youth passed half an hour in the midst of that city of palaces. He looked about him with his mouth open as he re-entered the coach, and all the while that we were driving away past the Ratcliffe Library, the Great Court of All-Souls, Exeter, Lincoln, Trinity, Balliol, and St. John's. When we were about a mile on the road he spoke the first words that I had heard him utter. "That was a pretty town enough. Pray, sir, what is it called?" I could not answer him for laughing; but he seemed quite unconscious of his own absurdity. Ever yours, T. B. M.

During all the period covered by this correspondence the town of Leeds was alive with the agitation of a turbulent but not very dubious contest. Macaulay's relations with the electors whose votes he was courting are too characteristic to be omitted altogether from the story of his life, though the style of his speeches and manifestoes is more likely to excite the admiring envy of modern members of Parliament than to be taken as a model for their communications to their own constituents. This young politician, who depended on office for his bread, and on a seat in the House of Commons for office, adopted from the first an attitude of high and almost peremptory independence which would have sat well on a prime minister in his grand climacteric. The following letter (some passages of which have been here omitted and others slightly condensed) is strongly marked in every line with the personal qualities of the writer:

London, August 3d, 1832.

My dear Sir,—I am truly happy to find that the opinion of my friends at Leeds on the subject of canvassing agrees with that which I have long entertained. The practice of begging for votes is, as it seems to me, absurd, pernicious, and altogether at variance with the true principles of representative government. The suffrage of an elector ought not to be asked, or to be given, as a personal favor. It is as much for the interest of constituents to choose well as it can be for the interest of a candidate to be chosen. To request an honest man to vote according to his conscience is superfluous. To request him to vote against his conscience is an insult. The practice of canvassing is quite reasonable under a system in which men are sent to Parliament to serve themselves. It is the height of absurdity under a system under which men are sent to Parliament to serve the public. While we had only a mock representation, it was natural enough that this practice should be carried to a great extent. I trust it will soon perish with the abuses from which it sprung. I trust that the great and intelligent body of people who have obtained the elective franchise will see that seats in the House of Commons ought not to be given, like rooms in an almshouse, to urgency of solicitation; and that a man who surrenders his vote to caresses and supplications forgets his duty as much as if he sold it for a bank-note. I hope to see the day when an Englishman will think it as great an affront to be courted and fawned upon in his capacity of elector as in his capacity of juryman. He would be shocked at the thought of finding an unjust verdict because the plaintiff or the defendant had been very civil and pressing; and, if he would reflect, he would, I think, be equally shocked at the thought of voting for a candidate for whose public character he felt no esteem, merely because that candidate had called upon him, and begged very hard, and had shaken his hand very warmly. My conduct is before the electors of Leeds. My opinions shall on all occasions be stated to them with perfect frankness. If they approve that conduct, if they concur in those opinions, they ought, not for my sake, but for their own, to choose me as their member. To be so chosen I should indeed consider as a high and enviable honor; but I should think it no honor to be returned to Parliament by persons who, thinking me destitute of the requisite qualifications, had yet been wrought upon by cajolery and importunity to poll for me in despite of their better judgment.

I wish to add a few words touching a question which has lately been much canvassed; I mean the question of pledges. In this letter, and in every letter which I have written to my friends at Leeds, I have plainly declared my *opinions*. But I think it, at this conjuncture, my duty to declare that I will give *no pledges*. I will not bind myself to make or to support any particular motion. I will state as shortly as I can some of the reasons which have induced me to form this determination. The great beauty of the representative system is, that it unites the advantages of popular control with the advantages arising from a division of labor. Just as a physician understands medicine better than an ordinary man, just as a shoe-maker makes shoes better than an ordinary man, so a person whose life is passed in transacting affairs of state becomes a better statesman than an ordinary man. In politics, as well as every other department of life, the public ought to have the means of checking those who serve it. If a man finds that he derives no benefit from the prescription of his physician, he calls in another. If his shoes do not fit him, he changes his shoemaker. But when he has called in a physician of whom he hears a good report, and whose general practice he believes to be judicious, it would be absurd in him to tie down that physician to order particular pills and particular draughts. While he continues to be the customer of a shoe-maker, it would be absurd in him to sit by and mete every motion of that shoemaker's hand. And in the same manner, it would, I think, be absurd in him to require positive pledges, and to exact daily and hourly obedience, from his representative. My opinion is, that electors ought at first to choose cautiously; then to confide liberally; and, when the term for which they have selected their member has expired, to review his conduct equitably, and to pronounce on the whole taken together.

If the people of Leeds think proper to repose in me that confidence which is necessary to the proper discharge of the duties of a representative, I hope that I shall not abuse it. If it be their pleasure to fetter their members by positive promises, it is in their power to do so. I can only say that on such terms I can not conscientiously serve them.

I hope, and feel assured, that the sincerity with which I make this explicit declaration will, if it deprive me of the votes of my friends at Leeds, secure to me what I value far more highly, their esteem. Believe me ever, my dear sir,

Your most faithful servant, T. B. MACAULAY.

This frank announcement, taken by many as a slight, and by some as a downright challenge, produced remonstrances which, after the interval of a week, were answered by Macaulay in a second letter; worth reprinting, if it were only for the sake of his fine parody upon the popular cry which for two years past had been the watch-word of Reformers.

I was perfectly aware that the avowal of my feelings on the subject of pledges was not likely to advance my interest at Leeds. I was perfectly aware that many of my most respectable friends were likely to differ from me; and therefore I thought it the more necessary to make, uninvited, an explicit declaration of my feelings. If ever there was a time when public men were in an especial measure bound to speak *the truth, the whole truth, and nothing but the truth*, to the people, this is that time. Nothing is easier than for a candidate to avoid unpopular topics as long as possible, and when they are forced on him, to take refuge in evasive and unmeaning phrases. Nothing is easier than for him to give extravagant promises while an election is depending, and to forget them as soon as the return is made. I will take no such course. I do not wish to obtain a single vote on false pretenses. Under the old system I have never been the flatterer of the great. Under the new system I will not be the flatterer of the people. The truth, or what appears to me to be such, may sometimes be distasteful to those whose good opinion I most value. I shall nevertheless always abide by it, and trust to their good sense, to their second thoughts, to the force of reason, and the progress of time. If, after all, their decision should be unfavorable to me, I shall submit to that decision with fortitude and good humor. It is not necessary to my happiness that I should sit in Parliament; but it is necessary to my happiness that I should possess, in Parliament or out of Parliament, the consciousness of having done what is right.

Macaulay had his own ideas as to the limits within which constituents are justified in exerting their privilege of questioning a candidate; and, on the first occasion when those limits were exceeded, he made a notable example of the transgressor. During one of his public meetings, a voice was heard to exclaim from the crowd in the body of the hall, "An elector wishes to know the religious creed of Mr. Marshall and Mr. Macaulay." The last-named gentleman was on his legs in a moment. "Let that man stand up!" he cried. "Let him stand on a form, where I can see him!" The offender, who proved to be a Methodist preacher, was hoisted on to a bench by his indignant neighbors; nerving himself even in that terrible moment by a lingering hope that he might yet be able to hold his own. But the unhappy man had not a chance against Macaulay, who harangued him as if he were the living embodiment of religious intolerance and illegitimate curiosity. "I have heard with the greatest shame and sorrow the question which has been proposed to me; and with peculiar pain do I learn that this question was proposed by a minister of religion. I do most deeply regret that any person should think it necessary to make a meeting like this an arena for theological discussion. I will not be a party to turning this assembly to such a purpose. My answer is short, and in one word. Gentlemen, I am a Christian." At this declaration the delighted audience began to cheer; but Macaulay would have none of their applause. "This is no subject," he said, "for acclamation. I will say no more. No man shall speak of me as the person who, when this disgraceful inquisition was entered upon in an assembly of Englishmen, brought forward the most sacred subjects to be canvassed here, and be turned into a matter for hissing or for cheering. If on any future occasion it should happen that Mr. Carlile should favor any large meeting with his infidel attacks upon the Gospel, he shall not have it to say that I set the example. Gentlemen, I have done; I tell you, I will say no more; and if the person who has thought fit to ask this question has the feelings worthy of a teacher of religion, he will not, I think, rejoice that he has called me forth."

This ill-fated question had been prompted by a report, diligently spread through the town, that the Whig candidates were Unitarians; a report which, even if correct, would probably have done little to damage their electioneering prospects. There are few general remarks which so uniformly hold good as the observation that men are not willing to attend the religious worship of people who believe less than themselves, or to vote at elections for people who believe more than themselves. While the congregations at a high Anglican service are in part composed of Low-churchmen and Broad-churchmen, while Presbyterians and Wesleyans have no objection to a sound discourse from a divine of the Establishment, it is seldom the case that any but Unitarians are seen inside a Unitarian chapel. On the other hand, at the general election of 1874, when not a solitary Roman Catholic was returned throughout the length and breadth of the island of Great Britain, the Unitarians retained their long-acknowledged preeminence as the most overrepresented sect in the kingdom.

While Macaulay was stern in his refusal to gratify his electors with the customary blandishments, he gave them plenty of excellent political instruction; which he conveyed to them in rhetoric, not premeditated with the care that alone makes speeches readable after a lapse of years, but for this very reason all the more effective when the passion of the moment was pouring itself from his lips in a stream of faultless, but unstudied, sentences. A course of mobs, which turned Cobden into an orator, made of Macaulay a Parliamentary debater; and the ear and eye of the House of Commons soon detected, in his replies from the Treasury bench, welcome signs of the invaluable training that can be got nowhere except on the hustings and the platform. There is no better sample of Macaulay's extempore speaking than the first words which he addressed to his committee at Leeds after the Reform Bill had received the royal assent. "I find it difficult to express my gratification at seeing such an assembly convened at such a time. All the history of our own country, all the history of other countries, furnishes nothing parallel to it. Look at the great events in our own former history, and in every one of them which, for importance, we can venture to compare with the Reform Bill, we shall find something to disgrace and tarnish the achievement. It was by the assistance of French arms and of Roman bulls that King John was harassed into giving the Great Charter. In the times of Charles I., how much injustice, how much crime, how much bloodshed and misery, did it cost to assert the liberties of England! But in this event, great and important as it is in substance, I confess I think it still more important from the manner in which it has been achieved. Other countries have obtained deliverances equally signal and complete, but in no country has that deliverance been obtained with such perfect peace; so entirely within the bounds of the Constitution; with all the forms of law observed; the government of the country proceeding in its regular course; every man going forth unto his labor until the evening. France boasts of her three days of July, when her people rose, when barricades fenced the streets, and the entire population of the capital in arms successfully vindicated their liberties. They boast, and justly, of those three days of July; but I will boast of our ten days of May. We, too, fought a battle, but it was with moral arms. We, too, placed an impassable barrier between ourselves and military tyranny; but we fenced ourselves only with moral barricades. Not one crime committed, not one acre confiscated, not one life lost, not one instance of outrage or attack on the authorities or the laws. Our victory has not left a single family in mourning. Not a tear, not a drop of blood, has sullied the pacific and blameless triumph of a great people."

The Tories of Leeds, as a last resource, fell to denouncing Macaulay as a placeman: a stroke of superlative audacity in a party which, during eight-and-forty years, had been out of office for only fourteen months. It may well be imagined that he found plenty to say in his own defense. "The only charge which malice can prefer against me is that I am a placeman. Gentlemen, is it your wish that those persons who are thought worthy of the public confidence should never possess the confidence of the king? Is it your wish that no men should be ministers but those whom no populous places will take as their representatives? By whom, I ask, has the Reform Bill been carried? By ministers. Who have raised Leeds into the situation to return members to Parliament? It is by the strenuous efforts of a patriotic ministry that that great result has been produced. I should think that the Reform Bill had done little for the people, if under it the service of the people was not consistent with the service of the crown."

Just before the general election Hyde Villiers died, and the secretaryship to the Board of Control became vacant. Macaulay succeeded his old college friend in an office that gave him weighty responsibility, defined duties, and, as it chanced, exceptional opportunities for distinction. About the same time, an event occurred which touched him more nearly than could any possible turn of fortune in the world of politics. His sisters, Hannah and Margaret, had for some months been almost domesticated among a pleasant nest of villas which lie in the southern suburb of Liverpool, on Dingle Bank: a spot whose natural beauty nothing can spoil, until in the fullness of time its inevitable destiny shall convert it into docks. The young ladies were the guests of Mr. John Cropper, who belonged to the Society of Friends, a circumstance which readers who have got thus far into the Macaulay correspondence will doubtless have discovered for themselves. Before the visit was over, Margaret became engaged to the brother of her host, Mr. Edward Cropper, a man in every respect worthy of the personal esteem and the commercial prosperity which have fallen to his lot.

There are many who will be surprised at finding in Macaulay's letters, both now and hereafter, indications of certain traits in his disposition with which the world, knowing him only through his political actions and his published works, may perhaps be slow to credit him; but which, taking his life as a whole, were predominant in their power to affect his happiness and give matter for his thoughts. Those who are least partial to him will allow that his was essentially a virile intellect. He wrote, he thought, he spoke, he acted, like a man. The public regarded him as an impersonation of vigor, vivacity, and self-reliance; but his own family, together with one, and probably only one of his friends, knew that his affections were only too tender and his sensibilities only too acute. Others may well be loath to parade what he concealed; but a portrait of Macaulay from which those features were omitted would be imperfect to the extent of misrepresentation; and it must be acknowledged that, where he loved, he loved more entirely, and more exclusively, than was well for himself. It was improvident in him to concentrate such intensity of feeling upon relations who, however deeply they were attached to him, could not always be in a position to requite him with the whole of their time and the whole of their heart. He suffered much for that improvidence; but he was too just and too kind to permit that others should suffer with him; and it is not for one who obtained by inheritance a share of his inestimable affection to regret a weakness to which he considers himself by duty bound to refer.

How keenly Macaulay felt the separation from his sister it is impossible to do more than indicate. He never again recovered that tone of thorough boyishness which had been produced by a long, unbroken habit of gay and affectionate intimacy with those younger than himself; indulged in without a suspicion on the part of any concerned that it was in its very nature transitory and precarious. For the first time he was led to doubt whether his scheme of life was indeed a wise one; or, rather, he began to be aware that he had never laid out any scheme of life at all. But with that unselfishness which was the key to his character and to much of his career, (resembling in its quality what we sometimes admire in a woman, rather than what we ever detect in a man), he took successful pains to conceal his distress from those over whose happiness it otherwise could not have failed to cast a shadow.

"The attachment between brothers and sisters," he writes

in November, 1832, "blameless, amiable, and delightful as it is, is so liable to be superseded by other attachments that no wise man ought to suffer it to become indispensable to him. That women shall leave the home of their birth, and contract ties dearer than those of consanguinity, is a law as ancient as the first records of the history of our race, and as unchangeable as the constitution of the human body and mind. To repine against the nature of things, and against the great fundamental law of all society, because, in consequence of my own want of foresight, it happens to bear heavily on me, would be the basest and most absurd selfishness.

"I have still one more stake to lose. There remains one event for which, when it arrives, I shall, I hope, be prepared. From that moment, with a heart formed, if ever any man's heart was formed, for domestic happiness, I shall have nothing left in this world but ambition. There is no wound, however, which time and necessity will not render endurable: and, after all, what am I more than my fathers—than the millions and tens of millions who have been weak enough to pay double price for some favorite number in the lottery of life, and who have suffered double disappointment when their ticket came up a blank?"

To Hannah M. Macaulay.

Leeds, December 12th, 1832.

MY DEAR SISTER,—The election here is going on as well as possible. To-day the poll stands thus:

Marshall, 1804.........Macaulay, 1792.........Sadler, 1353.

The probability is that Sadler will give up the contest. If he persists, he will be completely beaten. The voters are under 4000 in number; those who have already polled are 3100; and about 500 will not poll at all. Even if we were not to bring up another man, the probability is that we should win. On Sunday morning early I hope to be in London; and I shall see you in the course of the day.

I had written thus far when your letter was delivered to me. I am sitting in the midst of two hundred friends, all mad with exultation and party spirit, all glorying over the Tories, and thinking me the happiest man in the world. And it is all that I can do to hide my tears, and to command my voice, when it is necessary for me to reply to their congratulations. Dearest, dearest sister, you alone are now left to me. Whom have I on earth but thee? But for you, in the midst of all these successes, I should wish that I were lying by poor Hyde Villiers. But I can not go on. I am wanted to write an address to the electors; and I shall lay it on Sadler pretty heavily. By what strange fascination is it that ambition and resentment exercise such power over minds which ought to be superior to them? I despise myself for feeling so bitterly toward this fellow as I do. But the separation from dear Margaret has jarred my whole temper. I am cried up here to the skies as the most affable and kind-hearted of men, while I feel a fierceness and restlessness within me quite new and almost inexplicable. Ever yours, T. B. M.

To Hannah M. Macaulay.

London, December 24th, 1832.

My dear Sister,—I am much obliged to you for your letter, and am gratified by all its contents, except what you say about your own cough. As soon as you come back, you shall see Dr. Chambers, if you are not quite well. Do not oppose me in this, for I have set my heart on it.

I dined on Saturday at Lord Essex's in Belgrave Square. But never was there such a take-in. I had been given to understand that his lordship's *cuisine* was superintended by the first French artists, and that I should find there all the luxuries of the "Almanach des Gourmands." What a mistake! His lordship is luxurious indeed, but in quite a different way. He is a true Englishman. Not a dish on his table but what Sir Roger de Coverley, or Sir Hugh Tyrold,* might have set before his guests. A huge haunch of venison on the sideboard; a magnificent piece of beef at the bottom of the table; and before my lord himself smoked, not a *dindon aux truffes*,

* The uncle of Miss Burney's Camilla.

but a fat roasted goose stuffed with sage and onions. I was disappointed, but very agreeably; for my tastes are, I fear, incurably vulgar, as you may perceive by my fondness for Mrs. Meeke's novels.

Our party consisted of Sharp; Lubbock; Watson, M.P. for Canterbury; and Rich, the author of "What will the Lords do?" who wishes to be M.P. for Knaresborough. Rogers was to have been of the party; but his brother chose that very day to die upon, so that poor Sam had to absent himself. The chancellor was also invited, but he had scampered off to pass his Christmas with his old mother in Westmoreland. We had some good talk, particularly about Junius's Letters. I learned some new facts which I will tell you when we meet. I am more and more inclined to believe that Francis was one of the people principally concerned. Ever yours, T. B. M.

On the 29th of January, 1833, commenced the first session of the Reformed Parliament. The main incidents of that session, so fruitful in great measures of public utility, belong to general history; if indeed Clio herself is not fated to succumb beneath the stupendous undertaking of turning Hansard into a narrative imbued with human interest. O'Connell—criticising the king's speech at vast length, and passing in turns through every mood from the most exquisite pathos to downright and undisguised ferocity—at once plunged the House into a discussion on Ireland, which alternately blazed and smoldered through four live-long nights. Sheil and Grattan spoke finely; Peel and Stanley admirably; Bulwer made the first of his successes, and Cobbett the second of his failures; but the longest and the loudest cheers were those which greeted each of the glowing periods in which Macaulay, as the champion of the Whig party,* met the great agitator face to

* "We are called base, and brutal, and bloody. Such are the epithets which the honorable and learned member for Dublin thinks it becoming to pour forth against the party to which he owes every political privilege that he enjoys. The time will come when history will do justice to the Whigs of England, and will faithfully relate how much they did and suffered for Ireland. I see on the benches near me men who might, by utter-

face with high, but not intemperate, defiance. In spite of this flattering reception, he seldom addressed the House. A subordinate member of a government, with plenty to do in his own department, finds little temptation, and less encouragement, to play the debater. The difference of opinion between the two Houses concerning the Irish Church Temporalities Bill, which constituted the crisis of the year, was the one circumstance that excited in Macaulay's mind any very lively emotions; but those emotions, being denied their full and free expression in the oratory of a partisan, found vent in the doleful prognostications of a despairing patriot which fill his letters throughout the months of June and July. His abstinence from the passing topics of parliamentary controversy obtained for him a friendly as well as an attentive hearing from both sides of the House whenever he spoke on his own subjects; and did much to smooth the progress of those immense and salutary reforms with which the Cabinet had resolved to accompany the renewal of the India Company's charter.

So rapid had been the march of events under that strange imperial system established in the East by the enterprise and

ing one word against Catholic Emancipation—nay, by merely abstaining from uttering a word in favor of Catholic Emancipation—have been returned to this House without difficulty or expense, and who, rather than wrong their Irish fellow-subjects, were content to relinquish all the objects of their honorable ambition, and to retire into private life with conscience and fame untarnished. As to one eminent person, who seems to be regarded with especial malevolence by those who ought never to mention his name without respect and gratitude, I will only say this, that the loudest clamor which the honorable and learned gentleman can excite against Lord Grey will be trifling when compared with the clamor which Lord Grey withstood in order to place the honorable and learned gentleman where he now sits. Though a young member of the Whig party, I will venture to speak in the name of the whole body. I tell the honorable and learned gentleman, that the same spirit which sustained us in a just contest for him will sustain us in an equally just contest against him. Calumny, abuse, royal displeasure, popular fury, exclusion from office, exclusion from Parliament, we were ready to endure them all, rather than that he should be less than a British subject. We never will suffer him to be more.

valor of three generations of our countrymen, that each of the periodical revisions of that system was, in effect, a revolution. The legislation of 1813 destroyed the monopoly of the India trade. In 1833, the time had arrived when it was impossible any longer to maintain the monopoly of the China trade, and the extinction of this remaining commercial privilege could not fail to bring upon the company commercial ruin. Skill and energy, and caution, however happily combined, would not enable rulers who were governing a population larger than that governed by Augustus, and making every decade conquests more extensive than the conquests of Trajan, to compete with private merchants in an open market. England, mindful of the inestimable debt which she owed to the great company, did not intend to requite her benefactors by imposing on them a hopeless task. Justice and expediency could be reconciled by one course, and one only—that of buying up the assets and liabilities of the company on terms the favorable character of which should represent the sincerity of the national gratitude. Interest was to be paid from the Indian exchequer at the rate of ten guineas a year on every hundred pounds of stock; the company was relieved of its commercial attributes, and became a corporation charged with the function of ruling Hindoostan; and its directors, as has been well observed, remained princes, but merchant-princes no longer.

The machinery required for carrying into effect this gigantic metamorphosis was embodied in a bill every one of whose provisions breathed the broad, the fearless, and the tolerant spirit with which Reform had inspired our counsels. The earlier sections placed the whole property of the company in trust for the crown, and enacted that "from and after the 22d day of April, 1834, the exclusive right of trading with the dominions of the Emperor of China and of trading in tea shall cease;" and then came clauses which threw open the whole continent of India as a place of residence for all subjects of his majesty; which pronounced the doom of slavery; and which ordained that no native of the British territories in the East should, "by reason only of his religion, place of birth, descent, or color, be disabled from holding any place, office, or employment." The measure was introduced by Mr. Charles Grant, the President of the Board of Control, and was read a second time on Wednesday, the 10th of July. On that occasion Macaulay defended the bill in a thin House; a circumstance which may surprise those who are not aware that on a Wednesday, and with an Indian question on the paper, Cicero replying to Hortensius would hardly draw a quorum. Small as it was, the audience contained Lord John Russell, Peel, O'Connell, and other masters in the parliamentary craft. Their unanimous judgment was summed up by Charles Grant, in words which every one who knows the House of Commons will recognize as being very different from the conventional verbiage of mutual senatorial flattery: "I must embrace the opportunity of expressing, not what I felt (for language could not express it), but of making an attempt to convey to the House my sympathy with it in its admiration of the speech of my honorable and learned friend: a speech which, I will venture to assert, has never been exceeded within these walls for the development of statesmanlike policy and practical good sense. It exhibited all that is noble in oratory; all that is sublime, I had almost said, in poetry; all that is truly great, exalted, and virtuous in human nature. If the House at large felt a deep interest in this magnificent display, it may judge of what were my emotions when I perceived in the hands of my honorable friend the great principles which he expounded glowing with fresh colors and arrayed in all the beauty of truth."

There is no praise more gratefully treasured than that which is bestowed by a generous chief upon a subordinate with whom he is on the best of terms. Macaulay to the end entertained for Lord Glenelg that sentiment of loyalty* which a man of honor and feeling will always cherish with regard to the statesman under whom he began his career as a servant of the crown. The secretary repaid the president for his un-

* The affinity between this sentiment, and that of the quæstor toward his first proconsul, so well described in the orations against Verres, is one among the innumerable points of resemblance between the public life of ancient Rome and modern England.

varying kindness and confidence by helping him to get the bill through committee with that absence of friction which is the pride and delight of official men. The vexed questions of Establishment and Endowment (raised by the clauses appointing bishops to Madras and Bombay, and balancing them with as many salaried Presbyterian chaplains) increased the length of the debates and the number of the divisions; but the Government carried every point by large majorities, and, with slight modifications in detail and none in principle, the measure became law with the almost universal approbation both of Parliament and the country.

To Hannah M. Macaulay.

House of Commons, Monday Night, half-past 12.

MY DEAR SISTER,—The papers will scarcely contain any account of what passed yesterday in the House of Commons in the middle of the day. Grant and I fought a battle with Briscoe and O'Connell in defense of the Indian people, and won it by 38 to 6.* It was a rascally claim of a dishonest agent of the company against the employers whom he had cheated, and sold to their own tributaries. The nephew of the original claimant has been pressing his case on the Board most vehemently. He is an attorney living in Russell Square, and very likely hears the word at St. John's Chapel. He hears it, however, to very little purpose; for he lies as much as if he went to hear a "cauld clatter of morality" at the parish church.

I remember that when you were at Leamington two years ago I used to fill my letters with accounts of the people with

* In his great Indian speech Macaulay referred to this affair, in a passage, the first sentence of which has, by frequent quotation, been elevated into an apothegm: "A broken head in Cold Bath Fields produces a greater sensation than three pitched battles in India. A few weeks ago we had to decide on a claim brought by an individual against the revenues of India. If it had been an English question, the walls would scarcely have held the members who would have flocked to the division. It was an Indian question; and we could scarcely, by dint of supplication, make a House."

whom I dined. High life was new to me then; and now it has grown so familiar that I should not, I fear, be able, as I formerly was, to select the striking circumstances. I have dined with sundry great folks since you left London, and I have attended a very splendid rout at Lord Grey's. I stole thither, at about eleven, from the House of Commons, with Stewart Mackenzie. I do not mean to describe the beauty of the ladies, nor the brilliancy of stars and uniforms. I mean only to tell you one circumstance which struck, and even affected me. I was talking to Lady Charlotte Lindsay, the daughter of Lord North, a great favorite of mine, about the apartments and the furniture, when she said, with a good deal of emotion: "This is an interesting visit to me. I have never been in this house for fifty years. It was here that I was born; I left it a child when my father fell from power in 1782, and I have never crossed the threshold since." Then she told me how the rooms seemed dwindled to her; how the staircase, which appeared to her in recollection to be the most spacious and magnificent that she had ever seen, had disappointed her. She longed, she said, to go over the garrets and rummage her old nursery. She told me how, in the No-Popery riots of 1780, she was taken out of bed at two o'clock in the morning. The mob threatened Lord North's house. There were soldiers at the windows, and an immense and furious crowd in Downing Street. She saw, she said, from her nursery the fires in different parts of London; but she did not understand the danger, and only exulted in being up at midnight. Then she was conveyed through the Park to the Horse Guards as the safest place; and was laid, wrapped up in blankets, on the table in the guard-room in the midst of the officers. "And it was such fun," she said, "that I have ever after had rather a liking for insurrections."

I write in the midst of a crowd. A debate on slavery is going on in the Commons; a debate on Portugal in the Lords. The door is slamming behind me every moment, and people are constantly going out and in. Here comes Vernon Smith. "Well, Vernon, what are they doing?" "Gladstone has just made a very good speech, and Howick is answering him."

"Ay, but in the House of Lords?" "They will beat us by twenty, they say." "Well, I do not think it matters much." "No; nobody out of the House of Lords cares either for Don Pedro or for Don Miguel."

There is a conversation between two official men in the Library of the House of Commons on the night of the 3d of June, 1833, reported word for word. To the historian three centuries hence this letter will be invaluable. To you, ungrateful as you are, it will seem worthless. Ever yours,

T. B. M.

To Hannah M. Macaulay.

Smoking-room of the House of Commons, June 6th, 1833.

MY DARLING,—Why am I such a fool as to write to a gypsy at Liverpool, who fancies that none is so good as she if she sends one letter for my three? A lazy chit whose fingers tire with penning a page in reply to a quire! There, miss, you read all the first sentence of my epistle, and never knew that you were reading verse. I have some gossip for you about the *Edinburgh Review.* Napier is in London, and has called on me several times. He has been with the publishers, who tell him that the sale is falling off; and in many private parties, where he hears sad complaints. The universal cry is that the long dull articles are the ruin of the *Review.* As to myself, he assures me that my articles are the only things which keep the work up at all. Longman and his partners correspond with about five hundred book-sellers in different parts of the kingdom. All these book-sellers, I find, tell them that the *Review* sells, or does not sell, according as there are, or are not, articles by Mr. Macaulay. So, you see, I, like Mr. Darcy,* shall not care how proud I am. At all events, I can not but be pleased to learn that, if I should be forced to depend on my pen for subsistence, I can command what price I choose.

The House is sitting; Peel is just down; Lord Palmerston is speaking; the heat is tremendous; the crowd stifling; and

* The central male figure in "Pride and Prejudice."

so here I am in the smoking-room, with three Repealers making chimneys of their mouths under my very nose.

> To think that this letter will bear to my Anna
> The exquisite scent of O'Connor's Havana!

You know that the Lords have been foolish enough to pass a vote* implying censure on the ministers. The ministers do not seem inclined to take it of them. The king has snubbed their lordships properly; and in about an hour, as I guess (for it is near eleven), we shall have come to a resolution in direct opposition to that agreed to by the Upper House. Nobody seems to care one straw for what the Peers say about any public matter. A resolution of the Court of Common Council, or of a meeting at Freemasons' Hall, has often made a greater sensation than this declaration of a branch of the Legislature against the Executive Government. The institution of the peerage is evidently dying a natural death.

I dined yesterday—where, and on what, and at what price, I am ashamed to tell you. Such scandalous extravagance and gluttony I will not commit to writing. I blush when I think of it. You, however, are not wholly guiltless in this matter. My nameless offense was partly occasioned by Napier; and I have a very strong reason for wishing to keep Napier in good humor. He has promised to be at Edinburgh when I take a certain damsel thither; to look out for very nice lodgings for us in Queen Street; to show us every thing and every body; and to see us as far as Dunkeld on our way northward, if we do go northward. In general I abhor visiting; but at Edinburgh we must see the people as well as the walls and windows; and Napier will be a capital guide. Ever yours,

T. B. M.

---

* On June 3d, 1833, a vote of censure on the Portuguese policy of the ministry was moved by the Duke of Wellington, and carried in the Lords by 79 votes to 69. On June 6th a counter-resolution was carried in the Commons by 361 votes to 98.

To Hannah M. Macaulay.

London, June 14th, 1833.

My dear Sister,—I do not know what you may have been told. I may have grumbled, for aught I know, at not having more letters from you; but as to being angry, you ought to know by this time what sort of anger mine is when you are its object.

You have seen the papers, I dare say, and you will perceive that I did not speak yesterday night.* The House was thin. The debate was languid. Grant's speech had done our work sufficiently for one night; and both he and Lord Althorp advised me to reserve myself for the second reading.

What have I to tell you? I will look at my engagement-book, to see where I am to dine. Friday, June 14th, Lord Grey; Saturday, June 15th, Mr. Boddington; Sunday, June 16th, Mr. S. Rice; Saturday, June 22d, Sir R. Inglis; Thursday, June 27th, the Earl of Ripon; Saturday, June 29th, Lord Morpeth.

Read, and envy, and pine, and die. And yet I would give a large slice of my quarter's salary, which is now nearly due, to be at the Dingle. I am sick of lords with no brains in their heads, and ladies with paint on their cheeks, and politics, and politicians, and that reeking furnace of a House. As the poet says,

> Oh! rather would I see this day
> My little Nancy well and merry,
> Than the blue ribbon of Earl Grey,
> Or the blue stockings of Miss Berry.

Margaret tells us that you are better, and better, and better. I want to hear that you are well. At all events, our Scotch tour will set you up. I hope, for the sake of the tour, that we shall keep our places; but I firmly believe that, before many days have passed, a desperate attempt will be made in the House of Lords to turn us out. If we stand the shock, we shall be firmer than ever. I am not without anxiety as to the

* The night of the first reading of the India Bill.

result: yet I believe that Lord Grey understands the position in which he is placed; and as for the king, he will not forget his last blunder,* I will answer for it, even if he should live to the age of his father.

But why plague ourselves about politics when we have so much pleasanter things to talk of? "The Parson's Daughter:" don't you like "The Parson's Daughter?" What a wretch Harbottle was! And Lady Frances, what a sad worldly woman! But Mrs. Harbottle, dear suffering angel! And Emma Lovel, all excellence! Dr. MacGopus you doubtless like; but you probably do not admire the Duchess and Lady Catherine. There is a regular coze over a novel for you! But, if you will have my opinion, I think it Theodore Hook's worst performance; far inferior to "The Surgeon's Daughter;" a set of fools making themselves miserable by their own nonsensical fancies and suspicions. Let me hear your opinion; for I will be sworn that,

> In spite of all the serious world,
> Of all the thumbs that ever twirled,
> Of every broadbrim-shaded brow,
> Of every tongue that e'er said "thou,"
> You still read books in marble covers
> About smart girls and dapper lovers.

But what folly I have been scrawling! I must go to work.

> I can not all day
> Be neglecting Madras,
> And slighting Bombay
> For the sake of a lass.

Kindest love to Edward, and to the woman who owns him.

Ever yours, T. B. M.

London, June 17th, 1833.

Dear Hannah,—All is still anxiety here. Whether the House of Lords will throw out the Irish Church Bill, whether

* This "last blunder" was the refusal of the king to stand by his ministers in May, 1832. Macaulay proved a bad prophet; for after an interval of only three years, William the Fourth repeated his blunder in an aggravated form.

the king will consent to create new peers, whether the Tories will venture to form a ministry, are matters about which we are all in complete doubt. If the ministry should really be changed, Parliament will, I feel quite sure, be dissolved. Whether I shall have a seat in the next Parliament I neither know nor care. I shall regret nothing for myself but our Scotch tour. For the public I shall, if this Parliament be dissolved, entertain scarcely any hopes. I see nothing before us but a frantic conflict between extreme opinions; a short period of oppression; then a convulsive reaction; and then a tremendous crash of the Funds, the Church, the Peerage, and the Throne. It is enough to make the most strenuous royalist lean a little to republicanism to think that the whole question between safety and general destruction may probably, at this most fearful conjuncture, depend on a single man whom the accident of his birth has placed in a situation to which certainly his own virtues or abilities would never have raised him.

The question must come to a decision, I think, within the fortnight. In the mean time the funds are going down, the newspapers are storming, and the faces of men on both sides are growing day by day more gloomy and anxious. Even during the most violent part of the contest for the Reform Bill, I do not remember to have seen so much agitation in the political circles. I have some odd anecdotes for you, which I will tell you when we meet. If the Parliament should be dissolved, the West Indian and East Indian bills are of course dropped. What is to become of the slaves? What is to become of the tea-trade? Will the negroes, after receiving the resolutions of the House of Commons promising them liberty, submit to the cart-whip? Will our merchants consent to have the trade with China, which has just been offered to them, snatched away? The Bank charter, too, is suspended. But that is comparatively a trifle. After all, what is it to me who is in or out, or whether those fools of Lords are resolved to perish, and drag the king to perish with them, in the ruin which they have themselves made? I begin to wonder what the fascination is which attracts men, who could sit over their tea and their books in their own cool, quiet room, to breathe bad air, hear bad speeches, lounge up and down the long gallery, and doze uneasily on the green benches till three in the morning. Thank God, these luxuries are not necessary to me. My pen is sufficient for my support, and my sister's company is sufficient for my happiness. Only let me see her well and cheerful; and let offices in Government, and seats in Parliament, go to those who care for them. If I were to leave public life to-morrow, I declare that, except for the vexation which it might give you and one or two others, the event would not be in the slightest degree painful to me. As you boast of having a greater insight into character than I allow to you, let me know how you explain this philosophical disposition of mine, and how you reconcile it with my ambitious inclinations. That is a problem for a young lady who professes knowledge of human nature.

Did I tell you that I dined at the Duchess of Kent's, and sat next that loveliest of women, Mrs. Littleton? Her husband, our new Secretary for Ireland, told me this evening that Lord Wellesley, who sat near us at the duchess's, asked Mrs. Littleton afterward who it was that was talking to her. "Mr. Macaulay." "Oh!" said the marquess, "I am very sorry I did not know it. I have a most particular desire to be acquainted with that man." Accordingly, Littleton has engaged me to dine with him, in order to introduce me to the marquess. I am particularly curious, and always was, to know him. He has made a great and splendid figure in history, and his weaknesses, though they make his character less worthy of respect, make it more interesting as a study. Such a blooming old swain I never saw; hair combed with exquisite nicety, a waistcoat of driven snow, and a star and garter put on with rare skill.

To-day we took up our resolutions about India to the House of Lords. The two Houses had a conference on the subject in an old Gothic room called the Painted Chamber. The painting consists in a mildewed daub of a woman in the niche of one of the windows. The Lords sat in little cocked hats along a table; and we stood uncovered on the other side, and delivered in our resolutions. I thought that before long it may be our turn to sit, and theirs to stand.

Ever yours, T. B. M.

London, June 21st, 1833.

DEAR HANNAH,—I can not tell you how delighted I was to learn from Fanny this morning that Margaret pronounces you to be as well as she could wish you to be. Only continue so, and all the changes of public life will be as indifferent to me as to Horatio. If I am only spared the misery of seeing you suffer, I shall be found

> A man that fortune's buffets and rewards
> Has ta'en with equal thanks.

Whether we are to have buffets or rewards is known only to Heaven and to the Peers. I think that their lordships are rather cowed. Indeed, if they venture on the course on which they lately seemed bent, I would not give sixpence for a coronet or a penny for a mitre.

I shall not read "The Repealers;" and I think it very impudent in you to make such a request. Have I nothing to do but to be your novel-taster? It is rather your duty to be mine. What else have you to do? I have read only one novel within the last week, and a most precious one it was: "The Invisible Gentleman." Have you ever read it? But I need not ask. No doubt it has formed part of your Sunday studies. A wretched, trumpery imitation of Godwin's worst manner. What a number of stories I shall have to tell you when we meet!—which will be, as nearly as I can guess, about the 10th or 12th of August. I shall be as rich as a Jew by that time.

> Next Wednesday will be quarter-day;
> And then, if I'm alive,
> Of sterling pounds I shall receive
> Three hundred seventy-five.
>
> Already I possess in cash
> Two hundred twenty-four,
> Besides what I have lent to John,
> Which makes up twenty more.

Also the man who editeth
The "Yellow and the Blue"
Doth owe me ninety pounds at least,
All for my last review.

So, if my debtors pay their debts,
You'll find, dear sister mine,
That all my wealth together makes
Seven hundred pounds and nine.

Ever yours, T. B. M.

The rhymes in which Macaulay unfolds his little budget derive a certain dignity and meaning from the events of the ensuing weeks. The unparalleled labors of the antislavery leaders were at length approaching a successful issue, and Lord Grey's Cabinet had declared itself responsible for the emancipation of the West Indian negroes. But it was already beginning to be known that the ministerial scheme, in its original shape, was not such as would satisfy even the more moderate Abolitionists. Its most objectionable feature was shadowed forth in the third of the resolutions with which Mr. Stanley, who had the question in charge, prefaced the introduction of his bill: "That all persons, now slaves, be entitled to be registered as apprenticed laborers, and to acquire thereby all the rights and privileges of freemen, subject to the restriction of laboring, for a time to be fixed by Parliament, for their present owners." It was understood that twelve years would be proposed as the period of apprenticeship; although no trace of this intention could be detected in the wording of the resolution. Macaulay, who thought twelve years far too long, felt himself justified in supporting the Government during the preliminary stages; but he took occasion to make some remarks indicating that circumstances might occur which would oblige him to resign office and adopt a line of his own.

As time went on, it became evident that his firmness would be put to the test; and a severe test it was. A rising statesman, whose prospects would be irremediably injured by abruptly quitting a government that seemed likely to be in power for the next quarter of a century; a zealous Whig, who shrunk from the very appearance of disaffection to his party; a man of sense, with no ambition to be called Quixotic; a member for a large constituency, possessed of only seven hundred pounds in the world when his purse was at its fullest; above all, an affectionate son and brother, now, more than ever, the main hope and reliance of those whom he held most dear—it may well be believed that he was not in a hurry to act the martyr. His father's affairs were worse than bad. The African firm, without having been reduced to declare itself bankrupt, had ceased to exist as a house of business; or existed only so far that for some years to come every penny that Macaulay earned, beyond what the necessities of life demanded, was scrupulously devoted to paying, and at length to paying off, his father's creditors: a dutiful enterprise in which he was assisted by his brother Henry,* a young man of high spirit and excellent abilities, who had recently been appointed one of the commissioners of arbitration in the prize courts at Sierra Leone.

The pressure of pecuniary trouble was now beginning to make itself felt even by the younger members of the family. About this time, or perhaps a little earlier, Hannah Macaulay writes thus to one of her cousins: "You say nothing about coming to us. You must come in good health and spirits. Our trials ought not greatly to depress us; for, after all, all we want is money, the easiest want to bear; and, when we have so many mercies—friends who love us and whom we love; no bereavements; and, above all (if it be not our own fault), a hope full of immortality—let us not be so ungrateful as to repine because we are without what in itself can not make our happiness."

Macaulay's colleagues, who, without knowing his whole story, knew enough to be aware that he could ill afford to give up office, were earnest in their remonstrances; but he answered shortly, and almost roughly: "I can not go counter to my

---

* Henry Macaulay married, in 1841, a daughter of his brother's old political ally, Lord Denman. He died at Boa Vista in 1846.

father. He has devoted his whole life to the question, and I can not grieve him by giving way when he wishes me to stand firm." During the crisis of the West India Bill, Zachary Macaulay and his son were in constant correspondence. There is something touching in the picture which these letters present of the older man (whose years were coming to a close in poverty, which was the consequence of his having always lived too much for others), discussing quietly and gravely how, and when, the younger was to take a step that in the opinion of them both would be fatal to his career: and this with so little consciousness that there was any thing heroic in the course which they were pursuing, that it appears never to have occurred to either of them that any other line of conduct could possibly be adopted.

London, July 22d, 1833.

My dear Father,—We are still very anxious here. The Lords, though they have passed the Irish Church Bill through its first stage, will very probably mutilate it in committee. It will then be for the ministers to decide whether they can with honor keep their places. I believe that they will resign if any material alteration should be made; and then every thing is confusion.

These circumstances render it very difficult for me to shape my course right with respect to the West India Bill, the second reading of which stands for this evening. I am fully resolved to oppose several of the clauses. But to declare my intention publicly, at a moment when the Government is in danger, would have the appearance of ratting. I must be guided by circumstances; but my present intention is to say nothing on the second reading. By the time that we get into committee the political crisis will, I hope, be over; the fate of the Church Bill will be decided one way or the other; and I shall be able to take my own course on the slavery question without exposing myself to the charge of deserting my friends in a moment of peril. Ever yours, affectionately,

T. B. Macaulay.

Having made up his mind as to what he should do, Macaulay set about it with as good a grace as is compatible with the most trying position in which a man, and especially a young man, can find himself. Carefully avoiding the attitude of one who bargains or threatens, he had given timely notice in the proper quarter of his intentions and his views. At length the conjuncture arrived when decisive action could no longer be postponed. On the 24th of July Mr. Thomas Fowell Buxton moved an amendment in committee, limiting the apprenticeship to the shortest period necessary for establishing the system of free labor. Macaulay, whose resignation was already in Lord Althorp's hands, made a speech which produced all the more effect as being inornate, and, at times, almost awkward. Even if deeper feelings had not restrained the range of his fancy and the flow of his rhetoric, his judgment would have told him that it was not the moment for an oratorical display. He began by entreating the House to extend to him that indulgence which it had accorded on occasions when he had addressed it "with more confidence and with less harassed feelings." He then, at some length, exposed the effects of the Government proposal. "In free countries the master has a choice of laborers, and the laborer has a choice of masters; but in slavery it is always necessary to give despotic power to the master. This bill leaves it to the magistrate to keep peace between master and slave. Every time that the slave takes twenty minutes to do that which the master thinks he should do in fifteen, recourse must be had to the magistrate. Society would day and night be in a constant state of litigation, and all differences and difficulties must be solved by a judicial interference."

He did not share in Mr. Buxton's apprehension of gross cruelty as a result of the apprenticeship. "The magistrate would be accountable to the Colonial Office, and the Colonial Office to the House of Commons, in which every lash which was inflicted under magisterial authority would be told and counted. My apprehension is that the result of continuing for twelve years this dead slavery—this state of society destitute of any vital principle—will be that the whole negro population will sink into weak and drawling inefficacy, and will be much less fit for liberty at the end of the period than at the commencement. My hope is that the system will die a natural death; that the experience of a few months will so establish its utter inefficiency as to induce the planters to abandon it, and to substitute for it a state of freedom. I have voted," he said, "for the second reading, and I shall vote for the third reading; but, while the bill is in committee, I shall join with other honorable gentlemen in doing all that is possible to amend it."

Such a declaration, coming from the mouth of a member of the Government, gave life to the debate, and secured to Mr. Buxton an excellent division, which under the circumstances was equivalent to a victory. The next day Mr. Stanley rose; adverted shortly to the position in which the ministers stood; and announced that the term of apprenticeship would be reduced from twelve years to seven. Mr. Buxton, who, with equal energy and wisdom, had throughout the proceedings acted as leader of the antislavery party in the House of Commons, advised his friends to make the best of the concession; and his counsel was followed by all those abolitionists who were thinking more of their cause than of themselves. It is worthy of remark that Macaulay's prophecy came true, though not at so early a date as he ventured to anticipate. Four years of the provisional system brought all parties to acquiesce in the premature termination of a state of things which denied to the negro the blessings of freedom, and to the planter the profits of slavery.

"The papers," Macaulay writes to his father, "will have told you all that has happened, as far as it is known to the public. The secret history you will have heard from Buxton. As to myself, Lord Althorp told me yesterday night that the Cabinet had determined not to accept my resignation. I have therefore the singular good luck of having saved both my honor and my place, and of having given no just ground of offense either to the Abolitionists or to my party friends. I have more reason than ever to say that honesty is the best policy."

This letter is dated the 27th of July. On that day week, Wilberforce was carried to his grave in Westminster Abbey.

"We laid him," writes Macaulay, "side by side with Canning, at the feet of Pitt, and within two steps of Fox and Grattan." He died with the Promised Land full in view. Before the end of August Parliament abolished slavery, and the last touch was put to the work that had consumed so many pure and noble lives. In a letter of congratulation to Zachary Macaulay, Mr. Buxton says: "Surely you have reason to rejoice. My sober and deliberate opinion is that you have done more toward this consummation than any other man. For myself, I take pleasure in acknowledging that you have been my tutor all the way through, and that I could have done nothing without you." Such was the spirit of these men, who, while the struggle lasted, were prodigal of health and ease; but who, in the day of triumph, disclaimed, each for himself, even that part of the merit which their religion allowed them to ascribe to human effort and self-sacrifice.

London, July 11th, 1833.

DEAR HANNAH,—I have been so completely overwhelmed with business for some days that I have not been able to find time for writing a line. Yesterday night we read the India Bill a second time. It was a Wednesday, and the reporters gave hardly any account of what passed. They always resent being forced to attend on that day, which is their holiday. I made the best speech, by general agreement, and in my own opinion, that I ever made in my life. I was an hour and three-quarters up; and such compliments as I had from Lord Althorp, Lord Palmerston, Lord John Russell, Wynne, O'Connell, Grant, the Speaker, and twenty other people, you never heard. As there is no report of the speech, I have been persuaded, rather against my will, to correct it for publication. I will tell you one compliment that was paid me, and which delighted me more than any other. An old member said to me, "Sir, having heard that speech may console the young people for never having heard Mr. Burke."*

* A Tory member said that Macaulay resembled both the Burkes: that he was like the first from his eloquence, and like the second from his stopping other people's mouths.

The Slavery Bill is miserably bad. I am fully resolved not to be dragged through the mire, but to oppose, by speaking and voting, the clauses which I think objectionable. I have told Lord Althorp this, and have again tendered my resignation. He hinted that he thought that the Government would leave me at liberty to take my own line, but that he must consult his colleagues. I told him that I asked for no favor; that I knew what inconvenience would result if official men were allowed to dissent from ministerial measures, and yet to keep their places; and that I should not think myself in the smallest degree ill-used if the Cabinet accepted my resignation. This is the present posture of affairs. In the mean time the two Houses are at daggers drawn. Whether the Government will last to the end of the session I neither know nor care. I am sick of boards, and of the House of Commons; and pine for a few quiet days, a cool country breeze, and a little chatting with my dear sister. Ever yours, T. B. M.

To Hannah M. Macaulay.

London, July 19th, 1833.

My dear Sister,—I snatch a few minutes to write a single line to you. We went into committee on the India Bill at twelve this morning, sat till three, and are just set at liberty for two hours. At five we recommence, and shall be at work till midnight. In the interval between three and five I have to dispatch the current business of the office, which, at present, is fortunately not heavy; to eat my dinner, which I shall do at Grant's; and to write a short scrawl to my little sister.

My work, though laborious, has been highly satisfactory. No bill, I believe, of such importance—certainly no important bill in my time—has been received with such general approbation. The very cause of the negligence of the reporters, and of the thinness of the House, is that we have framed our measure so carefully as to give little occasion for debate. Littleton, Denison, and many other members, assure me that they never remember to have seen a bill better drawn or better conducted.

On Monday night, I hope, my work will be over. Our

Bill will have been discussed, I trust, for the last time in the House of Commons; and, in all probability, I shall within forty-eight hours after that time be out of office. I am fully determined not to give way about the West India Bill; and I can hardly expect—I am sure I do not wish—that the ministers should suffer me to keep my place and oppose their measure. Whatever may befall me or my party, I am much more desirous to come to an end of this interminable session than to stay either in office or in Parliament. The Tories are quite welcome to take every thing, if they will only leave me my pen and my books, a warm fireside, and you chattering beside it. This sort of philosophy, an odd kind of cross between Stoicism and Epicureanism, I have learned, where most people unlearn all their philosophy—in crowded senates and fine drawing-rooms.

But time flies, and Grant's dinner will be waiting. He keeps open house for us during this fight. Ever yours,

T. B. M.

To Hannah M. Macaulay.

London, July 24th, 1833.

MY DEAR SISTER,—You will have seen by the papers that the West India debate on Monday night went off very quietly in little more than a hour. To-night we expect the great struggle, and I fear that, much against my inclination, I must bear a part in it. My resignation is in Lord Althorp's hands. He assures me that he will do his utmost to obtain for me liberty to act as I like on this question; but Lord Grey and Stanley are to be consulted, and I think it very improbable that they will consent to allow me so extraordinary a privilege. I know that, if I were minister, I would not allow such latitude to any man in office; and so I told Lord Althorp. He answered in the kindest and most flattering manner; told me that in office I had surpassed their expectations, and that, much as they wished to bring me in last year, they wished much more to keep me in now. I told him, in reply, that the matter was one for the ministers to settle purely with a view to their own interest; that I asked for no indulgence; that I could make no terms; and that what I would not do to serve them, I certainly would not do to keep my place. Thus the matter stands. It will probably be finally settled within a few hours.

This detestable session goes on lengthening and lengthening, like a human hair in one's mouth. (Do you know that delicious sensation?) Last month we expected to have been up before the middle of August. Now we should be glad to be quite certain of being in the country by the 1st of September. One comfort I shall have in being turned out: I will not stay a day in London after the West India Bill is through committee; which I hope it will be before the end of next week.

The new *Edinburgh Review* is not much amiss; but I quite agree with the publishers, the editor, and the reading public generally, that the number would have been much the better for an article of thirty or forty pages from the pen of a gentleman who shall be nameless. Ever yours, T. B. M.

To Hannah M. Macaulay.

London, July 25th, 1833.

My dear Sister,—The plot is thickening. Yesterday Buxton moved an instruction to the Committee on the Slavery Bill, which the Government opposed, and which I supported. It was extremely painful to me to speak against all my political friends—so painful that at times I could hardly go on. I treated them as mildly as I could, and they all tell me that I performed my difficult task not ungracefully. We divided at two this morning, and were 151 to 158. The ministers found that if they persisted they would infallibly be beaten. Accordingly they came down to the House at twelve this day, and agreed to reduce the apprenticeship to seven years for the agricultural laborers, and to five years for the skilled laborers. What other people may do I can not tell; but I am inclined to be satisfied with this concession; particularly as I believe that if we press the thing further they will resign, and we shall have no bill at all, but instead of it a Tory ministry and a dissolution. Some people flatter me with the assurance that our large minority, and the consequent change in the bill, have been owing to me. If this be so, I have done one useful act, at least, in my life.

I shall now certainly remain in office; and if, as I expect, the Irish Church Bill passes the Lords, I may consider myself as safe till the next session; when Heaven knows what may happen. It is still quite uncertain when we may rise. I pine for rest, air, and a taste of family life, more than I can express. I see nothing but politicians, and talk about nothing but politics.

I have not read "Village Belles." Tell me, as soon as you can get it, whether it is worth reading. As John Thorpe* says: "Novels! Oh, Lord! I never read novels. I have something else to do." Farewell. T. B. M.

To Hannah M. Macaulay.

London, July 27th, 1833.

MY DEAR SISTER,—Here I am, safe and well, at the end of one of the most stormy weeks that the oldest man remembers in Parliamentary affairs. I have resigned my office, and my resignation has been refused. I have spoken and voted against the ministry under which I hold my place. The ministry has been so hard run in the Commons as to be forced to modify its plan; and has received a defeat in the Lords;† a slight one, to be sure, and on a slight matter, yet such that I, and many others, fully believed twenty-four hours ago that they would have resigned. In fact, some of the Cabinet—Grant among the rest, to my certain knowledge—were for resigning. At last Saturday has arrived. The ministry is as strong as ever. I am as good friends with the ministers as ever. The East India Bill is carried through our House. The West India Bill is so far modified that, I believe, it will be carried. The Irish Church Bill has got through the committee in the Lords; and we are all beginning to look forward to a prorogation in about three weeks.

* The young Oxford man in Northanger Abbey.

† On the 25th of July the Archbishop of Canterbury carried an amendment on the Irish Church Bill, against the Government, by 84 votes to 82.

To-day I went to Haydon's to be painted into his great picture of "The Reform Banquet." Ellis was with me, and declares that Haydon has touched me off to a nicety. I am sick of pictures of my own face. I have seen within the last few days one drawing of it, one engraving, and three paintings. They all make me a very handsome fellow. Haydon pronounces my profile a gem of art, perfectly antique; and, what is worth the praise of ten Haydons, I was told yesterday that Mrs. Littleton, the handsomest woman in London, had paid me exactly the same compliment. She pronounced Mr. Macaulay's profile to be a study for an artist. I have bought a new looking-glass and razor-case on the strength of these compliments, and am meditating on the expediency of having my hair cut in the Burlington Arcade, rather than in Lamb's, Conduit Street. As Richard says,

> Since I am crept in favor with myself,
> I will maintain it with some little cost.

I begin, like Sir Walter Elliot,* to rate all my acquaintance according to their beauty. But what nonsense I write, and in times that make merry men look grave! Ever yours,

T. B. M.

To Hannah M. Macaulay.

London, July 29th, 1833.

My dear Sister,—I dined last night at Holland House. There was a very pleasant party. My lady was courteous, and my lord extravagantly entertaining: telling some capital stories about old Bishop Horsley, which were set off with some of the drollest mimicry that I ever saw. Among many others, there were Sir James Graham; and Dr. Holland, who is a good scholar as well as a good physician; and Wilkie, who is a modest, pleasing companion, as well as an excellent artist. For ladies, we had her Grace of ——; and her daughter, Lady ——, a fine, buxom, sonsy lass, with more color than, I am sorry to say, is often seen among fine ladies. So our dinner and our soirée were very agreeable.

---

* The Baronet in "Persuasion."

We narrowly escaped a scene at one time. Lord —— is in the navy, and is now on duty in the fleet at the Tagus. We got into a conversation about Portuguese politics. His name was mentioned, and Graham, who is first lord of the admiralty, complimented the duchess on her son's merit, to which, he said, every dispatch bore witness. The duchess forthwith began to entreat that he might be recalled. He was very ill, she said. If he staid longer on that station she was sure that he would die; and then she began to cry. I can not bear to see women cry, and the matter became serious, for her pretty daughter began to bear her company. That hard-hearted Lord —— seemed to be diverted by the scene. He, by all accounts, has been doing little else than making women cry during the last five-and-twenty years. However, we all were as still as death while the wiping of eyes and the blowing of noses proceeded. At last Lord Holland contrived to restore our spirits; but before the duchess went away she managed to have a tête-à-tête with Graham, and, I have no doubt, begged and blubbered to some purpose. I could not help thinking how many honest, stout-hearted fellows are left to die on the most unhealthy stations, for want of being related to some duchess who has been handsome, or to some duchess's daughter who still is so.

The duchess said one thing that amused us. We were talking about Lady Morgan. "When she first came to London," said Lord Holland, "I remember that she carried a little Irish harp about with her wherever she went." Others denied this. I mentioned what she says in her "Book of the Boudoir." There she relates how she went one evening to Lady ——'s with her little Irish harp, and how strange every body thought it. "I see nothing very strange," said her grace, "in her taking her harp to Lady ——'s. If she brought it safe away with her, that would have been strange indeed." On this, as a friend of yours says, we la-a-a-a-a-a-a-ft.

I am glad to find that you approve of my conduct about the niggers. I expect, and indeed wish, to be abused by the Agency Society. My father is quite satisfied, and so are the best part of my Leeds friends.

I amuse myself, as I walk back from the House at two in the morning, with translating Virgil. I am at work on one of the most beautiful episodes, and am succeeding pretty well. You shall have what I have done when I come to Liverpool, which will be, I hope, in three weeks or thereanent.

Ever yours, T. B. M.

To Hannah M. Macaulay.

London, July 31st, 1833.

MY DEAR SISTER,—Political affairs look cheeringly. The Lords passed the Irish Church Bill yesterday, and mean, we understand, to give us little or no trouble about the India Bill. There is still a hitch in the Commons about the West India Bill, particularly about the twenty millions for compensation to the planters; but we expect to carry our point by a great majority. By the end of next week we shall be very near the termination of our labors. Heavy labors they have been.

So Wilberforce is gone! We talk of burying him in Westminster Abbey; and many eminent men, both Whigs and Tories, are desirous to join in paying him this honor. There is, however, a story about a promise given to old Stephen that they should both lie in the same grave. Wilberforce kept his faculties, and (except when he was actually in fits) his spirits, to the very last. He was cheerful and full of anecdote only last Saturday. He owned that he enjoyed life much, and that he had a great desire to live longer. Strange in a man who had, I should have said, so little to attach him to this world, and so firm a belief in another: in a man with an impaired fortune, a weak spine, and a worn-out stomach! What is this fascination which makes us cling to existence, in spite of present sufferings and of religious hopes? Yesterday evening I called at the house in Cadogan Place, where the body is lying. I was truly fond of him: that is "je l'aimais comme l'on aime." And how is that? How very little one human being generally cares for another! How very little the world misses any body! How soon the chasm left by the best and wisest men closes! I thought, as I walked back from Cadogan Place, that our own selfishness when others are taken away ought to teach us how little others will suffer at losing us. I thought that, if I were to die to-morrow, not one of the fine people whom I dine with every week will take a *côtelette aux petits pois* the less on Saturday at the table to which I was invited to meet them, or will smile less gayly at the ladies over the Champagne. And I am quite even with them. What are those pretty lines of Shelley?

> Oh, world, farewell!
> Listen to the passing bell.
> It tells that thou and I must part
> With a light and heavy heart.

There are not ten people in the world whose deaths would spoil my dinner; but there are one or two whose deaths would break my heart. The more I see of the world, and the more numerous my acquaintance becomes, the narrower and more exclusive my affection grows, and the more I cling to my sisters, and to one or two old tried friends of my quiet days. But why should I go on preaching to you out of Ecclesiastes? And here comes, fortunately, to break the train of my melancholy reflections, the proof of my East India speech from Hansard: so I must put my letter aside and correct the press. Ever yours, T. B. M.

To Hannah M. Macaulay.

London, August 2d, 1833.

MY DEAR SISTER,—I agree with your judgment on Chesterfield's "Letters." They are for the most part trash; though they contain some clever passages, and the style is not bad. Their celebrity must be attributed to causes quite distinct from their literary merit, and particularly to the position which the author held in society. We see in our own time that the books written by public men of note are generally rated at more than their value: Lord Granville's little compositions, for example; Canning's verses; Fox's history; Brougham's treatises. The writings of people of high fashion, also, have a value set on them far higher than that which intrinsically belongs to them. The verses of the late Duchess of Devonshire, or an occasional prologue by Lord Alvanley, attract a most undue share of attention. If the present Duke of Devonshire, who is the very "glass of fashion and mold of form," were to publish a book with two good pages, it would be extolled as a masterpiece in half the drawing-rooms of London. Now, Chesterfield was, what no person in our time has been or can be, a great political leader and at the same time the acknowledged chief of the fashionable world; at the head of the House of Lords and at the head of *ton;* Mr. Canning and the Duke of Devonshire in one. In our time the division of labor is carried so far that such a man could not exist. Politics require the whole of energy, bodily and mental, during half the year; and leave very little time for the bow-window at White's in the day, or for the crush-room of the opera at night. A century ago the case was different. Chesterfield was at once the most distinguished orator in the Upper House, and the undisputed sovereign of wit and fashion. He held this eminence for about forty years. At last it became the regular custom of the higher circles to laugh whenever he opened his mouth, without waiting for his *bonmot.* He used to sit at White's with a circle of young men of rank round him, applauding every syllable that he uttered. If you wish for a proof of the kind of position which Chesterfield held among his contemporaries, look at the prospectus of Johnson's "Dictionary." Look even at Johnson's angry letter. It contains the strongest admission of the boundless influence which Chesterfield exercised over society. When the letters of such a man were published, of course they were received more favorably by far than they deserved.

So much for criticism. As to politics, every thing seems tending to repose; and I should think that by this day fortnight we shall probably be prorogued. The Jew Bill was thrown out yesterday night by the Lords. No matter. Our turn will come one of these days.

If you want to see me puffed and abused by somebody who evidently knows nothing about me, look at the *New Monthly* for this month. Bulwer, I see, has given up editing it. I suppose he is making money in some other way; for his dress must cost as much as that of any five other members of Parliament.

To-morrow Wilberforce is to be buried. His sons acceded with great eagerness to the application made to them by a considerable number of the members of both Houses that the funeral should be public. We meet to-morrow at twelve at the House of Commons, and we shall attend the coffin into the Abbey. The Duke of Wellington, Lord Eldon, and Sir R. Peel have put down their names, as well as the ministers and the Abolitionists.

My father urges me to pay some tribute to Wilberforce in the House of Commons. If any debate should take place on the third reading of the West India Bill in which I might take part, I should certainly embrace the opportunity of doing honor to his memory. But I do not expect that such an occasion will arise. The House seems inclined to pass the bill without more contest; and my father must be aware that any thing like theatrical display—any thing like a set funeral oration not springing naturally out of the discussion of a question—is extremely distasteful to the House of Commons.

I have been clearing off a great mass of business which had accumulated at our office while we were conducting our bill through Parliament. To-day I had the satisfaction of seeing the green boxes, which a week ago were piled up with papers three or four feet high, perfectly empty. Admire my superhuman industry. This I will say for myself, that, when I do sit down to work, I work harder and faster than any person that I ever knew. Ever yours, T. B. M.

The next letter, in terms too clear to require comment, introduces the mention of what proved to be the most important circumstance in Macaulay's life.

To Hannah M. Macaulay.

London, August 17th, 1833.

My dear Sister,—I am about to write to you on a subject which to you and Margaret will be one of the most agitating interest; and which, on that account chiefly, is so to me.

By the new India Bill it is provided that one of the members of the Supreme Council, which is to govern our Eastern empire, is to be chosen from among persons who are not servants of the company. It is probable, indeed nearly certain, that the situation will be offered to me.

The advantages are very great. It is a post of the highest dignity and consideration. The salary is ten thousand pounds a year. I am assured by persons who know Calcutta intimately, and who have themselves mixed in the highest circles and held the highest offices at that presidency, that I may live in splendor there for five thousand a year, and may save the rest of the salary with the accruing interest. I may therefore hope to return to England at only thirty-nine, in the full vigor of life, with a fortune of thirty thousand pounds. A larger fortune I never desired.

I am not fond of money, or anxious about it. But, though every day makes me less and less eager for wealth, every day shows me more and more strongly how necessary a competence is to a man who desires to be either great or useful. At present the plain fact is that I can continue to be a public man only while I can continue in office. If I left my place in the Government, I must leave my seat in Parliament too. For I must live: I can live only by my pen: and it is absolutely impossible for any man to write enough to procure him a decent subsistence, and at the same time to take an active part in politics. I have not during this session been able to send a single line to the *Edinburgh Review;* and if I had been out of office, I should have been able to do very little. Edward Bulwer has just given up the *New Monthly Magazine* on the ground that he can not conduct it and attend to his Parliamentary duties. Cobbett has been compelled to neglect his *Register* so much that its sale has fallen almost to nothing. Now, in order to live like a gentleman, it would be necessary for me to write, not as I have done hitherto, but regularly, and even daily. I have never made more than two hundred a year by my pen. I could not support myself in comfort on less than five hundred; and I shall in all probability have many others to support. The prospects of our family are, if possible, darker than ever.

In the mean time my political outlook is very gloomy. A schism in the ministry is approaching. It requires only that common knowledge of public affairs which any reader of the newspapers may possess to see this; and I have more, much more, than common knowledge on the subject. They can not hold together. I tell you in perfect seriousness that my chance of keeping my present situation for six months is so small, that I would willingly sell it for fifty pounds down. If I remain in office, I shall, I fear, lose my political character. If I go out, and engage in opposition, I shall break most of the private ties which I have formed during the last three years. In England I see nothing before me, for some time to come, but poverty, unpopularity, and the breaking-up of old connections.

If there were no way out of these difficulties, I would encounter them with courage. A man can always act honorably and uprightly; and, if I were in the Fleet Prison or the rules of the King's Bench, I believe that I could find in my own mind resources which would preserve me from being positively unhappy. But if I could escape from these impending disasters, I should wish to do so. By accepting the post which is likely to be offered to me, I withdraw myself for a short time from the contests of faction here. When I return, I shall find things settled, parties formed into new combinations, and new questions under discussion. I shall then be able, without the scandal of a violent separation, and without exposing myself to the charge of inconsistency, to take my own line. In the mean time I shall save my family from distress; and shall return with a competence honestly earned, as rich as if I were Duke of Northumberland or Marquess of Westminster, and able to act on all public questions without even a temptation to deviate from the strict line of duty. While in India, I shall have to discharge duties not painfully laborious, and of the highest and most honorable kind. I shall have whatever that country affords of comfort or splendor; nor will my absence be so long that my friends, or the public here, will be likely to lose sight of me.

The only persons who know what I have written to you are Lord Grey, the Grants, Stewart Mackenzie, and George Babington. Charles Grant and Stewart Mackenzie, who know better than most men the state of the political world, think that I should act unwisely in refusing this post; and this though they assure me, and, I really believe, sincerely, that they shall feel the loss of my society very acutely. But what shall I feel? And with what emotions, loving as I do my country and my family, can I look forward to such a separation, enjoined, as I think it is, by prudence and by duty? Whether the period of my exile shall be one of comfort, and, after the first shock, even of happiness, depends on you. If, as I expect, this offer shall be made to me, will you go with me? I know what a sacrifice I ask of you. I know how many dear and precious ties you must, for a time, sunder. I know that the splendor of the Indian Court, and the gayeties of that brilliant society of which you would be one of the leading personages, have no temptation for you. I can bribe you only by telling you that, if you will go with me, I will love you better than I love you now, if I can.

I have asked George Babington about your health and mine. He says that he has very little apprehension for me, and none at all for you. Indeed, he seemed to think that the climate would be quite as likely to do you good as harm.

All this is most strictly secret. You may, of course, show the letter to Margaret, and Margaret may tell Edward; for I never cabal against the lawful authority of husbands. But further the thing must not go. It would hurt my father, and very justly, to hear of it from any body before he hears of it from myself; and if the least hint of it were to get abroad, I should be placed in a very awkward position with regard to the people at Leeds. It is possible, though not probable, that difficulties may arise at the India House; and I do not mean to say any thing to any person who is not already in the secret till the directors have made their choice, and till the king's pleasure has been taken.

And now think calmly over what I have written. I would not have written on the subject even to you till the matter was quite settled, if I had not thought that you ought to have full time to make up your mind. If you feel an insurmountable aversion to India, I will do all in my power to make your residence in England comfortable during my absence, and to enable you to confer instead of receiving benefits. But if my dear sister would consent to give me, at this great crisis of my life, that proof, that painful and arduous proof, of her affection which I beg of her, I think that she will not repent of it. She shall not, if the unbounded confidence and attachment of one to whom she is dearer than life can compensate her for a few years' absence from much that she loves.

Dear Margaret! She will feel this. Consult her, my love, and let us both have the advantage of such advice as her excellent understanding, and her warm affection for us, may furnish. On Monday next, at the latest, I expect to be with you. Our Scotch tour, under these circumstances, must be short. By Christmas it will be fit that the new councilor should leave England. His functions in India commence next April. We shall leave our dear Margaret, I hope, a happy mother.

Farewell, my dear sister. You can not tell how impatiently I shall wait for your answer. T. B. M.

This letter, written under the influence of deep and varied emotions, was read with feelings of painful agitation and surprise. India was not then the familiar name that it has become to a generation which regards a visit to Cashmere as a trip to be undertaken between two London seasons; and which discusses over its breakfast-table at home the decisions arrived at on the previous afternoon in the council-room of Simla or Calcutta. In those rural parsonages and middle-class households where service in our Eastern territories now presents itself in the light of a probable and desirable destiny for a promising son, those same territories were forty years ago regarded as an obscure and distant region of disease and death. A girl who had seen no country more foreign than Wales, and crossed no water broader and more tempestuous than the Mersey, looked forward to a voyage which (as she subsequently learned by melancholy experience) might extend over six weary months, with an anxiety that can hardly be imagined by us who spend only half as many weeks on the journey between Dover and Bombay. A separation from beloved relations under such conditions was a separation indeed; and if Macaulay and his sister could have foreseen how much of what they left at their departure they would fail to find on their return, it is a question whether any earthly consideration could have induced them to quit their native shore. But Hannah's sense of duty was too strong for these doubts and tremors; and, happily (for, on the whole, her resolution was a fortunate one), she resolved to accompany her brother in an expatriation which he never would have faced without her. With a mind set at ease by a knowledge of her intention, he came down to Liverpool as soon as the session was at an end; and carried her off on a jaunt to Edinburgh in a post-chaise, furnished with Horace Walpole's letters for their common reading, and Smollett's collected works for his own. Before October he was back at the Board of Control; and his letters recommenced, as frequent and rather more serious and business-like than of old.

London, October 5th, 1833.

Dear Hannah,—Life goes on so quietly here, or rather stands so still, that I have nothing, or next to nothing, to say. At the Athenæum I now and then fall in with some person passing through town on his way to the Continent or to Brighton. The other day I met Sharp, and had a long talk with him about every thing and every body—metaphysics, poetry, politics, scenery, and painting. One thing I have observed in Sharp, which is quite peculiar to him among town-wits and diners-out. He never talks scandal. If he can say nothing good of a man, he holds his tongue. I do not, of course, mean that in confidential communication about politics he does not speak freely of public men; but about the foibles of private individuals I do not believe that, much as I have talked with him, I ever heard him utter one word. I passed three or four hours very agreeably in his company at the club.

I have also seen Kenny for an hour or two. I do not know that I ever mentioned Kenny to you. When London is overflowing, I meet such numbers of people that I can not remember half their names. This is the time at which every acquaintance, however slight, attracts some degree of attention. In the desert island, even poor Poll was something of a companion to Robinson Crusoe. Kenny is a writer of a class which, in our time, is at the very bottom of the literary scale. He is a dramatist. Most of the farces and three-act plays which have succeeded during the last eight or ten years are, I am told, from his pen. Heaven knows that, if they are the farces and plays which I have seen, they do him but little honor. However, this man is one of our great comic writers. He has the merit, such as it is, of hitting the very bad taste of our modern audiences better than any other person who has stooped to that degrading work. We had a good deal of literary chat, and I thought him a clever, shrewd fellow.

My father is poorly: not that any thing very serious is the matter with him; but he has a cold, and is in low spirits.

Ever yours, T. B. M.

London, October 14th, 1833.

DEAR HANNAH,—I have just finished my article on Horace Walpole. This is one of the happy moments of my life: a stupid task performed; a weight taken off my mind. I should be quite joyous if I had only you to read it to. But to Napier it must go forthwith; and as soon as I have finished this letter, I shall put it into the general post with my own fair hands. I was up at four this morning to put the last touch to it. I often differ with the majority about other people's writings, and still oftener about my own, and therefore I may very likely be mistaken; but I think that this article will be a hit. We shall see. Nothing ever cost me more pains than the first half; I never wrote any thing so flowingly as the latter half; and I like the latter half the best. I have laid it on Walpole so unsparingly that I shall not be surprised if Miss Berry should cut me. You know she was Walpole's favorite in her youth. Neither am I sure that Lord and Lady Holland will be well pleased. But they ought to be obliged to me; for I refrained, for their sake, from laying a hand, which has been thought to be not a light one, on that old rogue, the first Lord Holland.*

Charles Grant is still at Paris; ill, he says. I never knew a man who wanted setting to rights so often. He goes as badly as your watch.

My father is at me again to provide for P——. What on earth have I to do with P——? The relationship is one which none but Scotchmen would recognize. The lad is such a fool that he would utterly disgrace my recommendation. And, as if to make the thing more provoking, his sisters say that he must be provided for in England, for that they can not think of parting with him. This, to be sure, matters little; for there is at present just as little chance of getting any thing in India as in England.

But what strange folly this is which meets me in every quarter—people wanting posts in the army, the navy, the public offices, and saying that if they can not find such posts they must starve! How do all the rest of mankind live? If I had not happened to be engaged in politics, and if my father had not been connected, by very extraordinary circumstances, with public men, we should never have dreamed of having places. Why can not P—— be apprenticed to some hatter or tailor? He may do well in such a business: he will do detestably ill as a clerk in my office. He may come to make good coats: he will never, I am sure, write good dispatches. There is nothing truer than Poor Richard's saw, "We are taxed twice as heavily by our pride as by the state." The curse of England is the obstinate determination of the middle classes to make their sons what they call gentlemen. So we are overrun by clergymen without livings; lawyers without briefs; physicians without patients; authors without readers; clerks soliciting employment, who might have thriven, and

* Lord Holland, once upon a time, speaking to Macaulay of his grandfather, said, "He had that temper which kind folks have been pleased to say belongs to my family; but he shared the fault that belonged to that school of statesmen, an utter disbelief in public virtue."

been above the world, as bakers, watch-makers, or innkeepers. The next time my father speaks to me about P——, I will offer to subscribe twenty guineas toward making a pastry-cook of him. He had a sweet tooth when he was a child.

So you are reading Burnet! Did you begin from the beginning? What do you think of the old fellow? He was always a great favorite of mine; honest, though careless; a strong party man on the right side, yet with much kind feeling toward his opponents, and even toward his personal enemies. He is to me a most entertaining writer; far superior to Clarendon in the art of amusing, though of course far Clarendon's inferior in discernment, and in dignity and correctness of style. Do you know, by-the-bye, Clarendon's life of himself? I like it, the part after the Restoration at least, better than his great History.

I am very quiet: rise at seven or half-past; read Spanish till ten; breakfast; walk to my office; stay there till four; take a long walk; dine toward seven; and am in bed before eleven. I am going through "Don Quixote" again, and admire it more than ever. It is certainly the best novel in the world, beyond all comparison. Ever yours, T. B. M.

To Hannah M. Macaulay.

London, October 21st, 1833.

My dear Sister,—Grant is here at last, and we have had a very long talk about matters both public and private. The Government would support my appointment, but he expects violent opposition from the Company. He mentioned my name to the Chairs,* and they were furious. They know that I have been against them through the whole course of the negotiations which resulted in the India Bill. They put their opposition on the ground of my youth—a very flattering objection to a man who this week completes his thirty-third year. They spoke very highly of me in other respects; but they seemed quite obstinate.

---

* The Chairman and Deputy Chairman of the East India Company were at that time Mr. Campbell Marjoribanks and Mr. Wigram.

The question now is whether their opposition will be supported by the other directors. If it should be so, I have advised Grant most strongly to withdraw my name, to put up some other man, and then to fight the battle to the utmost. We shall be suspected of jobbing if we proceed to extremities on behalf of one of ourselves; but we can do what we like, if it is in favor of some person whom we can not be suspected of supporting from interested motives. From the extreme unreasonableness and pertinacity which are discernible in every communication that we receive from the India House at present, I am inclined to think that I have no chance of being chosen by them, without a dispute in which I should not wish the Government to engage for such a purpose. Lord Grey says that I have a right to their support if I ask for it; but that, for the sake of his administration generally, he is very adverse to my going. I do not think that I shall go. However, a few days will decide the matter.

I have heard from Napier. He praises my article on Walpole in terms absolutely extravagant. He says that it is the best that I ever wrote, and, *entre nous*, I am not very far from agreeing with him. I am impatient to have your opinion. No flattery pleases me so much as domestic flattery. You will have the number within the week. Ever yours,

T. B. M.

To Macvey Napier, Esq.

London, October 21st, 1833.

Dear Napier,—I am glad to learn that you like my article. I like it myself, which is not much my habit. Very likely the public, which has often been kinder to my performances than I was, may on this, as on other occasions, differ from me in opinion. If the paper has any merit, it owes it to the delay of which you must, I am sure, have complained very bitterly in your heart. I was so thoroughly dissatisfied with the article as it stood at first that I completely rewrote it; altered the whole arrangement; left out ten or twelve pages in one part; and added twice as many in another. I never wrote any thing so slowly as the first half, or so rapidly as the last half.

You are in an error about Akenside, which I must clear up for his credit, and for mine. You are confounding the "Ode to Curio" and the "Epistle to Curio." The latter is generally printed at the end of Akenside's works, and is, I think, the best thing that he ever wrote. The "Ode" is worthless. It is merely an abridgment of the "Epistle," executed in the most unskillful way. Johnson says, in his "Life of Akenside,"* that no poet ever so much mistook his powers as Akenside when he took to lyric composition. "Having," I think the words are, "written with great force and poignancy his 'Epistle to Curio,' he afterward transformed it into an ode only disgraceful to its author."

When I said that Chesterfield† had lost by the publication of his "Letters," I of course considered that he had much to lose; that he has left an immense reputation, founded on the testimony of all his contemporaries of all parties, for wit, taste, and eloquence; that what remains of his Parliamentary oratory is superior to any thing of that time that has come down to us, except a little of Pitt's. The utmost that can be said of the letters is that they are the letters of a cleverish man; and there are not many which are entitled even to that praise. I think he would have stood higher if we had been left to judge of his powers—as we judge of those of Chatham, Mansfield, Charles Townshend, and many others—only by tradition, and by fragments of speeches preserved in Parliamentary reports.

I said nothing about Lord Byron's criticism on Walpole, because I thought it, like most of his lordship's criticism, below refutation. On the drama Lord Byron wrote more nonsense

---

* "Akenside was one of the fiercest and the most uncompromising of the young patriots out of Parliament. When he found that the change of administration had produced no change of system, he gave vent to his indignation in the 'Epistle to Curio,' the best poem that he ever wrote; a poem, indeed, which seems to indicate that if he had left lyrical composition to Gray and Collins, and had employed his powers in grave and elevated satire, he might have disputed the pre-eminence of Dryden."—*Macaulay's Essay on Horace Walpole.*

† "Lord Chesterfield stands much lower in the estimation of posterity than he would have done if his "Letters" had never been published.

than on any subject. He wanted to have restored the unities. His practice proved as unsuccessful as his theory was absurd. His admiration of "The Mysterious Mother" was of a piece with his thinking Gifford and Rogers greater poets than Wordsworth and Coleridge. Ever yours truly,

T. B. MACAULAY.

London, October 28th, 1833.

DEAR HANNAH,—I wish to have Malkin* as head of the commission at Canton, and Grant seems now to be strongly bent on the same plan. Malkin is a man of singular temper, judgment, and firmness of nerve. Danger and responsibility, instead of agitating and confusing him, always bring out whatever there is in him. This was the reason of his great success at Cambridge. He made a figure there far beyond his learning or his talents, though both his learning and his talents are highly respectable. But the moment that he sat down to be examined, which is just the situation in which all other people, from natural flurry, do worse than at other times, he began to do his very best. His intellect became clearer, and his manner more quiet, than usual. He is the very man to make up his mind in three minutes if the Viceroy of Canton were in a rage, the mob bellowing round the doors of the factory, and an English ship of war making preparations to bombard the town.

Apropos of places, my father has been at me again about P——. Would you think it? This lad has a hundred and twenty pounds a year for life! I could not believe my ears; but so it is; and I, who have not a penny, with half a dozen brothers and sisters as poor as myself, am to move heaven and earth to push this boy, who, as he is the silliest, is also, I think, the richest relation that I have in the world.

I am to dine on Thursday with the Fish-mongers' Company, the first company for gourmands in the world. Their magnificent hall near London Bridge is not yet built; but as re-

* Sir Benjamin Malkin, a college friend of Macaulay, was afterward a judge in the Supreme Court at Calcutta.

spects eating and drinking I shall be no loser, for we are to be entertained at the Albion Tavern. This is the first dinner-party that I shall have been to for a long time. There is nobody in town that I know except official men, and they have left their wives and households in the country. I met Poodle Byng, it is true, the day before yesterday in the street; and he begged me to make haste to Brooks's; for Lord Essex was there, he said, whipping up for a dinner-party, cursing and swearing at all his friends for being out of town, and wishing —what an honor!—that Macaulay was in London. I preserved all the dignity of a young lady in an *affaire du cœur.* "I shall not run after my lord, I assure you. If he wants me, he knows where he may hear of me." This nibble is the nearest approach to a dinner-party that I have had.

Ever yours, T. B. M.

London, November 1st, 1833.

Dear Hannah,—I have not much to add to what I told you yesterday; but every thing that I have to add looks one way. Marjoribanks and Wigram have resigned. We have a new chairman and deputy chairman, both very strongly in my favor. Sharp, by whom I sat yesterday at the Fish-mongers' dinner, told me that my old enemy, James Mill, had spoken to him on the subject. Mill is, as you have heard, at the head of one of the principal departments of the India House. The late chairman consulted him about me; hoping, I suppose, to have his support against me. Mill said, very handsomely, that he would advise the company to take me; for, as public men went, I was much above the average, and, if they rejected me, he thought it very unlikely that they would get any body so fit. This is all the news that I have for you. It is not much; but I wish to keep you as fully informed of what is going on as I am myself.

Old Sharp told me that I was acting quite wisely, but that he should never see me again;* and he cried as he said it. I encouraged him; and told him that I hoped to be in England

---

* Mr. Sharp died in 1837, before Macaulay's return from India.

again before the end of 1839, and that there was nothing impossible in our meeting again. He cheered up after a time; told me that he should correspond with me, and give me all the secret history both of politics and of society; and promised to select the best books, and send them regularly to me.

The Fish-mongers' dinner was very good, but not so profusely splendid as I had expected. There has been a change, I find, and not before it was wanted. They had got at one time to dining at ten guineas a head. They drank my health, and I harangued them with immense applause. I talked all the evening to Sharp. I told him what a dear sister I had, and how readily she had agreed to go with me. I had told Grant the same in the morning. Both of them extolled my good fortune in having such a companion. Ever yours,

T. B. M.

London, November —, 1833.

DEAR HANNAH,—Things stand as they stood, except that the report of my appointment is every day spreading more widely, and that I am beset by advertising dealers begging leave to make up a hundred cotton shirts for me, and fifty muslin gowns for you, and by clerks out of place begging to be my secretaries. I am not in very high spirits to-day, as I have just received a letter from poor Ellis, to whom I had not communicated my intentions till yesterday. He writes so affectionately and so plaintively that he quite cuts me to the heart. There are few, indeed, from whom I shall part with so much pain; and he, poor fellow, says that, next to his wife, I am the person for whom he feels the most thorough attachment, and in whom he places the most unlimited confidence.

On the 11th of this month there is to be a dinner given to Lushington by the electors of the Tower Hamlets. He has persecuted me with importunities to attend and make a speech for him, and my father has joined in the request. It is enough, in these times, Heaven knows, for a man who represents, as I do, a town of a hundred and twenty thousand people, to keep his own constituents in good humor; and the Spitalfields weavers and Whitechapel butchers are nothing to me. But, ever since I succeeded in what every body allows to have been the most hazardous attempt of the kind ever made—I mean, in persuading an audience of manufacturers, all Whigs or Radicals, that the immediate alteration of the corn laws was impossible—I have been considered as a capital physician for desperate cases in politics. However—to return from that delightful theme, my own praises—Lushington, who is not very popular with the rabble of the Tower Hamlets, thinks that an oration from me would give him a lift. I could not refuse him directly, backed as he was by my father. I only said that I would attend if I were in London on the 11th; but I added that, situated as I was, I thought it very probable that I should be out of town.

I shall go to-night to Miss Berry's soirée. I do not know whether I told you that she resented my article on Horace Walpole so much that Sir Stratford Canning advised me not to go near her. She was Walpole's greatest favorite. His "Reminiscences" are addressed to her in terms of the most gallant eulogy. When he was dying, at past eighty, he asked her to marry him, merely that he might make her a countess and leave her his fortune. You know that in "Vivian Grey" she is called Miss Otranto. I always expected that my article would put her into a passion, and I was not mistaken; but she has come round again, and sent me a most pressing and kind invitation the other day.

I have been racketing lately, having dined twice with Rogers and once with Grant. Lady Holland is in a most extraordinary state. She came to Rogers's, with Allen, in so bad a humor that we were all forced to rally and make common cause against her. There was not a person at table to whom she was not rude; and none of us were inclined to submit. Rogers sneered; Sydney made merciless sport of her; Tom Moore looked excessively impertinent; Bobus put her down with simple straightforward rudeness; and I treated her with what I meant to be the coldest civility. Allen flew into a rage with us all, and especially with Sydney, whose guffaws, as the Scotch say, were indeed tremendous. When she and all the rest were gone, Rogers made Tom Moore and me sit down with him for half an hour, and we coshered over the events of the evening. Rogers said that he thought Allen's firing-up in defense of his patroness the best thing that he had seen in him. No sooner had Tom and I got into the street than he broke forth: "That such an old stager as Rogers should talk such nonsense, and give Allen credit for attachment to any thing but his dinner! Allen was bursting with envy to see us so free, while he was conscious of his own slavery."

Her ladyship has been the better for this discipline. She has overwhelmed me ever since with attentions and invitations. I have at last found out the cause of her ill-humor, or at least of that portion of it of which I was the object. She is in a rage at my article on Walpole, but at what part of it I can not tell. I know that she is very intimate with the Waldegraves, to whom the manuscripts belong, and for whose benefit the letters were published. But my review was surely not calculated to injure the sale of the book. Lord Holland told me, in an aside, that he quite agreed with me, but that we had better not discuss the subject.

A note; and, by my life, from my Lady Holland: "Dear Mr. Macaulay, pray wrap yourself very warm, and come to us on Wednesday." No, my good lady. I am engaged on Wednesday to dine at the Albion Tavern with the Directors of the East India Company—now my servants; next week, I hope, to be my masters. Ever yours, T. B. M.

To Hannah M. Macaulay.

London, November 22d, 1833.

My dear Sister,—The decision is postponed for a week; but there is no chance of an unfavorable result. The Chairs have collected the opinions of their brethren; and the result is, that, of the twenty-four directors, only six or seven at the most will vote against me.

I dined with the directors on Wednesday at the Albion Tavern. We had a company of about sixty persons, and many eminent military men among them. The very courteous manner in which several of the directors begged to be introduced to me, and drank my health at dinner, led me to think that the Chairs have not overstated the feeling of the court. One of them, an old Indian and a great friend of our uncle, the general, told me in plain words that he was glad to hear that I was to be in their service. Another, whom I do not even know by sight, pressed the chairman to propose my health. The chairman with great judgment refused. It would have been very awkward to have had to make a speech to them in the present circumstances.

Of course, my love, all your expenses, from the day of my appointment, are my affair. My present plan, formed after conversation with experienced East Indians, is not to burden myself with an extravagant outfit. I shall take only what will be necessary for the voyage. Plate, wine, coaches, furniture, glass, china, can be bought in Calcutta as well as in London. I shall not have money enough to fit myself out handsomely with such things here; and to fit myself out shabbily would be folly. I reckon that we can bring our whole expense for the passage within the £1200 allowed by the company. My calculation is that our cabins and board will cost £250 apiece. The passage of our servants £50 apiece. That makes up £600. My clothes and etceteras, as Mrs. Meeke* observes, will, I am quite sure, come within £200. Yours will, of course, be more. I will send you £300 to lay out as you like; not meaning to confine you to it, by any means; but you would probably prefer having a sum down to sending in your milliner's bills to me. I reckon my servant's outfit at £50; your maid's at as much more. The whole will be £1200.

One word about your maid. You really must choose with great caution. Hitherto the company has required that all ladies who take maid-servants with them from this country to India should give security to send them back within two years. The reason was, that no class of people misconducted themselves so much in the East as female servants from this country. They generally treat the natives with gross inso-

* Mrs. Meeke was his favorite among bad novel-writers. See page 129.

lence; an insolence natural enough to people accustomed to stand in a subordinate relation to others when, for the first time, they find a great population placed in a servile relation toward them. Then, too, the state of society is such that they are very likely to become mistresses of the wealthy Europeans, and to flaunt about in magnificent palanquins, bringing discredit on their country by the immorality of their lives and the vulgarity of their manners. On these grounds the company has hitherto insisted upon their being sent back at the expense of those who take them out. The late act will enable your servant to stay in India, if she chooses to stay. I hope, therefore, that you will be careful in your selection. You see how much depends upon it. The happiness and concord of our native household, which will probably consist of sixty or seventy people, may be destroyed by her, if she should be ill-tempered and arrogant. If she should be weak and vain, she will probably form connections that will ruin her morals and her reputation. I am no preacher, as you very well know; but I have a strong sense of the responsibility under which we shall both lie with respect to a poor girl brought by us into the midst of temptations of which she can not be aware, and which have turned many heads that might have been steady enough in a quiet nursery or kitchen in England.

To find a man and wife, both of whom would suit us, would be very difficult; and I think it right, also, to offer to my clerk to keep him in my service. He is honest, intelligent, and respectful; and as he is rather inclined to consumption, the change of climate would probably be useful to him. I can not bear the thought of throwing any person who has been about me for five years, and with whom I have no fault to find, out of bread, while it is in my power to retain his services. Ever yours, T. B. M.

London, December 5th, 1833.

Dear Lord Lansdowne,—I delayed returning an answer to your kind letter till this day, in order that I might be able to send you definitive intelligence. Yesterday evening the directors appointed me to a seat in the council of India. The votes were nineteen for me, and three against me.

I feel that the sacrifice which I am about to make is great. But the motives which urge me to make it are quite irresistible. Every day that I live I become less and less desirous of great wealth. But every day makes me more sensible of the importance of a competence. Without a competence it is not very easy for a public man to be honest: it is almost impossible for him to be thought so. I am so situated that I can subsist only in two ways: by being in office, and by my pen. Hitherto, literature has been merely my relaxation—the amusement of perhaps a month in the year. I have never considered it as the means of support. I have chosen my own topics, taken my own time, and dictated my own terms. The thought of becoming a book-seller's hack; of writing to relieve, not the fullness of the mind, but the emptiness of the pocket; of spurring a jaded fancy to reluctant exertion; of filling sheets with trash merely that the sheets may be filled; of bearing from publishers and editors what Dryden bore from Tonson, and what, to my own knowledge, Mackintosh bore from Lardner, is horrible to me. Yet thus it must be, if I should quit office. Yet to hold office merely for the sake of emolument would be more horrible still. The situation in which I have been placed for some time back would have broken the spirit of many men. It has rather tended to make me the most mutinous and unmanageable of the followers of the Government. I tendered my resignation twice during the course of the last session. I certainly should not have done so if I had been a man of fortune. You, whom malevolence itself could never accuse of coveting office for the sake of pecuniary gain, and whom your salary very poorly compensates for the sacrifice of ease and of your tastes to the public service, can not estimate rightly the feelings of a man who knows that his circumstances lay him open to the suspicion of being actuated in his public conduct by the lowest motives. Once or twice, when I have been defending unpopular measures in the House of Commons, that thought has disordered my ideas and deprived me of my presence of mind.

If this were all, I should feel that, for the sake of my own happiness and of my public utility, a few years would be well spent in obtaining an independence. But this is not all. I am not alone in the world. A family which I love most fondly is dependent on me. Unless I would see my father left in his old age to the charity of less near relations; my youngest brother unable to obtain a good professional education; my sisters, who are more to me than any sisters ever were to a brother, forced to turn governesses or humble companions, I must do something, I must make some effort. An opportunity has offered itself. It is in my power to make the last days of my father comfortable, to educate my brother, to provide for my sisters, to procure a competence for myself. I may hope, by the time I am thirty-nine or forty, to return to England with a fortune of thirty thousand pounds. To me that would be affluence. I never wished for more.

As far as English politics are concerned, I lose, it is true, a few years. But, if your kindness had not introduced me very early to Parliament, if I had been left to climb up the regular path of my profession, and to rise by my own efforts—I should have had very little chance of being in the House of Commons at forty. If I have gained any distinction in the eyes of my countrymen, if I have acquired any knowledge of Parliamentary and official business, and any habitude for the management of great affairs, I ought to consider these things as clear gain.

Then, too, the years of my absence, though lost, as far as English politics are concerned, will not, I hope, be wholly lost as respects either my own mind or the happiness of my fellow-creatures. I can scarcely conceive a nobler field than that which our Indian empire now presents to a statesman. While some of my partial friends are blaming me for stooping to accept a share in the government of that empire, I am afraid that I am aspiring too high for my qualifications. I sometimes feel, I most unaffectedly declare, depressed and appalled by the immense responsibility which I have undertaken. You are one of the very few public men of our time who have bestowed on Indian affairs the attention which they deserve;

and you will therefore, I am sure, fully enter into my feelings.

And now, dear Lord Lansdowne, let me thank you most warmly for the kind feeling which has dictated your letter. That letter is, indeed, but a very small part of what I ought to thank you for. That at an early age I have gained some credit in public life; that I have done some little service to more than one good cause; that I now have it in my power to repair the ruined fortunes of my family, and to save those who are dearest to me from the misery and humiliation of dependence; that I am almost certain, if I live, of obtaining a competence by honorable means before I am past the full vigor of manhood—all this I owe to your kindness. I will say no more. I will only entreat you to believe that neither now, nor on any former occasion, have I ever said one thousandth part of what I feel.

If it will not be inconvenient to you, I propose to go to Bowood on Wednesday next. Labouchere will be my fellow-traveler. On Saturday we must both return to town. Short as my visit must be, I look forward to it with great pleasure.

Believe me ever yours most faithfully and affectionately,

T. B. Macaulay.

To Hannah M. Macaulay.

London, December 5th, 1833.

My dear Sister,—I am overwhelmed with business, clearing off my work here, and preparing for my new functions. Plans of ships, and letters from captains, pour in without intermission. I really am mobbed with gentlemen begging to have the honor of taking me to India at my own time. The fact is, that a member of council is a great catch, not merely on account of the high price which he directly pays for accommodation, but because other people are attracted by him. Every father of a young writer or a young cadet likes to have his son on board the same vessel with the great man, to dine at the same table, and to have a chance of attracting his notice. Every thing in India is given by the governor in council; and, though I have no direct voice in the disposal of patronage, my indirect influence may be great.

Grant's kindness through all these negotiations has been such as I really can not describe. He told me yesterday, with tears in his eyes, that he did not know what the Board would do without me. I attribute his feeling partly to Robert Grant's absence; not that Robert ever did me ill offices with him—far from it; but Grant's is a mind that can not stand alone. It is—begging your pardon for my want of gallantry—a feminine mind. It turns, like ivy, to some support. When Robert is near him, he clings to Robert. Robert being away, he clings to me. This may be a weakness in a public man, but I love him the better for it.

I have lately met Sir James Graham at dinner. He took me aside, and talked to me on my appointment with a warmth of kindness which, though we have been always on good terms, surprised me. But the approach of a long separation, like the approach of death, brings out all friendly feelings with unusual strength. The Cabinet, he said, felt the loss strongly. It was great at the India Board, but in the House of Commons (he used the word over and over) irreparable. They all, however, he said, agreed that a man of honor could not make politics a profession unless he had a competence of his own, without exposing himself to privation of the severest kind. They felt that they had never had it in their power to do all they wished to do for me. They had no means of giving me a provision in England, and they could not refuse me what I asked in India. He said very strongly that they all thought that I judged quite wisely; and added that, if God heard his prayers and spared my health, I should make a far greater figure in public life than if I had remained during the next five or six years in England.

I picked up in a print-shop the other day some superb views of the suburbs of Chowringhee, and the villas of the Garden Reach. Selina professes that she is ready to die with envy of the fine houses and verandas. I heartily wish we were back again in a nice plain brick house, three windows in front, in Cadogan Place or Russell Square, with twelve or fifteen hundred a year, and a spare bedroom (we, like Mrs. Norris,* must always have a spare bedroom) for Edward and Margaret. Love to them both. Ever yours, T. B. M.

To Macvey Napier, Esq.

London, December 5th, 1833.

DEAR NAPIER,—You are probably not unprepared for what I am about to tell you. Yesterday evening the Directors of the East India Company elected me one of the members of the Supreme Council. It will, therefore, be necessary that in a few weeks, ten weeks at furthest, I should leave this country for a few years.

It would be mere affectation in me to pretend not to know that my support is of some importance to the *Edinburgh Review*. In the situation in which I shall now be placed, a connection with the *Review* will be of some importance to me. I know well how dangerous it is for a public man wholly to withdraw himself from the public eye. During an absence of six years, I run some risk of losing most of the distinction, literary and political, which I have acquired. As a means of keeping myself in the recollection of my countrymen during my sojourn abroad, the *Review* will be invaluable to me; nor do I foresee that there will be the slightest difficulty in my continuing to write for you at least as much as ever. I have thought over my late articles, and I really can scarcely call to mind a single sentence in any one of them which might not have been written at Calcutta as easily as in London. Perhaps in India I might not have the means of detecting two or three of the false dates in Croker's Boswell; but that would have been all. Very little, if any, of the effect of my most popular articles is produced either by minute research into rare books, or by allusions to mere topics of the day.

I think, therefore, that we might easily establish a commerce mutually beneficial. I shall wish to be supplied with all the good books which come out in this part of the world. Indeed, many books which in themselves are of little value,

---

* A leading personage in Miss Austen's "Mansfield Park."

and which, if I were in England, I should not think it worth while to read, will be interesting to me in India; just as the commonest daubs and the rudest vessels at Pompeii attract the minute attention of people who would not move their eyes to see a modern sign-post or a modern kettle. Distance of place, like distance of time, makes trifles valuable.

What I propose, then, is that you should pay me for the articles which I may send you from India, not in money, but in books. As to the amount I make no stipulations. You know that I have never haggled about such matters. As to the choice of books, the mode of transmission, and other matters, we shall have ample time to discuss them before my departure. Let me know whether you are willing to make an arrangement on this basis.

I have not forgotten Chatham in the midst of my avocations. I hope to send you an article on him early next week.

Ever yours sincerely, T. B. MACAULAY.

From the Right Hon. Francis Jeffrey to Macvey Napier, Esq.

24 Moray Place, Saturday Evening, December 7th.

MY DEAR NAPIER,—I am very much obliged to you for the permission to read this. It is to me, I will confess, a solemn and melancholy announcement. I ought not, perhaps, so to consider it. But I can not help it. I was not prepared for six years, and I must still hope that it will not be so much. At my age, and with that climate for him, the chances of our ever meeting again are terribly endangered by such a term. He does not know the extent of the damage which his secession may be to the great cause of Liberal government. His anticipations and offers about the *Review* are generous and pleasing, and must be peculiarly gratifying to you. I think, if you can, you should try to see him before he goes, and I envy you the meeting. Ever very faithfully yours,

F. JEFFREY.

To Hannah M. Macaulay.

London, December 21st, 1833.

MY DEAR SISTER,—Yesterday I dined at Boddington's. We had a very agreeable party: Duncannon, Charles Grant,

Sharp, Chantrey the sculptor, Bobus Smith, and James Mill. Mill and I were extremely friendly, and I found him a very pleasant companion, and a man of more general information than I had imagined.

Bobus was very amusing. He is a great authority on Indian matters. He was during several years advocate general in Bengal, and made all his large fortune there. I asked him about the climate. Nothing, he said, could be pleasanter, except in August and September. He never eat or drank so much in his life. Indeed, his looks do credit to Bengal, for a healthier man of his age I never saw. We talked about expenses. "I can not conceive," he said, "how any body at Calcutta can live on less than £3000 a year, or can contrive to spend more than £4000." We talked of the insects and snakes, and he said a thing which reminded me of his brother Sydney, "Always, sir, manage to have at your table some fleshy, blooming young writer or cadet, just come out; that the mosquitoes may stick to him, and leave the rest of the company alone."

I have been with George Babington to the *Asia*. We saw her to every disadvantage, all litter and confusion; but she is a fine ship, and our cabins will be very good. The captain I like much. He is an agreeable, intelligent, polished man of forty; and very good-looking, considering what storms and changes of climate he has gone through. He advised me strongly to put little furniture into our cabins. I told him to have yours made as neat as possible, without regard to expense. He has promised to have it furnished simply, but prettily; and when you see it, if any addition occurs to you, it shall be made. I shall spare nothing to make a pretty little boudoir for you. You can not think how my friends here praise you. You are quite Sir James Graham's heroine.

To-day I breakfasted with Sharp, whose kindness is as warm as possible. Indeed, all my friends seem to be in the most amiable mood. I have twice as many invitations as I can accept, and I have been frequently begged to name my own party. Empty as London is, I never was so much beset with invitations. Sharp asked me about you. I told him how much I regretted my never having had any opportunity of showing you the best part of London society. He said that he would take care that you should see what was best worth seeing before your departure. He promises to give us a few breakfast-parties and dinner-parties, where you will meet as many as he can muster of the best set in town; Rogers, Luttrell, Rice, Tom Moore, Sydney Smith, Grant, and other great wits and politicians. I am quite delighted at this; both because you will, I am sure, be amused and pleased at a time when you ought to have your mind occupied, and because even to have mixed a little in a circle so brilliant will be of advantage to you in India. You have neglected, and very rightly and sensibly, frivolous accomplishments; you have not been at places of fashionable diversion; and it is, therefore, the more desirable that you should appear among the dancing, piano-forte-playing, opera-going damsels at Calcutta as one who has seen society better than any that they ever approached. I hope that you will not disapprove of what I have done. I accepted Sharp's offer for you eagerly. Ever yours,

T. B. M.

To Hannah M. Macaulay.

London, January 2d, 1834.

My dear Sister,—I am busy with an article* for Napier. I can not in the least tell at present whether I shall like it or not. I proceed with great ease; and in general I have found that the success of my writings has been in proportion to the ease with which they have been written.

I had a most extraordinary scene with Lady Holland. If she had been as young and handsome as she was thirty years ago, she would have turned my head. She was quite hysterical about my going; paid me such compliments as I can not repeat; cried; raved; called me dear, dear Macaulay. "You are sacrificed to your family. I see it all. You are too good to them. They are always making a tool of you; last session about the slaves; and now sending you to India!" I always do my best to keep my temper with Lady Holland, for three

* The first article on Lord Chatham.

reasons: because she is a woman; because she is very unhappy in her health, and in the circumstances of her position; and because she has a real kindness for me. But at last she said something about you. This was too much, and I was beginning to answer her in a voice trembling with anger, when she broke out again: "I beg your pardon. Pray forgive me, dear Macaulay. I was very impertinent. I know you will forgive me. Nobody has such a temper as you. I have said so a hundred times. I said so to Allen only this morning. I am sure you will bear with my weakness. I shall never see you again;" and she cried, and I cooled; for it would have been to very little purpose to be angry with her. I hear that it is not to me alone that she runs on in this way. She storms at the ministers for letting me go. I was told that at one dinner she became so violent that even Lord Holland, whose temper, whatever his wife may say, is much cooler than mine, could not command himself, and broke out: "Don't talk such nonsense, my lady. What, the devil! Can we tell a gentleman who has a claim upon us that he must lose his only chance of getting an independence in order that he may come and talk to you in an evening?"

Good-bye, and take care not to become so fond of your own will as my lady. It is now my duty to omit no opportunity of giving you wholesome advice. I am henceforward your sole guardian. I have bought Gisborne's "Duties of Women," Moore's "Fables for the Female Sex," Mrs. King's "Female Scripture Characters," and Fordyce's Sermons. With the help of these books I hope to keep my responsibility in order on our voyage, and in India. Ever yours, T. B. M.

To Hannah M. Macaulay.

London, January 4th, 1834.

MY DEAR SISTER,—I am now buying books; not trashy books which will only bear one reading, but good books for a library. I have my eye on all the book-stalls; and I shall no longer suffer you, when we walk together in London, to drag me past them as you used to do. Pray make out a list of any which you would like to have. The provision which I design for the voyage is Richardson, Voltaire's works, Gibbon, Sismondi's "History of the French," "Davila," "The Orlando" in Italian, "Don Quixote" in Spanish, Homer in Greek, Horace in Latin. I must also have some books of jurisprudence, and some to initiate me in Persian and Hindoostanee. Shall I buy "Dunallan" for you? I believe that in your eyes it would stand in the place of all the rest together. But, seriously, let me know what you would like me to procure.

Ellis is making a little collection of Greek classics for me. Sharpe has given me one or two very rare and pretty books, which I much wanted. All the *Edinburgh Reviews* are being bound, so that we shall have a complete set up to the forthcoming number, which will contain an article of mine on Chatham. And this reminds me that I must give over writing to you, and fall to my article. I rather think that it will be a good one. Ever yours, T. B. M.

London, February 13th, 1834.

Dear Napier,—It is true that I have been severely tried by ill-health during the last few weeks; but I am now rapidly recovering, and am assured by all my medical advisers that a week of the sea will make me better than ever I was in my life.

I have several subjects in my head. One is Mackintosh's "History;" I mean the fragment of the large work. Another plan which I have is a very fine one, if it could be well executed. I think that the time is come when a fair estimate may be formed of the intellectual and moral character of Voltaire. The extreme veneration with which he was regarded during his life-time has passed away; the violent reaction which followed has spent itself; and the world can now, I think, bear to hear the truth, and to see the man exhibited as he was—a strange mixture of greatness and littleness, virtues and vices. I have all his works, and shall take them in my cabin on the voyage. But my library is not particularly rich in those books which illustrate the literary history of his times. I have Rousseau and Marmontel's "Memoirs," and Madame du Deffand's "Letters," and perhaps a few other works which would be of use. But Grimm's "Correspondence," and several other volumes of memoirs and letters, would be necessary. If you would make a small collection of the works which would be most useful in this point of view, and send it after me as soon as possible, I will do my best to draw a good Voltaire. I fear that the article must be enormously long—seventy pages, perhaps; but you know that I do not run into unnecessary lengths.

I may perhaps try my hand on Miss Austen's novels. That is a subject on which I shall require no assistance from books.

Whatever volumes you may send me ought to be half-bound; or the white ants will devour them before they have been three days on shore. Besides the books which may be necessary for the *Review*, I should like to have any work of very striking merit which may appear during my absence. The particular department of literature which interests me most is history; above all, English history. Any valuable book on that subject I should wish to possess. Sharp, Miss Berry, and some of my other friends, will perhaps, now and then, suggest a book to you. But it is principally on your own judgment that I must rely to keep me well supplied.

Yours most truly, T. B. MACAULAY.

On the 4th of February Macaulay bid farewell to his electors, in an address which the Leeds Tories probably thought too high-flown* for the occasion. But he had not yet done

* "If, now that I have ceased to be your servant, and am only your sincere and grateful friend, I may presume to offer you advice which must, at least, be allowed to be disinterested, I would say to you: Act toward your future representatives as you have acted toward me. Choose them, as you chose me, without canvassing and without expense. Encourage them, as you encouraged me, always to speak to you fearlessly and plainly. Reject, as you have hitherto rejected, the wages of dishonor. Defy, as you have hitherto defied, the threats of petty tyrants. Never forget that the worst and most degrading species of corruption is the corruption which operates, not by hopes, but by fears. Cherish those noble and virtuous principles for which we have struggled and triumphed together—the principles of liberty and toleration, of justice and order. Support, as

with the House of Commons. Parliament met on the first Tuesday in the month; and, on the Wednesday, O'Connell, who had already contrived to make two speeches since the session began, rose for a third time to call attention to words uttered during the recess by Mr. Hill, the member for Hull. That gentleman, for want of something better to say to his constituents, had told them that he happened to know "that an Irish member, who spoke with great violence against every part of the Coercion Bill, and voted against every clause of it, went to ministers and said, 'Don't bate a single atom of that bill, or it will be impossible for any man to live in Ireland.'" O'Connell called upon Lord Althorp, as the representative of the Government, to say what truth there was in this statement. Lord Althorp, taken by surprise, acted upon the impulse of the moment, which in his case was a feeling of reluctance to throw over poor Mr. Hill to be bullied by O'Connell and his redoubtable tail. After explaining that no set and deliberate communication of the nature mentioned had been made to the ministers, his lordship went on to say that he "should not act properly if he did not declare that he had good reason to believe that some Irish members did, in private conversation, use very different language" from what they had employed in public.

It was chivalrously, but most unwisely, spoken. O'Connell at once gave the cue by inquiring whether he himself was among the members referred to, and Lord Althorp assured him that such was not the case. The Speaker tried to interfere; but the matter had gone too far. One Irish representative after another jumped up to repeat the same question with regard to his own case, and received the same answer. At length Sheil rose, and asked whether he was one of the

---

you have steadily supported, the cause of good government; and may all the blessings which are the natural fruits of good government descend upon you and be multiplied to you a hundred-fold! May your manufactures flourish; may your trade be extended; may your riches increase! May the works of your skill, and the signs of your prosperity, meet me in the farthest regions of the East, and give me fresh cause to be proud of the intelligence, the industry, and the spirit of my constituents!"

members to whom the noble lord had alluded. Lord Althorp replied: "Yes. The honorable and learned gentleman is one." Sheil, "in the face of his country, and the presence of his God," asserted that the individual who had given any such information to the noble lord was guilty of a "gross and scandalous calumny," and added that he understood the noble lord to have made himself responsible for the imputation. Then ensued one of those scenes in which the House of Commons appears at its very worst. All the busy-bodies, as their manner is, rushed to the front; and hour after hour slipped away in an unseemly, intricate, and apparently interminable wrangle. Sheil was duly called upon to give an assurance that the affair should not be carried beyond the walls of the House. He refused to comply, and was committed to the charge of the sergeant-at-arms. The Speaker then turned to Lord Althorp, who promised, in Parliamentary language, not to send a challenge. Upon this, as is graphically enough described in the conventional terms of Hansard, "Mr. O'Connell made some observation to the honorable member sitting next him which was not heard in the body of the House. Lord Althorp immediately rose, and amidst loud cheers, and with considerable warmth, demanded to know what the honorable and learned gentleman meant by his gesticulation;" and then, after an explanation from O'Connell, his lordship went on to use phrases which very clearly signified that, though he had no cause for sending a challenge, he had just as little intention of declining one; upon which he likewise was made over to the sergeant. Before, however, honorable members went to their dinners, they had the relief of learning that their refractory colleagues had submitted to the Speaker's authority, and had been discharged from custody.

There was only one way out of the difficulty. On the 10th of February a committee of investigation was appointed, composed of members who enjoyed a special reputation for discretion. Mr. Hill called his witnesses. The first had nothing relevant to tell. Macaulay was the second; and he forthwith cut the matter short by declaring that, on principle, he refused to disclose what had passed in private conversation: a sentiment which was actually cheered by the committee. One sentence of common sense brought the absurd embroilment to a rational conclusion. Mr. Hill saw his mistake; begged that no further evidence might be taken; and, at the next sitting of the House, withdrew his charge in unqualified terms of self-abasement and remorse. Lord Althorp readily admitted that he had acted "imprudently as a man, and still more imprudently as a minister," and stated that he considered himself bound to accept Sheil's denial; but he could not manage so to frame his remarks as to convey to his hearers the idea that his opinion of that honorable gentleman had been raised by the transaction. Sheil acknowledged the two apologies with effusion proportioned to their respective value; and so ended an affair which, at the worst, had evoked a fresh proof of that ingrained sincerity of character for the sake of which his party would have followed Lord Althorp to the death.*

Gravesend, February 15th, 1834.

Dear Lord Lansdowne,—I had hoped that it would have been in my power to shake hands with you once more before my departure; but this deplorably absurd affair in the House of Commons has prevented me from calling on you. I lost a whole day while the committee were deciding whether I should or should not be forced to repeat all the foolish, shabby things that I had heard Sheil say at Brooks's.

I can not leave England without sending a few lines to you, and yet they are needless. It is unnecessary for me to say with what feelings I shall always remember our connection, and with what interest I shall always learn tidings of you and of your family.

Yours most sincerely, T. B. Macaulay.

---

* In Macaulay's journal for June 3d, 1851, we read: "I went to breakfast with the Bishop of Oxford, and there learned that Sheil was dead. Poor fellow! We talked about Sheil, and I related my adventure of February, 1834. Odd that it should have been so little known, or so completely forgotten! Every body thought me right, as I certainly was."

CHAPTER VI.

1834-1838.

The Outward Voyage.—Arrival at Madras.—Macaulay is summoned to join Lord William Bentinck in the Neilgherries.—His Journey Up-country.—His Native Servant.—Arcot.—Bangalore.—Seringapatam.—Ascent of the Neilgherries.—First Sight of the Governor-general.—Letters to Mr. Ellis and the Miss Macaulays.—A Summer on the Neilgherries.—Native Christians.—Clarissa.—A Tragi-comedy.—Macaulay leaves the Neilgherries, travels to Calcutta, and there sets up House.—Letters to Mr. Napier and Mrs. Cropper.—Mr. Trevelyan.—Marriage of Hannah Macaulay.—Death of Mrs. Cropper.—Macaulay's Work in India.—His Minutes for Council.—Freedom of the Press.—Literary Gratitude.—Second Minute on the Freedom of the Press.—The Black Act.—A Calcutta Public Meeting.—Macaulay's Defense of the Policy of the Indian Government.—His Minute on Education.—He becomes President of the Committee of Public Instruction.—His Industry in discharging the Functions of that Post.—Specimens of his Official Writing.—Results of his Labors.—He is appointed President of the Law Commission, and recommends the Framing of a Criminal Code.—Appearance of the Code.—Comments of Mr. Fitzjames Stephen.—Macaulay's Private Life in India.—Oriental Delicacies.—Breakfast-parties.—Macaulay's Longing for England.—Calcutta and Dublin.—Departure from India.—Letters to Mr. Ellis, Mr. Sharp, Mr. Napier, and Mr. Z. Macaulay.

FROM the moment that a deputation of Falmouth Whigs, headed by their mayor, came on board to wish Macaulay his health in India and a happy return to England, nothing occurred that broke the monotony of an easy and rapid voyage. "The catching of a shark; the shooting of an albatross; a sailor tumbling down the hatchway and breaking his head; a cadet getting drunk and swearing at the captain," are incidents to which not even the highest literary power can impart the charm of novelty in the eyes of the readers of a sea-faring nation. The company on the quarter-deck was much on a level with the average society of an East Indiaman. "Hannah will give you the histories of all these good people at length, I dare say, for she was extremely social: danced with the gentlemen in the evenings, and read novels and sermons with the ladies in the mornings. I contented myself with being very civil whenever I was with the other passengers, and took care to be with them as little as I could. Except at meals, I hardly exchanged a word with any human being. I never was left for so long a time so completely to my own resources; and I am glad to say that I found them quite sufficient to keep me cheerful and employed. During the whole voyage I read with keen and increasing enjoyment. I devoured Greek, Latin, Spanish, Italian, French, and English; folios, quartos, octavos, and duodecimos."

On the 10th of June the vessel lay to off Madras; and Macaulay had his first introduction to the people for whom he was appointed to legislate, in the person of a boatman who pulled through the surf on his raft. "He came on board with nothing on him but a pointed yellow cap, and walked among us with a self-possession and civility which, coupled with his color and his nakedness, nearly made me die of laughing." This gentleman was soon followed by more responsible messengers, who brought tidings the reverse of welcome. Lord William Bentinck, who was then governor-general, was detained by ill-health at Ootacamund, in the Neilgherry Hills; a place which, by name at least, is now as familiar to Englishmen as Malvern; but which in 1834 was known to Macaulay, by vague report, as situated somewhere "in the mountains of Malabar, beyond Mysore." The state of public business rendered it necessary that the council should meet; and, as the governor-general had left one member of that body in Bengal as his deputy, he was not able to make a quorum until his new colleague arrived from England. A pressing summons to attend his lordship in the Hills placed Macaulay in some embarrassment on account of his sister, who could not with safety commence her Eastern experiences by a journey of four hundred miles up the country in the middle of June. Happily the second letter which he opened proved to be from Bishop Wilson; who insisted that the son and daughter of so eminent an Evangelical as the editor of the *Christian Observer*, themselves part of his old congregation in Bedford Row, should begin their Indian life nowhere except under his roof. Hannah, accordingly, continued her voyage, and made her appearance in Calcutta circles with the Bishop's palace as a home, and Lady William Bentinck as a kind, and soon an affectionate, chaperon; while her brother remained on shore at Madras, somewhat consoled for the separation by finding himself in a country where so much was to be seen, and where, as far as the English residents were concerned, he was regarded with a curiosity at least equal to his own.

During the first few weeks nothing came amiss to him. "To be on land after three months at sea is of itself a great change. But to be in such a land! The dark faces with white turbans and flowing robes: the trees not our trees: the very smell of the atmosphere that of a hot-house, and the architecture as strange as the vegetation." Every feature in that marvelous scene delighted him, both in itself and for the sake of the innumerable associations and images which it conjured up in his active and well-stored mind. The salute of fifteen guns that greeted him as he set his foot on the beach reminded him that he was in a region where his countrymen could exist only on the condition of their being warriors and rulers. When on a visit of ceremony to a dispossessed rajah or nabob, he pleased himself with the reflection that he was face to face with a prince who in old days governed a province as large as a first-class European kingdom, conceding to his suzerain, the mogul, no tribute beyond "a little outward respect such as the great Dukes of Burgundy used to pay to the Kings of France; and who now enjoyed the splendid and luxurious insignificance of an abdicated prince which fell to the lot of Charles the Fifth, or Queen Christina of Sweden," with a court that preserved the forms of royalty, the right of keeping as many badly armed and worse paid ragamuffins as he could retain under his tawdry standard, and the privilege of "occasionally sending letters of condolence and congratulation to the King of England, in which he calls himself his majesty's good brother and ally."

Macaulay set forth on his journey within a week from his landing, traveling by night, and resting while the sun was at its hottest. He has recorded his first impressions of Hindoostan in a series of journal letters addressed to his sister Margaret. The fresh and vivid character of those impressions, the genuine and multiform interest excited in him by all that met his ear or eye, explain the secret of the charm which enabled him in after-days to overcome the distaste for Indian literature entertained by that personage who, for want of a better, goes by the name of the general reader. Macaulay reversed in his own case the experience of those countless writers on Indian themes who have successively blunted their pens against the passive indifference of the British public; for his faithful but brilliant studies of the history of our Eastern empire are to this day incomparably the most popular* of his works. It may be possible, without injury to the fame of the author, to present a few extracts from a correspondence which is in some sort the raw material of productions that have already secured their place among our national classics.

"In the afternoon of the 17th of June I left Madras. My train consisted of thirty-eight persons. I was in one palanquin, and my servant followed in another. He is a half-caste. On the day on which we set out he told me he was a Catholic; and added, crossing himself and turning up the whites of his eyes, that he had recommended himself to the protection of his patron saint, and that he was quite confident that we should perform our journey in safety. I thought of Ambrose Llamela, Gil Blas's devout

---

* When published in a separate form, the articles on Lord Clive and Warren Hastings have sold nearly twice as well as the articles on Lord Chatham, nearly thrice as well as the article on Addison, and nearly five times as well as the article on Byron. The great Sepoy mutiny, while it something more than doubled the sale of the essay on Warren Hastings, all but trebled the sale of the essay on Lord Clive; but, taking the last twenty years together, there has been little to choose between the pair. The steadiness and permanence of the favor with which they are regarded may be estimated by the fact that, during the five years between 1870 and 1874, as compared with the five years between 1865 and 1869, the demand for them has been in the proportion of seven to three; and, as compared with the five years between 1860 and 1864, in the proportion of three to one.

valet, who arranges a scheme for robbing his master of his portmanteau, and, when he comes back from meeting his accomplices, pretends that he has been to the cathedral to implore a blessing on their voyage. I did him, however, a great injustice; for I have found him a very honest man, who knows the native languages; and who can dispute a charge, bully a negligent bearer, arrange a bed, and make a curry. But he is so fond of giving advice that I fear he will some day or other, as the Scotch say, raise my corruption, and provoke me to send him about his business. His name, which I never hear without laughing, is Peter Prim.

"Half my journey was by daylight, and all that I saw during that time disappointed me grievously. It is amazing how small a part of the country is under cultivation. Two-thirds at least, as it seemed to me, was in the state of Wandsworth Common, or, to use an illustration which you will understand better, of Chatmoss. The people whom we met were as few as in the Highlands of Scotland. But I have been told that in India the villages generally lie at a distance from the roads, and that much of the land, which when I passed through it looked like parched moor that had never been cultivated, would after the rains be covered with rice."

After traversing this landscape for fifteen hours, he reached the town of Arcot, which, under his handling, was to be celebrated far and wide as the cradle of our greatness in the East.

"I was most hospitably received by Captain Smith, who commanded the garrison. After dinner the palanquins went forward with my servant, and the captain and I took a ride to see the lions of the neighborhood. He mounted me on a very quiet Arab, and I had a pleasant excursion. We passed through a garden which was attached to the residence of the Nabob of the Carnatic, who anciently held his court at Arcot. The garden has been suffered to run to waste, and is only the more beautiful for having been neglected. Garden, indeed, is hardly a proper word. In England it would rank as one of our noblest parks, from which it differs principally in this, that most of the fine trees are fruit-trees. From this we came to a mountain pass which reminded me strongly of Borradaile near Derwentwater, and through this defile we struck into the road and rejoined the bearers."

And so he went forward on his way, recalling at every step the reminiscence of some place, or event, or person; and thereby doubling for himself, and perhaps for his correspondent, the pleasure which the reality was capable of affording. If he put up at a collector's bungalow, he liked to think that his host ruled more absolutely and over a larger population than "a Duke of Saxe-Weimar or a Duke of Lucca;" and when he came across a military man with a turn for reading, he pronounced him, "as Dominie Sampson said of another Indian colonel, 'a man of great erudition, considering his imperfect opportunities.'"

On the 19th of June he crossed the frontier of Mysore, reached Bangalore on the morning of the 20th, and rested there for three days in the house of the commandant.

"On Monday, the 23d, I took leave of Colonel Cubbon, who told me, with a warmth which I was vain enough to think sincere, that he had not passed three such pleasant days for thirty years. I went on all night, sleeping soundly in my palanquin. At five I was waked, and found that a carriage was waiting for me. I had told Colonel Cubbon that I very much wished to see Seringapatam. He had written to the British authorities at the town of Mysore, and an officer had come from the Residency to show me all that was to be seen. I must now digress into Indian politics; and let me tell you that, if you read the little that I shall say about them, you will know more on the subject than half the members of the Cabinet."

After a few pages occupied by a sketch of the history of Mysore during the preceding century, Macaulay proceeds:

"Seringapatam has always been a place of peculiar interest to me. It was the scene of the greatest events of Indian history. It was the residence of the greatest of Indian princes. From a child I used to hear it talked of every day. Our uncle Colin was imprisoned there for four years, and he was afterward distinguished at the siege. I remember that there was, in a shop-window at Clapham, a daub of the taking of Seringapatam, which, as a boy, I often used to stare at with the greatest interest. I was delighted to have an opportunity of seeing the place; and, though my expectations were high, they were not disappointed.

"The town is depopulated; but the fortress, which was one of the strongest in India, remains entire. A river almost as broad as the Thames at Chelsea breaks into two branches, and surrounds the walls, above which are seen the white minarets of a mosque. We entered, and found every thing silent and desolate. The mosque, indeed, is still kept up, and deserves to be so; but the palace of Tippoo has fallen into utter ruin. I saw, however, with no small interest, the air-holes of the dungeon in which the English prisoners were confined, and the water-gate leading down to the river where the body of Tippoo was found still warm by the Duke of Wellington, then Colonel Wellesley. The exact spot through which the English soldiers fought their way against desperate disadvantages into the fort is still perfectly discernible. But, though only thirty-five years have elapsed since the fall of the city, the palace is in the condition of Tintern Abbey and Melrose Abbey. The courts, which bear a great resemblance to those of the Oxford colleges, are completely overrun with weeds and flowers. The Hall of Audience, once considered the finest in India, still retains some very faint traces of its old magnificence. It is supported on a great number of light and lofty wooden pillars, resting on pedestals of black granite. These pillars were formerly covered with gilding, and here and there the glitter may still be perceived. In a few more years not the smallest trace of this superb chamber will remain. I am surprised that more care was not taken by the English to preserve so splendid a memorial of the greatness of him whom they had conquered. It was not like Lord Wellesley's general mode of proceeding; and I soon saw a proof of his taste and liberality. Tippoo raised a most sumptuous mausoleum to his father, and attached to it a mosque which he endowed. The buildings are carefully maintained at the expense of our Government. You walk up from the fort through a narrow path, bordered by flower-beds and cypresses, to the front of the mausoleum, which is very beautiful, and in general character closely resembles the most richly carved of our small Gothic chapels. Within are three tombs, all covered with magnificent palls embroidered in gold with verses from the Koran. In the centre lies Hyder; on his right the mother of Tippoo; and Tippoo himself on the left."

During his stay at Mysore, Macaulay had an interview with the deposed rajah; whose appearance, conversation, palace, furniture, jewels, soldiers, elephants, courtiers, and idols he depicts in a letter, intended for family perusal, with a minuteness that would qualify him for an Anglo-Indian Richardson. By the evening of the 24th of June he was once more on the road; and, about noon on the following day, he began to ascend the Neilgherries, through scenery which, for the benefit of readers who had never seen the Pyrenees or the Italian slopes of an Alpine pass, he likened to "the vegetation of Windsor Forest or Blenheim spread over the mountains of Cumberland." After reaching the summit of the table-land, he passed through a wilderness where for eighteen miles together he met nothing more human than a monkey, until a turn of the road disclosed the pleasant surprise of an amphitheatre of green hills encircling a small lake, whose banks were dotted with red-tiled cottages surrounding a pretty Gothic church. The whole station presented "very much the look of a rising English watering-place. The largest house is occupied by the governor-general. It is a spacious and handsome building of stone. To this I was carried, and immediately ushered into his lordship's presence. I found him sitting by a fire in a carpeted library. He received me with the greatest kindness, frankness, and hospitality. He is, as far as I can yet judge, all that I have heard; that is to say, rectitude, openness, and good nature personified." Many months of close friendship and common labors did but confirm Macaulay in this first view of Lord William Bentinck. His estimate of that singularly noble character survives in the closing sentence of the essay on Lord Clive; and is inscribed on the base of the statue which, standing in front of the Town Hall, may be seen far and wide over the great expanse of grass that serves as the park, the parade-ground, and the race-course of Calcutta.

To Thomas Flower Ellis.

Ootacamund, July 1st, 1834.

DEAR ELLIS,—You need not get your map to see where Ootacamund is, for it has not found its way into the maps. It is a new discovery; a place to which Europeans resort for their health, or, as it is called by the Company's servants—blessings on their learning!—a *sanaterion.* It lies at the height of seven thousand feet above the sea.

While London is a perfect gridiron, here am I, at 13° north from the equator, by a blazing wood-fire, with my windows closed. My bed is heaped with blankets, and my black servants are coughing round me in all directions. One poor fellow in particular looks so miserably cold that, unless the sun comes out, I am likely soon to see under my own roof the spectacle which, according to Shakspeare, is so interesting to the English*—a dead Indian.

I traveled the whole four hundred miles between this and Madras on men's shoulders. I had an agreeable journey, on the whole. I was honored by an interview with the Rajah of Mysore, who insisted on showing me all his wardrobe, and his

* "The Tempest," act ii., scene 2.

picture-gallery. He has six or seven colored English prints not much inferior to those which I have seen in the sanded parlor of a country inn: "Going to Cover," "The Death of the Fox," and so forth. But the bijou of his gallery, of which he is as vain as the grand duke can be of the "Venus," or Lord Carlisle of "The Three Maries," is a head of the Duke of Wellington, which has most certainly been on a sign-post in England.

Yet, after all, the rajah was by no means the greatest fool whom I found at Mysore. I alighted at a bungalow appertaining to the British Residency. There I found an Englishman who, without any preface, accosted me thus: "Pray, Mr. Macaulay, do not you think that Bonaparte was the Beast?" "No, sir, I can not say that I do." "Sir, he was the Beast. I can prove it. I have found the number 666 in his name. Why, sir, if he was not the Beast, who was?" This was a puzzling question, and I am not a little vain of my answer. "Sir," said I, "the House of Commons is the Beast. There are 658 members of the House; and these, with their chief officers—the three clerks, the sergeant and his deputy, the chaplain, the door-keeper, and the librarian—make 666." "Well, sir, that is strange. But I can assure you that, if you write Napoleon Bonaparte in Arabic, leaving out only two letters, it will give 666." "And, pray, sir, what right have you to leave out two letters? And, as St. John was writing Greek and to Greeks, is it not likely that he would use the Greek rather than the Arabic notation?" "But, sir," said this learned divine, "every body knows that the Greek letters were never used to mark numbers." I answered with the meekest look and voice possible: "I do not think that every body knows that. Indeed, I have reason to believe that a different opinion—erroneous, no doubt—is universally embraced by all the small minority who happen to know any Greek." So ended the controversy. The man looked at me as if he thought me a very wicked fellow; and, I dare say, has by this time discovered that, if you write my name in Tamul, leaving out T in Thomas, B in Babington, and M in Macaulay, it will give the number of this unfortunate Beast.

I am very comfortable here. The governor-general is the frankest and best-natured of men. The chief functionaries who have attended him hither are clever people, but not exactly on a par as to general attainments with the society to which I belonged in London. I thought, however, even at Madras, that I could have formed a very agreeable circle of acquaintance; and I am assured that at Calcutta I shall find things far better. After all, the best rule in all parts of the world, as in London itself, is to be independent of other men's minds. My power of finding amusement without companions was pretty well tried on my voyage. I read insatiably; the "Iliad" and "Odyssey," Virgil, Horace, Cæsar's "Commentaries," Bacon, "De Augmentis," Dante, Petrarch, Ariosto, Tasso, "Don Quixote," Gibbon's "Rome," Mill's "India," all the seventy volumes of Voltaire, Sismondi's "History of France," and the seven thick folios of the "Biographia Britannica." I found my Greek and Latin in good condition enough. I liked the "Iliad" a little less, and the "Odyssey" a great deal more, than formerly. Horace charmed me more than ever; Virgil not quite so much as he used to do. The want of human character, the poverty of his supernatural machinery, struck me very strongly. Can any thing be so bad as the living bush which bleeds and talks, or the Harpies who befoul Æneas's dinner? It is as extravagant as Ariosto, and as dull as Wilkie's "Epigoniad." The last six books which Virgil had not fully corrected pleased me better than the first six. I like him best on Italian ground. I like his localities; his national enthusiasm; his frequent allusions to his country, its history, its antiquities, and its greatness. In this respect he often reminded me of Sir Walter Scott, with whom, in the general character of his mind, he had very little affinity. The "Georgics" pleased me better; the "Eclogues" best—the second and tenth above all. But I think that the finest lines in the Latin language are those five which begin:

Sepibus in nostris parvam te roscida mala—*

I can not tell you how they struck me. I was amused to find

* Eclogue viii., 37.

that Voltaire pronounces that passage to be the finest in Virgil.

I liked the "Jerusalem" better than I used to do. I was enraptured with Ariosto; and I still think of Dante, as I thought when I first read him, that he is a superior poet to Milton; that he runs neck and neck with Homer; and that none but Shakspeare has gone decidedly beyond him.

As soon as I reach Calcutta I intend to read Herodotus again. By-the-bye, why do not you translate him? You would do it excellently; and a translation of Herodotus, well executed, would rank with original compositions. A quarter of an hour a day would finish the work in five years. The notes might be made the most amusing in the world. I wish you would think of it. At all events, I hope you will do something which may interest more than seven or eight people. Your talents are too great, and your leisure time too small, to be wasted in inquiries so frivolous (I must call them) as those in which you have of late been too much engaged—whether the Cherokees are of the same race with the Chickasaws; whether Van Diemen's Land was peopled from New Holland, or New Holland from Van Diemen's Land; what is the precise mode of appointing a head-man in a village in Timbuctoo. I would not give the worst page in Clarendon or Fra Paolo for all that ever was or ever will be written about the migrations of the Leleges and the laws of the Oscans.

I have already entered on my public functions, and I hope to do some good. The very wigs of the judges in the Court of King's Bench would stand on end if they knew how short a chapter my Law of Evidence will form. I am not without many advisers. A native of some fortune at Madras has sent me a paper on legislation. "Your honor must know," says this judicious person, "that the great evil is that men swear falsely in this country. No judge knows what to believe. Surely, if your honor can make men to swear truly, your honor's fame will be great, and the company will flourish. Now, I know how men may be made to swear truly; and I will tell your honor, for your fame, and for the profit of the company.

Let your honor cut off the great toe of the right foot of every man who swears falsely, whereby your honor's fame will be extended." Is not this an exquisite specimen of legislative wisdom?

I must stop. When I begin to write to England, my pen runs as if it would run on forever.

Ever yours affectionately, T. B. M.

To Miss Fanny and Miss Selina Macaulay.

Ootacamund, August 10th, 1834.

My dear Sisters,—I sent last month a full account of my journey hither, and of the place, to Margaret, as the most stationary of our family; desiring her to let you all see what I had written to her. I think that I shall continue to take the same course. It is better to write one full and connected narrative than a good many imperfect fragments.

Money matters seem likely to go on capitally. My expenses, I find, will be smaller than I anticipated. The rate of exchange, if you know what that means, is very favorable indeed; and, if I live, I shall get rich fast. I quite enjoy the thought of appearing in the light of an old hunks who knows on which side his bread is buttered; a warm man; a fellow who will cut up well. This is not a character which the Macaulays have been much in the habit of sustaining; but I can assure you that after next Christmas I expect to lay up on an average about seven thousand pounds a year, while I remain in India.

At Christmas I shall send home a thousand or twelve hundred pounds for my father, and you all. I can not tell you what a comfort it is to me to find that I shall be able to do this. It reconciles me to all the pains—acute enough, sometimes, God knows—of banishment. In a few years, if I live—probably in less than five years from the time at which you will be reading this letter—we shall be again together in a comfortable, though a modest, home; certain of a good fire, a good joint of meat, and a good glass of wine; without owing obligations to any body; and perfectly indifferent, at least as far as our pecuniary interest is concerned, to the changes of the political world. Rely on it, my dear girls, that there is no chance of my going back with my heart cooled toward you. I came hither principally to save my family, and I am not likely while here to forget them. Ever yours,

T. B. M.

The months of July and August Macaulay spent on the Neilgherries, in a climate equable as Madeira and invigorating as Braemar; where thickets of rhododendron fill the glades and clothe the ridges; and where the air is heavy with the scent of rose-trees of a size more fitted for an orchard than a flower-bed, and bushes of heliotrope thirty paces round. The glories of the forests and of the gardens touched him in spite of his profound botanical ignorance, and he dilates more than once upon his "cottage buried in laburnums, or something very like them, and geraniums which grow in the open air." He had the more leisure for the natural beauties of the place, as there was not much else to interest even a traveler fresh from England.

"I have as yet seen little of the idolatry of India; and that little, though excessively absurd, is not characterized by atrocity or indecency. There is nothing of the sort at Ootacamund. I have not, during the last six weeks, witnessed a single circumstance from which you would have inferred that this was a heathen country. The bulk of the natives here are a colony from the plains below, who have come up hither to wait on the European visitors, and who seem to trouble themselves very little about caste or religion. The Todas, the aboriginal population of these hills, are a very curious race. They had a grand funeral a little while ago. I should have gone if it had not been a council day; but I found afterward that I had lost nothing. The whole ceremony consisted in sacrificing bullocks to the manes of the defunct. The roaring of the poor victims was horrible. The people stood talking and laughing till a particular signal was made, and immediately all the ladies lifted up their voices and wept. I have not lived three-and-thirty years in this world without learning that a bullock roars when he is knocked down, and that a woman can cry whenever she chooses.

"By all that I can learn, the Catholics are the most respectable portion of the native Christians. As to Swartz's people in the Tanjore, they are a perfect scandal to the religion which they profess. It would have been thought something little short of blasphemy to say this a year ago; but now it is considered impious to say otherwise, for they have got into a violent quarrel with the missionaries and the bishop. The missionaries refused to recognize the distinctions of caste in the administration of the sacrament of the Lord's-supper, and the bishop supported them in the refusal. I do not pretend to judge whether this was right or wrong. Swartz and Bishop Heber conceived that the distinction of caste, however objectionable politically, was still only a distinction of rank; and that, as in English churches the gentlefolks generally take the sacrament apart from the poor of the parish, so the high-caste natives might be allowed to communicate apart from the pariahs.

"But, whoever was first in the wrong, the Christians of Tanjore took care to be most so. They called in the interposition of Government, and sent up such petitions and memorials as I never saw before or since; made up of lies, invectives, bragging, cant, bad grammar of the most ludicrous kind, and texts of Scripture quoted without the smallest application. I remember one passage by heart, which is really only a fair specimen of the whole: 'These missionaries, my lord, loving only filthy lucre, bid us to eat Lordsupper with pariahs as lives ugly, handling dead men, drinking rack and toddy, sweeping the streets, mean fellows altogether, base persons, contrary to that which Saint Paul saith: I determined to know nothing among you save Jesus Christ and Him crucified.'

"Was there ever a more appropriate quotation? I believe that nobody on either side of the controversy found out a text so much to the purpose as one which I cited to the Council of India when we were discussing this business: 'If this be a question of words, and names, and of your law, look ye to it; for I will be no judge of such matters.' But though, like Gallio, I drove them and their petitions from my judgment-seat, I could not help saying to one of the missionaries, who is here on the Hills, that I thought it a pity to break up the Church of Tanjore on account of a matter which such men as Swartz and Heber had not been inclined to regard as essential. 'Sir,' said the reverend gentleman, 'the sooner the Church of Tanjore is broken up, the better. You can form no notion of the worthlessness of the native Christians there.' I could not dispute this point with him; but neither could I help thinking, though I was too polite to say so, that it was hardly worth the while of so many good men to come fifteen thousand miles over sea and land in order to make proselytes, who, their very instructors being judges, were more children of hell than before."

Unfortunately, Macaulay's stay on the Neilgherries coincided with the monsoon. "The rain streamed down in floods. It was very seldom that I could see a hundred yards in front of me. During a month together I did not get two hours' walking." He began to be bored, for the first and last time in his life: while his companions, who had not his resources, were ready to hang themselves for very dullness. The ordinary amusements with which, in the more settled parts of India, our countrymen beguile the rainy season, were wanting in a settlement that had only lately been reclaimed from the desert; in the immediate vicinity of which you still ran the chance of being "trodden into the shape of half a crown by a wild elephant, or eaten by the tigers, which prefer this situation to the plains below for the same reason that takes so many Europeans to India: they encounter an uncongenial climate for the sake of what they can get." There were no books in the place except those that Macaulay had brought with him; among which, most luckily, was "Clarissa Harlowe." Aided by the rain outside, he soon talked his favorite romance into general favor. The reader will consent to put up with one or two slight inaccuracies in order to have the story told by Thackeray.

"I spoke to him once about 'Clarissa.' 'Not read "Clarissa!"' he cried out. 'If you have once read "Clarissa," and are infected by it, you can't leave it. When I was in India I passed one hot season in the Hills; and there were the governor-general, and the secretary of government, and the commander-in-chief, and their wives. I had "Clarissa" with me; and as soon as they began to read, the whole station was in a passion of excitement about Miss Harlowe, and her misfortunes, and her scoundrelly Lovelace. The governor's wife seized the book; the secretary waited for it; the chief-justice could not read it for tears.' He acted the whole scene: he paced up and down the Athenæum library. I dare say he could have spoken pages of the book: of that book, and of what countless piles of others!"

An old Scotch doctor, a Jacobin and a freethinker, who could only be got to attend church by the positive orders of the governor-general, cried over the last volume* until he was

* Degenerate readers of our own day have actually been provided with an abridgment of "Clarissa," itself as long as an ordinary novel. A wiser course than buying the abridgment would be to commence the original at the third volume. In the same way, if any one, after obtaining the outline of Lady Clementina's story from a more adventurous friend, will read "Sir Charles Grandison," skipping all letters from Italians to Italians, and about Italians, he will find that he has got hold of a delightful, and not unmanageable, book.

too ill to appear at dinner. The chief secretary—afterward, as Sir William Macnaghten, the hero and the victim of the darkest episode in our Indian history—declared that reading this copy of "Clarissa" under the inspiration of its owner's enthusiasm was nothing less than an epoch in his life. After the lapse of thirty years, when Ootacamund had long enjoyed the advantage of a book-club and a circulating library, the tradition of Macaulay and his novel still lingered on with a tenacity most unusual in the ever-shifting society of an Indian station.

"At length Lord William gave me leave of absence. My bearers were posted along the road; my palanquins were packed; and I was to start next day; when an event took place which may give you some insight into the state of the laws, morals, and manners among the natives.

"My new servant, a Christian, but such a Christian as the missionaries make in this part of the world, had been persecuted most unmercifully for his religion by the servants of some other gentlemen on the Hills. At last they contrived to excite against him (whether justly or unjustly, I am quite unable to say) the jealousy of one of Lord William's under-cooks. We had accordingly a most glorious tragi-comedy; the part of Othello by the cook aforesaid; Desdemona by an ugly, impudent pariah girl, his wife; Iago by Colonel Casement's servant; and Michael Cassio by my rascal. The place of the handkerchief was supplied by a small piece of sugar-candy which Desdemona was detected in the act of sucking, and which had found its way from my canisters to her fingers. If I had any part in the piece, it was, I am afraid, that of Roderigo, whom Shakspeare describes as a 'foolish gentleman,' and who also appears to have had 'money in his purse.'

"On the evening before my departure, my bungalow was besieged by a mob of blackguards. The native judge came with them. After a most prodigious quantity of jabbering, of which I could not understand one word, I called the judge, who spoke tolerable English, into my room, and learned from him the nature of the case. I was, and still am, in doubt as to the truth of the charge. I have a very poor opinion of my man's morals, and a very poor opinion also of the veracity of his accusers. It was, however, so very inconvenient for me to be just then deprived of my servant that I offered to settle the business at my own expense. Under ordinary circumstances this would have been easy enough, for the Hindoos of the lower castes have no delicacy on these subjects. The husband would gladly have taken a few rupees, and walked away; but the persecutors of my servant interfered, and insisted that he should be brought to trial in order that they might have the pleasure of smearing him with filth, giving him a flogging, beating kettles before him, and carrying him round on an ass with his face to the tail.

"As the matter could not be accommodated, I begged the judge to try the case instantly; but the rabble insisted that the trial should not take place for some days. I argued the matter with them very mildly, and told them that I must go next day, and that if my servant were detained, guilty or innocent, he must lose his situation. The gentle and reasoning tone of my expostulations only made them impudent. They are, in truth, a race so accustomed to be trampled on by the strong that they always consider humanity as a sign of weakness. The judge told me that he never heard a gentleman speak such sweet words to the people. But I was now at an end of my sweet words. My blood was beginning to boil at the undisguised display of rancorous hatred and shameless injustice. I sat down, and wrote a line to the commandant of the station, begging him to give orders that the case might be tried that very evening. The court assembled, and continued all night in violent contention. At last the judge pronounced my servant not guilty. I did not then know, what I learned some days after, that this respectable magistrate had received twenty rupees on the occasion.

"The husband would now gladly have taken the money which he refused the day before; but I would not give him a farthing. The rascals who had raised the disturbance were furious. My servant was to set out at eleven in the morning, and I was to follow at two. He had scarcely left the door when I heard a noise. I looked forth, and saw that the gang had pulled him out of his palanquin, torn off his turban, stripped him almost naked, and were, as it seemed, about to pull him to pieces. I snatched up a sword-stick, and ran into the middle of them. It was all I could do to force my way to him, and for a moment I thought my own person was in danger as well as his. I supported the poor wretch in my arms; for, like most of his countrymen, he is a chicken-hearted fellow, and was almost fainting away. My honest barber, a fine old soldier in the company's service, ran off for assistance, and soon returned with some police officers. I ordered the bearers to turn round, and proceeded instantly to the house of the commandant. I was not long detained here. Nothing can be well imagined more expeditious than the administration of justice in this country, when the judge is a colonel, and the plaintiff a councilor. I told my story in three words. In three minutes the rioters were marched off to prison, and my servant, with a sepoy to guard him, was fairly on his road and out of danger."

Early next morning Macaulay began to descend the pass.

"After going down for about an hour we emerged from the clouds and moisture, and the plain of Mysore lay before us—a vast ocean of foliage on which the sun was shining gloriously. I am very little given to cant about the beauties of nature, but I was almost moved to tears. I jumped off the palanquin, and walked in front of it down the immense declivity. In two hours we descended about three thousand feet. Every turning in the road showed the boundless forest below in some new point of view. I was greatly struck with the resemblance which this prodigious jungle, as old as the world, and planted by nature, bears to the fine works of the great English landscape gardeners. It was exactly a Wentworth Park as large as Devonshire. After reaching the foot of the hills, we traveled through a succession of scenes which might have been part of the Garden of Eden. Such gigantic trees I never saw. In a quarter of an hour I passed hundreds, the smallest of which would bear a comparison with any of those oaks which are shown as prodigious in England. The grass, the weeds, and the wild flowers grew as high as my head. The sun, almost a stranger to me, was now shining brightly; and, when late in the afternoon I again got out of my palanquin and looked back, I saw the large mountain ridge from which I had descended twenty miles behind me, still buried in the same mass of fog and rain in which I had been living for weeks.

"On Tuesday, the 16th, I went on board at Madras. I amused myself on the voyage to Calcutta with learning Portuguese, and made myself almost as well acquainted with it as I care to be. I read The "Lusiad," and am now reading it a second time. I own that I am disappointed in Camoens; but I have so often found my first impressions wrong on such subjects that I still hope to be able to join my voice to that of the great body of critics. I never read any famous foreign book which did not, in the first perusal, fall short of my expectations, except Dante's poem, and "Don Quixote," which were prodigiously superior to what I had imagined. Yet in these cases I had not pitched my expectations low."

He had not much time for his Portuguese studies. The run was unusually fast, and the ship only spent a week in the Bay of Bengal, and forty-eight hours in the Hooghly. He found his sister comfortably installed in Government House, where he himself took up his quarters during the next six weeks; Lady William Bentinck having been prepared to welcome him as a guest by her husband's letters, more than one of which ended with the words "è un miracolo." Toward the middle of November, Macaulay began housekeeping for himself; living, as he always loved to live, rather more generously than the strict necessities of his position demanded. His residence, then the best in Calcutta, has long since been converted into the Bengal Club.

To Macvey Napier, Esq.

Calcutta, December 10th, 1834.

DEAR NAPIER,—First to business. At length I send you the article on Mackintosh; an article which has the merit of length, whatever it may be deficient in. As I wished to transmit it to England in duplicate, if not in triplicate, I thought it best to have two or three copies coarsely printed here under the seal of strict secrecy. The printers at Edinburgh will, therefore, have no trouble in deciphering my manuscript, and the corrector of the press will find his word done to his hands.

The disgraceful imbecility, and the still more disgraceful malevolence, of the editor have, as you will see, moved my indignation not a little. I hope that Longman's connection with the *Review* will not prevent you from inserting what I have said on this subject. Murray's copy writers are unsparingly abused by Southey and Lockhart in the *Quarterly*; and it would be hard indeed if we might not in the *Edinburgh* strike hard at an assailant of Mackintosh.

I shall now begin another article. The subject I have not yet fixed upon; perhaps the romantic poetry of Italy, for which there is an excellent opportuuity, Panizzi's reprint of Boiardo; perhaps the little volume of Burnet's "Characters" edited by Bishop Jebb. This reminds me that I have to acknowledge the receipt of a box from Longman, containing this little book; and other books of much greater value, Grimm's "Correspondence," Jacquemont's "Letters," and several foreign works on jurisprudence. All that you have yet sent have been excellently chosen. I will mention, while I am on this subject, a few books which I want, and which I am not likely to pick up here: Daru's "Histoire de Venise;" St. Real's "Conjuration de Venise;" Fra Paolo's works; Monstrelet's "Chronicle;" and Coxe's book on the Pelhams. I should also like to have a really good edition of Lucian.

My sister desires me to send you her kind regards. She remembers her visit to Edinburgh, and your hospitality, with the greatest pleasure. Calcutta is called, and not without some reason, the City of Palaces; but I have seen nothing in the East like the view from the Castle Rock, nor expect to see any thing like it till we stand there together again. Kindest regards to Lord Jeffrey. Yours most truly,

T. B. MACAULAY.

To Mrs. Cropper.

Calcutta, December 7th, 1834.

DEAREST MARGARET,—I rather suppose that some late letters from Nancy may have prepared you to learn what I am now about to communicate. She is going to be married, and with my fullest and warmest approbation. I can truly say that, if I had to search India for a husband for her, I could have found no man to whom I could with equal confidence have intrusted her happiness. Trevelyan is about eight-and-twenty. He was educated at the Charter-house, and then went to Haileybury, and came out hither. In this country he has distinguished himself beyond any man of his standing by his great talent for business; by his liberal and enlarged views of policy; and by literary merit, which, for his opportunities, is considerable. He was at first placed at Delhi under Sir Edward Colebrooke, a very powerful and a very popular man, but extremely corrupt. This man tried to initiate Trevelyan in his own infamous practices; but the young fellow's spirit was too noble for such things. When only twenty-one years of age, he publicly accused Sir Edward, then almost at the head of the service, of receiving bribes from the natives. A perfect storm was raised against the accuser. He was almost everywhere abused, and very generally cut. But, with a firmness and ability scarcely ever seen in any man so young, he brought his proofs forward, and, after an inquiry of some weeks, fully made out his case. Sir Edward was dismissed in disgrace, and is now living obscurely in England. The Government here, and the directors at home, applauded Trevelyan in the highest terms; and from that time he has been considered as a man likely to rise to the very top of the service. Lord William told him to ask for any thing that he wished for. Trevelyan begged that something might be done for his elder brother, who is in the company's army. Lord William told him that he had richly earned that, or any thing else, and gave Lieutenant Trevelyan a very good diplomatic employment. Indeed Lord William, a man who makes no favorites, has always given to Trevelyan the strongest marks, not of a blind partiality, but of a thoroughly well-grounded and discriminating esteem.

Not long ago Trevelyan was appointed by him to the under secretaryship for foreign affairs, an office of a very important and confidential nature. While holding the place, he was commissioned to report to Government on the operation of the internal transit duties of India. About a year ago his report was completed. I shall send to England a copy or two of it by the first safe conveyance, for nothing that I can say of his abilities or of his public spirit will be half so satisfactory. I have no hesitation in affirming that it is a perfect masterpiece in its kind. Accustomed as I have been to public affairs, I never read an abler state paper; and I do not believe that there is, I will not say in India, but in England, another man of twenty-seven who could have written it. Trevelyan is a most stormy reformer. Lord William said to me before any one had observed Trevelyan's attentions to Nancy, "That man is almost always on the right side in every question; and it is well that he is so, for he gives a most confounded deal of trouble when he happens to take the wrong one."* He is quite at the head of that active party among the younger servants of the company who take the side of improvement. In particular, he is the soul of every scheme for diffusing education among the natives of this country. His reading has been very confined; but to the little that he has read he has brought a mind as active and restless as Lord Brougham's, and much more judicious and honest.

As to his person, he always looks like a gentleman, particularly on horseback. He is very active and athletic, and is re-

* Macaulay used to apply to his future brother-in-law the remark which Julius Cæsar made with regard to his young friend Brutus: "Magni refert hic quid velit. Quidquid volet, valdè volet."

nowned as a great master in the most exciting and perilous of field-sports, the spearing of wild boars. His face has a most characteristic expression of ardor and impetuosity, which makes his countenance very interesting to me. Birth is a thing that I care nothing about; but his family is one of the oldest and best in England.

During the important years of his life, from twenty to twenty-five, or thereabouts, Trevelyan was in a remote province of India, where his whole time was divided between public business and field-sports, and where he seldom saw a European gentleman, and never a European lady. He has no small talk. His mind is full of schemes of moral and political improvement, and his zeal boils over in his talk. His topics, even in courtship, are steam navigation, the education of the natives, the equalization of the sugar duties, the substitution of the Roman for the Arabic alphabet in the Oriental languages.

I saw the feeling growing from the first; for, though I generally pay not the smallest attention to those matters, I had far too deep an interest in Nancy's happiness not to watch her behavior to every body who saw much of her. I knew it, I believe, before she knew it herself; and I could most easily have prevented it by merely treating Trevelyan with a little coldness, for he is a man whom the smallest rebuff would completely discourage. But you will believe, my dearest Margaret, that no thought of such base selfishness ever passed through my mind. I would as soon have locked my dear Nancy up in a nunnery as have put the smallest obstacle in the way of her having a good husband. I therefore gave every facility and encouragement to both of them. What I have myself felt, it is unnecessary to say. My parting from you almost broke my heart. But when I parted from you I had Nancy; I had all my other relations; I had my friends; I had my country. Now I have nothing except the resources of my own mind, and the consciousness of having acted not ungenerously. But I do not repine. Whatever I suffer I have brought on myself. I have neglected the plainest lessons of reason and experience. I have staked my happiness without calculating the chances of the dice. I have hewn out broken cisterns; I have leaned on a reed; I have built on the sand; and I have fared accordingly. I must bear my punishment as I can; and, above all, I must take care that the punishment does not extend beyond myself.

Nothing can be kinder than Nancy's conduct has been. She proposes that we should form one family; and Trevelyan (though like most lovers, he would, I imagine, prefer having his goddess to himself), consented with strong expressions of pleasure. The arrangement is not so strange as it might seem at home. The thing is often done here; and those quarrels between servants, which would inevitably mar any such plan in England, are not to be apprehended in an Indian establishment. One advantage there will be in our living together of a most incontestable sort—we shall both be able to save more money. Trevelyan will soon be entitled to his furlough; but he proposes not to take it till I go home.

I shall write in a very different style from this to my father. To him I shall represent the marriage as what it is in every respect except its effect on my own dreams of happiness—a most honorable and happy event; prudent in a worldly point of view; and promising all the felicity which strong mutual affection, excellent principles on both sides, good temper, youth, health, and the general approbation of friends can afford. As for myself, it is a tragical dénouement of an absurd plot. I remember quoting some nursery rhymes, years ago, when you left me in London to join Nancy at Rothley Temple or Leamington, I forget which. Those foolish lines contain the history of my life.

> There were two birds that sat on a stone:
> One flew away, and there was but one.
> The other flew away, and then there was none;
> And the poor stone was left all alone.

Ever, my dearest Margaret, yours, T. B. MACAULAY.

A passage from a second letter to the same person deserves to be quoted, as an instance of how a good man may be unable to read aright his own nature, and a wise man to forecast his own future. "I feel a growing tendency to cynicism and suspicion. My intellect remains; and is likely, I sometimes think, to absorb the whole man. I still retain (not only undiminished, but strengthened by the very events which have deprived me of every thing else) my thirst for knowledge; my passion for holding converse with the greatest minds of all ages and nations; my power of forgetting what surrounds me, and of living with the past, the future, the distant, and the unreal. Books are becoming every thing to me. If I had at this moment my choice of life, I would bury myself in one of those immense libraries that we saw together at the universities, and never pass a waking hour without a book before me." So little was he aware that, during the years which were to come, his thoughts and cares would be less than ever for himself, and more for others; and that his existence would be passed amidst a bright atmosphere of affectionate domestic happiness, which, until his own death came, no accident was henceforward destined to overcloud.

But, before his life assumed the equable and prosperous tenor in which it continued to the end, one more trouble was in store for him. Long before the last letters to his sister Margaret had been written, the eyes which were to have read them had been closed forever. The fate of so young a wife and mother touched deeply all who had known her, and some who knew her only by name.* When the melancholy news arrived in India, the young couple were spending their honeymoon in a lodge in the governor-general's part at Barrackpore. They immediately returned to Calcutta, and, under the shad-

---

* Moultrie made Mrs. Cropper's death the subject of some verses on which her relatives set a high value. He acknowledges his little poem to be the tribute of one who had been a stranger to her whom it was written to commemorate.

And yet methinks we are not strange: so many claims there be
Which seem to weave a viewless band between my soul and thee.
Sweet sister of my early friend, the kind, the single-hearted,
Than whose remembrance none more bright still gilds the days departed!
Beloved, with more than sister's love, by some whose love to me
Is now almost my brightest gem in this world's treasury.

ow of a great sorrow,* began their sojourn in their brother's house; who, for his part, did what he might to drown his grief in floods of official work.

The narrative of that work may well be the despair of Macaulay's biographer. It would be inexcusable to slur over what in many important respects was the most honorable chapter of his life; while, on the other hand, the task of interesting Englishmen in the details of Indian administration is an undertaking which has baffled every pen except his own. In such a dilemma the safest course is to allow that pen to tell the story for itself; or, rather, so much of the story as, by concentrating the attention of the reader upon matters akin to those which are in frequent debate at home, may enable him to judge whether Macaulay at the council-board and the bureau was the equal of Macaulay in the senate and the library.

Examples of his minute-writing may with some confidence be submitted to the criticism of those whose experience of public business has taught them in what a minute should differ from a dispatch, a memorial, a report, and a decision. His method of applying general principles to the circumstances of a special case, and of illustrating those principles with just so much literary ornament as would place his views in a pictorial form before the minds of those whom it was his business to convince, is strikingly exhibited in the series of papers by means of which he reconciled his colleagues in the Council, and his masters in Leadenhall Street, to the removal of the modified censorship which existed in India previously to the year 1835.

"It is difficult," he writes, "to conceive that any measures can be more indefensible than those which I propose to repeal. It has always been the practice of politic rulers to disguise their arbitrary measures under pop-

---

* "*April 8th, Lichfield, Easter-Sunday.*—After the service was ended, we went over the cathedral. When I stood before the famous children by Chantrey, I could think only of one thing; that, when last I was there, in 1832, my dear sister Margaret was with me, and that she was greatly affected. I could not command my tears, and was forced to leave our party and walk about by myself."—*Macaulay's Journal for the year* 1849.

ular forms and names. The conduct of the Indian Government with respect to the Press has been altogether at variance with this trite and obvious maxim. The newspapers have for years been allowed as ample a measure of practical liberty as that which they enjoy in England. If any inconveniences arise from the liberty of political discussion, to those inconveniences we are already subject. Yet while our policy is thus liberal and indulgent, we are daily reproached and taunted with the bondage in which we keep the Press. A strong feeling on this subject appears to exist throughout the European community here; and the loud complaints which have lately been uttered are likely to produce a considerable effect on the English people, who will see at a glance that the law is oppressive, and who will not know how completely it is inoperative.

"To impose strong restraints on political discussion is an intelligible policy, and may possibly—though I greatly doubt it—be in some countries a wise policy. But this is not the point at issue. The question before us is not whether the Press shall be free, but whether, being free, it shall be called free. It is surely mere madness in a government to make itself unpopular for nothing; to be indulgent, and yet to disguise its indulgence under such outward forms as bring on it the reproach of tyranny. Yet this is now our policy. We are exposed to all the dangers—dangers, I conceive, greatly overrated—of a free Press; and at the same time we contrive to incur all the opprobrium of a censorship. It is universally allowed that the licensing system, as at present administered, does not keep any man who can buy a press from publishing the bitterest and most sarcastic reflections on any public measure or any public functionary. Yet the very words 'license to print' have a sound hateful to the ears of Englishmen in every part of the globe. It is unnecessary to inquire whether this feeling be reasonable; whether the petitioners who have so strongly pressed this matter on our consideration would not have shown a better judgment if they had been content with their practical liberty, and had reserved their murmurs for practical grievances. The question for us is not what they ought to do, but what we ought to do; not whether it be wise in them to complain when they suffer no injury, but whether it be wise in us to incur odium unaccompanied by the smallest accession of security or of power.

"One argument only has been urged in defense of the present system. It is admitted that the Press of Bengal has long been suffered to enjoy practical liberty, and that nothing but an extreme emergency could justify the Government in curtailing that liberty. But, it is said, such an emergency may arise, and the Government ought to retain in its hands the power of adopting, in that event, the sharp, prompt, and decisive measures which may be necessary for the preservation of the empire. But when we consider with what vast powers, extending over all classes of people, Parliament has armed the governor-general in council, and, in extreme cases, the governor-general alone, we shall probably be inclined to allow little weight to this argument. No government in the world is better provided with the means of meeting extraordinary dangers by extraordinary precautions. Five persons, who may be brought together in half an hour, whose deliberations are secret, who are not shackled by any of those forms which elsewhere delay legislative measures, can, in a single sitting, make a law for stopping every press in India. Possessing as we do the unquestionable power to interfere, whenever the safety of the state may require it, with overwhelming rapidity and energy, we surely ought not, in quiet times, to be constantly keeping the offensive form and ceremonial of despotism before the eyes of those whom, nevertheless, we permit to enjoy the substance of freedom."

Eighteen months elapsed, during which the Calcutta Press found occasion to attack Macaulay with a breadth and ferocity of calumny such as few public men, in any age and country, have ever endured, and none, perhaps, have ever forgiven. There were many mornings when it was impossible for him to allow the newspapers to lie about his sister's drawing-room. The editor of the periodical which called itself, and had a right to call itself, the *Friend of India*, undertook to shame his brethren by publishing a collection of their invectives; but it was very soon evident that no decent journal could venture to foul its pages by reprinting the epithets and the anecdotes which constituted the daily greeting of the literary men of Calcutta to their fellow-craftsmen of the *Edinburgh Review*. But Macaulay's cheery and robust common sense carried him safe and sound through an ordeal which has broken down sterner natures than his, and imbittered as stainless lives. The allusions in his correspondence, all the more surely because they are brief and rare, indicate that the torrent of obloquy to which he was exposed interfered neither with his temper nor with his happiness; and how little he allowed it to disturb his judgment, or distort his public spirit, is proved by the tone of a state paper, addressed to the Court of Directors in September, 1836, in which he eagerly vindicates the freedom of the Calcutta Press, at a time when the writers of that Press, on the days when they were pleased to be decent, could find for him no milder appellations than those of cheat, swindler, and charlatan.

"I regret that on this, or on any subject, my opinion should differ from that of the honorable court. But I still conscientiously think that we acted wisely when we passed the law on the subject of the Press; and I am quite certain that we should act most unwisely if we were now to repeal that law.

"I must, in the first place, venture to express an opinion that the importance of that question is greatly overrated by persons, even the best informed and the most discerning, who are not actually on the spot. It is most justly observed by the honorable court that many of the arguments which may be urged in favor of a free Press at home do not apply to this country. But it is, I conceive, no less true that scarcely any of those arguments which have been employed in Europe to defend restrictions on the Press apply to a press such as that of India.

"In Europe, and especially in England, the Press is an engine of tremendous power, both for good and for evil. The most enlightened men, after long experience both of its salutary and of its pernicious operation, have come to the conclusion that the good, on the whole, preponderates. But that there is no inconsiderable amount of evil to be set off against the good has never been disputed by the warmest friend to freedom of discussion.

"In India the Press is comparatively a very feeble engine. It does far less good, and far less harm, than in Europe. It sometimes renders useful services to the public. It sometimes brings to the notice of the Government evils the existence of which would otherwise have been unknown. It operates, to some extent, as a salutary check on public functionaries. It does something toward keeping the administration pure. On the other hand, by misrepresenting public measures, and by flattering the prejudices of those who support it, it sometimes produces a slight degree of excitement in a very small portion of the community.

"How slight that excitement is, even when it reaches its greatest height, and how little the Government has to fear from it, no person whose observation has been confined to European societies will readily believe. In this country the number of English residents is very small, and of that small number a great proportion are engaged in the service of the state, and are most deeply interested in the maintenance of existing institutions. Even those English settlers who are not in the service of the Government have a strong interest in its stability. They are few: they are thinly scattered among a vast population with whom they have neither language, nor religion, nor morals, nor manners, nor color, in common: they feel that any convulsion which should overthrow the existing order of things would be ruinous to themselves. Particular acts of the Government—especially acts which are mortifying to the pride of caste naturally felt by an Englishman in India—are often angrily condemned by these persons. But every indigo-planter in Tirhoot, and every shop-keeper in Calcutta, is perfectly aware that the downfall of the Government would be attended with the destruction of his fortune, and with imminent hazard to his life.

"Thus, among the English inhabitants of India, there are no fit subjects for that species of excitement which the Press sometimes produces at home. There is no class among them analogous to that vast body of English laborers and artisans whose minds are rendered irritable by frequent distress and privation, and on whom, therefore, the sophistry and rhetoric of bad men often produce a tremendous effect. The English papers here might be infinitely more seditious than the most seditious that were ever printed in London without doing harm to any thing but their own circulation. The fire goes out for want of some combustible material on which to seize. How little reason would there be to apprehend danger to order and property in England from the most inflammatory writings, if those writings were read only by ministers of state, commissioners of the customs and excise, judges and masters in chancery, upper clerks in Government offices, officers in the army, bankers, landed proprietors, barristers, and master-manufacturers! The most timid politician would not anticipate the smallest evil from the most seditious libels, if the circulation of those libels were confined to such a class of readers; and it is to such a class of readers that the circulation of the English newspapers in India is almost entirely confined."

The motive for the scurrility with which Macaulay was assailed by a handful of sorry scribblers was his advocacy of the act, familiarly known as the Black Act, which withdrew from British subjects resident in the provinces their so-called privilege of bringing civil appeals before the Supreme Court at Calcutta. Such appeals were thenceforward to be tried by the Sudder Court, which was manned by the company's judges, "all of them English gentlemen of liberal education: as free as even the judges of the Supreme Court from any imputation of personal corruption, and selected by the Government from a body which abounds in men as honorable and as intelligent as ever were employed in the service of any state." The change embodied in the act was one of little practical moment; but it excited an opposition based upon arguments and assertions of such a nature that the success or failure of the proposed measure became a question of high and undeniable importance.

"In my opinion," writes Macaulay, "the chief reason for preferring the Sudder Court is this—that it is the court which we have provided to administer justice, in the last resort, to the great body of the people. If it is not fit for that purpose, it ought to be made so. If it is fit to administer justice to the great body of the people, why should we exempt a mere handful of settlers from its jurisdiction? There certainly is, I will not say the reality, but the semblance, of partiality and tyranny in the distinction made by the Charter Act of 1813. That distinction seems to indicate a notion that the natives of India may well put up with something less than justice, or that Englishmen in India have a title to something more than justice. If we give our own countrymen an appeal to the King's Courts, in cases in which all others are forced to be contented with the Company's Courts, we do, in fact, cry down the Company's Courts. We proclaim to the Indian people that there are two sorts of justice—a coarse one, which we think good enough for them, and another of superior quality, which we keep for ourselves. If we take pains to show that we distrust our highest courts, how can we expect that the natives of the country will place confidence in them?

"The draft of the act was published, and was, as I fully expected, not unfavorably received by the British in the Mofussil.* Seven weeks have elapsed since the notification took place. Time has been allowed for petitions from the farthest corners of the territories subject to this presidency. But I have heard of only one attempt in the Mofussil to get up a remonstrance; and the Mofussil newspapers which I have seen, though generally disposed to cavil at all the acts of the Government, have spoken favorably of this measure.

"In Calcutta the case has been somewhat different; and this is a remarkable fact. The British inhabitants of Calcutta are the only British-born subjects in Bengal who will not be affected by the proposed act, and they are the only British subjects in Bengal who have expressed the smallest objection to it. The clamor, indeed, has proceeded from a very small portion of the society of Calcutta. The objectors have not ventured to call a public meeting, and their memorial has obtained very few signatures; but they have attempted to make up by noise and virulence for what has been wanting in strength. It may at first sight appear strange that a law, which is not unwelcome to those who are to live under it, should excite such acrimonious feelings among people who are wholly exempted from its operation. But the explanation is simple. Though nobody who resides at Calcutta will be sued in the Mofussil courts, many people who reside at Calcutta have, or wish to have, practice in the Supreme Court. Great exertions have accordingly been made, though with little success, to excite a feeling against this measure among the English inhabitants of Calcutta.

---

* The term "Mofussil" is used to denote the provinces of the Bengal Presidency, as opposed to the capital.

The political phraseology of the English in India is the same with the political phraseology of our countrymen at home; but it is never to be forgotten that the same words stand for very different things at London and at Calcutta. We hear much about public opinion, the love of liberty, the influence of the Press. But we must remember that public opinion means the opinion of five hundred persons who have no interest, feeling, or taste in common with the fifty millions among whom they live; that the love of liberty means the strong objection which the five hundred feel to every measure which can prevent them from acting as they choose toward the fifty millions; that the Press is altogether supported by the five hundred, and has no motive to plead the cause of the fifty millions.

"We know that India can not have a free government. But she may have the next best thing—a firm and impartial despotism. The worst state in which she can possibly be placed is that in which the memorialists would place her. They call on us to recognize them as a privileged order of freemen in the midst of slaves. It was for the purpose of averting this great evil that Parliament, at the same time at which it suffered Englishmen to settle in India, armed us with those large powers which, in my opinion, we ill deserve to possess if we have not the spirit to use them now."

Macaulay had made two mistakes. He had yielded to the temptation of imputing motives, a habit which the *Spectator* newspaper has pronounced to be his one intellectual vice, finely adding that it is "the vice of rectitude;" and he had done worse still, for he had challenged his opponents to a course of agitation. They responded to the call. After preparing the way by a string of communications to the public journals, in which their objections to the act were set forth at enormous length, and with as much point and dignity as can be obtained by a copious use of italics and capital letters, they called a public meeting, the proceedings at which were almost too ludicrous for description. "I have seen," said one of the speakers, "at a Hindoo festival, a naked, disheveled figure, his face painted with grotesque colors, and his long hair besmeared with dirt and ashes. His tongue was pierced with an iron bar, and his breast was scorched by the fire from the burning altar which rested on his stomach. This revolting figure, covered with ashes, dirt, and bleeding voluntary wounds, may the next moment ascend the Sudder bench, and in a suit between a Hindoo and an Englishman think it an act of sanctity to decide against law in favor of the professor of the true faith."

Another gentleman, Mr. Longueville Clarke, reminded "the tyrant" that

There yawns the sack, and yonder rolls the sea.

"Mr. Macaulay may treat this as an idle threat; but his knowledge of history will supply him with many examples of what has occurred when resistance has been provoked by milder instances of despotism than the decimation of a people." This pretty explicit recommendation to lynch a member of council was received with rapturous applause.

At length arose a Captain Biden, who spoke as follows: "Gentlemen, I come before you in the character of a British seaman, and on that ground claim your attention for a few moments. Gentlemen, there has been much talk during the evening of laws, and regulations, and rights, and liberties; but you all seem to have forgotten that this is the anniversary of the glorious Battle of Waterloo. I beg to propose, and I call on the statue of Lord Cornwallis and yourselves to join me in, three cheers for the Duke of Wellington and the Battle of Waterloo." The audience, who by this time were pretty well convinced that no grievance which could possibly result under the Black Act could equal the horrors of a crowd in the Town-hall of Calcutta during the latter half of June, gladly caught at the diversion, and made noise enough to satisfy even the gallant orator. The business was brought to a hurried close, and the meeting was adjourned till the following week.

But the luck of Macaulay's adversaries pursued them still. One of the leading speakers at the adjourned meeting, himself a barrister, gave another barrister the lie, and a tumult ensued which Captain Biden in vain endeavored to calm by his favorite remedy. "The opinion at Madras, Bombay, and Canton," said he (and in so saying he uttered the only sentence of wisdom which either evening had produced), "is that there is no public opinion at Calcutta but the lawyers. And now—who has the presumption to call it a burlesque?—let's give three cheers for the Battle of Waterloo, and then I'll propose an amendment which shall go into the whole question." The chairman, who certainly had earned the vote of thanks for "his very extraordinary patience" which Captain Biden was appropriately selected to move, contrived to get resolutions passed in favor of petitioning Parliament and the Home Government against the obnoxious act.

The next few weeks were spent by the leaders of the movement in squabbling over the preliminaries of duels that never came off, and applying for criminal informations for libel against each other, which their beloved Supreme Court very judiciously refused to grant; but in the course of time the petitions were signed, and an agent was selected who undertook to convey them to England. On the 22d of March, 1838, a committee of inquiry into the operation of the act was moved for in the House of Commons; but there was nothing in the question which tempted honorable members to lay aside their customary indifference with regard to Indian controversies, and the motion fell through without a division. The House allowed the Government to have its own way in the matter; and any possible hesitation on the part of the ministers was borne down by the emphasis with which Macaulay claimed their support. "I conceive," he wrote, "that the act is good in itself, and that the time for passing it has been well chosen. The strongest reason, however, for passing it, is the nature of the opposition which it has experienced. The organs of that opposition repeated every day that the English were the conquerors and the lords of the country; the dominant race; the electors of the House of Commons, whose power extends both over the company at home and over the governor-general in council here. The constituents of the British Legislature, they told us, were not to be bound by laws made by any inferior authority. The firmness with which the Government withstood the idle outcry of two or three hundred people, about a matter with which they had nothing to do, was designated as insolent defiance of public opinion. We were enemies of freedom, because we would not suffer a small white aristocracy to domineer over millions. How utterly at variance these principles are with reason, with justice, with the honor of the British Government, and with the dearest interests of the Indian people, it is unnecessary for me to point out. For myself, I can only say that if the Government is to be conducted on such principles, I am utterly disqualified, by all my feelings and opinions, from bearing any part in it, and can not too soon resign my place to some person better fitted to hold it."

It is fortunate for India that a man with the tastes and the training of Macaulay came to her shores as one vested with authority, and that he came at the moment when he did; for that moment was the very turning-point of her intellectual progress. All educational action had been at a stand for some time back, on account of an irreconcilable difference of opinion in the Committee of Public Instruction; which was divided, five against five, on either side of a controversy, vital, inevitable, admitting of neither postponement nor compromise, and conducted by both parties with a pertinacity and a warmth that was nothing but honorable to those concerned. Half of the members were for maintaining and extending the old scheme of encouraging Oriental learning by stipends paid to students in Sanscrit, Persian, and Arabic; and by liberal grants for the publication of works in those languages. The other half were in favor of teaching the elements of knowledge in the vernacular tongues, and the higher branches in English. On his arrival, Macaulay was appointed president of the committee; but he declined to take any active part in its proceedings until the Government had finally pronounced on the question at issue. Late in January, 1835, the advocates of the two systems, than whom ten abler men could not be found in the service, laid their opinions before the Supreme Council; and, on the 2d of February, Macaulay, as a member of that council, produced a minute in which he adopted and defended the views of the English section in the committee.

"How stands the case? We have to educate a people who can not at present be educated by means of their mother tongue. We must teach them some foreign language. The claims of our own language it is hardly necessary to recapitulate. It stands pre-eminent even among the languages of the West. It abounds with works of imagination not inferior to the noblest which Greece has bequeathed to us; with models of every species of eloquence; with historical compositions, which, considered merely as narratives, have seldom been surpassed, and which, considered as vehicles of ethical and political instruction, have never been equaled; with just and lively representations of human life and human nature; with the most profound speculations on metaphysics, morals, government, jurisprudence, and trade; with full and correct information respecting every experimental science which tends to preserve the health, to increase the comfort, or to expand the intellect of man. Whoever knows that language has ready access to all the vast intellectual wealth which all the wisest nations of the earth have created and hoarded in the course of ninety generations. It may safely be said that the literature now extant in that language is of far greater value than all the literature which three hundred years ago was extant in all the languages of the world together. Nor is this all. In India, English is the language spoken by the ruling class. It is spoken by the higher class of natives at the seats of government. It is likely to become the language of commerce throughout the seas of the East. It is the language of two great European communities which are rising, the one in the south of Africa, the other in Australasia; communities which are every year becoming more important, and more closely connected with our Indian empire. Whether we look at the intrinsic value of our literature, or at the particular situation of this country, we shall see the strongest reason to think that, of all foreign tongues, the English tongue is that which would be the most useful to our native subjects.

"The question now before us is simply whether, when it is in our power to teach this language, we shall teach languages in which, by universal confession, there are no books on any subject which deserve to be compared to our own; whether, when we can teach European science, we shall teach systems which, by universal confession, whenever they differ from those of Europe, differ for the worse; and whether, when we can patronize sound philosophy and true history, we shall countenance, at the public expense, medical doctrines which would disgrace an English farrier—astronomy, which would move laughter in the girls at an English boarding-school—history, abounding with kings thirty feet high, and reigns thirty thousand years long—and geography, made up of seas of treacle and seas of butter.

"We are not without experience to guide us. History furnishes several analogous cases, and they all teach the same lesson. There are in modern times, to go no further, two memorable instances of a great impulse given to the mind of a whole society—of prejudice overthrown—of knowledge diffused—of taste purified—of arts and sciences planted in countries which had recently been ignorant and barbarous.

"The first instance to which I refer is the great revival of letters among the Western nations at the close of the fifteenth and the beginning of the sixteenth century. At that time almost every thing that was worth reading was contained in the writings of the ancient Greeks and Romans. Had our ancestors acted as the Committee of Public Instruction has hitherto acted; had they neglected the language of Cicero and Tacitus; had they confined their attention to the old dialects of our own island; had they printed nothing and taught nothing at the universities but chronicles in Anglo-Saxon and romances in Norman-French, would England have been what she now is? What the Greek and Latin were to the contemporaries of More and Ascham, our tongue is to the people of India. The literature of England is now more valuable than that of classical antiquity. I doubt whether the Sanscrit literature be as valuable as that of our Saxon and Norman progenitors. In some departments—in history, for example—I am certain that it is much less so.

"Another instance may be said to be still before our eyes. Within the last hundred and twenty years, a nation which had previously been in a state as barbarous as that in which our ancestors were before the Crusades, has gradually emerged from the ignorance in which it was sunk, and has taken its place among civilized communities. I speak of Russia. There is now in that country a large educated class, abounding with persons fit to serve the state in the highest functions, and in no wise inferior to the most accomplished men who adorn the best circles of Paris and London. There is reason to hope that this vast empire, which in the time of our grandfathers was probably behind the Punjab, may, in the time of our grandchildren, be pressing close on France and Britain in the career of improvement. And how was this change effected? Not by flattering national prejudices; not by feeding the mind of the young Muscovite with the old woman's stories which his rude fathers had believed; not by filling his head with lying legends about St. Nicholas; not by encouraging him to study the great question, whether the world was or was not created on the 13th of September; not by calling him 'a learned native' when he has mastered all these points of knowledge; but by teaching him those foreign languages in which the greatest mass of information had been laid up, and thus putting all that information within his reach. The languages of Western Europe civilized Russia. I can not doubt that they will do for the Hindoo what they have done for the Tartar."

This minute, which in its original shape is long enough for an article in a quarterly review, and as business-like as a report of a royal commission, set the question at rest at once and forever. On the 7th of March, 1835, Lord William Bentinck decided that "the great object of the British Government ought to be the promotion of European literature and science among the natives of India;" two of the Orientalists retired from the Committee of Public Instruction; several new members, both English and native, were appointed; and Macaulay entered upon the functions of president with an energy and assiduity which in his case were an infallible proof that his work was to his mind.

The post was no sinecure. It was an arduous task to plan, found, and construct, in all its grades, the education of such a country as India. The means at Macaulay's disposal were utterly inadequate for the undertaking on which he was engaged. Nothing resembling an organized staff was as yet in existence. There were no inspectors of schools. There were no training colleges for masters. There were no boards of experienced managers. The machinery consisted of voluntary committees acting on the spot, and corresponding directly with the superintending body at Calcutta. Macaulay rose to the occasion, and threw himself into the routine of administration and control with zeal sustained by diligence and tempered by tact. "We were hardly prepared," said a competent critic, "for the amount of conciliation which he evinces in dealing with irritable colleagues and subordinates, and for the strong, sterling, practical common sense with which he sweeps away rubbish, or cuts the knots of local and departmental problems." The value which a man sets upon the objects of his pursuit is generally in proportion to the mastery which he exercises over himself, and the patience and forbearance displayed in his dealings with others. If we judge Macaulay by this standard, it is plain that he cared a great deal more for providing our Eastern empire with an educational outfit that would work and wear than he ever cared for keeping his own seat in Parliament, or pushing his own fortunes in Downing Street. Throughout his innumerable minutes, on all subjects, from the broadest principles to the narrowest detail, he is everywhere free from crotchets and susceptibilities; and everywhere ready to humor any person who will make himself useful, and to adopt any appliance which can be turned to account.

"I think it highly probable that Mr. Nicholls may be to blame, because I have seldom known a quarrel in which both parties were not to blame. But I see no evidence that he is so. Nor do I see any evidence which tends to prove that Mr. Nicholls leads the Local Committee by the nose. The Local Committee appear to have acted with perfect propriety, and I can not consent to treat them in the manner recommended by Mr. Sutherland. If we appoint the colonel to be a member of their body, we shall, in effect, pass a most severe censure on their proceedings. I dislike the suggestion of putting military men on the committee as a check on the civilians. Hitherto we have never, to the best of my belief, been troubled by any such idle jealousies. I would appoint the fittest men, without caring to what branch of the service they belonged, or whether they belonged to the service at all."*

Exception had been taken to an applicant for a mastership, on the ground that he had been a preacher with a strong turn for proselytizing.

"Mr. —— seems to be so little concerned about proselytizing, that he does not even know how to spell the word; a circumstance which, if I did not suppose it to be a slip of the pen, I should think a more serious objection than the Reverend which formerly stood before his name. I am quite content with his assurances."

In default of better, Macaulay was always for employing the tools which came to hand. A warm and consistent advocate of appointment by competitive examination, wherever a field for competition existed, he was no pedantic slave to a theory. In the dearth of school-masters, which is a feature in every infant educational system, he refused to reject a candidate who "mistook Argos for Corinth," and backed the claims of any aspirant of respectable character who could "read, write, and work a sum."

"By all means accept the King of Oude's present, though, to be sure, more detestable maps were never seen. One would think that the revenues of Oude and the treasures of Saadut Ali might have borne the expense of producing something better than a map in which Sicily is joined on to the toe of Italy, and in which so important an Eastern island as Java does not appear at all."

---

* This and the following extracts are taken from a volume of Macaulay's Minutes, "now first collected from Records in the Department of Public Instruction, by H. Woodrow, Esq., M.A., Inspector of Schools at Calcutta, and formerly Fellow of Caius College, Cambridge." The collection was published in India.

"As to the corrupting influence of the zenana, of which Mr. Trevelyan speaks, I may regret it; but I own that I can not help thinking that the dissolution of the tie between parent and child is as great a moral evil as can be found in any zenana. In whatever degree infant schools relax that tie, they do mischief. For my own part, I would rather hear a boy of three years old lisp all the bad words in the language, than that he should have no feelings of family affection—that his character should be that which must be expected in one who has had the misfortune of having a schoolmaster in place of a mother."

"I do not see the reason for establishing any limit as to the age of scholars. The phenomena are exactly the same which have always been found to exist when a new mode of education has been rising into fashion. No man of fifty now learns Greek with boys; but in the sixteenth century it was not at all unusual to see old doctors of divinity attending lectures side by side with young students."

"With respect to making our college libraries circulating libraries, there is much to be said on both sides. If a proper subscription is demanded from those who have access to them, and if all that is raised by this subscription is laid out in adding to the libraries, the students will be no losers by the plan. Our libraries, the best of them at least, would be better than any which would be readily accessible at an up-country station; and I do not know why we should grudge a young officer the pleasure of reading our copy of Boswell's 'Life of Johnson,' or 'Marmontel's Memoirs,' if he is willing to pay a few rupees for the privilege."

These utterances of cultured wisdom, or homely mother wit, are sometimes expressed in phrases almost as amusing, though not so characteristic, as those which Frederic the Great used to scrawl on the margin of reports and dispatches for the information of his secretaries.

"We are a little too indulgent to the whims of the people in our employ. We pay a large sum to send a master to a distant station. He dislikes the place. The collector is uncivil; the surgeon quarrels with him; and he must be moved. The expenses of the journey have to be defrayed. Another man is to be transferred from a place where he is comfortable and useful. Our masters run from station to station at our cost, as vaporized ladies at home run about from spa to spa. All situations have their discomforts; and there are times when we all wish that our lot had been cast in some other line of life, or in some other place."

With regard to a proposed coat of arms for Hooghly College, he says:

"I do not see why the mummeries of European heraldry should be introduced into any part of our Indian system. Heraldry is not a science which has any eternal rules. It is a system of arbitrary canons, originating in pure caprice. Nothing can be more absurd and grotesque than armorial bearings, considered in themselves. Certain recollections, certain associations, make them interesting in many cases to an Englishman; but in those recollections and associations the natives of India do not participate. A lion rampant, with a folio in his paw, with a man standing on each side of him, with a telescope over his head, and with a Persian motto under his feet, must seem to them either very mysterious or very absurd."

In a discussion on the propriety of printing some books of Oriental science, Macaulay writes:

"I should be sorry to say any thing disrespectful of that liberal and generous enthusiasm for Oriental literature which appears in Mr. Sutherland's minute; but I own that I can not think that we ought to be guided in the distribution of the small sum which the Government has allotted for the purpose of education by considerations which seem a little romantic. That the Saracens a thousand years ago cultivated mathematical science is hardly, I think, a reason for our spending any money in translating English treatises on mathematics into Arabic. Mr. Sutherland would probably think it very strange if we were to urge the destruction of the Alexandrian Library as a reason against patronizing Arabic literature in the nineteenth century. The undertaking may be, as Mr. Sutherland conceives, a great national work. So is the breakwater at Madras. But under the orders which we have received from the Government, we have just as little to do with one as with the other."

Now and then a stroke aimed at Hooghly College hits nearer home. That men of thirty should be bribed to continue their education into mature life "seems very absurd. Moghal Jan has been paid to learn something during twelve years. We are told that he is lazy and stupid; but there are hopes that in four years more he will have completed his course of study. We have had quite enough of these lazy, stupid school-boys of thirty."

"I must frankly own that I do not like the list of books. Grammars of rhetoric and grammars of logic are among the most useless furniture of a shelf. Give a boy 'Robinson Crusoe.' That is worth all the grammars of rhetoric and logic in the world. We ought to procure such books as are likely to give the children a taste for the literature of the West; not books filled with idle distinctions and definitions which every man who has learned them makes haste to forget. Who ever reasoned better for having been taught the difference between a syllogism and an enthymeme? Who ever composed with greater spirit and elegance because he could define an oxymoron or an aposiopesis? I am not joking, but writing quite seriously, when I say that I would much rather order a hundred copies of 'Jack the Giant-killer' for our schools than a hundred copies of any grammar of rhetoric or logic that ever was written."

"Goldsmith's Histories of Greece and Rome are miserable performances, and I do not at all like to lay out £50 on them, even after they have received all Mr. Pinnock's improvements. I must own, too, that I think the order for globes and other instruments unnecessarily large. To lay out £324 at once on globes alone, useful as I acknowledge those articles to be, seems exceedingly profuse, when we have only about £3000 a year for all purposes of English education. One twelve-inch or eighteen-inch globe for each school is quite enough; and we ought not, I think, to order sixteen such globes when we are about to establish only seven schools. Useful as the telescopes, the theodolites, and the other scientific instruments mentioned in the indent undoubtedly are, we must consider that four or five such instruments run away with a year's salary of a school-master, and that if we purchase them it will be necessary to defer the establishment of schools."

At one of the colleges at Calcutta the distribution of prizes was accompanied by some histrionic performances on the part of the pupils.

"I have no partiality," writes Macaulay, "for such ceremonies. I think it a very questionable thing whether, even at home, public spouting and acting ought to form part of the system of a place of education. But in this country such exhibitions are peculiarly out of place. I can conceive nothing more grotesque than the scene from the 'Merchant of Venice,' with Portia represented by a little black boy. Then, too, the subjects of recitation were ill chosen. We are attempting to introduce a great nation to a knowledge of the richest and noblest literature in the world. The society of Calcutta assemble to see what progress we are making; and we produce as a sample a boy who repeats some blackguard doggerel of George Colman's, about a fat gentleman who was put to bed over an oven, and about a man-midwife who was called out of his bed by a drunken man at night. Our disciple tries to hiccough, and tumbles and staggers about in imitation of the tipsy English sailors whom he has seen at the punch-houses. Really, if we can find nothing better worth reciting than this trash, we had better give up English instruction altogether."

"As to the list of prize books, I am not much better satisfied. It is absolutely unintelligible to me why Pope's works, and my old friend Moore's 'Lalla Rookh,' should be selected from the whole mass of English poetry to be prize books. I will engage to frame, *currente calamo*, a better list. Bacon's 'Essays,' Hume's 'England,' Gibbon's 'Rome,' Robertson's 'Charles V.,' Robertson's 'Scotland,' Robertson's 'America,' Swift's 'Gulliver,' 'Robinson Crusoe,' Shakspeare's works, 'Paradise Lost,' Milton's smaller poems, 'Arabian Nights,' Park's 'Travels,' Anson's 'Voyage,' the 'Vicar of Wakefield,' Johnson's 'Lives,' 'Gil Blas,' Voltaire's 'Charles XII.,' Southey's 'Nelson,' Middleton's 'Life of Cicero.'

"This may serve as a specimen. These are books which will amuse and interest those who obtain them. To give a boy 'Abercrombie on the Intellectual Powers,' Dick's 'Moral Improvement,' Young's 'Intellectual Philosophy,' Chalmers's 'Poetical Economy'!!! (in passing, I may be allowed to ask what that means), is quite absurd. I would not give orders at random for books about which we know nothing. We are under no necessity of ordering at haphazard. We know 'Robinson Crusoe,' and 'Gulliver,' and the 'Arabian Nights,' and Anson's 'Voyage,' and many other delightful works which interest even the very young, and which do not lose their interest to the end of our lives. Why should we order blindfold such books as Markham's 'New Children's Friend,' the 'Juvenile Scrap-book,' the 'Child's Own Book,' Niggens's 'Earth,' Mudie's 'Sea,' and somebody else's 'Fire and Air'?—books which, I will be bound for it, none of us ever opened.

"The list ought in all its parts to be thoroughly recast. If Sir Benjamin Malkin will furnish the names of ten or twelve works of a scientific kind which he thinks suited for prizes, the task will not be difficult; and, with his help, I will gladly undertake it. There is a marked distinction between a prize book and a school book. A prize book ought to be a book which a boy receives with pleasure, and turns over and over, not as a task, but spontaneously. I have not forgotten my own school-boy feelings on this subject. My pleasure at obtaining a prize was greatly enhanced by the knowledge that my little library would receive a very agreeable addition. I never was better pleased than when at fourteen I was master of Boswell's 'Life of Johnson,' which I had long been wishing to read. If my master had given me, instead of Boswell, a critical pronouncing dictionary, or a geographical class-book, I should have been much less gratified by my success."

The idea had been started of paying authors to write books in the languages of the country. On this Macaulay remarks:

"To hire four or five people to make a literature is a course which never answered and never will answer, in any part of the world. Languages grow. They can not be built. We are now following the slow but sure course on which alone we can depend for a supply of good books in the vernacular languages of India. We are attempting to raise up a large class of enlightened natives. I hope that, twenty years hence, there will be hundreds, nay thousands, of natives familiar with the best models of composition, and well acquainted with Western science. Among them some persons will be found who will have the inclination, and the ability, to exhibit European knowledge in the vernacular dialects. This I believe to be the only way in which we can raise up a good vernacular literature in this country."

These hopeful anticipations have been more than fulfilled. Twice twenty years have brought into existence, not hundreds or thousands, but hundreds of thousands, of natives who can appreciate European knowledge when laid before them in the English language, and can reproduce it in their own. Taking one year with another, upward of a thousand works of literature and science are published annually in Bengal alone, and at least four times that number throughout the entire continent. Our colleges have more than six thousand students on their books, and two hundred thousand boys are receiving a liberal education in schools of the higher order. For the improvement of the mass of the people, nearly seven thousand young men are in training as certificated masters. The amount allotted in the budget to the item of Public Instruction has increased more than seventy-fold since 1835; and is largely supplemented by the fees which parents of all classes willingly contribute, when once they have been taught the value of a commodity the demand for which is created by the supply. During many years past the generosity of wealthy natives has to a great extent been diverted from the idle extravagance of pageants and festivals, to promote the intellectual advancement of their fellow-countrymen. On several different occasions, at a single stroke of the pen, our Indian universities have been endowed with twice, three times, four times the amount of the slender sum which Macaulay had at his command. But none the less was he the master-engineer, whose skill and foresight determined the direction of the channels along which this stream of public and private munificence was to flow for the regeneration of our Eastern empire.

It may add something to the merit of Macaulay's labors in

the cause of education that those labors were voluntary and unpaid; and voluntary and unpaid likewise was another service which he rendered to India, not less durable than the first, and hardly less important. A clause in the act of 1833 gave rise to the appointment of a commission to inquire into the jurisprudence and jurisdiction of our Eastern empire. Macaulay, at his own instigation, was appointed president of that commission. He had not been many months engaged in his new duties before he submitted a proposal, by the adoption of which his own industry, and the high talents of his colleagues, Mr. Cameron and Sir John Macleod, might be turned to the best account by being employed in framing a criminal code for the whole Indian empire. "This code," writes Macaulay, "should not be a mere digest of existing usages and regulations, but should comprise all the reforms which the commission may think desirable. It should be framed on two great principles—the principle of suppressing crime with the smallest possible amount of suffering, and the principle of ascertaining truth at the smallest possible cost of time and money. The commissioners should be particularly charged to study conciseness, as far as it is consistent with perspicuity. In general, I believe, it will be found that perspicuous and concise expressions are not only compatible, but identical."

The offer was eagerly accepted, and the commission fell to work. The results of that work did not show themselves quickly enough to satisfy the most practical and (to its credit be it spoken) the most exacting of governments; and Macaulay was under the necessity of explaining and excusing a procrastination which was celerity itself as compared with any codifying that had been done since the days of Justinian.

"During the last rainy season—a season, I believe, peculiarly unhealthy—every member of the commission except myself was wholly incapacitated for exertion. Mr. Anderson has been twice under the necessity of leaving Calcutta, and has not, till very lately, been able to labor with his accustomed activity. Mr. Macleod has been, till within the last week or ten days, in so feeble a state that the smallest effort seriously disordered him; and his health is so delicate that, admirably qualified as he is by very rare talents for the discharge of his functions, it would be imprudent, in forming any prospective calculation, to reckon on much service from him. Mr. Cameron, of the importance of whose assistance I need not speak, has been during more than four months utterly unable to do any work, and has at length been compelled to ask leave of absence, in order to visit the Cape for the recovery of his health. Thus, as the governor-general has stated, Mr. Millett and myself have, during a considerable time, constituted the whole effective strength of the commission. Nor has Mr. Millett been able to devote to the business of the commission his whole undivided attention.

"I must say that, even if no allowance be made for the untoward occurrences which have retarded our progress, that progress can not be called slow. People who have never considered the importance and difficulty of the task in which we are employed are surprised to find that a code can not be spoken off extempore, or written like an article in a magazine. I am not ashamed to acknowledge that there are several chapters in the code on which I have been employed for months; of which I have changed the whole plan ten or twelve times; which contain not a single word as it originally stood; and with which I am still very far indeed from being satisfied. I certainly shall not hurry on my share of the work to gratify the childish impatience of the ignorant. Their censure ought to be a matter of perfect indifference to men engaged in a task, on the right performing of which the welfare of millions may, during a long series of years, depend. The cost of the commission is as nothing when compared with the importance of such a work. The time during which the commission has sat is as nothing compared with the time during which that work will produce good, or evil, to India.

"Indeed, if we compare the progress of the 'Indian Code' with the progress of codes under circumstances far more favorable, we shall find little reason to accuse the Law Commission of tardiness. Bonaparte had at his command the services of experienced jurists to any extent to which he chose to call for them; yet his legislation proceeded at a far slower rate than ours. The 'French Criminal Code' was begun, under the Consulate, in March, 1801; and yet the 'Code of Criminal Procedure' was not completed till 1808, and the 'Penal Code' not till 1810. The 'Criminal Code of Louisiana' was commenced in February, 1821. After it had been in preparation during three years and a half, an accident happened to the papers which compelled Mr. Livingstone to request indulgence for another year. Indeed, when I remember the slow progress of law reforms at home, and when I consider that our code decides hundreds of questions, every one of which, if stirred in England, would give occasion to voluminous controversy and to many animated debates, I must acknowledge that I am inclined to fear that we have been guilty rather of precipitation than of delay."

This minute was dated the 2d of January, 1837; and in

the course of the same year the code appeared, headed by an introductory report in the shape of a letter to the governor-general, and followed by an appendix containing eighteen notes, each in itself an essay. The most readable of all digests, its pages are alive with illustrations drawn from history, from literature, and from the habits and occurrences of everyday life. The offense of fabricating evidence is exemplified by a case which may easily be recognized as that of Lady Macbeth and the grooms;* and the offense of voluntary culpable homicide, by an imaginary incident of a pit covered with sticks and turf, which irresistibly recalls a reminiscence of "Jack the Giant-killer." The chapters on theft and trespass establish the rights of book-owners as against book-stealers, book-borrowers, and book-defacers,† with an affectionate precision which would have gladdened the heart of Charles Lamb or Sir Walter Scott. In the chapter on manslaughter, the judge is enjoined to treat with lenity an act done in the first anger of a husband or father, provoked by the intolerable outrage of a certain kind of criminal assault. "Such an assault produced the Sicilian Vespers. Such an assault called forth the memorable blow of Wat Tyler." And, on the question whether the severity of a hurt should be considered in apportioning the punishment, we are reminded of "examples which

---

* "A, after wounding a person with a knife, goes into the room where Z is sleeping, smears Z's clothes with blood, and lays the knife under Z's pillow; intending not only that suspicion may thereby be turned away from himself, but also that Z may be convicted of voluntarily causing grievous hurt. A is liable to punishment as a fabricator of false evidence."

† "A, being on friendly terms with Z, goes into Z's library, in Z's absence, and takes a book without Z's express consent. Here, it is probable that A may have conceived that he had Z's implied consent to use Z's books. If this was A's impression, A has not committed theft."

"A takes up a book belonging to Z, and reads it, not having any right over the book, and not having the consent of any person entitled to authorize A so to do. A trespasses."

"A, being exasperated at a passage in a book which is lying on the counter of Z, snatches it up and tears it to pieces. A has not committed theft, as he has not acted fraudulently, though he may have committed criminal trespass and mischief."

are universally known. Harley was laid up more than twenty days by the wound which he received from Guiscard;" while "the scratch which Damien gave to Louis the Fifteenth was so slight that it was followed by no feverish symptoms." Such a sanguine estimate of the diffusion of knowledge with regard to the details of ancient crimes could proceed from no pen but that of the writer who endowed school-boys with the erudition of professors, and the talker who, when he poured forth the stores of his memory, began each of his disquisitions with the phrase "Don't you remember?"

If it be asked whether or not the "Penal Code" fulfills the ends for which it was framed, the answer may safely be left to the gratitude of Indian civilians, the younger of whom carry it about in their saddle-bags, and the older in their heads. The value which it possesses in the eyes of a trained English lawyer may be gathered from the testimony of Macaulay's eminent successor, Mr. Fitzjames Stephen:

"In order to appreciate the importance of the 'Penal Code,' it must be borne in mind what crime in India is. Here, in England, order is so thoroughly well established that the crime of the country is hardly more than an annoyance. In India, if crime is allowed to get to a head, it is capable of destroying the peace and prosperity of whole tracts of country. The mass of the people in their common moods are gentle, submissive, and disposed to be innocent; but, for that very reason, bold and successful criminals are dangerous in the extreme. In old days, when they joined in gangs or organized bodies, they soon acquired political importance. Now, in many parts of India, crime is quite as uncommon as in the least criminal parts of England; and the old high-handed, systematized crime has almost entirely disappeared. This great revolution (for it is nothing less) in the state of society of a whole continent has been brought about by the regular administration of a rational body of criminal law.

"The administration of criminal justice is intrusted to a very small number of English magistrates, organized according to a carefully devised system of appeal and supervision which represents the experience of a century. This system is not unattended by evils; but it is absolutely necessary, to enable a few hundred civilians to govern a continent. Persons in such a position must be provided with the plainest instructions as to the nature of their duties. These instructions, in so far as the administration of criminal justice is concerned, are contained in the 'Indian Penal Code' and the 'Code of Criminal Procedure.' The 'Code of Criminal Procedure' contains 541 sections, and forms a pamphlet of 210 widely printed octavo pages. The 'Penal Code' consists of 510 sections. Pocket editions of these codes are published, which may be carried about as easily as a pocket Bible; and I doubt whether, even in Scotland, you would find many people who know their Bibles as Indian civilians know their codes."

After describing the confusion and complication of the criminal law of our Indian empire before it was taken in hand by the Commission of 1834, Mr. Stephen proceeds to say:

"Lord Macaulay's great work was far too daring and original to be accepted at once. It was a draft when he left India in 1838. His successors made remarks on it for twenty-two years. Those years were filled with wars and rumors of wars. The Afghan disasters and triumphs, the war in Central India, the wars with the Sikhs, Lord Dalhousie's annexations, threw law reform into the background, and produced a state of mind not very favorable to it. Then came the Mutiny, which in its essence was the breakdown of an old system; the renunciation of an attempt to effect an impossible compromise between the Asiatic and the European view of things, legal, military, and administrative. The effect of the Mutiny on the statute-book was unmistakable. The 'Code of Civil Procedure' was enacted in 1859. The 'Penal Code' was enacted in 1860, and came into operation on the 1st of January, 1862. The credit of passing the 'Penal Code' into law, and of giving to every part of it the improvements which practical skill and technical knowledge could bestow, is due to Sir Barnes Peacock, who held Lord Macaulay's place during the most anxious years through which the Indian empire has passed. The draft and the revision are both eminently creditable to their authors; and the result of their successive efforts has been to reproduce in a concise and even beautiful form the spirit of the law of England; the most technical, the most clumsy, and the most bewildering of all systems of criminal law, though I think, if its principles are fully understood, it is the most rational. If any one doubts this assertion, let him compare the 'Indian Penal Code' with such a book as Mr. Greaves's edition of 'Russell on Crimes.' The one subject of homicide, as treated by Mr. Greaves and Russell, is, I should think, twice as long as the whole 'Penal Code;' and it does not contain a tenth part of the matter."

"The point which always has surprised me most in connection with the 'Penal Code' is, that it proves that Lord Macaulay must have had a knowledge of English criminal law which, considering how little he had practiced it,* may fairly be called extraordinary. He must have possessed the

---

* Macaulay's practice at the bar had been less than little, according to

gift of going at once to the very root of the matter, and of sifting the corn from the chaff to a most unusual degree; for his draft gives the substance of the criminal law of England, down to its minute working details, in a compass which by comparison with the original may be regarded as almost absurdly small. The 'Indian Penal Code' is to the English criminal law what a manufactured article ready for use is to the materials out of which it is made. It is to the French 'Code Pénal,' and, I may add, to the 'North German Code' of 1871, what a finished picture is to a sketch. It is far simpler, and much better expressed, than Livingston's 'Code for Louisiana;' and its practical success has been complete. The clearest proof of this is that hardly any questions have arisen upon it which have had to be determined by the courts; and that few and slight amendments have had to be made in it by the Legislature."

Without troubling himself unduly about the matter, Macaulay was conscious that the world's estimate of his public services would be injuriously affected by the popular notion, which he has described as "so flattering to mediocrity," that a great writer can not be a great administrator; and it is possible that this consciousness had something to do with the heartiness and fervor which he threw into his defense of the author of "Cato" against the charge of having been an inefficient secretary of state. There was much in common between his own lot and that of the other famous essayist who had been likewise a Whig statesman; and this similarity in their fortunes may account in part for the indulgence, and almost tenderness, with which he reviewed the career and character of Addison. Addison himself, at his villa in Chelsea, and still more amidst the gilded slavery of Holland House, might have envied the literary seclusion, ample for so rapid a reader, which the usages of Indian life permitted Macaulay to enjoy. "I have a very pretty garden," he writes, "not unlike our little grass-plot at Clapham, but larger. It consists of a fine sheet of turf, with a gravel walk round it, and flower-beds scattered over it. It looks beautiful just now after the rains, and I

---

an account which he gave of it at a public dinner: "My own forensic experience, gentlemen, has been extremely small; for my only recollection of an achievement that way is that at quarter sessions I once convicted a boy of stealing a parcel of cocks and hens."

hear that it keeps its verdure during a great part of the year. A flight of steps leads down from my library into the garden, and it is so well shaded that you may walk there till ten o'clock in the morning."

Here, book in hand, and in dressing-gown and slippers, he would spend those two hours after sunrise which Anglo-Indian gentlemen devote to riding, and Anglo-Indian ladies to sleeping off the arrears of the sultry night. Regularly, every morning, his studies were broken in upon by the arrival of his baby niece, who came to feed the crows with the toast which accompanied his early cup of tea; a ceremony during which he had much ado to protect the child from the advances of a multitude of birds, each almost as big as herself, which hopped and fluttered round her as she stood on the steps of the veranda. When the sun drove him indoors (which happened sooner than he had promised himself, before he had learned by experience what the hot season was), he went to his bath and toilet, and then to breakfast; "at which we support nature under the exhausting effects of the climate by means of plenty of eggs, mango-fish, snipe-pies, and frequently a hot beefsteak. My cook is renowned through Calcutta for his skill. He brought me attestations of a long succession of gourmands, and among them one from Lord Dalhousie,* who pronounced him decidedly the first artist in Bengal. This great man, and his two assistants, I am to have for thirty rupees a month. While I am on the subject of the cuisine, I may as well say all that I have to say about it at once. The tropical fruits are wretched. The best of them is inferior to our apricot or gooseberry. When I was a child, I had a notion of its being the most exquisite of treats to eat plantains and yams, and to drink palm-wine. How I envied my father for having enjoyed these luxuries! I have now enjoyed them all, and I have found, like much greater men on much more important occasions, that all is vanity. A plantain is very like a rotten pear—so like, that I would lay twen-

* Lord Dalhousie, the father of the governor-general, was commander-in-chief in India during the years 1830 and 1831.

ty to one that a person blindfolded would not discover the difference. A yam is better. It is like an indifferent potato. I tried palm-wine at a pretty village near Madras, where I slept one night. I told Captain Barron that I had been curious to taste that liquor ever since I first saw, eight or nine and twenty years ago, the picture of the negro climbing the tree in Sierra Leone. The next morning I was roused by a servant, with a large bowl of juice fresh from the tree. I drank it, and found it very like ginger-beer in which the ginger has been sparingly used."

Macaulay necessarily spent away from home the days on which the Supreme Council, or the Law Commission, held their meetings; but the rest of his work, legal, literary, and educational, he carried on in the quiet of his library. Now and again, a morning was consumed in returning calls; an expenditure of time which it is needless to say that he sorely grudged. "Happily the good people here are too busy to be at home. Except the parsons, they are all usefully occupied somewhere or other, so that I have only to leave cards; but the reverend gentlemen are always within doors in the heat of the day, lying on their backs, regretting breakfast, longing for tiffin, and crying out for lemonade." After lunch he sat with Mrs. Trevelyan, translating Greek or reading French for her benefit; and Scribe's comedies and Saint Simon's "Memoirs" beguiled the long, languid leisure of the Calcutta afternoon, while the punka swung overhead, and the air came heavy and scented through the moistened grass matting which shrouded the windows. At the approach of sunset, with its attendant breeze, he joined his sister in her drive along the banks of the Hooghly; and they returned by starlight, too often to take part in a vast banquet of forty guests, dressed as fashionably as people can dress at ninety degrees east from Paris; who, one and all, had far rather have been eating their curry and drinking their bitter beer at home, in all the comfort of muslin and nankeen. Macaulay is vehement in his dislike of "those great formal dinners, which unite all the stiffness of a levee to all the disorder and discomfort of a two-shilling ordinary. Nothing can be duller. Nobody speaks except to the person next him. The conversation is the most deplorable twaddle; and, as I always sit next to the lady of the highest rank, or, in other words, to the oldest, ugliest, and proudest woman in the company, I am worse off than my neighbors."

Nevertheless he was far too acute a judge of men to undervalue the special type of mind which is produced and fostered by the influences of an Indian career. He was always ready to admit that there is no better company in the world than a young and rising civilian; no one who has more to say that is worth hearing, and who can say it in a manner better adapted to interest those who know good talk from bad. He delighted in that freedom from pedantry, affectation, and pretension which is one of the most agreeable characteristics of a service to belong to which is in itself so effectual an education, that a bore is a phenomenon notorious everywhere within a hundred miles of the station which has the honor to possess him, and a fool is quoted by name throughout all the three presidencies. Macaulay writes to his sisters at home: "The best way of seeing society here is to have very small parties. There is a little circle of people whose friendship I value, and in whose conversation I take pleasure: the chief-justice, Sir Edward Ryan; my old friend, Malkin;* Cameron and Macleod, the law commissioners; Macnaghten, among the older servants of the company, and Mangles, Colvin, and John Peter Grant, among the younger. These, in my opinion, are the flower of Calcutta society, and I often ask some of them to a quiet dinner." On the Friday of every week these chosen few met round Macaulay's breakfast-table to discuss

* It can not be said that all the claims made upon Macaulay's friendship were acknowledged as readily as those of Sir Benjamin Malkin. "I am dunned unmercifully by place-hunters. The oddest application that I have received is from that rascal ——, who is somewhere in the interior. He tells me that he is sure that prosperity has not changed me; that I am still the same John Macaulay who was his dearest friend, his more than brother; and that he means to come up and live with me at Calcutta. If he fulfills his intention, I will have him taken before the police-magistrates."

the progress which the Law Commission had made in its labors; and each successive point which was started opened the way to such a flood of talk, legal, historical, political, and personal, that the company would sit far on toward noon over the empty tea-cups, until an uneasy sense of accumulating dispatch-boxes drove them, one by one, to their respective offices.

There are scattered passages in these letters which prove that Macaulay's feelings during his protracted absence from his native country were at times almost as keen as those which racked the breast of Cicero when he was forced to exchange the triumphs of the forum, and the cozy suppers with his brother augurs, for his hateful place of banishment at Thessalonica, or his hardly less hateful seat of government at Tarsus. The complaints of the English statesman do not, however, amount in volume to a fiftieth part of those reiterated outpourings of lachrymose eloquence with which the Roman philosopher bewailed an expatriation that was hardly one-third as long. "I have no words," writes Macaulay, very much underestimating the wealth of his own vocabulary, "to tell you how I pine for England, or how intensely bitter exile has been to me, though I hope that I have borne it well. I feel as if I had no other wish than to see my country again, and die. Let me assure you that banishment is no light matter. No person can judge of it who has not experienced it. A complete revolution in all the habits of life; an estrangement from almost every old friend and acquaintance; fifteen thousand miles of ocean between the exile and every thing that he cares for; all this is, to me at least, very trying. There is no temptation of wealth or power which would induce me to go through it again. But many people do not feel as I do. Indeed, the servants of the company rarely have such a feeling; and it is natural that they should not have it, for they are sent out while still school-boys, and when they know little of the world. The moment of emigration is to them also the moment of emancipation; and the pleasures of liberty and affluence to a great degree compensate them for the loss of their home. In a few years they become Orientalized and, by the time that they are of my age, they would generally prefer India, as a residence, to England. But it is a very different matter when a man is transplanted at thirty-three."

Making, as always, the best of every thing, he was quite ready to allow that he might have been placed in a still less agreeable situation. In the following extract from a letter to his friend, Mrs. Drummond, there is much which will come home to those who are old enough to remember how vastly the Dublin of 1837 differed, for the worse, from the Dublin of 1875: "It now seems likely that you may remain in Ireland for years. I can not conceive what has induced you to submit to such an exile. I declare, for my own part, that, little as I love Calcutta, I would rather stay here than be settled in the Phœnix Park. The last residence which I would choose would be a place with all the plagues, and none of the attractions, of a capital; a provincial city on fire with factions political and religious, peopled by raving Orangemen and raving Repealers, and distracted by a contest between Protestantism as fanatical as that of Knox, and Catholicism as fanatical as that of Bonner. We have our share of the miseries of life in this country. We are annually baked four months, boiled four more, and allowed the remaining four to become cool if we can. At this moment the sun is blazing like a furnace. The earth, soaked with oceans of rain, is steaming like a wet blanket. Vegetation is rotting all round us. Insects and undertakers are the only living creatures which seem to enjoy the climate. But, though our atmosphere is hot, our factions are lukewarm. A bad epigram in a newspaper, or a public meeting attended by a tailor, a pastry-cook, a reporter, two or three barristers, and eight or ten attorneys, are our most formidable annoyances. We have agitators in our own small way, Tritons of the minnows, bearing the same sort of resemblance to O'Connell that a lizard bears to an alligator. Therefore Calcutta for me, in preference to Dublin."

He had good reason for being grateful to Calcutta, and still better for not showing his gratitude by prolonging his stay there over a fourth summer and autumn. "That tremendous crash of the great commercial houses which took place a few years ago has produced a revolution in fashions. It ruined one half of the English society in Bengal, and seriously injured the other half. A large proportion of the most important functionaries here are deeply in debt, and, accordingly, the mode of living is now exceedingly quiet and modest. Those immense subscriptions, those public tables, those costly equipages and entertainments of which Heber, and others who saw Calcutta a few years back, say so much, are never heard of. Speaking for myself, it was a great piece of good fortune that I came hither just at the time when the general distress had forced every body to adopt a moderate way of living. Owing very much to that circumstance (while keeping house, I think, more handsomely than any other member of council), I have saved what will enable me to do my part toward making my family comfortable; and I shall have a competency for myself, small indeed, but quite sufficient to render me as perfectly independent as if I were the possessor of Burleigh or Chatsworth."*

"The rainy season of 1837 has been exceedingly unhealthy. Our house has escaped as well as any; yet Hannah is the only one of us who has come off untouched. The baby has been repeatedly unwell. Trevelyan has suffered a good deal, and is kept right only by occasional trips in a steamer down to the mouth of the Hooghly. I had a smart touch of fever, which happily staid but an hour or two, and I took such vigorous measures that it never came again; but I remained unnerved and exhausted for nearly a fortnight. This was my first, and I hope my last, taste of Indian maladies. It is a happy thing for us all that we are not to pass another year in the reek of this deadly marsh." Macaulay wisely declined to set the hope of making another lac of rupees against the risk, to himself and others, of such a fate as subsequently befell

* Macaulay writes to Lord Mahon on the last day of December, 1836: "In another year I hope to leave this country, with a fortune which you would think ridiculously small, but which will make me as independent as if I had all that Lord Westminster has above the ground, and Lord Durham below it. I have no intention of again taking part in politics; but I can not tell what effect the sight of the old Hall and Abbey may produce on me."

Lord Canning and Mr. James Wilson. He put the finishing stroke to his various labors; resigned his seat in the council, and his presidentships of the Law Commission and the Committee of Public Instruction; and, in company with the Trevelyans, sailed for England in the first fortnight of the year 1838.

To Mr. Thomas Flower Ellis.

Calcutta, December 15th, 1834.

Dear Ellis,—Many thanks for your letter. It is delightful in this strange land to see the handwriting of such a friend. We must keep up our spirits. We shall meet, I trust, in little more than four years, with feelings of regard only strengthened by our separation. My spirits are not bad; and they ought not to be bad. I have health, affluence, consideration, great power to do good; functions which, while they are honorable and useful, are not painfully burdensome; leisure for study, good books, an unclouded and active mind, warm affections, and a very dear sister. There will soon be a change in my domestic arrangements. My sister is to be married next week. Her lover, who is lover enough to be a knight of the Round Table, is one of the most distinguished of our young civilians. I have the very highest opinion of his talents both for action and for discussion. Indeed, I should call him a man of real genius. He is also, what is even more important, a man of the utmost purity of honor, of a sweet temper, and of strong principle. His public virtue has gone through very severe trials, and has come out resplendent. Lord William, in congratulating me the other day, said that he thought my destined brother-in-law the ablest young man in the service. His name is Trevelyan. He is a nephew of Sir John Trevelyan, a baronet—in Cornwall, I suppose, by the name; for I never took the trouble to ask.

He and my sister will live with me during my stay here. I have a house about as large as Lord Dudley's in Park Lane, or rather larger, so that I shall accommodate them without the smallest difficulty. This arrangement is acceptable to me, because it saves me from the misery of parting with my sister in this strange land; and is, I believe, equally gratifying to

Trevelyan, whose education, like that of other Indian servants, was huddled up hastily at home; who has an insatiable thirst for knowledge of every sort; and who looks on me as little less than an oracle of wisdom. He came to me the other morning to know whether I would advise him to keep up his Greek, which he feared he had nearly lost. I gave him Homer, and asked him to read a page; and I found that, like most boys of any talent who had been at the Charter-house, he was very well grounded in that language. He read with perfect rapture, and has marched off with the book, declaring that he shall never be content till he has finished the whole. This, you will think, is not a bad brother-in-law for a man to pick up in 22 degrees of north latitude, and 100 degrees of east longitude.

I read much, and particularly Greek; and I find that I am, in all essentials, still not a bad scholar. I could, I think, with a year's hard study, qualify myself to fight a good battle for a Craven's scholarship. I read, however, not as I read at college, but like a man of the world. If I do not know a word, I pass it by unless it is important to the sense. If I find, as I have of late often found, a passage which refuses to give up its meaning at the second reading, I let it alone. I have read during the last fortnight, before breakfast, three books of Herodotus, and four plays of Æschylus. My admiration of Æschylus has been prodigiously increased by this reperusal. I can not conceive how any person of the smallest pretension to taste should doubt about his immeasurable superiority to every poet of antiquity, Homer only excepted. Even Milton, I think, must yield to him. It is quite unintelligible to me that the ancient critics should have placed him so low. Horace's notice of him in the "Ars Poetica" is quite ridiculous. There is, to be sure, the "magnum loqui;" but the great topic insisted on is the skill of Æschylus as a manager, as a property-man; the judicious way in which he boarded the stage; the masks, the buskins, and the dresses.* And, after all, the

* Post hunc personæ pallæque repertor honestæ
Æschylus et modicis instravit pulpita tignis,
Et docuit magnumque loqui, nitique cothurno.

"magnum loqui," though the most obvious characteristic of Æschylus, is by no means his highest or his best. Nor can I explain this by saying that Horace had too tame and unimaginative a mind to appreciate Æschylus. Horace knew what he could himself do, and, with admirable wisdom, he confined himself to that; but he seems to have had a perfectly clear comprehension of the merit of those great masters whom he never attempted to rival. He praised Pindar most enthusiastically. It seems incomprehensible to me that a critic who admired Pindar should not admire Æschylus far more.

Greek reminds me of Cambridge and of Thirlwall, and of Wordsworth's unutterable baseness and dirtiness.* When you see Thirlwall, tell him that I congratulate him from the bottom of my soul on having suffered in so good a cause; and that I would rather have been treated as he has been treated, on such an account, than have the mastership of Trinity. There would be some chance for the Church, if we had more Churchmen of the same breed, worthy successors of Leighton and Tillotson.

From one Trinity fellow I pass to another. (This letter is quite a study to a metaphysician who wishes to illustrate the law of association.) We have no official tidings yet of Malkin's appointment to the vacant seat on the bench at Calcutta. I can not tell you how delighted I am at the prospect of having him here. An honest, enlightened judge, without professional narrowness, is the very man whom we want, on public grounds. And as to my private feelings, nothing could be more agreeable to me than to have an old friend, and so es-

* The subjoined extract from the letter of a leading member of Trinity College explains Macaulay's not unrighteous indignation: "Thirlwall published a pamphlet in 1834, on the admission of Dissenters to the university. The result was that he was either deprived of his assistant tutorship by the master, Wordsworth, or had to give it up. Whewell, also, was supposed to have behaved badly in not standing up for him. Thirlwall left Cambridge soon afterward. I suppose that if he had remained he would have been very possibly Wordsworth's successor in the mastership."

timable a friend, brought so near to me in this distant country. Ever, dear Ellis, yours very affectionately,

T. B. MACAULAY.

Calcutta, February 8th, 1835.

DEAR ELLIS,—The last month has been the most painful that I ever went through. Indeed, I never knew before what it was to be miserable. Early in January, letters from England brought me news of the death of my youngest sister. What she was to me no words can express. I will not say that she was dearer to me than any thing in the world, for my sister who was with me was equally dear; but she was as dear to me as one human being can be to another. Even now, when time has begun to do its healing office, I can not write about her without being altogether unmanned. That I have not utterly sunk under this blow I owe chiefly to literature. What a blessing it is to love books as I love them—to be able to converse with the dead, and to live amidst the unreal! Many times during the last few weeks I have repeated to myself those fine lines of old Hesiod:

εἰ γάρ τις καὶ πένθος ἔχων νεοκηδέϊ θυμῷ
ἄζηται κραδίην ἀκαχήμενος, αὐτὰρ ἀοιδὸς
μουσάων θεράπων κλεῖα προτέρων ἀνθρώπων
ὑμνήσῃ, μάκαράς τε θεοὺς οἳ Ὄλυμπον ἔχουσι,
αἶψ' ὅγε δυσφρονέων ἐπιλήθεται, οὐδέ τι κηδέων
*μέμνηται· ταχέως δὲ παρέτραπε δῶρα θεάων.**

I have gone back to Greek literature with a passion quite astonishing to myself. I have never felt any thing like it. I was enraptured with Italian during the six months which I gave up to it; and I was little less pleased with Spanish. But when I went back to the Greek, I felt as if I had nev-

* "For if to one whose grief is fresh, as he sits silent with sorrow-stricken heart, a minstrel, the henchman of the Muses, celebrates the men of old and the gods who possess Olympus, straightway he forgets his melancholy, and remembers not at all his grief, beguiled by the blessed gift of the goddesses of song." In Macaulay's Hesiod this passage is scored with three lines in pencil.

er known before what intellectual enjoyment was. Oh that wonderful people! There is not one art, not one science, about which we may not use the same expression which Lucretius has employed about the victory over superstition, "Primum Graius homo—"

I think myself very fortunate in having been able to return to these great masters while still in the full vigor of life, and when my taste and judgment are mature. Most people read all the Greek that they ever read before they are five-and-twenty. They never find time for such studies afterward till they are in the decline of life; and then their knowledge of the language is in a great measure lost, and can not easily be recovered. Accordingly, almost all the ideas that people have of Greek literature are ideas formed while they were still very young. A young man, whatever his genius may be, is no judge of such a writer as Thucydides. I had no high opinion of him ten years ago. I have now been reading him with a mind accustomed to historical researches and to political affairs, and I am astonished at my own former blindness, and at his greatness. I could not bear Euripides at college. I now read my recantation. He has faults, undoubtedly. But what a poet! The "Medea," the "Alcestis," the "Troades," the "Bacchæ," are alone sufficient to place him in the very first rank. Instead of depreciating him, as I have done, I may, for aught I know, end by editing him.

I have read Pindar—with less pleasure than I feel in reading the great Attic poets, but still with admiration. An idea occurred to me which may very likely have been noticed by a hundred people before. I was always puzzled to understand the reason for the extremely abrupt transitions in those "Odes" of Horace which are meant to be particularly fine. The "justum et tenacem" is an instance. All at once you find yourself in heaven, Heaven knows how. What the firmness of just men in times of tyranny or of tumult has to do with Juno's oration about Troy, it is hardly possible to conceive. Then, again, how strangely the fight between the Gods and the Giants is tacked on to the fine hymn to the Muses in that noble ode, "Descende cœlo et dic age tibiâ!" This always struck me as a great fault, and an inexplicable one; for it is peculiarly alien from the calm good sense and good taste which distinguish Horace.

My explanation of it is this: The "Odes" of Pindar were the acknowledged models of lyric poetry. Lyric poets imitated his manner as closely as they could; and nothing was more remarkable in his compositions than the extreme violence and abruptness of the transitions. This in Pindar was quite natural and defensible. He had to write an immense number of poems on subjects extremely barren, and extremely monotonous. There could be little difference between one boxing-match and another. Accordingly, he made all possible haste to escape from the immediate subject, and to bring in, by hook or by crook, some local description; some old legend; something or other, in short, which might be more susceptible of poetical embellishment, and less utterly threadbare, than the circumstances of a race or a wrestling-match. This was not the practice of Pindar alone. There is an old story which proves that Simonides did the same, and that sometimes the hero of the day was nettled at finding how little was said about him in the ode for which he was to pay. This abruptness of transition was, therefore, in the Greek lyric poets, a fault rendered inevitable by the peculiarly barren and uniform nature of the subjects which they had to treat. But, like many other faults of great masters, it appeared to their imitators a beauty; and a beauty almost essential to the grander ode. Horace was perfectly at liberty to choose his own subjects, and to treat them after his own fashion. But he confounded what was merely accidental in Pindar's manner with what was essential; and because Pindar, when he had to celebrate a foolish lad from Ægina who had tripped up another's heels at the Isthmus, made all possible haste to get away from so paltry a topic to the ancient heroes of the race of Æacus, Horace took it into his head that he ought always to begin as far from the subject as possible, and then arrive at it by some strange and sudden bound. This is my solution. At least I can find no better. The most obscure passage — at least the strangest passage — in all Horace may be explained by supposing that he was misled by Pindar's example: I mean that odd parenthesis in the "Qualem Ministrum:"

quibus
Mos unde deductus per omne—

This passage,* taken by itself, always struck me as the harshest, queerest, and most preposterous digression in the world. But there are several things in Pindar very like it.

You must excuse all this, for I labor at present under a suppression of Greek, and am likely to do so for at least three years to come. Malkin may be some relief; but I am quite unable to guess whether he means to come to Calcutta. I am in excellent bodily health, and I am recovering my mental health; but I have been sorely tried. Money matters look well. My new brother-in-law and I are brothers in more than law. I am more comfortable than I expected to be in this country; and, as to the climate, I think it, beyond all comparison, better than that of the House of Commons.

Yours affectionately, T. B. MACAULAY.

Writing three days after the date of the foregoing letter, Macaulay says to his old friend Mr. Sharp: "You see that my mind is not in great danger of rusting. The danger is that I may become a mere pedant. I feel a habit of quotation growing on me; but I resist that devil, for such it is, and it flees from me. It is all that I can do to keep Greek and Latin out of all my letters. Wise sayings of Euripides are even now at my fingers' ends. If I did not maintain a constant struggle against this propensity, my correspondence would resemble the notes to the 'Pursuits of Literature.' It is a dangerous thing for a man with a very strong memory to read very much. I could give you three or four quotations this moment in support of that proposition; but I will bring the vicious propensity under subjection, if I can."

---

* Orelli makes an observation much to the same effect in his note on this passage in his edition of 1850.

Calcutta, May 29th, 1835.

DEAR ELLIS,—I am in great want of news. We know that the Tories dissolved at the end of December, and we also know that they were beaten toward the end of February.* As to what passed in the interval, we are quite in the dark. I will not plague you with comments on events which will have been driven out of your mind by other events before this reaches you, or with prophecies which may be falsified before you receive them. About the final issue I am certain. The language of the first great reformer is that which I should use in reply to the exultation of our Tories here, if there were any of them who could understand it:

σέβου, προσεύχου, θῶπτε τὸν κρατοῦντ' ἀεί·
ἐμοὶ δ' ἔλασσον Ζηνὸς, ἢ μηδὲν, μέλει.
δράτω· κρατείτω τόνδε τὸν βραχὺν χρόνον
ὅπως θέλει· δαρὸν γὰρ οὐκ ἄρξει θεοῖς.†

As for myself, I rejoice that I am out of the present storm. "Suave mari magno;" or, as your new premier, if he be still premier, construes, "It is a source of melancholy satisfaction." I may, indeed, feel the effects of the changes here, but more on public than private grounds. A Tory governor-general is not very likely to agree with me about the very important law reforms which I am about to bring before the council. But he is not likely to treat me ill personally, or if he do,

ἀλλ' οὔ τι χαίρων, ἢν τόδ' ὀρθωθῇ βέλος,‡

---

* In November, 1834, the king called Sir Robert Peel to power, after having, of his own accord, dismissed the Whig ministry. Parliament was dissolved, but the Tories did not succeed in obtaining a majority. After three months of constant and angry fighting, Peel was driven from office in April, 1835.

† "Worship thou, adore, and flatter the monarch of the hour. To me Jove is of less account than nothing. Let him have his will, and his sceptre, for this brief season; for he will not long be the ruler of the gods." It is needless to say that poor William the Fourth was the Jove of the Whig Prometheus.

‡ "It shall be to his cost, so long as this bow carries true."

as Philoctetes says. In a few months I shall have enough to enable me to live, after my very moderate fashion, in perfect independence at home; and whatever debts any governor-general may choose to lay on me at Calcutta shall be paid off, he may rely on it, with compound interest, at Westminster.

My time is divided between public business and books. I mix with society as little as I can. My spirits have not yet recovered—I sometimes think that they will never wholly recover—from the shock which they received five months ago. I find that nothing soothes them so much as the contemplation of those miracles of art which Athens has bequeathed to us. I am really becoming, I hope not a pedant, but certainly an enthusiast about classical literature. I have just finished a second reading of Sophocles. I am now deep in Plato, and intend to go right through all his works. His genius is above praise. Even where he is most absurd, as, for example, in the "Cratylus," he shows an acuteness and an expanse of intellect which are quite a phenomenon by themselves. The character of Socrates does not rise upon me. The more I read about him, the less I wonder that they poisoned him. If he had treated me as he is said to have treated Protagoras, Hippias, and Gorgias, I could never have forgiven him.

Nothing has struck me so much in Plato's dialogues as the raillery. At college, somehow or other, I did not understand or appreciate it. I can not describe to you the way in which it now tickles me. I often sink forward on my huge old "Marsilius Ficinus" in a fit of laughter. I should say that there never was a vein of ridicule so rich, and at the same time so delicate. It is superior to Voltaire's; nay, to Pascal's. Perhaps there are one or two passages in Cervantes, and one or two in Fielding, that might give a modern reader a notion of it.

I have very nearly finished Livy. I never read him through before. I admire him greatly, and would give a quarter's salary to recover the lost Decades. While I was reading the earlier books I went again through Niebuhr; and I am sorry to say that, having always been a little skeptical about his merits, I am now a confirmed unbeliever. I do not, of course, mean that he has no merit. He was a man of immense learning and of great ingenuity; but his mind was utterly wanting in the faculty by which a demonstrated truth is distinguished from a plausible supposition. He is not content with suggesting that an event may have happened. He is certain that it happened, and calls on the reader to be certain too (though not a trace of it exists in any record whatever), because it would solve the phenomena so neatly. Just read over again, if you have forgotten it, the conjectural restoration of the inscription in page 126 of the second volume; and then, on your honor as a scholar and a man of sense, tell me whether in Bentley's edition of Milton there is any thing which approaches to the audacity of that emendation. Niebuhr requires you to believe that some of the greatest men in Rome were burned alive in the Circus; that this event was commemorated by an inscription on a monument, one-half of which is still in existence; but that no Roman historian knew any thing about it; and that all tradition of the event was lost, though the memory of anterior events much less important has reached our time. When you ask for a reason, he tells you plainly that such a thing can not be established by reason; that he is sure of it; and that you must take his word. This sort of intellectual despotism always moves me to mutiny, and generates a disposition to pull down the reputation of the dogmatist. Niebuhr's learning was immeasurably superior to mine; but I think myself quite as good a judge of evidence as he was. I might easily believe him if he told me that there were proofs which I had never seen; but, when he produces all his proofs, I conceive that I am perfectly competent to pronounce on their value.

As I turned over his leaves just now, I lighted on another instance of what I can not but call ridiculous presumption. He says that Martial committed a blunder in making the penultimate of Porsena short. Strange that so great a scholar should not know that Horace had done so too!

Minacis aut Etrusca Porsenæ manus.

There is something extremely nauseous to me in a German

professor telling the world, on his own authority, and without giving the smallest reason, that two of the best Latin poets were ignorant of the quantity of a word which they must have used in their exercises at school a hundred times.

As to the general capacity of Niebuhr for political speculations, let him be judged by the preface to the second volume. He there says, referring to the French Revolution of July, 1830, that "unless God send us some miraculous help, we have to look forward to a period of destruction similar to that which the Roman world experienced about the middle of the third century." Now, when I see a man scribble such abject nonsense about events which are passing under our eyes, what confidence can I put in his judgment as to the connection of causes and effects in times very imperfectly known to us?

But I must bring my letter, or review, to a close. Remember me most kindly to your wife. Tell Frank that I mean to be a better scholar than he when I come back, and that he must work hard if he means to overtake me. Ever, dear Ellis,

Your affectionate friend, T. B. Macaulay.

Calcutta, August 25th, 1835.

Dear Ellis,—Cameron arrived here about a fortnight ago, and we are most actively engaged in preparing a complete criminal code for India. He and I agree excellently. Ryan, the most liberal of judges, lends us his best assistance. I heartily hope, and fully believe, that we shall put the whole penal law, and the whole law of criminal procedure, into a moderately sized volume. I begin to take a very warm interest in this work. It is, indeed, one of the finest employments of the intellect that it is easy to conceive. I ought, however, to tell you that the more progress I make as a legislator, the more intense my contempt for the mere technical study of law becomes.

I am deep in the examination of the political theories of the old philosophers. I have read Plato's "Republic," and his "Laws;" and I am now reading Aristotle's "Politics;" after which I shall go through Plato's two treatises again. I every now and then read one of Plutarch's Lives on an idle afternoon; and in this way I have got through a dozen of them. I like him prodigiously. He is inaccurate, to be sure, and a romancer; but he tells a story delightfully, and his illustrations and sketches of character are as good as any thing in ancient eloquence. I have never till now rated him fairly.

As to Latin, I am just finishing Lucan, who remains pretty much where he was in my opinion; and I am busily engaged with Cicero, whose character, moral and intellectual, interests me prodigiously. I think that I see the whole man through and through. But this is too vast a subject for a letter. I have gone through all Ovid's poems. I admire him; but I was tired to death before I got to the end. I amused myself one evening with turning over the "Metamorphoses," to see if I could find any passage of ten lines which could, by possibility, have been written by Virgil. Whether I was in ill luck or no, I can not tell; but I hunted for half an hour without the smallest success. At last I chanced to light on a little passage more Virgilian, to my thinking, than Virgil himself. Tell me what you say to my criticism. It is part of Apollo's speech to the laurel.

> Semper habebunt
> Te coma, te citharæ, te nostræ, laure, pharetræ.
> Tu ducibus Latiis aderis, cum læta triumphum
> Vox canet, et longas visent Capitolia pompas.
> Portibus Augustis eadem fidissima custos
> Ante fores stabis, mediamque tuebere quercum.

As to other Latin writers, Sallust has gone sadly down in my opinion. Cæsar has risen wonderfully. I think him fully entitled to Cicero's praise.* He has won the honor of

* In the dialogue "De Claris Oratoribus" Cicero makes Atticus say that a consummate judge of style (who is evidently intended for Cicero himself) pronounces Cæsar's Latin to be the most elegant, with one implied exception, that had ever been heard in the Senate or the Forum. Atticus then goes on to detail at full length a compliment which Cæsar had paid to Cicero's powers of expression; and Brutus declares with enthusiasm that such praise, coming from such a quarter, is worth more than a Triumph, as Triumphs were then given; and inferior in value only to the honors which were voted to the statesman who had baffled Catiline. The whole passage is a model of self-glorification, exquisite in skill and finish.

an excellent historian while attempting merely to give hints for history. But what are they all to the great Athenian? I do assure you that there is no prose composition in the world, not even the "De Coronâ," which I place so high as the seventh book of Thucydides. It is the *ne plus ultra* of human art. I was delighted to find in Gray's letters the other day this query to Wharton: "The retreat from Syracuse—Is it, or is it not, the finest thing you ever read in your life?"

Did you ever read Athenæus through? I never did; but I am meditating an attack on him. The multitude of quotations looks very tempting; and I never open him for a minute without being paid for my trouble.

Yours very affectionately, T. B. Macaulay.

Calcutta, December 30th, 1835.

Dear Ellis,—What the end of the Municipal Reform Bill is to be I can not conjecture. Our latest English intelligence is of the 15th of August. The Lords* were then busy in rendering the only great service that I expect them ever to render to the nation; that is to say, in hastening the day of reckoning. But I will not fill my paper with English politics.

I am in excellent health. So are my sister and brother-in-law, and their little girl, whom I am always nursing; and of whom I am becoming fonder than a wise man, with half my experience, would choose to be of any thing except himself. I have but very lately begun to recover my spirits. The tremendous blow which fell on me at the beginning of this year has left marks behind it which I shall carry to my grave. Literature has saved my life and my reason. Even now, I dare not, in the intervals of business, remain alone for a minute without a book in my hand. What my course of life will be when I return to England is very doubtful. But I am more than half determined to abandon politics, and to give myself wholly to letters; to undertake some great historical

---

* In the middle of August the Irish Tithe Bill went up to the House of Lords, where it was destined to undergo a mutilation which was fatal to its existence.

work which may be at once the business and the amusement of my life; and to leave the pleasures of pestiferous rooms, sleepless nights, aching heads, and diseased stomachs, to Roebuck and to Praed.

In England I might probably be of a very different opinion. But, in the quiet of my own little grass-plot—when the moon, at its rising, finds me with the "Philoctetes" or the "De Finibus" in my hand—I often wonder what strange infatuation leads men who can do something better, to squander their intellect, their health, their energy, on such objects as those which most statesmen are engaged in pursuing. I comprehend perfectly how a man who can debate, but who would make a very indifferent figure as a contributor to an annual or a magazine—such a man as Stanley, for example—should take the only line by which he can attain distinction. But that a man before whom the two paths of literature and politics lie open, and who might hope for eminence in either, should choose politics, and quit literature, seems to me madness. On the one side are health, leisure, peace of mind, the search after truth, and all the enjoyments of friendship and conversation. On the other side are almost certain ruin to the constitution, constant labor, constant anxiety. Every friendship which a man may have becomes precarious as soon as he engages in politics. As to abuse, men soon become callous to it; but the discipline which makes them callous is very severe. And for what is it that a man, who might, if he chose, rise and lie down at his own hour, engage in any study, enjoy any amusement, and visit any place, consents to make himself as much a prisoner as if he were within the rules of the Fleet; to be tethered during eleven months of the year within the circle of half a mile round Charing Cross; to sit, or stand, night after night for ten or twelve hours, inhaling a noisome atmosphere, and listening to harangues of which nine-tenths are far below the level of a leading article in a newspaper? For what is it that he submits, day after day, to see the morning break over the Thames, and then totters home, with bursting temples, to his bed? Is it for fame? Who would compare the fame of Charles Townshend to that of Hume, that of Lord North to that of Gibbon, that of Lord Chatham to that of Johnson? Who can look back on the life of Burke, and not regret that the years which he passed in ruining his health and temper by political exertions were not passed in the composition of some great and durable work? Who can read the letters to Atticus, and not feel that Cicero would have been an infinitely happier and better man, and a not less celebrated man, if he had left us fewer speeches, and more Academic Questions and Tusculan Disputations? if he had passed the time which he spent in brawling with Vatinius and Clodius in producing a history of Rome superior even to that of Livy? But these, as I said, are meditations in a quiet garden, situated far beyond the contagious influence of English faction. What I might feel if I again saw Downing Street and Palace Yard is another question. I tell you sincerely my present feelings.

I have cast up my reading account, and brought it to the end of the year 1835. It includes December, 1834; for I came into my house and unpacked my books at the end of November, 1834. During the last thirteen months I have read Æschylus twice; Sophocles twice; Euripides once; Pindar twice; Callimachus; Apollonius Rhodius; Quintus Calaber; Theocritus twice; Herodotus; Thucydides; almost all Xenophon's works; almost all Plato; Aristotle's "Politics," and a good deal of his "Organon," besides dipping elsewhere in him; the whole of Plutarch's "Lives;" about half of Lucian; two or three books of Athenæus; Plautus twice; Terence twice; Lucretius twice; Catullus; Tibullus; Propertius; Lucan; Statius; Silius Italicus; Livy; Velleius Paterculus; Sallust; Cæsar; and, lastly, Cicero. I have, indeed, still a little of Cicero left; but I shall finish him in a few days. I am now deep in Aristophanes and Lucian. Of Aristophanes I think as I always thought; but Lucian has agreeably surprised me. At school I read some of his "Dialogues of the Dead" when I was thirteen; and, to my shame, I never, to the best of my belief, read a line of him since. I am charmed with him. His style seems to me to be superior to that of any extant writer who lived later than the age of Demosthenes and Theophrastus. He has a most peculiar and delicious vein of humor. It is not the humor of Aristophanes; it is not that of Plato; and yet it is akin to both: not quite equal, I admit, to either, but still exceedingly charming. I hardly know where to find an instance of a writer, in the decline of a literature, who has shown an invention so rich and a taste so pure. But if I get on these matters I shall fill sheet after sheet. They must wait till we take another long walk, or another tavern dinner, together; that is, till the summer of 1838.

I had a long story to tell you about a classical examination here; but I have not time. I can only say that some of the competitors tried to read the Greek with the papers upside down; and that the great man of the examination, the Thirlwall of Calcutta, a graduate of Trinity College, Dublin, translated the words of Theophrastus, *ὅσας λειτουργίας λελειτούργηκε*,* "how many times he has performed divine service."

Ever yours affectionately, T. B. MACAULAY.

That the enormous list of classical works recorded in the foregoing letter was not only read through, but read with care, is proved by the pencil-marks, single, double, and treble, which meander down the margin of such passages as excited the admiration of the student; and by the remarks, literary, historical, and grammatical, with which the critic has interspersed every volume, and sometimes every page. In the case of a favorite writer, Macaulay frequently corrects the errors of the press, and even the punctuation, as minutely as if he were preparing the book for another edition. He read Plautus,† Terence, and Aristophanes four times through at Calcutta, and Euripides thrice. In his copy of Quintus Ca-

* "How many public services he had discharged at his own expense." Macaulay used to say that a lady who dips into Mr. Grote's history, and learns that Alcibiades won the heart of his fellow-citizens by the novelty of his theories and the splendor of his liturgies, may get a very false notion of that statesman's relations with the Athenian public.

† See the Appendix at the end of this volume.

laber (a versifier who is less unknown by the title of Quintus Smyrnæus), appear the entries,

"September 22d, 1835.
Turned over, July 13th, 1837."

It may be doubted whether the "Pandects" would have attained the celebrity which they enjoy, if, in the course of the three years during which Justinian's Law Commission was at work, the president, Tribonian, had read Quintus Smyrnæus twice.

Calcutta, May 30th, 1836.

Dear Ellis,—I have just received your letter dated December 28th. How time flies! Another hot season has almost passed away, and we are daily expecting the beginning of the rains. Cold season, hot season, and rainy season are all much the same to me. I shall have been two years on Indian ground in less than a fortnight, and I have not taken ten grains of solid, or a pint of liquid, medicine during the whole of that time. If I judged only from my own sensations, I should say that this climate is absurdly maligned; but the yellow, spectral figures which surround me serve to correct the conclusions which I should be inclined to draw from the state of my own health.

One execrable effect the climate produces. It destroys all the works of man with scarcely one exception. Steel rusts; razors lose their edge; thread decays; clothes fall to pieces; books molder away and drop out of their bindings; plaster cracks; timber rots; matting is in shreds. The sun, the steam of this vast alluvial tract, and the infinite armies of white ants, make such havoc with buildings that a house requires a complete repair every three years. Ours was in this situation about three months ago; and, if we had determined to brave the rains without any precautions, we should, in all probability, have had the roof down on our heads. Accordingly, we were forced to migrate for six weeks from our stately apartments and our flower-beds to a dungeon where we were stifled with the stench of native cookery, and deafened by the noise of native music. At last we have returned to our house.

We found it all snow-white and pea-green; and we rejoice to think that we shall not again be under the necessity of quitting it till we quit it for a ship bound on a voyage to London.

We have been for some months in the middle of what the people here think a political storm. To a person accustomed to the hurricanes of English faction this sort of tempest in a horse-pond is merely ridiculous. We have put the English settlers up the country under the exclusive jurisdiction of the company's courts in civil actions in which they are concerned with natives. The English settlers are perfectly contented; but the lawyers of the Supreme Court have set up a yelp which they think terrible, and which has infinitely diverted me. They have selected me as the object of their invectives, and I am generally the theme of five or six columns of prose and verse daily. I have not patience to read a tenth part of what they put forth. The last ode in my praise which I perused began,

> Soon we hope they will recall ye,
> Tom Macaulay, Tom Macaulay.

The last prose which I read was a parallel between me and Lord Strafford.

My mornings, from five to nine, are quite my own. I still give them to ancient literature. I have read Aristophanes twice through since Christmas; and have also read Herodotus, and Thucydides, again. I got into a way last year of reading a Greek play every Sunday. I began on Sunday, the 18th of October, with the "Prometheus," and next Sunday I shall finish with the "Cyclops" of Euripides. Euripides has made a complete conquest of me. It has been unfortunate for him that we have so many of his pieces. It has, on the other hand, I suspect, been fortunate for Sophocles that so few of his have come down to us. Almost every play of Sophocles which is now extant was one of his masterpieces. There is hardly one of them which is not mentioned with high praise by some ancient writer. Yet one of them, the "Trachiniæ," is, to my thinking, very poor and insipid. Now, if we had nineteen plays of Sophocles, of which twelve or thirteen should be no better than the "Trachiniæ"—and if, on the other hand, only seven pieces of Euripides had come down to us, and if those seven had been the "Medea," the "Bacchæ," the "Iphigenia in Aulis," the "Orestes," the "Phœnissæ," the "Hippolytus," and the "Alcestis"—I am not sure that the relative position which the two poets now hold in our estimation would not be greatly altered.

I have not done much in Latin. I have been employed in turning over several third-rate and fourth-rate writers. After finishing Cicero, I read through the works of both the Senecas, father and son. There is a great deal in the "Controversiæ" both of curious information and of judicious criticism. As to the son, I can not bear him. His style affects me in something the same way with that of Gibbon. But Lucius Seneca's affectation is even more rank than Gibbon's. His works are made up of mottoes. There is hardly a sentence which might not be quoted; but to read him straight forward is like dining on nothing but anchovy sauce. I have read, as one does read such stuff, Valerius Maximus, Annæus Florus, Lucius Ampelius, and Aurelius Victor. I have also gone through Phædrus. I am now better employed. I am deep in the "Annals" of Tacitus, and I am at the same time reading Suetonius.

You are so rich in domestic comforts that I am inclined to envy you. I am not, however, without my share. I am as fond of my little niece as her father. I pass an hour or more every day in nursing her, and teaching her to talk. She has got as far as Ba, Pa, and Ma; which, as she is not eight months old, we consider as proofs of a genius little inferior to that of Shakspeare or Sir Isaac Newton.

The municipal elections have put me in good spirits as to English politics. I was rather inclined to despondency.

Ever yours affectionately, T. B. MACAULAY.

Calcutta, July 25th, 1836.

MY DEAR ELLIS,—I have heard from you again, and glad I always am to hear from you. There are few things to which I look forward with more pleasure than to our meeting. It is really worth while to go into banishment for a few years for the pleasure of going home again. Yet that home will in some things be a different home—oh, how different a home!—from that to which I expected to return. But I will not stir up the bitterness of sorrow which has at last subsided.

You take interest, I see, in my Greek and Latin studies. I continue to pursue them steadily and actively. I am now reading Demosthenes with interest and admiration indescribable. I am slowly, at odd minutes, getting through the stupid trash of Diodorus. I have read through Seneca, and an affected, empty scribbler he is. I have read Tacitus again, and, by-the-bye, I will tell you a curious circumstance relating to that matter. In my younger days I always thought the "Annals" a prodigiously superior work to the "History." I was surprised to find that the "Annals" seemed cold and poor to me on the last reading. I began to think that I had overrated Tacitus. But, when I began the "History," I was enchanted, and thought more highly of him than ever. I went back to the "Annals," and liked them even better than the "History." All at once the explanation of this occurred to me. While I was reading the "Annals" I was reading Thucydides. When I began the "History," I began the "Hellenics." What made the "Annals" appear cold and poor to me was the intense interest which Thucydides inspired. Indeed, what coloring is there which would not look tame when placed side by side with the magnificent light and the terrible shade of Thucydides? Tacitus was a great man; but he was not up to the Sicilian expedition. When I finished Thucydides, and took up Xenophon, the case was reversed. Tacitus had been a foil to Thucydides. Xenophon was a foil to Tacitus.

I have read Pliny the Younger. Some of the "Epistles" are interesting. Nothing more stupid than the "Panegyric" was ever preached in the University church. I am reading the "Augustan History," and Aulus Gellius. Aulus is a favorite of mine. I think him one of the best writers of his class.

I read in the evenings a great deal of English, French, and Italian, and a little Spanish. I have picked up Portuguese enough to read Camoens with care, and I want no more. I have adopted an opinion about the Italian historians quite different from that which I formerly held, and which, I believe, is generally considered as orthodox. I place Fra Paolo decidedly at the head of them, and next to him Davila, whom I take to be the best modern military historian except Colonel Napier. Davila's battle of Ivry is worthy of Thucydides himself. Next to Davila I put Guicciardini, and last of all Machiavelli. But I do not think that you ever read much Italian.

The English poetry of the day has very few attractions for me. "Van Artevelde" is far the best specimen that I have lately seen. I do not much like Talfourd's "Ion," but I mean to read it again. It contains pretty lines; but, to my thinking, it is neither fish nor flesh. There is too much, and too little, of the antique about it. Nothing but the most strictly classical costume can reconcile me to a mythological plot; and Ion is a modern philanthropist, whose politics and morals have been learned from the publications of the Society for the Diffusion of Useful Knowledge.

I do not know whether the noise which the lawyers of the Supreme Court have been raising against our legislative authority has reached, or will reach, England. They held a public meeting, which ended or rather began, continued, and ended—in a riot; and ever since then the leading agitators have been challenging each other, refusing each other's challenges, libeling each other, swearing the peace against each other, and blackballing each other. Mr. Longueville Clarke, who aspires to be the O'Connell of Calcutta, called another lawyer a liar. The last-mentioned lawyer challenged Mr. Longueville Clarke. Mr. Longueville Clarke refused to fight, on the ground that his opponent had been guilty of hugging attorneys. The Bengal Club accordingly blackballed Longueville. This, and some other similar occurrences, have made the opposition here thoroughly ridiculous and contemptible. They will probably send a petition home; but, unless the House of Commons has undergone a great change since 1833, they have no chance there.

I have almost brought my letter to a close without mentioning the most important matter about which I had to write. I dare say you have heard that my uncle, General Macaulay, who died last February, has left me £10,000. This legacy, together with what I shall have saved by the end of 1837, will make me quite a rich man; richer than I even wish to be as a single man; and every day renders it more unlikely that I should marry.

We have had a very unhealthy season; but sickness has not come near our house. My sister, my brother-in-law, and their little child, are as well as possible. As to me, I think that, as Bonaparte said of himself after the Russian campaign, "J'ai le diable au corps." Ever yours affectionately,

T. B. MACAULAY.

To Macvey Napier, Esq.

Calcutta, November 26th, 1836.

DEAR NAPIER,—At last I send you an article of interminable length about Lord Bacon. I hardly know whether it is not too long for an article in a *Review;* but the subject is of such vast extent that I could easily have made the paper twice as long as it is.

About the historical and political part there is no great probability that we shall differ in opinion; but what I have said about Bacon's philosophy is widely at variance with what Dugald Stewart and Mackintosh have said on the same subject. I have not your essay; nor have I read it since I read it at Cambridge, with very great pleasure, but without any knowledge of the subject. I have at present only a very faint and general recollection of its contents, and have in vain tried to procure a copy of it here. I fear, however, that, differing widely as I do from Stewart and Mackintosh, I shall hardly agree with you. My opinion is formed, not at second hand, like those of nine-tenths of the people who talk about Bacon, but after several very attentive perusals of his greatest works, and after a good deal of thought. If I am in the wrong, my errors may set the minds of others at work, and may be the means of bringing both them and me to a knowledge of the truth. I never bestowed so much care on any thing that I have written. There is not a sentence in the latter half of the article which has not been repeatedly recast. I have no expectation that the popularity of the article will bear any proportion to the trouble which I have expended on it. But the trouble has been so great a pleasure to me that I have already been greatly overpaid. Pray look carefully to the printing.

In little more than a year I shall be embarking for England, and I have determined to employ the four months of my voyage in mastering the German language. I should be much obliged to you to send me out, as early as you can, so that they may be certain to arrive in time, the best grammar, and the best dictionary, that can be procured; a German Bible; Schiller's works; Goethe's works; and Niebuhr's "History," both in the original and in the translation. My way of learning a language is always to begin with the Bible, which I can read without a dictionary. After a few days passed in this way, I am master of all the common particles, the common rules of syntax, and a pretty large vocabulary. Then I fall on some good classical work. It was in this way that I learned both Spanish and Portuguese, and I shall try the same course with German.

I have little or nothing to tell you about myself. My life has flown away here with strange rapidity. It seems but yesterday that I left my country; and I am writing to beg you to hasten preparations for my return. I continue to enjoy perfect health, and the little political squalls which I have had to weather here are mere capfuls of wind to a man who has gone through the great hurricanes of English faction.

I shall send another copy of the article on Bacon by another ship. Yours very truly, T. B. MACAULAY.

Calcutta, November 28th, 1836.

DEAR NAPIER,—There is an oversight in the article on Bacon which I shall be much obliged to you to correct. I have said that Bacon did not deal at all in idle rants "like those in which Cicero and Mr. Shandy sought consolation for the loss of Tullia and of Bobby." Nothing can, as a general remark, be more true, but it escaped my recollection that two or three of Mr. Shandy's consolatory sentences are quoted from Bacon's "Essays." The illustration, therefore, is singularly unfortunate. Pray alter it thus: "in which Cicero vainly sought consolation for the loss of Tullia." To be sure, it is idle to correct such trifles at a distance of fifteen thousand miles.

Yours ever, T. B. MACAULAY.

From Lord Jeffrey to Macvey Napier, Esq.

May 2d, 1837.

MY DEAR N.,—What mortal could ever dream of cutting out the least particle of this precious work, to make it fit better into your *Review?* It would be worse than paring down the Pitt diamond to fit the old setting of a dowager's ring. Since Bacon himself, I do not know that there has been any thing so fine. The first five or six pages are in a lower tone, but still magnificent, and not to be deprived of a word.

Still, I do not object to consider whether it might not be best to serve up the rich repast in two courses; and on the whole I incline to that partition. One hundred and twenty pages might cloy even epicures, and would be sure to surfeit the vulgar; and the biography and philosophy are so entirely distinct, and of not very unequal length, that the division would not look like a fracture. FRANCIS JEFFREY.

In the end, the article appeared entire, occupying one hundred and four pages of the *Review;* and accompanied by an apology for its length in the shape of one of those editorial appeals to "the intelligent scholar," and "the best class of our readers," which never fail of success.

The letters addressed to Zachary Macaulay are half filled with anecdotes of the nursery; pretty enough, but such as only a grandfather could be expected to read. In other respects, the correspondence is chiefly remarkable for the affectionate ingenuity with which the son selects such topics as would interest the father.

Calcutta, October 12th, 1836.

MY DEAR FATHER,—We were extremely gratified by receiving, a few days ago, a letter from you which, on the whole, gave a good account of your health and spirits. The day after to-morrow is the first anniversary of your little granddaughter's birthday. The occasion is to be celebrated with a sort of droll puppet-show, much in fashion among the natives; an exhibition much in the style of Punch in England, but more dramatic and more showy. All the little boys and girls from the houses of our friends are invited, and the party will, I have no doubt, be a great deal more amusing than the stupid dinners and routs with which the grown-up people here kill the time.

In a few months—I hope, indeed, in a few weeks—we shall send up the "Penal Code" to Government. We have got rid of the punishment of death, except in the case of aggravated treason and willful murder. We shall also get rid indirectly of every thing that can properly be called slavery in India. There will remain civil claims on particular people for particular services, which claims may be enforced by civil action; but no person will be entitled, on the plea of being the master of another, to do any thing to that other which it would be an offense to do to a free man.

Our English schools are flourishing wonderfully. We find it difficult—indeed, in some places impossible—to provide instruction for all who want it. At the single town of Hooghly fourteen hundred boys are learning English. The effect of this education on the Hindoos is prodigious. No Hindoo who has received an English education ever remains sincerely attached to his religion. Some continue to profess it as a matter of policy; but many profess themselves pure Deists, and some embrace Christianity. It is my firm belief that, if our plans of education are followed up, there will not be a single idolater among the respectable classes in Bengal thirty years hence. And this will be effected without any efforts to proselytize; without the smallest interference with religious liberty; merely by the natural operation of knowledge and reflection. I heartily rejoice in the prospect.

I have been a sincere mourner for Mill. He and I were on the best terms, and his services at the India House were never so much needed as at this time. I had a most kind letter from him a few weeks before I heard of his death. He has a son just come out, to whom I have shown such little attentions as are in my power.

Within half a year after the time when you read this we shall be making arrangements for our return. The feelings with which I look forward to that return I can not express. Perhaps I should be wise to continue here longer, in order to enjoy during a greater number of months the delusion—for I know that it will prove a delusion—of this delightful hope. I feel as if I never could be unhappy in my own country; as if to exist on English ground and among English people, seeing the old familiar sights and hearing the sound of my mother tongue, would be enough for me. This can not be; yet some days of intense happiness I shall surely have; and one of those will be the day when I again see my dear father and sisters. Ever yours most affectionately, T. B. MACAULAY.

Calcutta, November 30th, 1836.

DEAR ELLIS,—How the months run away! Here is another cold season: morning fogs, cloth coats, green pease, new potatoes, and all the accompaniments of a Bengal winter. As to my private life, it has glided on, since I wrote to you last, in the most peaceful monotony. If it were not for the books which I read, and for the bodily and mental growth of my dear little niece, I should have no mark to distinguish one part of the year from another. Greek and Latin, breakfast, business, an evening walk with a book, a drive after sunset, dinner, coffee, my bed—there you have the history of a day. My classical studies go on vigorously. I have read Demosthenes twice—I need not say with what delight and admiration. I am now deep in Isocrates; and from him I shall pass to Lysias. I have finished Diodorus Siculus at last, after dawdling over him at odd times ever since last March. He is a stupid, credulous, prosing old ass; yet I heartily wish that we had a good deal more of him. I have read Arrian's expedition of Alexander, together with Quintus Curtius. I have at stray hours read Longus's "Romance" and Xenophon's "Ephesiaca," and I mean to go through Heliodorus and Achilles Tatius in the same way. Longus is prodigiously absurd; but there is often an exquisite prettiness in the style. Xenophon's novel* is the basest thing to be found in Greek. It was discovered at Florence, little more than a hundred years ago, by an English envoy. Nothing so detestable ever came from the Minerva Press. I have read Theocritus again, and like him better than ever.

As to Latin, I made a heroic attempt on Pliny's "Natural History;" but I stuck after getting through about a quarter of it. I have read Ammianus Marcellinus, the worst-written book in ancient Latin. The style would disgrace a monk of the tenth century; but Marcellinus has many of the substantial qualities of a good historian. I have gone through the Augustan history, and much other trash relating to the lower empire; curious as illustrating the state of society, but utterly worthless as composition. I have read Statius again, and thought him as bad as ever. I really found only two lines worthy of a great poet in all the "Thebäis." They are these (what do you think of my taste?):

> Clamorem, bello qualis supremus apertis
> Urbibus, aut pelago jam descendente carinâ.

I am now busy with Quintilian and Lucan, both excellent writers. The dream of Pompey, in the seventh book of the "Pharsalia," is a very noble piece of writing. I hardly know an instance in poetry of so great an effect produced by means so simple. There is something irresistibly pathetic in the lines:

> Qualis erat populi facies, clamorque faventum
> Olim cum juvenis—

---

* Xenophon the Ephesian lived in the third or fourth century of the Christian era. At the end of his work Macaulay has written, "A most stupid, worthless performance, below the lowest trash of an English circulating library." Achilles Tatius he disposes of with the words "Detestable trash;" and the "Æthiopics" of Heliodorus, which he appears to have finished on Easter-day, 1837, he pronounces "the best of the Greek romances, which is not saying much for it."

and something unspeakably solemn in the sudden turn which follows:

Crastina dira quies—

There are two passages in Lucan which surpass in eloquence any thing that I know in the Latin language. One is the enumeration of Pompey's exploits:

Quod si tam sacro dignaris nomine saxum—

The other is the character which Cato gives of Pompey,

Civis obît, inquit—

a pure gem of rhetoric, without one flaw, and, in my opinion, not very far from historical truth.* When I consider that Lucan died at twenty-six, I can not help ranking him among the most extraordinary men that ever lived.

I am glad that you have so much business, and sorry that you have so little leisure. In a few years you will be a baron of the exchequer, and then we shall have ample time to talk

---

* The following remarks occur at the end of Macaulay's copy of the "Pharsalia:"

"August 30th, 1835.

"When Lucan's age is considered, it is impossible not to allow that the poem is a very extraordinary one: more extraordinary, perhaps, than if it had been of a higher kind; for it is more common for the imagination to be in full vigor at an early time of life than for a young man to obtain a complete mastery of political and philosophical rhetoric. I know no declamation in the world, not even Cicero's best, which equals some passages in the 'Pharsalia.' As to what were meant for bold poetical flights—the sea-fight at Marseilles, the Centurion who is covered with wounds, the snakes in the Libyan desert—it is all as detestable as Cibber's 'Birthday Odes.' The furious partiality of Lucan takes away much of the pleasure which his talents would otherwise afford. A poet who is, as has often been said, less a poet than a historian, should to a certain degree conform to the laws of history. The manner in which he represents the two parties is not to be reconciled with the laws even of fiction. The senators are demi-gods; Pompey, a pure lover of his country; Cato, the abstract idea of virtue; while Cæsar, the finest gentleman, the most humane conqueror, and the most popular politician that Rome ever produced, is a blood-thirsty ogre. If Lucan had lived, he would probably have improved greatly. Again, December 9th, 1836."

over our favorite classics. Then I will show you a most superb emendation of Bentley's in Ampelius, and I will give you unanswerable reasons for pronouncing that Gibbon was mistaken in supposing that Quintus Curtius wrote under Gordian.

Remember me most kindly to Mrs. Ellis. I hope that I shall find Frank writing as good Alcaics as his father.

Ever yours affectionately, T. B. MACAULAY.

Calcutta, March 8th, 1837.

DEAR ELLIS,—I am at present very much worked, and have been so for a long time past. Cameron, after being laid up for some months, sailed at Christmas for the Cape, where I hope his health will be repaired; for this country can very ill spare him. However, we have almost brought our great work to a conclusion. In about a month we shall lay before the Government a complete penal code for a hundred millions of people, with a commentary explaining, and defending, the provisions of the text. Whether it is well or ill done, Heaven knows. I only know that it seems to me to be very ill done when I look at it by itself; and well done when I compare it with "Livingstone's Code," with the "French Code," or with the English statutes which have been passed for the purpose of consolidating and amending the "Criminal Law." In health I am as well as ever I was in my life. Time glides fast. One day is so like another that, but for a habit which I acquired soon after I reached India of penciling in my books the date of my reading them, I should have hardly any way of estimating the lapse of time. If I want to know when an event took place, I call to mind which of Calderon's plays, or of Plutarch's "Lives," I was reading on that day. I turn to the book, find the date, and am generally astonished to see that what seems removed from me by only two or three months really happened nearly a year ago.

I intend to learn German on my voyage home, and I have indented largely (to use our Indian official term) for the requisite books. People tell me that it is a hard language; but I can not easily believe that there is a language which I can not master in four months, by working ten hours a day. I promise myself very great delight and information from German literature; and, over and above, I feel a sort of presentiment, a kind of admonition of the Deity, which assures me that the final cause of my existence—the end for which I was sent into this vale of tears—was to make game of certain Germans. The first thing to be done in obedience to this heavenly call is to learn German; and then I may perhaps try, as Milton says,

Frangere Saxonicas Britonum sub Marte phalanges.

Ever yours affectionately, T. B. MACAULAY.

The years which Macaulay spent in India formed a transition period between the time when he kept no journal at all and the time when the daily portion of his journal was completed as regularly as the daily portion of his "History." Between 1834 and 1838, he contented himself with jotting down any circumstance that struck his fancy in the book which he happened to have in hand. The records of his Calcutta life, written in half a dozen different languages, are scattered throughout the whole range of classical literature from Hesiod to Macrobius. At the end of the seventy-ninth Epistle of Seneca we read: "April 14th, 1836. Hodie præmia distribui τοις ἐν τῳ μουσειῳ Σανσκριτικῳ νεανισκοις."*

On the last page of the "Birds" of Aristophanes: "Jan. 16th, 1836. οἱ πρεσβεῖς οἱ παρὰ τοῦ βασιλέως τῶν Νηπαυλιτων εἰσήγοντο χθες ἐς Καλκουτταν."†

On the first page of Theocritus: "March 20th, 1835. Lord W. Bentinck sailed this morning."

On the last page of the "De Amicitiâ:" "March 5th, 1836. Yesterday Lord Auckland arrived at Government House, and was sworn in."

Beneath an idyl of Moschus, of all places in the world, Mac-

---

* "To-day I distributed the prizes to the students of the Sanscrit College."

† "The embassadors from the King of Nepaul entered Calcutta yesterday." It may be observed that Macaulay wrote Greek with or without accents, according to the humor or hurry of the moment.

aulay notes the fact of Peel being First Lord of the Treasury; and he finds space, between two quotations in Athenæus, to commemorate a ministerial majority of 29 on the second reading of the Irish Church Bill.

A somewhat nearer approach to a formal diary may be found in his Catullus, which contains a catalogue of the English books that he read in the cold season of 1835–'36; as, for instance, Gibbon's "Answer to Davis," November 6th and 7th; Gibbon on Virgil's VI. Æneid, November 7th; Whately's "Logic," November 15th; Thirlwall's "Greece," November 22d; *Edinburgh Review*, November 29th. And all this was in addition to his Greek and Latin studies, to his official work, to the French that he read with his sister, and the unrecorded novels that he read to himself; which last would alone have afforded occupation for two ordinary men, unless this month of November was different from every other month of his existence since the day that he left Mr. Preston's school-room. There is something refreshing, amidst the long list of graver treatises, to light upon a periodical entry of "Πικυικινα," the immortal work of a classic who has had more readers in a single year than Statius and Seneca in all their eighteen centuries together. Macaulay turned over with indifference, and something of distaste, the earlier chapters of that modern "Odyssey." The first touch which came home to him was Jingle's "Handsome Englishman!" In that phrase he recognized a master; and, by the time that he landed in England, he knew his "Pickwick" almost as intimately as his "Grandison."

Calcutta, June 15th, 1837.

Dear Napier,—Your letter about my review of Mackintosh miscarried, vexatiously enough. I should have been glad to know what was thought of my performance among friends and foes, for here we have no information on such subjects. The literary correspondents of the Calcutta newspapers seem to be penny-a-line men whose whole stock of literature comes from the conversations in the Green Room.

My long article on Bacon has, no doubt, been in your hands some time. I never, to the best of my recollection, proposed to review Hannah More's "Life" or "Works." If I did, it must have been in jest. She was exactly the very last person in the world about whom I should choose to write a critique. She was a very kind friend to me from childhood. Her notice first called out my literary tastes. Her presents laid the foundation of my library. She was to me what Ninon was to Voltaire—begging her pardon for comparing her to a bad woman, and yours for comparing myself to a great man. She really was a second mother to me. I have a real affection for her memory. I therefore could not possibly write about her unless I wrote in her praise; and all the praise which I could give to her writings, even after straining my conscience in her favor, would be far indeed from satisfying any of her admirers.

I will try my hand on Temple, and on Lord Clive. Shaftesbury I shall let alone. Indeed, his political life is so much connected with Temple's that, without endless repetition, it would be impossible for me to furnish a separate article on each. Temple's "Life and Works;" the part which he took in the controversy about the ancients and moderns; the Oxford confederacy against Bentley; and the memorable victory which Bentley obtained, will be good subjects. I am in training for this part of the subject, as I have twice read through the Phalaris controversy since I arrived in India.

I have been almost incessantly engaged in public business since I sent off the paper on Bacon; but I expect to have comparative leisure during the short remainder of my stay here. The "Penal Code of India" is finished, and is in the press. The illness of two of my colleagues threw the work almost entirely on me. It is done, however; and I am not likely to be called upon for vigorous exertion during the rest of my Indian career. Yours ever, T. B. MACAULAY.

If you should have assigned Temple or Clive to any body else, pray do not be uneasy on that account. The pleasure of writing pays itself.

Calcutta, December 18th, 1837.

DEAR ELLIS,—My last letter was on a deeply melancholy subject—the death of our poor friend Malkin. I have felt very much for his widow. The intensity of her affliction, and the fortitude and good feeling which she showed as soon as the first agony was over, have interested me greatly in her. Six or seven of Malkin's most intimate friends here have joined with Ryan and me in subscribing to put up a plain marble tablet in the cathedral, for which I have written an inscription.*

My departure is now near at hand. This is the last letter which I shall write to you from India. Our passage is taken in the *Lord Hungerford*, the most celebrated of the huge floating hotels which run between London and Calcutta. She is more renowned for the comfort and luxury of her internal arrangements than for her speed. As we are to stop at the Cape for a short time, I hardly expect to be with you till the end of May or the beginning of June. I intend to make myself a good German scholar by the time of my arrival in England. I have already, at leisure moments, broken the ice. I have read about half of the New Testament in Luther's translation; and am now getting rapidly, for a beginner, through Schiller's "History of the Thirty Years' War." My German library consists of all Goethe's works, all Schiller's works, Müller's "History of Switzerland," some of Tieck, some of Lessing, and other works of less fame. I hope to dispatch them all on my way home. I like Schiller's style exceedingly. His history contains a great deal of very just and deep thought, conveyed in language so popular and agreeable that dunces would think him superficial.

I lately took it into my head to obtain some knowledge of the Fathers, and I read therefore a good deal of Athanasius, which by no means raised him in my opinion. I procured the magnificent edition of Chrysostom by Montfaucon from a public library here, and turned over the eleven huge folios, reading wherever the subject was of peculiar interest. As to reading him through, the thing is impossible. These volumes contain matter at least equal to the whole extant literature of the best times of Greece, from Homer to Aristotle inclusive.

---

* This inscription appears in Lord Macaulay's "Miscellaneous Works."

There are certainly some very brilliant passages in his homilies. It seems curious that, though the Greek literature began to flourish so much earlier than the Latin, it continued to flourish so much later. Indeed, if you except the century which elapsed between Cicero's first public appearance and Livy's death, I am not sure that there was any time at which Greece had not writers equal, or superior, to their Roman contemporaries. I am sure that no Latin writer of the age of Lucian is to be named with Lucian; that no Latin writer of the age of Longinus is to be named with Longinus; that no Latin prose of the age of Chrysostom can be named with Chrysostom's compositions. I have read Augustine's "Confessions." The book is not without interest; but he expresses himself in the style of a field-preacher.

Our "Penal Code" is to be published next week. It has cost me very intense labor; and, whatever its faults may be, it is certainly not a slovenly performance. Whether the work proves useful to India or not, it has been of great use, I feel and know, to my own mind. Ever yours affectionately,

T. B. MACAULAY.

APPENDIX.

A FEW extracts from the notes penciled in Macaulay's Greek and Latin books may interest any one who is wise enough to have kept up his classics, or young enough for it to be still his happy duty to read them. The number of the dates scribbled at the conclusion of each volume, and their proximity in point of time, are astonishing when we reflect that every such memorandum implies a separate perusal.

"This day I finished Thucydides, after reading him with inexpressible interest and admiration. He is the greatest historian that ever lived.—*February 27th*, 1835."

"I am still of the same mind.—*May 30th*, 1836."

At the end of Xenophon's "Anabasis" may be read the words:

"Decidedly his best work.—*December 17th*, 1835."

"Most certainly.—*February 24th*, 1837."

"One of the very first works that antiquity has left us. Perfect in its kind.—*October 9th*, 1837."

"I read Plautus four times at Calcutta.

"The first, in November and December, 1834.

"The second, in January and the beginning of February, 1835.

"The third, on the Sundays from the 24th of May to the 23d of August, 1835.

"The fourth, on the Sundays beginning from the 1st of January, 1837.

"I have since read him in the Isle of Wight (1850), and in the South of France (1858)."

"Finished the second reading of Lucretius this day, March 24th, 1835. It is a great pity that the poem is in an unfinished state. The philosophy is for the most part utterly worthless; but in energy, perspicuity, variety of illustration, knowledge of life and manners, talent for description, sense of the beauty of the external world, and elevation and dignity of moral feeling, he had hardly ever an equal."

"Finished Catullus August 3d, 1835. An admirable poet. No Latin writer is so Greek. The simplicity, the pathos, the perfect grace, which I find in the great Athenian models are all in Catullus, and in him alone of the Romans."

To the "Thebaïs" of Statius are simply appended the dates "October 26th, 1835." "October 31st, 1836." The expressions "Stuff!" and "Trash!" occur frequently enough throughout the dreary pages of the poem; while evidence of the attention with which those pages were studied is afforded by such observations as "Gray has translated this passage;" "Racine took a hint here;" and "Nobly imitated—indeed, far surpassed—by Chaucer."

"Finished Silius Italicus; for which Heaven be praised! December 24th, 1835. Pope must have read him before me. In the 'Temple of Fame,' and the 'Essay on Criticism,' are some touches plainly suggested by Silius."

In the last page of Velleius Paterculus come the following comments: "Vile flatterer! Yet, after all, he could hardly help it. But how the strong, acute, cynical mind of Tiberius must have been revolted by adulation, the absence of which he would probably have punished! Velleius Paterculus seems to me a remarkably good epitomist. I hardly know any historical work of which the scale is so small, and the subject so extensive. The Bishop of London admires his style. I do not. There are sentences worthy of Tacitus; but there is an immense quantity of rant, and far too much ejaculation and interrogation for oratory, let alone history.—*June 6th*, 1835; again, *May 14th*, 1836."

"I think Sallust inferior to both Livy and Tacitus in the talents of an historian. There is a lecturing, declaiming tone about him which would suit a teacher of rhetoric better than a statesman engaged in recording great events. Still, he is a good writer; and the view which he here gives of the state of parties at Rome, and the frightful demoralization of the aristocracy, is full of interest.—*June* 10*th*, 1835; *May* 6*th*, 1837."

"I do not think that there is better evidence of the genuineness of any book in the world than of the first seven books of Cæsar's 'Commentaries.' To doubt on that subject is the mere rage of skepticism."

After Cæsar's "De Bello Civili:" "He is an admirable writer, worth ten of Sallust. His manner is the perfection of good sense and good taste. He rises on me, also, as a man. He was on the right side, as far as in such a miserable government there could be a right side. He used his victory with glorious humanity. Pompey, whether he inclined to it or not, must have established a reign of terror to gratify the execrable aristocracy whose tool he had stooped to be."

To the "De Bello Alexandrino:" "This is not a bad history. Hirtius is a very respectable writer. The Alexandrian affair is a curious episode in Cæsar's life. No doubt the influence of Cleopatra was the real cause of his strange conduct. He was not a man to play Charles XII. at Bender, except when under the tyranny of some strong passion. The ability with which he got out of scrapes is some set-off against the rashness with which he got into them."

To the "De Bello Hispaniensi:" "This book must have been written by some sturdy old centurion, who fought better than he composed."

The odds and ends of Cæsar's conversation, gathered far and wide from classical literature into what is perhaps the most tantalizing biographical fragment in the world, are characterized by Macaulay as "Disjecta membra gigantis."

The three volumes of Macaulay's Ovid are enlivened, throughout, with pencil-notes charming in their vivacity and versatility. At the conclusion of the fifteenth and last book he writes: "There are some very fine things in this poem; and in ingenuity, and the art of doing difficult things in expression and versification as if they were the easiest in the world, Ovid is quite incomparable. But, on the whole, I am much disappointed. I like the romantic poets of Italy far better; not only Ariosto, but Boiardo, and even Forteguerri. The second book of the 'Metamorphoses' is by far the best. Next to that comes the first half of the thirteenth.

"Finished at Calcutta April 28th, 1835."

"I like it better this second time of reading.—*January 14th*, 1837."

He was evidently surfeited by the "Heroides," and pleased by the "Amores;" though he read them both twice through with the strictest impartiality. Of the "Ars Amatoria" he says: "Ovid's best. The subject did not require the power, which he did not possess, of moving the passions. The love, which he has reduced to a system, was little more than the mere sexual appetite, heightened by the art of dress, manner, and conversation. This was an excellent subject for a man so witty and so heartless."

The "Fasti" were almost too much for him. "June 30th, 1835.—It is odd that I should finish the 'Fasti' on the very day with which the 'Fasti' terminate. I am cloyed with Ovid. Yet I can not but admire him."

"Finished the 'Fasti' again.—*February 26th*, 1837."

After the "Tristia:" "A very melancholy set of poems. They make me very sad, and the more so because I am myself an exile, though in far happier circumstances, externally, than those of Ovid. It is impossible not to feel contempt, mingled with a sort of pitying kindness, for a man so clever, so accomplished, so weak-spirited and timid, placed, unjustly as it should seem, in so painful a situation. It is curious that the three most celebrated Roman writers who were banished, and whose compositions written in exile have come down to us—Cicero, Seneca, and Ovid—have all shown an impatience and pusillanimity which lower their characters;" and which, he might have added, are strangely at variance with the proverbial manliness and constancy of the Roman nature.

At the end of the last volume: "I have now gone through the whole of Ovid's works, and heartily tired I am of him and them. Yet he is a wonderfully clever man. But he has two insupportable faults. The one is that he will always be clever; the other that he never knows when to have done. He is rather a rhetorician than a poet. There is little feeling in his poems; even in those which were written during his exile. The pathetic effect of his supplications and lamentations is injured by the ingenious turns of expression, and by the learned allusions, with which he sets off his sorrow."

"He seems to have been a very good fellow: rather too fond of women; a flatterer and a coward; but kind and generous; and free from envy, though a man of letters, and though sufficiently vain of his literary performances. The 'Art of Love,' which ruined poor Ovid, is, in my opinion, decidedly his best work."

"I finished Livy, after reading him with the greatest delight, interest, and admiration, May 31st, 1835; again, April 29th, 1837."

At the end of Livy's twenty-seventh book there appear the following remarks; which, in a letter to Mr. Ellis, Macaulay entitles "Historic Doubts touching the Battle of the Metaurus:" "I suspect that the whole narrative is too highly colored, and that far too large a share of the praise is allotted to Nero. Who was Nero? What did he ever do before or after this great achievement? His conduct in Spain had been that of an incapable driveler, and we hear of nothing to set off against that conduct till he was made consul. And, after his first consulship, why was he not re-elected? All ordinary rules about succession to offices were suspended while Hannibal was in Italy. Fabius, Fulvius, Marcellus, were elected consuls over and over. The youth of Scipio did not keep him from holding the highest commands. Why was Nero, who, if Livy can be trusted, was a far abler man than any general whom Rome employed in that war—who outgeneraled Hasdrubal, who saved the republic from the most imminent danger—never re-employed against the Carthaginians?

"And then, how strange is the silence of the Latin writers anterior to the Augustan age! There does not exist, as far as I recollect, a single allusion to Nero in all Cicero's works. But, when we come to the time at which Tiberius was rising to the first importance in the State, we find Nero represented as the most illustrious captain of his age. The earliest panegyric on him that I know is in Horace's fine ode, 'Qualem Ministrum.' That ode was written to the praise and glory of Tiberius and Drusus—both Neros. Livy wrote when Tiberius was partner with Augustus in the Empire; Velleius Paterculus, when Tiberius was sovereign. They seem to me to have looked back into history for the purpose of finding some topic flattering to the house of Nero; and they found a victory—certainly a considerable victory—gained in the consulship of a Nero, and by an army, part of which he commanded. Accordingly, they ascribed to him all the glory of the success. They represented him as having contrived the whole plan; as having executed it on his own responsibility; as having completely outwitted both the Carthaginian generals. Yet, after all, the Senate would not let him enter Rome in triumph, but gave all the honor of the victory to his colleague Livius; and I can not find in Polybius any compliment whatsoever to Nero's generalship on this occasion.

"I dare say that, if the truth were known, it would be something of this sort. The Senate ordered Nero to march, and to effect a junction with Livius. The direction of the operations subsequent to that junction probably lay with Livius; as the province was especially his, and as he was general of by far the larger force. In the action, Livy himself tells us that Livius was opposed to Hasdrubal, which was doubtless the most important post. The universal impression at the time was that the glory of the day belonged to Livius. He alone triumphed for the victory; and no Roman writer, for many generations, ranked Nero with Fabius or Marcellus. But, when the house of Nero acquired supreme power, men of letters employed all their talents in extolling the only Nero of whom it was possible to make a great man; and they have described his conduct in such a way that he appears to have been a greater man than Scipio, and fully a match for Hannibal."

At the end of each drama of the Greek tragedians Macaulay wrote with a pencil (and, unfortunately, not a very good pencil) a little critical essay, from three to twenty lines in length.

"The first part of the Ajax is prodigiously fine. I do not know that the agonies of wounded honor have ever been so sublimely represented. Basil, in one of Miss Baillie's best plays, is a faint shadow of this grand creation of Sophocles. But the interest of the piece dies with Ajax. In the debates which follow, Sophocles does not succeed as well as Euripides would have done. The odes, too, are not very good."

"I have been less pleased with this perusal of the 'Œdipus Tyrannus' than I was when I read it in January; perhaps because I then read it all at one sitting. The construction seems to me less perfect than I formerly thought it. But nothing can exceed the skill with which the discovery is managed. The agony of Œdipus is so unutterably grand; and the tender sorrow, in which his mind at last reposes after his daughters have been brought to him, is as moving as any thing in the Greek drama."

"The 'Philoctetes' is a most noble play; conspicuous even among the works of Sophocles for the grace and majesty of effect produced by the most simple means. There is more character in it than in any play in the Greek language; two or three of Euripides's best excepted."

"The first half of the 'Eumenides' is equal to any thing in poetry. The close is also very fine."

"The 'Seven against Thebes' is a noble poem; full of dramatic improprieties; but all on fire with the finest poetical spirit.—*October 25th*, 1835 (my birthday).

> μὴ φῦναι τὸν ἅπαντα νικᾷ λόγον·
> τὸ δ', ἐπεὶ φανῇ,
> βῆναι κεῖθεν, ὅθενπερ ἥκει,
> πολὺ δεύτερον, ὡς τάχιστα."*

"The 'Agamemnon' is indeed very fine. From the king's entrance into the house to the appearance on the stage of Ægistheus, it is beyond all praise. I shall turn it over again next week."

To the "Prometheus" are appended the words, "One of the greatest of human compositions."

"The 'Orestes' is one of the very finest plays in the Greek language. Among those of Euripides, I should place it next to the 'Medea' and the 'Bacchæ.'† It has some very real faults; but it pos-

---

* "The happiest destiny is never to have been born; and the next best, by far, is to return, as swiftly as may be, to the bourn whence we came." The wound caused by his sister Margaret's death was then ten months old.

† Macaulay ranked the plays of Euripides thus: The "Medea;" the "Bacchæ;" the "Orestes;" the "Iphigenia in Aulis;" the "Alcestis;" the "Phœnissæ;" the "Troades;" the "Hippolytus."

sesses that strong human interest which neither Æschylus nor Sophocles—poets in many respects far superior to Euripides—ever gave to their dramas. 'Orestes' and 'Electra' keep a very strong hold on our sympathy. The friendship of Pylades is more amiably represented here than anywhere else. Menelaus keeps the character which the Athenian dramatists have agreed to give him. The sick-chamber scene, and the scene after the trial, are two of the finest things in ancient poetry. When Milton designated Euripides 'sad Electra's poet,' he was thinking of the 'Orestes,' I suppose, and not of the 'Electra.' Schlegel says (and he is perfectly right) that the 'Electra' is Euripides's worst play. It is quite detestable."

"I can hardly account for the contempt which, at school and college, I felt for Euripides. I own that I like him now better than Sophocles. The 'Alcestis' has faults enough; but there are scenes in it of surpassing beauty and tenderness. The choruses, too, are very fine. Fox thought it the best of Euripides's plays. I can not like it so well as the 'Medea.' The odious baseness of Admetus, in accepting the sacrifice of his wife, is a greater drawback than even the absurd machinery. Thomson avoided this very happily in his imitation, by making Eleanora suck the poison while Edward is sleeping."

"The 'Bacchæ' is a most glorious play. I doubt whether it be not superior to the 'Medea.' It is often very obscure; and I am not sure that I fully understand its general scope. But, as a piece of language, it is hardly equaled in the world. And, whether it was intended to encourage or to discourage fanaticism, the picture of fanatical excitement which it exhibits has never been rivaled."

END OF THE FIRST VOLUME.